ADVANCE PRAISE FOR

The Rights of Women
Reclaiming a Lost Vision

"Erika Bachiochi is one of the most brilliant and refreshingly original feminist legal scholars writing today. Uncowed by today's momentary orthodoxies, Bachiochi blends a rich understanding of tradition with compelling insights into present-day issues. No one writing in the field exceeds her gifts of insight, clarity, and scholarly fearlessness."

—Michael Stokes Paulsen, co-author of
The Constitution: An Introduction

"Bachiochi flips effortlessly from legal analysis to philosophical arguments to sociological observations to characters from classic literature in a way that is almost invisible to the reader . . . in a work that I would describe as, in many places, almost achingly beautiful."

—Elizabeth R. Schiltz, co-editor of
Feminism, Law, and Religion

"With clarity and boldness, Erika Bachiochi shows how the moral purpose underlying the case for truly equal rights has been lost even as those rights have been gained. Although it recounts a story of decline, *The Rights of Women* is ultimately filled with hope because it offers an alternative—a way to recapture the ideal of dignity that gives meaning to equality by grasping that the ultimate purpose of freedom is human flourishing and excellence."

—Yuval Levin, author of *A Time to Build*

"Bachiochi adds an important new voice to the conversation criticizing the nation's turn to revering market profit and the freedom to be left alone above all else. Feminists may not agree with all of her critique of contemporary feminism, but they would do well to engage with her powerful argument that conceptualizing the movement's goal as sex equality in the workplace is too narrow."

—Maxine Eichner, author of *The Free-Market Family*

"*The Rights of Women* brilliantly articulates what should be a central concern and debate for feminists today."

—Helen M. Alvaré, author of *Putting Children's Interests First in U.S. Family Law and Policy*

"Rights cannot flourish alone. They need to be embedded in a thicker moral context that gives voice to the goods that they should serve, the social duties that govern their exercise, and the virtues that enable respect for them. In this book, Erika Bachiochi recovers a tradition of thought about women's rights that fully recognizes this and, with Mary Wollstonecraft at one end and Mary Ann Glendon at the other, offers an important, salutary correction, not only to libertarian feminism in particular but also to contemporary rights-talk in general."

—Nigel Biggar, author of *What's Wrong with Rights?*

The Rights of Women

CATHOLIC IDEAS FOR A SECULAR WORLD

O. Carter Snead, *series editor*

DE NICOLA CENTER
for ETHICS AND CULTURE

Under the sponsorship of the de Nicola Center for Ethics and
Culture at the University of Notre Dame, the purpose of this
interdisciplinary series is to feature authors from around the world
who will expand the influence of Catholic thought on the most
important conversations in academia and the public square. The series
is "Catholic" in the sense that the books will emphasize and engage
the enduring themes of human dignity and flourishing, the common
good, truth, beauty, justice, and freedom in ways that reflect and
deepen principles affirmed by the Catholic Church for millennia.
It is not limited to Catholic authors or even works that explicitly
take Catholic principles as a point of departure. Its books are
intended to demonstrate the diversity and enhance the relevance
of these enduring themes and principles in numerous subjects,
ranging from the arts and humanities to the sciences.

THE RIGHTS
OF WOMEN

• • •

Reclaiming a Lost Vision

ERIKA BACHIOCHI

University of Notre Dame Press
Notre Dame, Indiana

University of Notre Dame Press
Notre Dame, Indiana 46556
undpress.nd.edu

Copyright © 2021 by the University of Notre Dame

Published in the United States of America

Library of Congress Control Number: 2021939573

ISBN: 978-0-268-20081-7 (Hardback)
ISBN: 978-0-268-20082-4 (Paperback)
ISBN: 978-0-268-20083-1 (WebPDF)
ISBN: 978-0-268-20080-0 (Epub)

For my daughters, Anna, Gabriella, Lucy, and Charlotte,
and my sons, Peter, JJ, and Luke—

in search of better ways to live, work, and love

If you wish to make your son rich, pursue one course—
if you are only anxious to make him virtuous, you must take
another; but do not imagine that you can bound from one
road to the other without losing your way.

—Mary Wollstonecraft,
A Vindication of the Rights of Woman

For where your treasure is, there also will your heart be.

—Matthew 6:21

CONTENTS

ILLUSTRATIONS

ACKNOWLEDGMENTS

This book was long in the dreaming and in the making, and it could never have come to be without the support, guidance, and assistance of many people.

I will be ever grateful for the early support and encouragement that Lisa Schiltz, Mary Hasson, and Carol Crossed offered me during the beginning stages of the research. I'm thankful too to Ed Whelan of the Ethics & Public Policy Center for taking a chance on the project, and on me. Years later, as the contours of my argument had grown and changed, but little output could yet be shared, Lisa, Mary, Carol, and Ed remained ever supportive and encouraging.

The year I spent as a visiting scholar at Harvard Law School, through a research fellowship provided by the Abigail Adams Institute (AAI) in Cambridge, Massachusetts, was pivotal. My gratitude to Bill English, Mike Marcucci, Mike Paulsen, Rick Garnett, Adrian Vermeule, Jeff Shafer, and especially AAI's director, Danilo Petranovich, for supporting the venture in the various ways they did. Danilo was unflaggingly hospitable to me and provided wisdom and a space to write. Fortuitously, an AAI event also introduced an early chapter to then Harvard graduate students Tiernan Kane and Dimitrios Halikiass, who went on to read each chapter of the manuscript, invariably almost as soon as I had completed them. Such intelligent and insightful readers are a writer's dream, and the book is far better for having experienced Tiernan's and Dimitri's red pens.

I was also grateful to call upon the expertise and advice of Allan Carlson, Mary Eberstadt, Helen Alvaré, Adam MacLeod, Jim Stoner, Deborah Savage, Leslie Nagel, Fr. Jeff Langan, Angela Franks, Clarke Forsythe, Elizabeth Kirk, Andrew Beauchamp, Sarah White, and

Catherine Pakaluk at various points in the project. Their careful consideration of my ideas and arguments (and correction when needed) was much appreciated. My dear friends Katie and Kevin Elrod were also especially intelligent sounding boards, as were the wonderfully bright students in my AAI seminar, "Man, Woman, Body, Soul in the Western Tradition." The inspiring women of the Catholic Women's Forum deserve my gratitude too.

Thanks too for the guidance that George Weigel, Yuval Levin, and Nick Mullendore offered me in my early hunt for a publisher. Happily, Carter Snead convinced me of the merits of the University of Notre Dame Press with but a phone call—and Carter, Margaret Cabaniss, and Steve Wrinn and his team graciously put up with me ever since.

The assistance I received from undergraduate, graduate, and postgrad students was outstanding. Sally Crippen's early research was particularly thorough, helping me to believe the heavy lift I had taken on was possible. Much-appreciated help also came from Bridget Rose, John Henry Hobgood, and Lauren Konkol, as well as Amanda Bernard and Brandi Marulli at the University Archives of the Catholic University of America. Gabrielle Landry joined the project as an intern just out of high school; she was preparing to enter Harvard, and I was half way through my tenure at Harvard Law. Thanks to the support of AAI and a happy extension of my fellowship beyond the first year, Gabby stayed on as my research assistant for two full academic years and was truly magnificent. Her diligence, attention to detail, keen intelligence, editorial expertise, and cheerful disposition made each and every interaction a joy. I've often thought that, with Gabby at my side, I could do anything. She is sure to take the world by storm.

It was a special privilege to witness the unfailing assistance of my family and friends as I undertook this project, especially as it wore on year after year. My eldest daughter, barely a teenager when I began research, transformed over the years into a mature, philosophically astute young woman and was among the first to read (and critique) the opening chapter of the manuscript. My younger children likely wondered about "mom's book," but as they grew older, their support and prayers for the project grew too. When baby Charlotte arrived (before the manuscript was finished and no doubt to prod it on), my stepmother,

Cheryl, dear cousin Maya, friend and neighbor Eileen Ford, and a handful of other very close friends (you know who you are) took their support of me, my work, and our family to an extraordinary level. My mere gratitude, great though it is, hardly seems sufficient for such remarkable generosity.

When all is said and done, two people remained, from the first day to the last, the source of inspiration for this work. The first, Mary Ann Glendon, turned my world upside down when, at twenty years old, I read *Rights Talk* as a pro-choice feminist with a heart for the poor who had recently volunteered for then U.S. Rep. Bernie Sanders (I-VT). I just could not shake the appeal of Mary Ann's arguments. As time went on, her thoroughgoing dignitarian vision was to pervade my own thinking and, eventually, my scholarship. I have relished each and every conversation we have had over these last few years and count myself among the truly blessed to have shared the company of this most gracious, wise, and spirited woman.

If Mary Ann Glendon and Mary Wollstonecraft provide the theoretical foundations for the vision laid out in this book, my husband, Dan, brings it concretely to life in our own home. He is a man whose integrity, selflessness, and tireless devotion to our family make every other good work possible. If I have set the bar high in these pages, it is because Dan has shown it altogether possible to attain.

Introduction

On the day before the inauguration of Woodrow Wilson in March 1913, a grand parade marched on Washington, DC, featuring mounted brigades, ornate floats, musical bands, and thousands of predominantly women marchers in distinctive occupational garb. As the procession reached the U.S. Treasury building, the parade turned allegorical pageant, with costumed actors representing in turn Charity, Liberty, Justice, Peace, and Hope, "those ideals toward which both men and women have been struggling through the ages and toward which, in co-operation and equality, they will continue to strive," according to the official program.[1] The *New York Times* chronicled the pageant as "one of the most impressively beautiful spectacles ever staged in this country."[2]

Seven years later, after nearly sixty years of advocacy, the Nineteenth Amendment to the U.S. Constitution was ratified, granting women in every state the right to vote. Nearly one hundred years after the Woman Suffrage Procession—just three years shy of the centennial celebration of the Nineteenth Amendment—another massive gathering in support of women's rights was organized in Washington, DC, this time the day after the inauguration of Donald Trump as president. If high ideals were present that day (represented, perhaps, by the slogan "Love Not Hate Makes America Great"), these were overwhelmed by the march's official panel of speakers, who extolled "nasty" women, made generous use of expletives, and engaged in insult, threat, and ad

FIGURE I.I. Scene from a tableau held on the U.S. Treasury steps in Washington, DC, in conjunction with the Woman Suffrage Procession on March 3, 1913. Credit: Library of Congress (public domain).

hominem attack on the new president. The symbol of the march—the female genitalia—was depicted throughout the day in various manifestations on poster board and costume, but most memorably atop participants' heads in the form of a pink "pussy hat."

Enduring moral principles, which women's rights advocates in earlier days would have employed to make a reasoned critique of the controversial new president, had given way to vulgar irony: "This pussy grabs back." Something significant had changed over the intervening century in the cause of women's rights. And it wasn't only that participants to the more recent Women's March arrived by bus rather than on horseback, or that the women marching were as educated and professionally competent as the men, impressive though these changes are. Rather, the underlying rationale for women's rights—for civil and political freedom and equality as such—has shifted profoundly. But this shift has occurred subtly and over time, such that many now falsely assume that an unbroken line can be traced from those who today agitate for women's rights to those who argued that women had the right to do so in the first place.

This shift can be detected in the changed meanings of words used in the mission statement of the Women's March; words that have long represented American ideals, such as "self-determination," "liberty,"

FIGURE I.2. Women's March on Washington, January 21, 2017.
Credit: public domain.

and "dignity," even "love" (rendered "charity" in 1913), do not mean today what they signified in earlier days. Today, these words connote an indeterminacy that would strike previous generations of women's rights advocates as bereft of noble purpose, and ultimately dangerous. Self-determination and liberty—for what end? Dignity—according to what measure? Love—as evident in what kinds of acts? The moral vacuity implicit in the present meanings of these age-old terms is something altogether new.

To be sure, the Woman Suffrage Procession in 1913 was itself not morally impeccable, and the women's suffragist movement as a whole did not perfectly embody the noble ideals depicted imaginatively that day. Although key leadership had drawn inspiration for their cause from participation in the abolitionist movement, some leaders wished the parade, and the movement too, to be racially segregated. The nation's original sin had infected its people deeply, and the cause of women's civil and political freedom and equality was sadly no exception. Yet, the parade's ideals, manifest in both word and dress, spoke a paramount truth to the nation and its leaders, the truth that had prevailed, albeit imperfectly, in the nation's founding era, and then also in the U.S. Congress and in the states ratifying amendments to the Constitution in the decades following the Civil War. The truth was this: the nation was founded upon and is ever measured by the moral proposition that all human beings are of equal dignity and worth.

The women suffragists had argued, like the Black suffragists before them, that by excluding women from full participation in civil and political life, the nation was not living up to its own founding principles. More, the suffragists suggested, in the later years of their campaign especially, that by their engagement in the public realm, women could raise the moral tenor of politics and help a still young nation to embrace more faithfully those principles. The rancorous and occasionally violent reaction to the suffragists' high-minded procession proved the suffragists right that day. By 2017, one could no longer be so sure.

Certainly much has been gained for women's rights in the last century, but something essential has been lost. It's worth pondering what that something is, and whether it is worth recovering today. Mining the intellectual history of the cause of women's rights can shed light on how a philosophical and political principle—equal citizenship for women—has morphed into something that nearly contradicts its original moral vision, a vision first fully articulated by English philosopher Mary Wollstonecraft in *A Vindication of the Rights of Woman* more than two centuries ago. For Wollstonecraft, political freedom and legal equality were not ends in themselves but necessary *means* to higher human *ends*: the common human pursuit of intellectual and moral excellence.

The political and civil rights Wollstonecraft claimed for women in the late eighteenth century have been over time and with great struggle steadily secured in modern democracies around the world. In the West, however, the *ennobling moral vision* upon which she built her rights claims has largely been abandoned. With the stark moral failures of so many of our political, economic, and cultural leaders, the sexual exploitation of women and children through pornography and sex trafficking, the relentless violence that increasingly targets the most vulnerable human beings, the abject poverty of so many even amid ever-growing wealth, and the materialism and consumerism that works to corrupt the soul of the West, Wollstonecraft's substantive vision is needed now more than ever.

For Wollstonecraft, women's capacity to reason, and thus to pursue reason to its proper ends, namely, *virtue* (imitation of divine perfection) and *wisdom* (imitation of divine reason), was the very foundation for women's just claims to political freedom and equality. But not just for women: freedom as such was a necessary means to these higher human ends. It was the forgetfulness of these noble ends, on the part of men especially, that facilitated the subjugation and victimization of women, even in their own homes.

A freedom bereft of wisdom and virtue reduces men to beasts, Wollstonecraft claimed. And this was especially true in intimate relations between men and women, the wellspring of the domestic affections she recognized as the source of every public virtue. Chastity was not to be abandoned in the pursuit of equality between the sexes, nor was this virtue specially required of women, as was the convention of the day. Rather, it was men who, in pursuing self-serving indulgence without habitual respect for women or a regard for the noble purposes of sex and the goods of shared domestic life, had too often failed to treat women with the dignity they deserved. Women, for their part, had too often acquiesced, fashioning themselves more pleasing to the eyes than strong in the mind. Indeed, the eighteenth-century philosopher identifies want of chastity in men as the single most consequential offense against women. Wollstonecraft's radical vision of sexual integrity for both sexes, with a view toward virtuous friendships of mutual trust and collaboration, poses an especially striking challenge to a modern-day women's movement shaped, since the 1970s, by a very different kind of sexual revolution.

Wollstonecraft's best-known work, *A Vindication of the Rights of Woman*, was published in 1792, just two years after she published *A Vindication of the Rights of Men*, the first widely read critique of Edmund Burke's famous 1790 defense of the British monarchy. Wollstonecraft wrote these treatises during a time of marked political and social change, as the American and then French revolutions threw off old forms of hereditary rule in their respective attempts (with greater and lesser success) to enact altogether new forms of republican government based on God-given rights, derived from the moral status of human beings as rational creatures.

In both the *Rights of Men* and the *Rights of Woman*, Wollstone-craft articulated this now-familiar rationale for civil and political rights in the modern era, artfully extending its reach to women. But unlike most of her contemporaries, Wollstonecraft's defense of rights was inspired by an ancient view of the human person, one that exalted the common human pursuit of wisdom and virtue above all else. She thus offered a unique synthesis of ancient wisdom and modern political insight, correcting errors she saw among philosophers of her day, and proposing a program that in its fullness remains still yet untried today.

Like her fellow travelers in the Enlightenment period, Wollstone-craft extolled freedom from illegitimate and arbitrary power, but not a freedom left to its own devices. Civil and political rights for both men and women (men without property at the time fared little better than women, and slaves often fared far worse) were essential to human dignity and political progress. But such rights were themselves born of moral duties to self, family, fellow citizens, and God. That is, political freedom was at the service of the moral development of each person, which consisted, in large measure, of virtuously fulfilling the ordinary duties of life. By assigning women to a dependent state, ill formed both intellectually and morally, social convention had rendered them incapable of fulfilling their familial and social duties as well as they might. Wollstonecraft argued that women ought to be freed from those social conventions that judged them less capable than men (and created only to please them). Such freedom ought to be extended not so that women might pursue a life of moral mediocrity, or worse, vulgarity, which would be no freedom at all. Wollstonecraft's was a freedom *for excellence*.

Wollstonecraft was strongly influenced by the classical republican tradition that was experiencing a renaissance in her time, and so she was persuaded that new forms of republican government would require civic virtue. But she did not recommend virtue for its social utility. Indeed, she railed against utilitarian views of virtue, especially as conceived in aristocratic society as mere decorum or manners; such displays too often lacked an interior disposition of authentic benevolence toward fellow creatures. Nor did she hesitate to repudiate the view, then current in the writings of Jean-Jacques Rousseau and others, that virtue was bifurcated by sex, with women devoted to developing only those "feeling" virtues most pleasing to "rational" men. Rather, for Wollstonecraft, personal virtue, most highly manifest in benevolence, represented the highest attainment of human life, for men and women in equal measure. All institutions in society ought to be designed according to, and measured against, this highest human ideal.

Wollstonecraft did not preach sanctity in a religious sense, but a religious perspective did inform her thinking. She sought instead to enunciate the moral duties that characterized rational creatures, duties to self (to develop one's rational faculties and master one's appetites), to family (to care for one's dependent children, spouse, and elderly parents), to fellow creatures (to be useful in one's work and respect the human dignity of all others, regardless of social status), and to God (to pursue truth and goodness and to trust in his providential designs). As the content of her children's stories attest, Wollstonecraft viewed the affectionate inculcation of virtue in children to be among the most essential of all social duties, and so motherhood and fatherhood the very highest of callings.

Wollstonecraft's appeal for women's education is her most remembered contribution today; her rationale perhaps less so. The self-taught philosopher believed that if women, like men, were afforded both intellectual and moral formation and the opportunities to engage in more serious-minded occupations, they would enjoy greater independence of mind and in turn better appreciate their distinctive duties to their families and beyond. Wollstonecraft's view of marriage in her *Rights of Woman*—a relationship of reciprocity and friendship between equals, a shared project for the upbringing of children, and the best means to restore harmony between the sexes—remains the treatise's most farsighted vision. Given the dangerous political upheaval that served as the context of her first romance, the unjust marital laws that existed in her time, the cruel abandonment she experienced at the hands of her first child's father, and her untimely death just after the birth of her second child, Wollstonecraft was unable to live out this vision for long. But her vision still has much to teach us today.

Wollstonecraft became a scandal in her day, less for her revolutionary ideas than for the incomplete picture of her tragic personal life imprudently published by her bereaved husband, William Godwin, in the months following her death. But although many of the themes Wollstonecraft first articulated in *Rights of Woman* emerged energetically in the political and legal writings of generations of women's rights advocates, in her own country, and particularly in the young United States, she proposed a far more substantive moral vision than what is often represented today as a treatise in favor of women's rights in marriage, education, employment, and political participation. Now, more than two hundred years later, we may yet be ready to hear all she had to say. Emboldened by her insights on work, marriage, children, virtue, and rights, a renewed women's movement might make itself a catalyst for the regeneration of marriages and families, the revaluing of caregiving and the reshaping of work, and the reconstituting of a morally embattled nation.

Sometime in the last half century, the women's movement lost its way. This book represents one woman's attempt to reclaim Wollstonecraft's lost vision for our day.

In 1966, Betty Friedan founded the National Organization for Women (NOW). Her blockbuster book, *The Feminine Mystique*, had three years earlier ushered in the modern-day women's movement, challenging the women of her station to broaden their focus beyond exclusive identification with their homes, husbands, and children. Friedan reminded her readers that American women from earlier generations had helped to build townships, run family farms and shops, staff and reform factories, win suffrage and other rights for women and children, all while tending to their families and homes. Friedan extolled the mid-nineteenth and early twentieth-century advocates of the "first wave" of the women's movement and noted the revolutionary writings of late eighteenth-century proto-feminist Mary Wollstonecraft.

Friedan maintained that suburban housewives in the postindustrial, postwar era were feeling incomplete, unfulfilled, and left out of the rest of life, especially as their young children left home during the day to attend school. Not all women were experiencing this feminine malaise, of course, but enough were to make Friedan's book an immediate best seller. When, a few years later, Friedan penned NOW's original

Statement of Purpose with civil rights attorney Pauli Murray, the two declared that "women . . . are human beings, who, like all other people in our society, must have the chance to develop their fullest human potential."[3] Sagely, they sought to connect the development of human potential with the acceptance of "the challenges and responsibilities [women] share with all other people in our society," and included several mentions of their "responsibilities as mothers and homemakers." Though the pursuit of wisdom and virtue were not foremost on their pens, the proposal represented a thin but decent reprisal of Wollstonecraft's more thoroughgoing vision: NOW pushed for an end to educational and workplace discrimination, a cultural recognition of the "economic and social value" of caregiving in (and of) the home, and creative solutions to promote the partnership of men and women in the family and in society. It was a modern vision that women (and men) of nearly all backgrounds could support.

But as NOW's priorities shifted sharply in the years and decades that followed, some observers, initially sympathetic to the "second wave" feminist cause, began to express their skepticism. By 1996, for instance, Elizabeth Fox-Genovese, the founder of the Women's Studies Department at Emory University, who was also an eminent historian of the American South, published *Feminism Is Not the Story of My Life*, in which she recounts the personal stories of scores of ordinary women—as Friedan herself had done in 1963—but this time to showcase a critique of what had since become of modern feminism. In Fox-Genovese's view, Friedan's "second wave" movement, three decades in, had given way to an all-encompassing, individualistic dedication to pursuit of success in the workplace, too often at the expense of familial relationships, and of particular harm, in Fox-Genovese's assessment, to underprivileged women and their children.

To be sure, Fox-Genovese, who had five years earlier published the learned feminist treatise *Feminism without Illusions*, celebrated how the modern-day women's movement had successfully torn down artificial barriers to allow women all the opportunities once available only to men. But now she and other social thinkers were lamenting that the movement had also seemed to cast away cultural norms that once taught young people how to forge and sustain enduring relationships with one another, and with those who depended upon them. Young

women were becoming just as adept as their male counterparts at negotiating the educational and professional landscape. But both sexes had
lost an important cultural inheritance that, from time immemorial, had
given priority to the longings for deep companionship and the duties
of care within the family. These were the longings and duties that Wollstonecraft herself had made so central to her program, for both women
and men. By 1981, Friedan herself had even begun to wonder if her
original vision had gone astray.[4]

Fox-Genovese's *Feminism Is Not the Story of My Life* sold a frac-
tion of the numbers Friedan's book had sold, but the historian's critique
was poignant and rang true for many in the 1990s. It certainly rang true
for me. As a middle-class white woman born in the mid-1970s, I profited
where the modern-day women's movement had made its most obvious
gains: by my late twenties, I had competed athletically at the collegiate
level and had earned two graduate degrees. A one-time women's studies
student, I had read Wollstonecraft and Friedan among the other feminist
greats and counted myself lucky to be born in the late twentieth century.

Indeed, elite women overall are doing better educationally and professionally than ever before, and in many fields increasingly outperform
their male counterparts. Wollstonecraft had claimed, like advocates of
women's equality in the Middle Ages and Renaissance before her, and
John Stuart Mill after, that women's true intellectual capacity would remain unknown until women had equal access to education and more serious-minded occupations.[5] Thanks to decades of educational and workplace reforms in the mid- to late twentieth century, false assumptions of
woman's inferior nature finally have been put to rest. But my generation
was also the first to experience the divorce revolution of my parents'
generation—propelled by 1970s feminist activists of their day—and it
took a toll on me personally just as it had taken its toll on many others
my age. As a teen and young adult, I lacked the confident sense of self-
worth and self-possession that I witness in my own children, instilled
imperceptibly by familial stability in their formative years.

The divorce rate has plateaued in recent years, but increasing rates
of cohabitation have consolidated a decades-long flight from marriage,
most notably among the poor and working classes. Children who grow
up in single-parent families can show impressive resilience, and many
flourish throughout their lives, but researchers from across the political

spectrum confirm what Wollstonecraft had intuited: children develop best when they have secured loving relationships with both of their parents, and in particular when their parents are committed to (and deeply respect) one another in marriage.

The trouble with the women's movement today, therefore, lies not with its most basic critique, as embodied in the myriad antidiscrimination measures brought about in the 1960s and 1970s. Few today would dispute the view that rigid social norms had confined women unfairly to domestic roles that limited their opportunity to use their talents to contribute to both their families' well-being and the broader community at large. Two hundred years after Wollstonecraft's *Rights of Woman*, women are enjoying civil and political liberties, at least in the most advanced democracies in the world.

The trouble with the women's movement today lies, rather, in its near abandonment of Wollstonecraft's original moral vision, one that championed women's rights so that women, with men, could virtuously fulfill their familial and social duties. Nowhere is such an abandonment clearer than in the revolutionary assault on the mutual responsibilities that inhere in sex, childbearing, and marriage that began in the 1960s and 70s. The modern-day fusion of the women's movement with the sexual revolution is one that most regard, for good or ill, as intrinsic to the cause of women's rights. But it is not. Rather, it is a great departure from Wollstonecraft's original moral vision and that of the early women's rights advocates in the United States too: it has cheapened sex and objectified women, belittled the essential contributions of both mothers and fathers, and has contributed to upending the American promise of equal opportunity for the most disadvantaged men, women, and children today.

Disentangling the original vision of the rights of women from the excesses of the sexual revolution may sound unlikely, but if rehabilitated, it's a vision both women and men could embrace today. Indeed, it's one that is already taking shape among some of the most well-off and educated in our society, as they increasingly embrace a vision of marriage as a friendship of equals, and shape their progressively flexible work lives around the caregiving needs of their families. And, in the most rudimentary of ways, it is a vision that is being articulated by some powerful women, even if they would themselves spurn what I regard to be some of its most necessary elements.

It now has become common practice for some very influential women in the professional world to acknowledge and even extol caregiving in the home and the important familial relationships that such caregiving presupposes. Consider, for instance, the rebranding of Hillary Clinton during the 2016 presidential campaign. This most prominent figure of a feminist movement once insistent on the need to refer to married women primarily as independent individuals—coining the term Ms. to replace Mrs. in the early 1970s—cast herself, on social media, first as "wife, mom, and grandma" and only then in terms of her professional achievements and aspirations, "lawyer . . . SecState . . . 2016 presidential candidate."

Princeton professor Anne-Marie Slaughter, one of Secretary Clinton's top aides at the State Department, became, with her widely read *Atlantic* article, "Why Women Still Can't Have It All," an outspoken proponent of a revaluation of caregiving and a prioritizing of the family within the women's movement. In her popular book *Unfinished Business*, Slaughter argues that the women's movement has mistakenly "left caregiving behind, valuing it less and less as a meaningful and important endeavor."[6] Now, Slaughter is not calling for a return to the 1950s. Few of us are. But Slaughter writes glowingly of her own happy marriage, and forthrightly acknowledges that women today still tend to place the care of their families ahead of their own professional advancement. She seeks instead to invite men into the caregiving enterprise, suggesting that if our society better valued caregiving, then perhaps men would do more of it, and we'd see greater equity in both the home and the workplace.

Slaughter follows a long line of scholars and advocates who have been working toward just this substantive goal, with the celebrated women's rights advocate and late Supreme Court Justice Ruth Bader Ginsburg at the very forefront. Justice Ginsburg, who died in September 2020, just as this book was going to press, undoubtedly wished for more couples to enjoy the happy situation that she and her beloved husband of fifty-six years enjoyed: a marriage of equals in which each spouse dedicates oneself to work and family with deep respect for the joys and duties of both avenues of fulfillment. Indeed, Ginsburg herself would seem to be the leading icon of Wollstonecraft's vision for women.

But as inspiring as women like Ginsburg and Slaughter are to many up-and-coming young professionals, *theirs are stories of great privilege*, and not just in terms of the resources and flexibility that come with high-status work. Their stories share a profound appreciation for and dedication to marriage at their very core. Indeed, it is hard to read the stories of these successful women, both mothers, without underscoring the relentless support and fidelity of their husbands. And not just women at the pinnacle of their professions. Marriage and child-rearing go hand in hand among the wealthier across the board, and women of all professions, including "at-home mothers," are the better for it. These women's success stories, then, are not first about sexual freedom and equality as individual autonomy, whatever their personal philosophies may tell us otherwise. They are the stories of the excesses of the sexual revolution spurned.

Ordinary women have not been so lucky. Solid marital ties that, for most of our country's history, bound men and women together with their dependent children—collaborative, loyal bonds of kinship and care that enabled working-class and immigrant families to rise into the middle class and enjoy the "American dream"—are no longer holding sway. Growing income inequality, economic insecurity, and threats to social cohesion have many causes, but the diametric trajectories of the marrying rich and unmarrying poor bear a good share of the blame. Economists and other social scientists have offered various explanations over the last several decades for the sharp decline in marriage, the rise in nonmarital childbearing among disadvantaged women, and the feminization of poverty that has accompanied both. But what has become increasingly difficult to ignore is the way in which the sexual revolution of the 1960s and 70s dramatically altered the circumstances in which poor women bear and raise their children. The decoupling of sex from marriage and marriage from childbearing, ushered in by the sexual revolution, unraveled a working-class culture of once-stable marital bonds that children need and both mothers and fathers once relied upon for their success at home and at work, and in all of life.

Women in the United States and other Western nations now enjoy untold educational and employment opportunities, won through landmark advances in antidiscrimination law and other state protections and cultural gains. But unmarried women who raise children without the emotional and financial supports of their children's fathers are at a stark disadvantage on any number of measures when compared to those women who raise their children within the marital bond. Again, the most well-educated women in the United States have not abandoned marriage in favor of total independence from men, as more radical feminists, insistent on the inherent patriarchal nature of marriage, suggested in the 1970s that they do. No, college-educated American women ("the most economically independent women in the history of the nation," according to a noted scholar at the Brookings Institution) are getting and staying married at the highest rates of all demographic groups today.[7] Whether working outside of the home or exclusively within it, these elite women well understand the unique contributions their husbands make to their children's well-being and to their own happiness. They also understand the central Wollstonecraftian principle that collaboration and reciprocity in their marriages is the surest ticket to their children's well-being—and to their own.

Slaughter's efforts to elevate the culturally essential work of caregiving, built upon the scholarship and advocacy of decades of "relational feminists" before her, are an advance for modern feminism, and so too an advance for women and for families. But a deep contradiction still riddles the modern-day women's movement from within. And without an understanding of the nature of the contradiction, even this newfound appreciation for duties of care—including Slaughter's own invitation to men to take part in more caregiving—will not set modern feminism aright. The cause of women's rights will only become what Wollstonecraft envisioned, a cause that honors both caregiving within the home and professional work without, when it disentangles itself from the excesses of the sexual revolution, and so firmly reestablishes the responsibilities that accompany sex.

Well before Slaughter called for a new men's movement to better value the work of caregiving, generations of men were already doing so, albeit in more traditional settings than many are today. Devoted husbands and fathers, both traditionally and often today, sacrifice time with their families to earn a living for their families so that the essential duties of nurturing and caregiving, so often managed primarily (and often quite happily) by women, are protected and preserved. These men understand what Wollstonecraft hoped they would, namely, that marital and paternal responsibilities accompany marriage and childbearing, and the sexual act has an intimate connection to both. Indeed, it is precisely this connection, between sexual activity and potential fatherhood, that Wollstonecraft strongly defended, and that the sexual revolution devastatingly eclipsed. And it has left the most vulnerable of women (and their children too) more vulnerable today than nearly anytime in modern U.S. history.

The contradiction deep at the heart of the modern-day women's movement is a tale plainly told because it is a great departure from Wollstonecraft's original moral vision and from that of the early women's rights advocates of the mid-nineteenth and early twentieth centuries, and it also departs from NOW's founding statement in 1966.

The departure took shape the day the modern women's movement wholeheartedly embraced abortion as a remedy, not just for life-threatening risks facing pregnant women, but as the sine qua non *of women's freedom and equality.*

Once understood as the necessary means toward the higher human goods of virtue and wisdom, goods first learned through the interdependent bonds of familial solidarity and affection, we are now told that freedom and equality ought to include that act that tears at the first bond of human affection, between a mother and her unborn child. But easy abortion access has not rendered women freer or more equal, as much as the U.S. Supreme Court in *Planned Parenthood v. Casey* suggested it might have. Instead, it has distorted the shared responsibilities that adhere in male–female sexual relationships, promoted a view of childbearing as one consumer choice among many, and has greatly contributed to the dim view of caregiving ever since.

More still, the relentless quest for abortion rights over the last several decades has placed the modern-day women's movement squarely on the side of the individualistic and consumerist economy, ever hostile to the priorities of the child-rearing family, and so diametrically at odds with the market-resistant logic for which the women's movement originally stood. Before the late 1960s, those advocating abortion mainly had done so for eugenic and population-control reasons, with women's rights advocates standing historically opposed to the practice in promoting an ethic of solidarity, care, and the shared duties of both mothers and fathers. Nineteenth-century women's rights advocates, who had won for women the right to vote, regarded abortion as an act of violence against an innocent unborn child, a reality advances in modern science have only made clearer. They, like Wollstonecraft before them, also intuited what social scientists have described in our time: that sex unmoored from its reproductive potential would increase sexual risk-taking, particularly among men, and that the negative effects of what economists now call "low-cost" sex would redound disproportionately to women, especially among the most vulnerable.

Like today's feminists, both Wollstonecraft and early women's rights advocates were deeply critical of the sexual double standard that shamed women for behaviors that men freely indulged in. But these early generations of women's advocates worked not for women to imitate dissolute men, as organizers of the 2017 Women's March seemed keen to do. Instead, Wollstonecraft and the suffragists argued for sexual integrity for both sexes. "Votes for women, chastity for men" was actually a suffragist slogan. Indeed, out of respect for both the reproductive potential of sex and women's distinctive reproductive capacity, many nineteenth-century women's rights advocates and their husbands practiced periodic abstinence, what they called "voluntary motherhood," an early precursor, not to abortion (or even contraception, which most of them opposed for the selfsame reasons), but to natural methods of fertility regulation, which have only grown more scientific and effective in our day. Sexual integrity, on this account, was a necessary precondition to authentic equality, and harmonious companionship, between women and men. It's worth asking whether this belief could still be true today.

In this book, I trace the intellectual history of that once-predominant vision of women's rights, one that honored the reproductive asymmetries of men and women but that also sought to promote shared concern and mutual collaboration in all spheres of life. Beginning with Mary Wollstonecraft's moral, familial, and political vision; through the champions of joint property rights, suffrage, "voluntary motherhood," and workers' rights in the mid-nineteenth and early twentieth centuries; then as articulated in NOW's original 1966 platform; and culminating in the landmark sex-discrimination legislation and high court rulings of the 1970s, chapters 1 through 7 detail how efforts for women's legal and social equality not only acknowledged and celebrated embodied sexual differences and the responsibilities they entailed, but also argued that these ought not disparage women's distinctive contributions or confine women to maternity alone.

Women's reproductive powers had historically given rise to women's legal, political, social, and economic subordination. The early women's right advocates said no more but sought not to reject the consequences of reproduction outright—arguing that such rejection would denigrate women by freeing men from their familial responsibilities. They sought instead to elevate women's dignity, legal status, and contributions in all realms of life.

Justice Ginsburg stands at the very center of the story, as both the rightly celebrated protagonist of the Supreme Court's sex-discrimination jurisprudence in the 1970s and then, as a Supreme Court justice, the Court's fiercest defender of abortion rights. In chapter 8, I suggest that the tension between these two pillars of Ginsburg's legal thought—antidiscrimination and pro-abortion rights—has contributed to what some have called the "stalled gender revolution," where women, thanks in large part to Ginsburg's trailblazing work in the 1970s, have achieved remarkable gains educationally and professionally, but without a concomitant valuing of the essential caregiving work that both mothers and fathers undertake in the home. "Reproductive choice" may have offered women a means to accommodate their bodies to fit the ideal unencumbered (male) worker with whom they seek to compete in the workplace, but it has delayed dramatically the workplace's acknowledgment of the essential cultural reality that most working persons are (or ought to be) deeply encumbered by their obligations to their families, and to the dependent and vulnerable at large.

Ginsburg's 1970s advocacy pushed law and culture to rethink the ways in which women traditionally had been pigeonholed as caregivers and men as providers, opening up a new era in which both men and women could respectably and responsibly engage in both avenues of fulfillment, according to their personal talents and family circumstances. But by constitutionalizing the right to abortion in the very same era, the

Supreme Court imposed a new and disputed view of liberty (as coincident with radical autonomy) onto the nation, liberating men, but never women, from the consequences of sex, with ramifications that are especially rife for poor single mothers today. Doubling down on its error, the Court appropriated a recently popularized theory of equality (with a very brief heritage) into the Court's interpretation of the Fourteenth Amendment. It thereby short-circuited more humane and creative responses to the asymmetries that naturally exist, and socially persist, because of women's disproportionate role in reproduction.

In chapter 9, I begin to put the pieces back together in both law and culture to set up an affirmative vision for women and men today inspired by Wollstonecraft's original vision. I take as my guide the prolific work of internationally acclaimed legal scholar Mary Ann Glendon. Glendon's thought, like that of Wollstonecraft, is steeped deeply in the Western tradition, culling from sources both ancient and modern. She and Wollstonecraft share a keen insight into the priority of the moral development of persons and the domestic affections that make the attainment of such virtue possible. Glendon is notably among the world's leading thinkers on the foundations of law and human rights. She has thought long and hard about the moral preconditions of liberty and equality, preconditions that Wollstonecraft too understood to be necessary to the flourishing of both individuals and republics. But Glendon, an ambassador, Harvard Law professor, and celebrated public intellectual, offers us something Wollstonecraft cannot: insight into how their shared moral vision can help us today.

Bringing the themes of the book sharply into our own time, I seek to explore how Glendon's dignitarian vision, as developed from her writing in a variety of areas of legal and political thought, is a crucial corrective to the irreconcilable tensions that exist in Justice Ginsburg's more libertarian strain of thought. Not only does Glendon's vision rehabilitate the neglected insights of Wollstonecraft, early women's rights advocates, and the drafters of the original NOW platform in their acknowledgment of reproductive asymmetry and our shared responsibilities for human dependency, but it also, in my view, offers a more authentic completion of both Wollstonecraft's vision and Ginsburg's 1970s antidiscrimination advocacy than Ginsburg's own equality arguments for abortion rights do.

Glendon questions the elevation of individual autonomy, or freedom as its own end, as our preeminent constitutional value. Rather, she suggests that the liberties necessary for the full flourishing and collaboration of women and men, and of a constitutional form of government that encourages such flourishing, rest upon cultural preconditions that freedom itself does not provide. If these preconditions are not furnished by the family and other mediating institutions, the overweening forces of both the market and the state necessarily step in, elevating individualism and materialism, eroding the moral development of, and solidarity with, persons that makes authentic freedom possible. Glendon suggests that law must properly acknowledge and respect human dependency, the maternal and paternal duties that dependency demands, and the mediating structures of civil society that have always taken up the task of forming persons to embrace responsibly their duties of care.

In chapter 10, I end with a lengthy treatment of authentic freedom and reproductive justice. Lamenting our culture's modern tendency to view freedom in a consumerist vein, I return once again to propose Wollstonecraft's vision anew: freedom for the sake of human excellence. I then sketch out the path to a feminism reimagined upon this philosophical foundation, looking first to the duties of care of mothers and fathers in the family, upon which every other public good rests. I conclude with some general suggestions drawn from the extraordinary women highlighted in this book and others, too, as to how workplaces and the community at large might better value the culturally essential work of the home and in so doing rewire the world of work so that human persons are served above all else.

In 1792, Mary Wollstonecraft called for a revolution of female manners: in reforming themselves, she thought, women would go on to reform the world. One need not go beyond the territorial limits of the Unites States to recognize that the world needs reforming today: though we often hesitate to use such language, those in powerful positions at all levels of society have shown significant moral failure. It is time to reexamine a cause originally inspired by an imperfect woman with a noble vision. What follows is the history of her idea and the blueprint to take it forward.

CHAPTER 1

Mary Wollstonecraft's Moral Vision

In 1785, John Adams, his wife, Abigail, and their two eldest children departed from his diplomatic post in Paris to travel to Britain, where he served as the first U.S. ambassador to the Court of St. James. Adams, together with Benjamin Franklin and John Jay, had successfully negotiated the Treaty of Paris in 1783, formally ending the Revolutionary War and acknowledging the existence of the United States as a sovereign country. Adams now hoped to mend broken ties between the two countries as the new republic's first foreign minister. When they arrived in London, Adams and his family joined the congregation of a learned intellectual Adams had long admired, Reverend Richard Price. Twenty-six-year-old Mary Wollstonecraft was among Price's most devoted congregants.

Price was a Unitarian minister, an old friend of Franklin's, and a stalwart supporter of the American Revolution. He had penned a number of important pamphlets in support of the American cause for freedom and corresponded with several American leaders, among them Adams himself, Thomas Jefferson, and George Washington. In a 1784 pamphlet, Price had declared that "next to the introduction of Christianity among mankind, the American Revolution may prove the most important step in the progressive course of human improvement."[1]

Years after the revolution, as the debates at the Constitutional Convention raged and drafts for the new nation's fundamental laws were drawn up, Price applauded the Americans' desire to build a federal

system, protecting the liberty of the people while assuring greater authority in the central government. But Price also challenged his American peers on what he regarded as the working document's two fundamental flaws: the failure to grant political equality to women and, more
egregious still, the perpetuation of the slave trade, which Price decried
as "cruel, wicked, and diabolical."[2] These deficiencies struck at the heart
of the moral project Price believed the Americans had undertaken. Writing to John Jay in 1785, Price lamented: "It will appear that the [Ameri-
can] people who have struggled so bravely against being enslaved themselves are ready enough to enslave others: the event which has raised
my hopes of seeing a better state of human affairs will prove only an
introduction to a new scene of aristocratical tyranny and human de-
basement: and the friends of liberty and virtue in Europe will be sadly
disappointed and mortified."[3] The American founders obviously did
not heed Price's admonition.

But the young English schoolmistress was listening. Wollstonecraft had met the Unitarian minister in 1784, the year before the Adams
family arrived. She was teaching at a small school in the area, which she
had founded with one of her sisters. Although Anglican in religious
practice, she also attended Price's political sermons during her two-
year stay in Newington. His theological and philosophical tutelage was
coincident with the development of Wollstonecraft's educational philosophy, one that prioritized the moral formation of the young and the
importance of educating girls alongside boys with an equally rigorous
curriculum. She wrote her first book, *Thoughts on the Education of
Daughters*, on these themes, themes that reemerged more fully in her
most famous work, *A Vindication of the Rights of Woman*.

A well-read and deeply intelligent woman, Wollstonecraft developed her thought from manifold influences throughout her life, but perhaps none was as foundational as that of Richard Price. Offering in both
word and deed an account of God as the providential source of all goodness and truth, Price advocated political liberty as a means for all human
beings to make moral progress through the imitation of divine attributes,
a calling befitting rational creatures dignified by the divine image implanted in them. In a letter to her son John Quincy, Abigail Adams
wrote of Price: "He has a Charity which embraces all mankind."[4]

FIGURE 1.1. Mary Wollstonecraft, unknown date.
Credit: After a painting by John Opie (public domain).

The young Wollstonecraft found no reason women ought not be included in Price's ennobling mission: they were, after all, rational creatures made in the divine image. Eight years later, after Wollstonecraft published her groundbreaking treatise on women, Abigail Adams, who, as Price did, had impressed upon her husband to "remember the ladies," declared herself a "pupil of Wollstonecraft."[5] Neither Price nor Abigail convinced John Adams (or the other American founders) of the import of women's civil and political equality with men. But, happily for Abigail and the American women who followed her, Wollstonecraft was to develop Price's moral and political philosophy into her own magnificent treatise on women's rights.

In this chapter I delve deeply into this development. First, I seek to uncover Wollstonecraft's understanding of the nature of the human person and the development of virtue, key themes she develops from Price's work. I then proceed in this chapter and the next to explore how this ethical theory influences her views of education, gender, sex, marriage, parenting, law, and government. My focus is on Wollstonecraft's moral philosophy as articulated in the *Rights of Men* and the *Rights of Woman*, but I also reference other works on occasion.

Until quite recently, the full import of her philosophical ideas had been obscured by a preoccupation with the intimate (and not altogether accurate) details of her life that her short-time husband, the anarchist William Godwin, publicly memorialized almost immediately after her death.[6] Over the course of more than two hundred years, she has been both scorned and lionized for her alleged love affairs and suicide attempts, but seldom recognized as a serious philosopher in her own right.

When she wrote the *Rights of Woman*, Wollstonecraft was a thirty-two-year-old virgin theorist who had yet to encounter the embrace of a man whom she loved. She met her first love, an American entrepreneur named Gilbert Imlay, nearly two years later after having traveled to Paris to report on the French Revolution. Though she fell in love with Imlay and wished for commitment, she refused to put herself under the unjust marital laws of the time. Yet, seeking the refuge those laws provided her as an Englishwoman in France during the revolution, she took her beloved's name and nationality, making her in social circles his American wife, but they did not legally exchange marital vows. Still, their "marriage" began with deep love and affection—captured in a series of beautiful love letters—and brought forth a beloved child, Fanny.[7] For a year, the new mother nursed her child and wrote little, depending for her keep upon Imlay's provision.

It was not long before Imlay's commercial ventures and philandering caused him to abandon Wollstonecraft and their child, resulting in her emotional breakdown and two suicide attempts. In one of many despairing letters to Imlay, Wollstonecraft writes:

> I will not distress you by talking of the depression of my spirits, or the struggle I had to keep alive my dying heart.—It is even now too full to allow me to write with composure . . .—am I always to be tossed about thus?—shall I never find an asylum to rest *contented* in? How can you love to fly about continually . . . every other day? Why do you not attach those tender emotions round the idea of home, which even now dim my eyes? This alone is affection—every thing else is only humanity, electrified by sympathy.[8]

Wollstonecraft's love for her child—and a chance rescue—kept her alive.

Still despondent some years later, she fell for the intellectual Godwin, despite their seemingly stark philosophical differences. Wollstonecraft conceived a child with Godwin, and then married him, just before she died in childbirth. That child, Mary Shelley, became more famous perhaps than even her mother as the celebrated author of *Frankenstein* and the spouse of the Romantic poet Percy Shelley. Still, Wollstonecraft's dramatic biography has too often distracted attention away from the merit of her own thought. Only in recent decades have a handful of historians and philosophers begun to fill in the scholarly void, focusing less on Wollstonecraft's personal history to give more extensive consideration to the foundational principles of her moral and political program.[9] This new scholarly literature is curiously coincident with a recent resurgence of "virtue ethics" in academic philosophy. Both are suggestive of the view that Wollstonecraft's theory of moral development falls squarely within the virtue ethics—or Aristotelian—tradition. Her theory of gender, however, represents a great advance from that of the ancient Greek philosopher, who famously referred to females as "deformed males."[10]

I suggest throughout this book that Wollstonecraft's insights about sex, gender, work, marriage, virtue, and rights are just as cogent, compelling, and revolutionary today as they were in the late eighteenth century. Given the disparaging views of women in both antiquity and during the Enlightenment period, and the Cartesian dualism that has haunted the philosophy of sex and gender since the seventeenth century, it's not surprising that Wollstonecraft's full program has been derailed. In putting the philosophical pieces back together, one finds in Wollstonecraft's work an ancient appreciation for moral excellence in harmony with a modern respect for human dignity and political freedom and equality. This synthesis, and its notable application in Wollstonecraft's vision of sex and marriage, serves as a sharp corrective to conceptions of freedom as radical autonomy today, even as it seeks a fuller recognition of the equal dignity of men and women.

In this chapter and the next, I showcase the great philosopher's lost vision. The chapters that follow recount how closely her successors in the cause of women's rights followed or how they strayed from her thought, and how we might reclaim that vision today.

THE *RIGHTS OF WOMAN* AND WOLLSTONECRAFT'S VIEW OF HUMAN NATURE

Wollstonecraft began her political writings with hope in the progressive potential of politics. The American Revolution, with its inspired Declaration of Independence and written constitution, had offered a humanizing picture of governance, extolling both liberty and, in the speeches and letters of many of the Founders, the virtue needed to sustain it. In Price's and Wollstonecraft's view, the Americans were building, however imperfectly, upon the tradition of ordered liberty rooted in the constitutional traditions of their British ancestors: the Glorious Revolution of 1688, which limited the absolute power of the British monarch, had represented a first reforming stage. The French Revolution was still in its early stage when she published the *Rights of Woman* in 1792; the Reign of Terror, which she witnessed in Paris, was months away. For republicans such as Wollstonecraft, hope was in the air.

Wollstonecraft's *Rights of Woman* represented, at the political level, an extended plea to expand on the revolution in political thinking that had taken root in America and then in France: to include women in political efforts to secure "the rights of man." But, even a cursory reading of the *Rights of Woman* reveals it is scarcely about rights at all, and her plea for women's political equality is not why her treatise remains so original. Others besides her, as far back as Christine de Pisan in medieval France and as recently as Olympe de Gouges's *Declaration of the Rights of Woman and the Female Citizen* in 1791, had made similar claims for women's equality.[11] Rather, Wollstonecraft's political argument, like that of Price before her, was most centrally concerned with the advance of intellectual and moral virtue, an advance they believed would be enabled by a universal share in liberty and equality among all men and women. "Unless virtue be nursed by liberty, it will never attain due strength,"[12] she writes in the *Rights of Woman*. Human beings' progress in virtue—not their attainment of property, wealth, or status—would guarantee personal, familial, and societal happiness. This was her claim.

Her philosophical case was robust, grounded in what she took to be the unalterable truth about God and the wondrous capacities of his human creation. Human beings are endowed with the ennobling capacity to reason, "to rise in excellence by the exercise of powers implanted for that purpose."[13] This capacity is what makes them distinct from the animals. Thus, the ultimate purpose of every human life is to use one's own reason to submit to the "unerring reason" of God, to conform oneself to the nature of things as God has designed them, and thus to unfold one's human faculties in order to better oneself and to be of service to others. Goodness has but one eternal standard— God—thus, all of his creatures, regardless of sex, are to seek to attain to that standard.

In Wollstonecraft's view, women in her time had been discouraged from "unfold[ing] their faculties" by their lack of intellectual and moral formation and by social conventions that had rendered their minds dependent and their cares frivolous.[14] Women had been kept from attaining the very purpose Providence had ordained: to make all human creatures wise and virtuous, seeking after truth, understanding, generosity, modesty, and humanity, instead of vain beauty, elegance, and worldly recognition. Such was the nature of Wollstonecraft's charge.

Wollstonecraft well understood that not all human beings would attain an equal share of wisdom and virtue; for her, the only truly just hierarchy was one based on these merited attainments. But she did believe that all human beings—male or female, rich or poor—were equally capable of trying. Indeed, it was their common nature as creatures endowed with rational powers capable of moral development that gave human beings their equal worth. Their common rational nature was also what enabled them to discern God's existence and the nature of the moral order. The existence of God and of the human soul were then not matters of blind religious faith for Wollstonecraft. She believed them to be discernable by the reasonable person's observation of the dynamic coherence and unity in nature and of the internal order and fitness of things, both natural and moral. God's harmonious design could be seen in his creation; the faculties of the human mind, as they reflected and sought truth, also revealed for her a single source. "The more man discovers of the nature of his mind and body, the more clearly he is convinced, that to act according to the dictates of reason is to conform to the will of God,"[15] she says in the *Rights of Men*.

Reason for Wollstonecraft, as for Price, was not mechanistic or calculating, nor was the intellect disconnected in any way from the body through which it worked, Descartes's increasingly popular theories notwithstanding. Those various views of reason, held by leading Enlightenment thinkers, promoted far too reductive a view of human capabilities. Rather, the human mind ceaselessly sought after truth and so was properly open to all of reality, including what transcended the merely visible. The reasoning power had the capacity to draw principles from the nature of things as they were impressed upon the mind through embodied experience, acquired knowledge, and contemplation of God. Hers was a far more ancient view.

Cultivating one's reason was "an arduous task," because the intellect represented the governing power of the person by regulating the emotions, passions, and appetites so these might become "necessary auxiliaries of reason."[16] The passions were neither good nor evil for Wollstonecraft; they were human dispositions that "push . . . us forward," but they must receive proper direction toward benevolence and imitation of the highest good, God.[17] In a well-integrated person, then, human appetites provided motivation and inspiration to seek the goods of life, but they did not direct it. Reason, naturally ordered to goodness and truth, and properly instructed in sound principles inculcated by high-minded parents and teachers, provided that direction. Wollstonecraft would have agreed with Cicero that virtue is "fully developed reason."[18]

But without reason directing the passions toward virtue, one's animal instincts could "run wild,"[19] rendering a person impulsive, selfish, even brutal. Not governing passions the way one should, he or she becomes a slave to those passions, and thus not independent and free. Wollstonecraft describes reason as the "light" to the passions' "heat," or the "rudder" to the passions' "winds": "But if virtue is to be acquired by experience, or taught by example, reason, perfected by reflection, must be the director of the whole host of passions, which produce a fructifying heat, but no light, that you would exalt into her place.—She must hold the rudder, or, let the wind blow which way it list, the vessel will never advance smoothly to its destined port; for the time lost in tacking about would dreadfully impede its progress."[20] Wollstonecraft's view of the proper interplay of the person's intellect and passions—the path, if well-trodden, that brings about self-possession, interior freedom, and independence of mind—can be traced to the great thinkers of antiquity.

One recalls Plato's chariot allegory in the *Phaedrus* as teaching a similar hierarchy in the rational soul: the charioteer, or reason, must guide the horses, the passions, to achieve interior order and peace. Aristotle famously taught that the life of virtue consisted in self-government, in the "active exercise of the soul's faculties in conformity to rational principle."[21] And, here is Cicero's rendition of this teaching: "For when appetites overstep their bounds and, galloping away, so to speak, whether in desire or aversion, are not well held in hand by reason, they clearly overleap all bound and measure; for they throw obedience off and leave it behind and refuse to obey the reins of reason, to which they are subject by Nature's laws."[22] Interior freedom and independence of mind, for the ancients and Wollstonecraft too, was found in self-mastery. Notably, contemporary researchers are beginning to corroborate and rehabilitate this ancient wisdom: character development outperforms cognitive development in studies of adult success over time.[23]

This ancient view is a far cry from that of the philosopher David Hume, a contemporary of Wollstonecraft's, who advanced a position that has only grown stronger in recent times: reason is the "slave of the passions."[24] Reason merely exists to provide a *post hoc* rationalization of the desires of the ruling passions. Wollstonecraft responded to such a degradation of the human person: "In what respect are we superior to the brute creation, if intellect is not allowed to be the guide of passion? Brutes hope and fear, love and hate; but, without a capacity to improve, a power of turning these passions to good or evil, they neither acquire virtue nor wisdom.—Why? Because the Creator has not given them reason."[25]

Wollstonecraft was not naïve to the fragility and fallibility of human reason; she well knew even well-disciplined human beings could err, and often do. Her view of human reason's propensity to err, especially when swept up in vengeful emotion, grew in its political manifestation as the Reign of Terror in Paris erupted. But until that life-changing experience, she did not believe human beings acted out of purely evil motives.[26] Indeed, here is Wollstonecraft writing in an especially Aristotelian vein, quite contrary to the deeply pessimistic Calvinist anthropology that, in post-Reformation Europe, had taken hold of many Christians' sensibilities: "It may be confidently asserted that no man chooses evil, because it is evil; he only mistakes it for happiness, the good he seeks."[27] With more hopeful a view still, Wollstonecraft believed that reason, if accompanied by humility, also had the capacity for self-correction: with reflection and guidance from wise teachers, and a faith-filled disposition, one could learn from one's experiences and gain wisdom to choose better the next time. This was life's struggle: to cooperate with God on the path toward moral perfection: "He has told us not only that we may inherit eternal life, but that we shall be changed, if we do not perversely reject the offered grace."[28]

EDUCATION: TO LIBERATE THE PERSON

It follows that the very purpose of education for Wollstonecraft, as for the ancient thinkers, was to cultivate in young persons their rational capacities and governance over the passions: "Into this error men have, probably, been led by viewing education in a false light; not considering it as the first step to form a being advancing gradually towards perfection; but only as a preparation for life."[29] "Liberal education," as opposed to mere technical training (for a job or even a profession), was designed to liberate the rational human being from the enslavement of the passions, so that he or she might be truly free—in whatever occupation he or she might enjoy.

Although many institutions of higher learning today still call themselves "liberal," most no longer understand their mission this way; rather, Hume's philosophy—and the ascendency of the passions—has gained currency, reducing the role of reason to the mere servant of the passions. The ancient idea of the properly ordered soul has not been discarded; it simply has been reversed, with the passions now serving as commander and reason the mere servant. And the passions' commands tend to be relentless and all-encompassing, the very adverse of liberation. Wollstonecraft believed that the inculcation of good intellectual and moral habits at a young age would allow the person to become free, with earned independence of mind. He or she then would possess an intellect capable of critical judgment, not merely imitative of groupthink or blindly obedient to prevailing authority. But independence of mind and good habits do not spring forth organically from the child: one must be taught; desires must be schooled; the familial environment and society in which he or she lives must encourage each child's intellectual and moral development. Her advice in this regard to parents was plentiful: "If you wish to make your son rich, pursue one course—if you are only anxious to make him virtuous, you must take another; but do not imagine that you can bound from one road to the other without losing your way."[30]

The personal and societal benefits of such moral development would be profound, Wollstonecraft thought. A person freed from the incessant desire to indulge one's various appetites would be more properly focused on the good of others, and thus engage in a much more meritorious undertaking through benevolence. Indeed, she believed strongly that it was each person's highest human end to imitate God's goodness through benevolence toward others. One's treatment

of fellow human beings—whatever their social status—was the best indicator of one's identification with God. From the lips of a protagonist
in one of Wollstonecraft's short children's stories: "If I behave improperly to servants, I am really their inferior, as I abuse trust, and imitate
not the Being, whose servant I am, without a shadow of equality."[31]

HUMAN HAPPINESS: PARTICIPATING IN GOD'S PERFECTION

Despite her own difficult upbringing with an abusive and alcoholic father, she thoroughly imbibed Price's view of the goodness of God's
providential design, drawn from deep within the Christian tradition.
Suffering thus was not a punishment from on high but was permitted
for one's edification: "Why should he lead us from love of ourselves to
the sublime emotions which the discovery of his wisdom and goodness
excites, if these feelings were not set in motion to improve our nature,
of which they make a part, and render us capable of enjoying a more
godlike portion of happiness? Firmly persuaded that no evil exists in
the world that God did not design to take place, I build my belief on
the perfection of God."[32] Wollstonecraft's moral norms were philosophically grounded in God's perfection, of which all human goods are
but a participation or a "shadow." The protagonist of one of her novels
states, "The same turn of mind which leads me to adore the Author of
all Perfection—which leads me to conclude that he only can fill my
soul; forces me to admire the faint image—the shadows of his attributes here below."[33]

Wollstonecraft thus regarded worship and imitation of the divine
perfection as the path to human excellence and happiness:

> The only solid foundation for morality appears to be the character
> of the supreme Being. . . .
>
> It seems natural for man to search for excellence, and either to
> trace it in the object that he worships, or blindly to invest it with
> perfection, as a garment. But what good effect can the latter mode
> of worship have on the moral conduct of a rational being? . . .
>
> For to love God as the fountain of wisdom, goodness, and
> power, appears to be the only worship useful to a being who

wishes to acquire either virtue or knowledge. A blind unsettled affection may, like human passions, occupy the mind and warm the heart, whilst, to do justice, love mercy, and walk humbly with our God, is forgotten.[34]

Humility was especially important in an ethic that sought to imitate God's goodness. Wollstonecraft believed that "the humble mind that seek[s] to find favor in His sight" will recognize one's own propensity to fall short of God's loving standard and so be quicker to forgive the failings of others: "I . . . have vices, hid, perhaps, from human eye, that bend me to the dust before God, and loudly tell me, when all is mute, that we are formed of the same earth, and breathe the same element. Humanity thus rises naturally out of humility, and twists the cords of love that in various convolutions entangle the heart."[35]

Wollstonecraft, again following Price, rejected voluntarism outright. Rather than a pronouncement of God's arbitrary will, the moral law is a participation in God's goodness, discernable through contemplation and right reason. For Wollstonecraft, God's unerring reason commanded submission: "I submit to the moral laws which my reason deduces from this view of my dependence on him.—It is not his power that I fear—it is not to an arbitrary will, but to unerring reason I submit."[36] Were God's goodness not sought as the "eternal rule of right," that by which we should judge all other claims of right, expediency and power would be all that remains to guide human actions.[37] Indeed, man's arbitrary claims of power, heeding not the higher authority of God, were the source of every oppression, in Wollstonecraft's view. And it was here that she made an important advance for women, articulating an ancient truth that still admonishes today: were there no higher standard of truth or virtue, human beings would base their actions on what is most useful, pleasing, or convenient to them, and the weak would fall prey to the strong. Wollstonecraft concludes: "For man and woman, truth, if I understand the meaning of the word, must be the same; yet . . . virtue becomes a relative idea, having no other foundation than utility, and of that utility men pretend arbitrarily to judge, shaping it to their own convenience."[38]

She regarded this utilitarian view as especially prevalent and harmful in moral considerations about women. It seemed plain to her that women were also rational creatures with equal dignity, responsible to that single standard of truth and virtue, but they were depicted culturally as fragile, emotional, and dependent, merely useful playthings for men. She points to Rousseau as the main culprit of a gendered theory of virtue. In Rousseau's view, Wollstonecraft paraphrased, "Man was made to reason, woman to feel; and that together, flesh and spirit, they make the most perfect whole, by blending happily reason and sensibility into one character."[39] Through this view of women, Wollstonecraft retorts, society tended to "render women pleasing at the expense of every solid virtue."[40] No, Wollstonecraft demanded, women were meant to strive for intellectual and moral excellence too.

Anticipating centuries of debate about whether women's equality with men would imply a claim to "sameness," Wollstonecraft was explicit about her views. Importantly, men and women share a common human nature ordered to wisdom and virtue, and the virtues are singular in their unitary source: God. But she was quick to note that by this she was not suggesting women and men are identical or that their responsibilities in life are the same. That is, the duties by which men and women endeavor to grow in wisdom and virtue will likely be different; this is most evident when it comes to their asymmetrical contributions to human reproduction. But, and this is the key to her ennobling theory of sexual equality, they are to meet whatever responsibilities they have with the same human virtues. Wollstonecraft affirms that "women, I allow, may have different duties to fulfill; but they are *human* duties, and the principles that should regulate the discharge of them, I sturdily maintain, must be the same."[41] Moral excellence might manifest itself differently in different persons, and childbearing and breastfeeding presented particular opportunities for excellence in women. But all such excellence, exhibited by a man or woman, is an imitation of the one perfect God. Thus, virtue has no sex: justice is not masculine, nor is mercy feminine; all must simply strive to imitate God's goodness as they carry out the particular duties of life.

Wollstonecraft was also clear about the means to develop virtue, which is a good practice repeated over time with such intentionality that it becomes a habitual disposition of the person. Virtue is inculcated and practiced in and through one's work, through carrying out one's particular duties, according to one's state in life. But if work was the means, idleness, for Wollstonecraft, was the undoing of moral development: "The human character has ever been formed by the employments the individual, or class, pursues; and if the faculties are not sharpened by necessity, they must remain obtuse."[42] Wollstonecraft complained that women's uneducated and dependent state had rendered them ill fit to undertake serious occupations. Because they were not formed to take their work seriously, they languished morally, dedicating their time and attention to trivialities rather than to their duties.

This view accords well with Wollstonecraft's core belief in self-determination and independence, or, in today's parlance, human agency. In a just society, each man or woman, as a rational creature, is free to determine the course of his or her life in and through one's personal circumstances. But, for Wollstonecraft, self-determination and agency, in a word, personal freedom, is found not in whimsical self-creation or the abdication of given obligations according to the dictate of one's passions. Rather, one creates one's life through growth in wisdom and virtue, achieved through sustained intellectual and moral formation and circumscribed by one's familial and social obligations. Such a course allows one to choose day by day, and with increasing freedom and independence, against decadence, self-regard, and mediocrity, for a life uniquely one's own, dedicated to human excellence, whatever one's personal circumstances. Wollstonecraft maintained, most paradoxically to our modern ears, that "the being who discharges the duties of its station is independent."[43] A life bereft of such a thoroughly human vision, one drawn instead to the pursuit of self-seeking unadorned by affections and obligations, would be neither authentically human nor authentically free.

THE PRIMACY OF DOMESTIC AFFECTIONS FOR WOMEN AND MEN

For Wollstonecraft, then, the very first duty of a human being is to develop his or her capacities as a rational creature, to grow in virtue and wisdom. Women and men accomplish this common aim through their particular duties in life. For married women with children, motherhood ranked first. She did not limit women's work to motherhood, but she gave it top priority. But here's the thing: she gave fatherhood top priority for married men. Wollstonecraft believed that domestic affections should take priority for both men and women, as therein lay the happiness of the couple, their children, and the world into which well-loved, self-possessed persons would go.

Wollstonecraft often laments the vices spawned in the idleness of the aristocratic rich: the fact that they could push off life's ordinary work to servants compromised their own potential growth in virtue, and gave poor example to the lower classes: "In the superior ranks of life, every duty is done by deputies, as if duties could ever be waved, and the vain pleasures which consequent idleness forces the rich to pursue, appear so enticing to the next rank, that the numerous scramblers for wealth sacrifice every thing to tread on their heels."[44] She was especially critical of the propensity of the rich to delegate their parental duties to servants. She warned of the regret they would experience when their children would not return their affections later in life: "Parental affection produces filial duty."[45] More so, she worried that parents who had abdicated the important task of parenting had also abdicated their first duty as citizens: to transform private persons into public citizens, capable of respect and benevolence toward their fellow creatures, especially the weak and vulnerable.

And so "domestic" (or family) duties and affections rank first; if self-mastery and independence of mind is not habituated in children when they are young, harder still will it be to practice virtue later. Again, emphasizing this point, Wollstonecraft writes, "It is the indispensable duty of men and women to fulfil the duties which give birth to affections that are the surest preservatives against vice."[46] Personal virtue and familial affections, cultivated in the domestic sphere, are the means to public virtue, to societal order and beatitude. The benefits of a rich domestic life for society were manifold, as these remarks found throughout her work make clear:

> If you wish to make good citizens, you must first exercise the affections of a son and a brother. This is the only way to expand the heart; for public affections, as well as public virtue, must ever grow out of private character. . . .

Few, I believe, have had much affection for mankind, who did not first love their parents, their brothers, sisters, and even the domestic brutes, whom they first played with. The exercise of youthful sympathies forms the moral temperature; and it is the recollection of these first affections and pursuits that gives life to those that are afterwards more under the direction of reason.[47]

I have endeavored to show that private duties are never properly fulfilled unless the understanding enlarges the heart; and that public virtue is only an aggregate of private.[48]

We ought to recall that the inculcation of virtue in the young is not utilitarian for Wollstonecraft: the very purpose as human beings is to achieve the self-mastery that allows them to be independent thinkers and benevolent to others. The benefits to society as a whole are not secondary, though; they are all of a piece. Well-integrated human beings make for a well-ordered society.

WOMEN'S WORK

Wollstonecraft appreciated the capacity of able women to be educated for serious occupations other than motherhood, and advocated training for women in medicine, journalism, politics, and business, to name a few. She recommended that girls and boys be educated together, so that girls would be privy to the same rigorous course of liberal education that boys were. Scientific study and public-minded occupations would broaden their minds and develop women intellectually and morally, advancing the development of the women themselves and of society. These benefits would redound to women's familial relationships too. In fact, undertakings outside of the home would complement women's domestic duties: "Women cannot be confined to merely domestic pursuits, for they will not fulfill family duties, unless their minds take a wider range, and while they are kept in ignorance they become in the same proportion the slaves of pleasure as they are the slaves of man. Nor can they be shut out of great enterprises."[49] Extraordinary women might even forgo marriage and family life altogether to focus with singularity on professional enterprises: "Certainly the best works, and of greatest merit for the public, have proceeded from the unmarried or childless men. I say the same of women."[50] But, again returning to the great good that ordinary domestic affections do for the world, she notes that "the welfare of society is not built on extraordinary exertions."[51]

She rings the same note when discussing professional occupations undertaken by mothers: they must not distract from maternal affections. Wollstonecraft recognized women's great capacity for multitasking (how could any student of history not), but she wished to ensure that one's familial affections and duties were always given primary importance: "No employment of the mind is a sufficient excuse for neglecting domestic duties, and I cannot conceive that they are incompatible."[52]

This is an encouraging note for what has become the perennial question for women (and increasingly men) in late modern capitalist societies: how to balance work and family without sacrificing the wellbeing of either. Of course, one recalls that Wollstonecraft lived before the Industrial Revolution; whatever the advances industrialization have brought to the work in the home and work outside the home, it has surely made combining the two a more trying task, a central theme to which we will return throughout this book.

Wollstonecraft extolled independence of mind, believing that a well-developed and disciplined mind would enable one to think for oneself and make good and prudent judgments, independent especially of the strength of the emotions and appetites directing them elsewhere. Thus, she worried extensively about how women's economic dependence upon men rendered them too often dependent on their husbands' minds also. When women lacked true independence of mind, and so personal ownership of their proper duties as rational creatures, women could be "cunning, mean, and selfish" toward their husbands, manipulating them rather than loving them.[53] Not only were young women at the time trained only to fit themselves, and their figures, for an advantageous marriage; once married, they lacked the intellectual and moral resources to undertake properly the important responsibilities of motherhood, and beyond: "To be a good mother—a woman must have sense, and that independence of mind which few women possess who are taught to depend entirely on their husbands. Meek wives are, in general, foolish mothers. . . . Unless the understanding of woman be enlarged, and her character rendered more firm, by being allowed to govern her own conduct, she will never have sufficient sense or command of temper to manage her children properly."[54]

Lest it sound as though Wollstonecraft were only concerned with domesticity for women, it must be repeated again and again that her concern was an improved domestic life, period. She did not erect an impenetrable public/private divide as so many before and since have been wont to do. Though she observed that the rearing of young children justly appeared to be the "peculiar destination of women," and she valorized breastfeeding as the best means to instill early on shared maternal and filial affections, she did not regard "women's role" as confined to the private sphere.[55] No, she simply regarded domestic life as the most important sphere in society. It was the seedbed for the cultivation of virtue in children, and in their parents: "The wisdom of the Almighty has so ordered things, that one cause produces many effects. While we are looking into another's mind, and forming their temper, we are insensibly correcting our own; and every act of benevolence which we exert to our fellow creatures, does ourselves the most essential services."[56] Here, she enunciates the great insight of seasoned parents: as mothers and fathers concern themselves with forming good habits in their children, they are awoken simultaneously to the myriad ways in which they themselves might improve their character too.

Wollstonecraft also anticipated the backlash that was to attend women's enhanced educational opportunities, notably in the mid-twentieth century. If highly educated women had become unsatisfied with motherhood in the 1960s, then perhaps they should not have attended college, suggested some traditionalists. However, Wollstonecraft blamed not the prospect of better education but rather the lack of virtue in those who would go on to prize public accomplishments over domestic affections. Whatever serious responsibilities women might undertake in the professional world, the primacy of domestic affections properly works against preferring public commendations over the needs of the family. But such an affective prioritizing of the prime good of the home takes discipline and virtue, however one arranges one's time in and outside the home:

> It is the want of domestic taste, and not the acquirement of knowledge, that takes women out of their families, and tears the smiling babe from the breast that ought to afford it nourishment. Women have been allowed to remain in ignorance, and slavish dependence, many, very many years . . . and vanity makes them value accomplishments more than virtues. . . .
>
> An active mind embraces the whole circle of its duties, and finds time enough for all. It is not, I assert . . . the enchantment of literary pursuits, or the steady investigation of scientific subjects, that lead women astray from duty. No, it is indolence and vanity— the love of pleasure and the love of sway, that will rain paramount in an empty mind.[57]

Wollstonecraft thus urged women to take seriously the essential work that happened in the home ("ennobling duties which equally require exertion and self-denial"[58]), and she believed a woman of purpose would undertake her familial duties and, under the right circumstances, create time for other pursuits. To do so required a sense of order and determination: "To fulfill domestic duties much resolution is necessary, and a serious kind of perseverance that requires a more firm support than emotions. . . . Whoever rationally means to be useful must have a plan of conduct."[59] The rearing of children was not for the meek or overly emotional; it was, again, serious work, and must be treated as such. She advises: "The management of the temper, the first, and most important branch of education, requires the sober steady eye of reason; a plan of conduct equally distant from tyranny and indulgence: yet these are the extremes that people of sensibility alternately fall into; always shooting beyond the mark."[60] Children were not a burden or impediment to a woman's "real" work; they were her real work, and an ennobling and important work they were. But they might not be her *only* work. And they were not only *her* work.

Wollstonecraft thought that women would not be successful and happy as they carried out their familial duties unless men turned their

first affections there too. Again, her emphasis is not so much on particular roles but rather primary affections and virtuous, benevolent dispositions in undertaking one's "respective duties of station." In Wollstonecraft's writings the proper role of a father in the lives of his wife
and children is not extensively delineated, but then, apart from childbearing and breastfeeding, and so the nurture of very young children,
neither does Wollstonecraft offer a list of proper duties for the mother.
Virtue prevails for Wollstonecraft, transforming the person into one
eager to be useful, to carry out the tasks at hand with good sense, and
to be benevolent, undertaking one's day-to-day duties with deep affection and respect for others. The parents' own moral development depends upon it too.

And this is certainly not only true for women. Wollstonecraft
viewed attentive fatherhood as deeply transformative of men: "The
character of . . . a husband, and a father, forms the citizen imperceptibly, by producing a sober manliness of thought, and orderly behavior;
but, from the lax morals and depraved affections of the libertine, what
results?—a finical man of taste, who is only anxious to secure his own
private gratifications, and to maintain his rank in society."[61] Wollstonecraft sensed a truth that, in our age of sociological data, would be proven
thus: men who are husbands and fathers are more successful at work and
have better health and less substance abuse issues and criminal activity.[62]
Wollstonecraft anticipated other recent sociological findings too: fathers
who are attentive to their children, and, even more importantly, to their
children's mothers not only have happier children but their children also
have happier mothers. Indeed, studies have found that the single best
predictor of a happy mother is an emotionally attentive father.[63] Wollstonecraft observed: "The affection of her husband [is] one of the comforts that render her task less difficult and her life happier."[64]

But men who did not prioritize domestic affections could hardly
expect women to do so either, thought Wollstonecraft: "Till men become attentive to the duty of a father, it is vain to expect women to
spend that time in their nursery which [men] choose to spend at their
glass."[65] This certainly would not be the last time an advocate for women
would point to liquor as what kept a father from the responsibilities of
his family. Engaged and attentive fatherhood was the best means to

transform men's desires by bringing them into a life of shared domesticity. With so much at stake for the men themselves, and for women,
children, and society more broadly, it really is no surprise then that the
single most important theme in Wollstonecraft's *Rights of Woman*—a
book far more about virtue than it is about rights—is men, and their
moral character.

It is to that theme that we now turn.

CHAPTER 2

Men, Marriage, Law, and Government

Having now understood the priority of virtue in Wollstonecraft's philosophy, its cultivation in a happy home, and the consequences of that state of domestic affairs for society at large, we can begin to appreciate the attention the late eighteenth-century philosopher pays to the intimate relationships between men and women. If "respect for man, as man, is the foundation of every noble sentiment," disrespect of men for women or women for men would surely be ruinous to the whole program. And so, she thought it was. Her aim was to set things between the sexes aright, for in doing that the whole human race, divided as it was between the sexes, might have a hope of progressing in virtue, and thus finding happiness: "The two sexes mutually corrupt and improve each other. This I believe to be an indisputable truth, extending it to every virtue."[1]

Let us now dig a bit deeper. Just what state of affairs corrupts relationships between the sexes, and what might improve them? The place to begin, strange as it may sound to many modern ears, is Wollstonecraft's consideration of the virtue of chastity, or sexual integrity, thought by most in our day to be wholly passé or simple prudery. To fully appreciate Wollstonecraft's vision in its fullness, however, we must not allow our preconceptions to cloud our understanding. If we miss her meaning here, casting it aside as a mere historical concern of no relevance to us today, we deprive ourselves of the wisdom she offers.

Wollstonecraft had a clear target in view when she "[threw] down [her] gauntlet" in an effort to "deny the existence of sexual virtues."[2] In her time, the association of women with "virtue" was confined to this single theme: chastity. And, in general, a real virtue it was not. The conventional concern, Wollstonecraft tells us, was to preserve a woman's reputation, not her dignity as a human being or her authentic moral development as a person. Since the societal emphasis in general was on appearances—and, for women, on appearing to have this particular "feminine" virtue—women missed the opportunity to develop the full panoply of virtues, and thus were deprived of real moral and intellectual development.

The apparent social reasons for keeping a woman's reputation as a "chaste woman" untarnished were at least twofold, according to Wollstonecraft. First, a woman's chastity within marriage held firm the hereditary dispensation of titles and property to the rightful heirs of the biological father. Second, a yet unmarried woman's pure reputation inspired the game of "valor" libertine men played, in which "chaste women" were worth the greatest catch. Little consideration was given in her time to the effect a woman's sexual experience inside and outside of marriage might have on the woman herself, but that was one of Wollstonecraft's chief concerns. She showed great pity for women who were drawn into prostitution (or even marriage) merely to make a living (since most other occupations were closed to them). She regarded such occupational decisions as endemic to a situation in which women were only educated to be sexually attractive to men, and so could only support themselves through their capacity to do so.

More egregious still, women who were poorly educated tended to attract libertine men who were least apt to care for them as persons and so were most dangerous to them. She worried about rape (even within marriage, since one could marry a libertine too), and the dangers of pregnancy, which at that time posed a life-threatening risk to women. Her closest friend, Fanny Blood, died in childbirth, as Wollstonecraft herself did years later. Clearly, sexual intercourse did not affect women and men equally; the burdens upon women then (and now too) were far more consequential, and the societal and marital power men wielded over women aggravated this asymmetry even further.

To be clear, Wollstonecraft valued chastity just as much as any other virtue, and because its absence struck at the heart of domestic life, perhaps even more so. But she was most eager to correct the lopsided (or "sexual") approach to virtue, wherein women were meant to conform to this virtue alone (and do so inauthentically), while men ignored their own need for sexual integrity entirely, assuming it the sole duty of women. She was especially impatient to correct this ironic state of affairs, since clearly men were "more under the influence of their appetites than women." She writes in full: "But, in proportion as this regard for the reputation of chastity is prized by women, it is despised by men: and the two extremes are equally destructive to morality. Men are certainly more under the influence of their appetites than women; and their appetites are more depraved by unbridled indulgence and the fastidious contrivances of satiety."[3]

Men's libidos were clearly stronger than women's, and yet men excused their own libertine behavior, assuming such desires must always be satiated, whatever the cost to women, and put the duty of chastity (and blame for any breach thereof) on women alone. But in Wollstonecraft's view, sexual integrity was good for both men and women and for society at large: "Chastity, modesty, public spirit, and all the noble train of virtues, on which social virtue and happiness are built, should be understood and cultivated by all mankind, or they will be cultivated to little effect."[4] This puzzling social convention (which we now refer to as the "sexual double standard") was bolstered, in Wollstonecraft's view, by the then popular gender theory of Rousseau, a deeply influential thinker at the time (and ever since). Rousseau suggested that women, though legally subordinate to men, commanded power over men through women's sexual purity. Their softening, moral influence within the private sphere civilized corruptible men; it followed for Rousseau that women's lack of chastity (or entrance into the public sphere, for that matter) sowed moral corruption as a matter of course. But Rousseau did not expect the same integrity from men. Indeed, the "natural man" of his *Second Discourse* famously "bedded down at random and often for one night only . . . according to chance encounters, opportunity, and desire."[5] Meanwhile, women in this natural state cared for the children whom, we later learn, their fathers "did not even recognize." Perhaps it is no surprise then when we recall that the author of *Emile*, the celebrated book on education, abandoned his own five children to an orphanage.

Wollstonecraft's theory of private virtue informing public virtue may remind us of Rousseau, as it well should. Rousseau here followed the ancients, and both were an influence upon Wollstonecraft. But with regard to the relations between the sexes, she disagreed with Rousseau fiercely. Women may indeed wield some sort of erotic power over men because of men's stronger desire for them, but, for Wollstonecraft, such power asymmetries ought never be encouraged, even if it is women who in some cases enjoy the upper hand. Power itself is corrupting of relationships, she thought, leading toward mutual manipulation and distrust. It is thus corrupting of individuals too. She instead urged affection and mutual respect, the fruits of *self*-mastery, not mastery over the other. Wollstonecraft famously writes: "I do not wish [women] to have power over men; but over themselves."[6] And this was her hope for men too. If men were more self-possessed, with a greater respect for the well-being of women as rational creatures made in God's image, women would not feel the need to self-objectify, degrading themselves into mere objects for men's arousal: "I know of no other way of preserving the chastity of mankind, than that of rendering women rather objects of love than desire. The difference is great. Yet, while women are encouraged to ornament their persons at the expense of their minds . . . they will be, generally speaking, only objects of desire; and, to such women, men cannot be constant. Men, accustomed only to have their senses moved, merely seek for a selfish gratification in the society of women, and their sexual instinct, being neither supported by the understanding nor the heart, must be excited by variety."[7]

With this theme, we reach the most significant unsung project of the *Rights of Woman*: to denounce the want of chastity in men. Two of the thirteen chapters are dedicated to bemoaning the state of this virtue in men. And beyond those two, she broaches the theme early in her introduction, returns to it at the very end of her conclusion, and discusses it in the chapter on education. But even counting references does not do justice to the prevalence of the theme. She states its centrality quite bluntly: "For I will venture to assert, that all the causes of female weakness, as well as depravity, which I have already enlarged

A

VINDICATION

OF THE

RIGHTS OF WOMAN:

WITH

STRICTURES

ON

POLITICAL AND MORAL SUBJECTS,

BY MARY WOLLSTONECRAFT.

PRINTED AT BOSTON,
BY PETER EDES FOR THOMAS AND ANDREWS,
FAUST's Statue, No. 45, Newbury-Street,
MDCCXCII.

FIGURE 2.1. Book cover, *A Vindication of the Rights of Woman*, printed in Boston, 1792. Credit: Library of Congress (public domain).

on, branch out of *one grand cause*—want of chastity in men."[8] And again, but now including the effect the vice has on all of "mankind": "The little respect paid to chastity in the male world is, I am persuaded, *the grand source* of many of the physical and moral evils that torment mankind, as well as of the vices and follies that degrade and destroy women."[9] Though she was an expressive writer, the superlatives here are not stylistic. Only women's "neglected education"—an equally impor-tant (and not unconnected) theme for which Wollstonecraft has received just accolades over the centuries—receives nearly as much attention.[10]

It's unfortunate that, over the last half century, women's rights advo-cates have not taken Wollstonecraft's admonitions about sex seriously, with some accusing her of "assailing female sexuality," while others ignore her manifest concern for sexual integrity and draw conclusions only from her ambiguous life choices.[11] But to miss the earnestness with which she treats the virtue of chastity is to miss a central theme of the *Rights of Woman*. Indeed, it is with regard to this theme that her most cogent moral aphorism is concerned: "Cherish such an habitual respect for mankind as may prevent us from disgusting a fellow-creature for the sake of a present indulgence." With the sex crimes that continue to beset women in our time—women who notably wield far more soci-etal influence than women in the late eighteenth century did—we best pay her some serious attention. She wished not for sexual repression, but for growth in self-mastery, for both women and men.

Wollstonecraft believed that many men did not arrive at true maturity because of sexual misadventures early on: "Thanks to early debauchery, [they are] scarcely men in their outward form."[12] These "overgrown children" had missed an essential schooling of their de-sires that ought to have taken place in their youth. She writes in a later letter to Imlay: "It is the rarest thing in the world to meet with a man with sufficient delicacy of feeling to govern desire."[13] Especially because of the power men possess in society, the inattention to boys' authentic moral development was ruinous to public virtue at large:

At school, boys infallibly lose that decent bashfulness, which might have ripened into modesty, at home. And what nasty inde-cent tricks do they not also learn from each other, when a number of them pig together in the same bedchamber, not to speak of the vices, which render the body weak, whilst they effectually prevent the acquisition of any delicacy of mind. The little attention paid to the cultivation of modesty, amongst men, produces great depravity in all the relationships of society; for, not only love—love that ought to purify the heart, and first call forth all the youthful powers, to prepare the man to discharge the benevolent duties of life, is sacrificed to premature lust; but, all the social affections are deadened by the selfish gratifications, which very early pollute the mind, and dry up the generous juices of the heart.[14]

In accord with her general theory of the passions, she regarded sexual desire as a natural appetite, but one that needs reason and principle to govern it. Otherwise, like the unbridled desire for food or drink, it becomes antisocial and selfish, even brutal: "Women as well as men ought to have the common appetites and passions of their nature, they are only brutal when unchecked by reason."[15] And as with these other passions, the sexual appetite has certain ends knowable to the intellect, ends that can be respected, or thwarted. The purpose of the sexual appetite, according to Wollstonecraft, is evident in the goods that underlie the sexual act itself: it nourishes intimate affections and encourages procreation: "This [sexual] intemperance, so prevalent, depraves the appetite to such a degree, that a wanton stimulus is necessary to rouse it; but the parental design of nature is forgotten, and the mere person, and that for a moment, alone engrosses the thoughts."[16]

Pleasure, a happy ancillary of the appetites (and of the sexual appetites more so than the others), tended to trump purpose, according to Wollstonecraft. But remember, for Wollstonecraft, the appetites do not lead, even if they serve to motivate and inspire; rather, for the person to be fully human, the appetites must be directed by the intellect, the governor of the passions. Otherwise, one's animal instincts, in themselves neither good nor bad, can become "depraved" and "run wild," rendering the person impulsive and selfish, rather than focused on the good of the other, and so, benevolent and free. Thus, in addition to teaching self-mastery to young children to prepare them to respond properly to their appetites, Wollstonecraft suggested that children well understand the ends of sex in an age-appropriate way, just as they would the purpose of other organs of their bodies: "Speak to children of the organs of generation as freely as we speak of other parts of the body, and explain to them the noble use which they were designed for, and how they may be injured."[17] So that all might guard against the consequences of sex, young men and women ought to be fully informed about what "the Creator has implanted in them for wise purposes."[18]

The ends of sex, as with food and drink, give way to guiding principles and moral duties, for *both women and men*: "the obligation to check [the appetites] is the duty of mankind, not a sexual [woman's] duty."[19] Libertine men's ill respect for both women's reproductive capacity and sex's "parental design" can place women in especially precarious situations, after all. Forgetting the "noble use" of sex, men with women indulge their desires, sometimes leaving women "too weak" to carry out the maternal duties that sexual intercourse potentially sets before them. They have "sacrifice[d] to lasciviousness the parental affection, that ennobles instinct," and the woman, now pregnant and abandoned by her sexual partner, may seek "either [to] destroy the embryo in the womb, or cast it off when born."[20]

Wollstonecraft blasts the idea that humanity had come so far from the "barbarism of antiquity," at which time parents routinely exposed children who were born but unwanted. She returns to the ends of sex implanted by nature: "Nature in every thing demands respect, and those who violate her laws seldom violate them with impunity. . . . Surely nature never intended that women, by satisfying an appetite, should frustrate the very purpose for which it was implanted!"[21] She expresses particular contempt for the woman who, seemingly without a thought, "smiles on the libertine while she spurns the victims of his lawless appetites and their own folly."[22] Wollstonecraft demanded instead that in situations such as this the father ought to maintain both mother and child. Such an expectation of paternal responsibility, she argues, might well bring an end to "an abuse that has an equally fatal effect on population and morals."[23] An advocate of sexual integrity and responsible fatherhood she was; of abortion, she was not. And this, we ought to remember, was at a time when pregnancy was far more hazardous to women—and embryonic development far less understood—than in our own day.

Wollstonecraft sought to transform intimate relationships between men and women into those governed by mutual respect and affection; in her view, these relationships had too often become manipulative and transactional, like a commercial enterprise, or, worse, entirely destructive of human dignity. True domestic affections, man for woman and woman for man, could channel sexual energies away from the pursuit of pleasure to something that could transform society itself. Thus, once a young man had learned deep personal respect for women and a mastery over his sexual impulses, the best course of action he could take to maintain his sexual integrity was, again, fatherhood. A man would only be moved to channel his affections properly, Wollstonecraft thought, when his sexual desire was supported by the nobility of a pure heart: "The tenderness which a man will feel for the mother of his children is an excellent substitute for the ardor of unsatisfied passion."[24] A man's love for his wife and children could expand his heart, and so free him from narrow self-regard. According to Wollstonecraft, "Cold would be the heart of a husband, were he not rendered unnatural by early debauchery, who did not feel more delight at seeing his child suckled by its mother, than the most artful wanton tricks could ever raise. . . . The maternal solicitude of a reasonable affectionate woman is very interesting, and the chastened dignity with which a mother returns the caresses that she and her child receive from a father who has been fulfilling the serious duties of his station, is not only a respectable, but a beautiful sight."[25]

By trading the libertine lifestyle for that first, domestic affection, a man could refine his humanity, and become a better man for the world.

MARRIAGE

Wollstonecraft therefore praised marriage in theory, but not as legally instituted and practiced in her time. As with all other matters, she judged the institution as it was designed in her day by its capacity to promote the moral development of persons. She thought it failed most miserably in this regard. It was the very potential she saw in the institution of marriage, were it designed with virtue and equal dignity in mind, that caused her scathing critique. The dependency and vulnerability of children made the marital relationship an essential one for human beings, after all: "The long and helpless state of infancy seems to point [them] out as particularly impelled to pair."[26] And this paramount responsibility for the nurture and education of children informed her thinking about the purposes of sex, particularly within marriage. The "animal instinct" became dignified: "The feelings of a parent mingling with an instinct merely animal, give it dignity; and the man and woman often meeting on account of the child, a mutual interest and affection is excited by the exercise of a common sympathy."[27]

The mutual long-term interest needed for the exercise of the couple's common project could not spring from mere sexual attraction or the "fever of love." Friendship and mutual respect would have to replace such fleeting emotion for the true benefits of marriage to emerge: "Were women more rationally educated, could they take a more comprehensive view of things, they would be contented to love but once in their lives; and after marriage calmly let passion subside into friendship—into that tender intimacy, which is the best refuge from care; yet is built on such pure, still affections, that idle jealousies would not be allowed to disturb the discharge of the sober duties of life, or to engross the thoughts that ought to be otherwise employed."[28] A marital relationship between equals, in which each was perfected by the other through their growth in the virtue of friendship, had great potential. Wollstonecraft urged couples to love the other not out of selfish designs, but "on account of [their] virtues."[29] She could scarcely imagine a state better suited to the human capacities of both men and women. Her happy depiction continues: "A couple of this description, equally necessary and independent of each other, because each fulfilled the respective duties of their station, possessed all that life could give. . . . I know not what is wanted to render this the happiest as well as the most respectable situation in the world."[30] And yet, a marriage without mutual love, respect, and affection would not be happy at all, and would render the wife but a mistress.

Her edifying vision of marriage may sound like a common aspiration to us now, two hundred years on, but in her time, among the more well-off, family law had become a function of property distribution more than anything else. Thus, she believed marriages among the wealthy to often be nothing but legal prostitution, a commercial venture in which young women were bartered by their fathers to the most advantageous bidder. Women of her day prepared from their youth for the day of their wedding, which provoked them to be self-focused and consumed with appearances rather than interiorly strong. They developed these vicious habits, which they then brought into marriage, opting for strategies of manipulation with their new spouses rather than authentic love. She bemoans the situation thus: "Strength of body and mind are sacrificed to libertine notions of beauty, to the desire of establishing themselves,—the only way women can rise in the world,—by marriage. And this desire making mere animals of them, when they marry they act as such children may be expected to act."[31] The ill foundation in youth from which both men and women often went into marriage—promiscuity for men, self-objectification for women— rendered them incapable of the benevolent love, simplicity of affection, and virtue of friendship that a good marriage required. And good marriages were the centerpiece of mutual improvement for men and women; bad marriages, a ruinous fall into corruption.

Indeed, marriage was so essential to the domestic affections that Wollstonecraft regarded as the primary instruments of both personal and societal happiness that the moral corruption of the institution was "more universally injurious to morality than all the other vices of mankind collectively considered."[32] She writes at the very end of the *Rights of Woman*:

> For as marriage has been termed the parent of those endearing charities which draw man from the brutal herd, the corrupting intercourse that wealth, idleness, and folly, produce between the sexes, is *more universally injurious to morality than all the other vices of mankind collectively considered.* To adulterous lust the most sacred duties are sacrificed, because before marriage, men, by a promiscuous intimacy with women, learned to consider love as a selfish gratification—learned to separate it not only from esteem, but from the affection merely built on habit, which mixes a little humanity with it. Justice and friendship are also set at defiance, and that purity of taste is vitiated which would naturally lead a man to relish an artless display of affection rather than affected airs.

But that noble simplicity of affection, which dares to appear un-adorned, has few attractions for the libertine, though it be the charm, which by cementing the matrimonial tie, secures to the pledges of a warmer passion the necessary parental attention; for children will never be properly educated till friendship subsists between parents. Virtue flies from a house divided against itself—and a whole le-gion of devils take up their residence there.[33]

Women who before marriage had prized their capacity to please men became, once they entered marriage, unfit intellectual companions for them, and, worse, had few moral and intellectual resources at their disposal for educating their children. Thus, lamented Wollstonecraft, women too often passed off this sublime duty to servants and reduced themselves to groveling like children before their husbands, upon whom they were entirely dependent. Marital laws at the time, after all, treated women not as full legal persons in their own right, but as "incorporated" into their husbands; the legal rights they enjoyed to own property and make contracts as single women were abrogated upon marriage by the law of coverture (the common law doctrine that governed married women's legal status). This was not always so: in medieval times, when the assets of the family were owned in common by the family—rather than solely by the individuals in it—married women often worked side by side with their husbands in business enterprises, learning their hus-band's craft or trade as their own and taking full responsibility for their affairs at their husband's absence or death. More still, customary law in many localities enabled married women to conduct the business of their own craft or trade as though they were single.[34] Married men, for their part, were expected to be deeply engaged in domestic life, especially in the education of their children. Medievalist Eileen Power writes that, practically speaking, medieval woman

> had a full share in the private rights and duties arising out of the possession of land and played a considerable part in industry, in spite of the handicap of low wages and sometimes masculine ex-clusiveness. The education of the average laywoman compared very favorably with that of her husband, and some ladies of rank were

leaders of culture. . . . In every class of the community the life of the married woman gave her a great deal of scope, since . . . the home of this period was a very wide sphere; social and economic conditions demanded that a wife should always be ready to perform the husband's duties as well as her own, and that a large range of activities should be carried on inside the home under her direction.[35]

And, of course, within monarchical regimes, women had been known to rule as (great) queens.

Yet by Sir William Blackstone's writing of the *Commentaries on the Laws of England* in the late eighteenth century, married (and unmarried) men were considered (potentially) "rights-bearing individuals," while married women were denied any legal recognition of their own. As I detail further in chapter 3, they neither earned a common share in the marital property by their productive work in the home, nor did any of their earnings outside the home (sparse though they were) fix to the common family name. Everything was legally held in the husband's name alone. Should their husbands be libertine men, women had no recourse in law or custom. They were first bartered by their fathers (assuming they could offer a dowry), and then in marriage their bodies were no longer their own.[36] Should they wish to protect themselves or their children from an abusive man, the law offered them nothing: the children were legally their fathers', so to abandon an abusive marriage was to abandon one's children.

Wollstonecraft argued that marriage ought to be entered voluntarily for companionship and the rearing of children, not so women might be autonomous individuals, free to abandon their families, but so that women could be equal partners in the soul-shaping, society-forming domestic tasks the husband and wife would engage in together: "The conclusion which I wish to draw, is obvious; make women rational creatures, and free citizens, and they will quickly become good wives, and mothers; that is—if men do not neglect the duties of husbands and fathers."[37] Wollstonecraft deeply valued the love and affection between a man and woman, but she valued each person in her own dignity too. Confronting the law of coverture head-on, she says that "man and woman were made for each other, though not to become one being."[38]

She had known too many bad men who had abused or abandoned their wives to be naïve: her own father, her sister's husband, and later she too would be abandoned with her first child by that child's father. Rather than treat their wives with care and concern, these men abused their privilege for their own pleasures or walked out on them with other women.

Though virtuous men may have ruled their wives and children with benevolence, the hierarchy in the home caused by great, legally enforced power differentials could not be entrusted to fallible men. Just as political thinkers of the time were seeking a form of government whose just authority did not rely entirely on the virtue of the monarch (and whose institutional safeguards protected against excessive political power in the hands of a bad man), Wollstonecraft was subjecting the legal situation of marriage to a similar critique. The woman's position of legal and economic dependency in marriage tended to corrupt both husband and wife; neither could develop the friendship (born of equality) and other virtues needed for a relationship in which the common good of the family might be promoted. Moreover, a dependent woman might not only be abandoned by a bad man, reasoned Wollstonecraft, but rather by a good man's ill-timed death. Left a widow, with no legal standing or prior experience in the world with which to provide for her children, she was more vulnerable still. She movingly described such a woman, "trained up to obedience, . . . married to a sensible man," but left alone with her children by the death of her husband, for "she cannot ensure the life of her protector."[39] Marriage was too important an institution—for men, women, children, society at large—for the laws to get it wrong.

When she met the American entrepreneur Imlay, she thought she had found herself a new kind of man whose first affections would be directed toward that shared domestic life about which she had theorized. For a time, it seemed so, and even after a number of misadventures on his part, she sought to persuade him of fidelity, and fatherhood: "You have a heart, my friend, yet . . . you have sought in vulgar excesses, for that gratification only the heart can bestow. . . . Why I cannot help thinking that it is possible for you, having great strength of mind, to return to nature, and regain a sanity of constitution, and purity of feeling—which would open your heart to me."[40] In time she realized that she had fallen for precisely the kind of man about whom she had warned others in her *Rights of Woman*. Imlay left Wollstonecraft and their child for another woman, and the laws, had she acceded to them, would have done nothing to protect her. She had intended to pen a follow-up to the *Rights of Woman* with a more direct treatment of the unjust effect of the laws upon women themselves, but she never did. Instead, she returned to the theme indirectly in fictional form, especially in her unfinished manuscript, published posthumously, *The Wrongs of Women*. Still, both the *Rights of Woman* itself and her earlier *Rights of Men* give us some indications of her views of justice, law, and the proper ends of government.

LAW AND THE ENDS OF GOVERNMENT

Clearly nature had made human beings unequal in talent, intelligence, and physical strength, among other attributes and capacities. Wollstonecraft believed that laws should be designed not to promote these natural inequalities but rather to encourage progress in virtue, for each and every person, whatever their station or starting point. Thus, law ought not be designed to maintain the strong and rich in their positions, but to promote the moral progress of all, especially the weak and vulnerable. So although Wollstonecraft shared the ancient view of human excellence as coincident with wisdom and virtue, she sought to universalize that characteristically human quest beyond the landed classes, recognizing a common human dignity in each person. If the equal dignity and human potential of each was recognized, and their liberal education and moral formation promoted, she believed that each person could make moral progress, and all of society would benefit. For Wollstonecraft, political and civil rights, properly understood, would promote the social freedom and legal equality needed for this ennobling human project.

Wollstonecraft's interlocutors took clear sides in modernity's central political debate about the existence of "natural rights" in a "state of nature." Her contemporary Thomas Paine, and just earlier Rousseau, followed Thomas Hobbes and John Locke in conceiving such a prepolitical state, even as each differed starkly as to its attributes. Still, to counter the divine right of kings, they agreed that a myth of origin was needed to provide a theoretical foundation for a new kind of government. Edmund Burke, on the other hand, repudiated the "state of nature" altogether, and so too did he repudiate the modern idea of abstract natural rights. The "rights of man" were well protected by the English common law and constitutional traditions, or they weren't protected at all. Wollstonecraft took a middle route between the liberal state of nature theorists and the conservative defender of English traditions: political society need not look back to a myth of origin for its moral foundations; our given human nature as rational creatures supplied a principled criterion by which to judge edifying traditions from old prejudices based solely on consolidated power: "We ought to respect old opinions; though prejudices, blindly adopted, lead to error and preclude the exercise of reason."[41]

And so she agreed that men were often "brutish" (Hobbes), that society grew out of man's perfectibility (Rousseau), and that a main purpose of government was to protect each person's God-given rights (Locke), but she did not believe any of this required an abstract "state of nature" to discern. Importantly, neither did she believe the "natural" states, discerned so dissimilarly by Hobbes and Rousseau, for instance, even explained human nature adequately. Rather, human beings were rational creatures created by God who required moral education and practice in self-mastery to perfect their given dispositions and act with virtue and benevolence toward others. From the person's given nature as a rational, moral, social being sprang forth certain discernable duties to self, family, society, and God. Civil and political rights vis-à-vis government were derived, therefore, not from theoretical abstractions but from actual moral duties to others. A good and just government enabled and encouraged the fulfillment of each person's concrete duties, in part, through the protection of his or her rights: a person must be free to pursue the right course of action. Rights were thus not freewheeling abstractions or self-defined prerogatives, as they are often conceived of today, but concrete and particular liberties derived from antecedent duties. And rights were not absolute. Thinking of parents' duties to their children especially, she maintains that those who "do not fulfill the duty" can "forfeit the right."[42]

Because political and civil institutions were properly in the service of these prior human duties, any institution that obstructed their proper fulfillment ought to be reconstituted with these more authentic human ends in mind: "I mean, therefore, to infer that the society is not properly organized which does not compel men and women to discharge their respective duties, by making it the only way to acquire that countenance from their fellow-creatures, which every human being wishes some way to attain."[43] The duty of the rational creature to follow the truth is the principle that underlay Wollstonecraft's tolerance of religious pluralism and her sympathy with the dissenting sects of her time. Still, she did not view religion as at all out of place in the encouragement of moral duties: "The wisest laws would not be sufficient to restrain men within the bounds of morality without those powerful motives, which religion affords to interest the affections, and enlighten the understanding."[44]

Although Burke's defense of the monarchy was the target of Wollstonecraft's *Vindication of the Rights of Men*, she took no issue with Burke's more fundamental view that natural, unchosen, binding obligations—the family, first and foremost—were both the foundation and happiness of society. They were speaking out of the same tradition, against the more liberal theorists, even as Wollstonecraft sought far more substantial reforms, including to the family, than Burke would have allowed. She thus would have agreed with Burke's description of moral duties here: "But out of physical causes, unknown to us, perhaps unknowable, arise moral duties, which, as we are able perfectly to comprehend, we are bound indispensably to perform. Parents may not be consenting to their moral relation; but consenting or not, they are bound to a long train of burthensome duties towards those with whom they have never made a convention of any sort. Children are not consenting to their relation, but their relation, without their actual consent, binds them to its duties."[45] And she similarly states: "The simple definition of the reciprocal duty, which naturally subsists between parent and child, may be given in a few words: The parent who pays proper attention to helpless infancy has a right to require the same attention when the feebleness of age comes upon him. . . . The parent who sedulously endeavors to form the heart and enlarge the understanding of his child, has given that dignity to the discharge of a duty, common to the whole animal world."[46]

Wollstonecraft thus agreed with Burke on the givenness of moral duties, but she disagreed fiercely (and at times via inelegant ad hominem attacks) about whether the aristocratic system was the best means to meet these moral obligations. Indeed, her main argument against Burke's defense of both monarchy and aristocracy was that hereditary distinctions in both government and property inheritance corrupted the morals of both the rulers and the ruled, the propertied and those without such holdings; few men with such honors and power could attain the humility necessary for the wisdom and virtue needed to carry out their moral obligations. She charged that "it is impossible for any man . . . to acquire [the] strength of mind to discharge the duties of a king, entrusted with uncontrolled power . . . his very elevation is an insuperable bar to the attainment of either wisdom or virtue. . . . for all power inebriates weak man."[47]

The problem with aristocracy as Wollstonecraft saw it consisted of basing distinctions of honor on birth rather than virtue. Whereas Burke feared losing the "pleasing illusions" that exalted the virtuous life putatively honored by the aristocracy, Wollstonecraft thought such illusions actually compelled neither the rich nor the poor to seek virtue. More often than not the aristocrat sought honor from his status or holdings; he did not, to her mind, seek virtue. Her critique of aristocracy was thus not based on abstractions or even the "natural rights" of the people, but on how static social hierarchies—with honors based on property distinctions—harmed the development of virtue in actual human beings.

Like other republicans of the time, especially in the newly formed United States, she thought property ownership a good, a means to develop virtue, and so the protection of property rights was a proper end of government: "Civilization is a blessing, so far as it gives security to person and property."[48] But gross inequality of property ownership kept the rich idle and the poor without a means to better themselves. Property as improperly determinative of just honors also invested the poor in a materialistic game of imitation in which they could never make progress. Wollstonecraft argued:

It would be an arduous task to trace all the vice and misery that arise in society from the middle class of people apeing the manners of the great. All are aiming to procure respect on account of their property. . . . The grand concern of three parts out of four is to contrive to live above their equals, and to appear to be richer than they are. How much domestic comfort and private satisfaction is sacrificed to this irrational ambition! It is a destructive mildew that blights the fairest virtues; benevolence, friendship, generosity, and all those endearing charities which bind human hearts together, and the pursuits which raise the mind to higher contemplations, all that were not cankered in the bud by the false notions that 'grew with its growth and strengthened with its strength,' are crushed by the iron hand of property![49]

Because the development of virtue was of singular importance in her moral philosophy, she repeatedly expressed concern with the rising avarice she saw among the men of commerce in her day. Though she greatly preferred an economic system in which work and merit rather than name and rank gave one access to property and wealth, she did not see an advance in the growing commercial mentality. In the traditional aristocratic system, honors and property represented virtue; in the new commercial system, wealth was taking their place. Here again, she followed her mentor, Richard Price. In a 1785 letter to Thomas Jefferson, Price had written: "The character . . . of popular governments depending on the character of the people; if the people deviate from simplicity of manners into luxury, the love of show, and extravagance[,] the governments must become corrupt and tyrannical."[50]

Wollstonecraft feared the new "aristocracy of wealth" even more than the aristocracy of old: "The narrow principle of commerce . . . seems every where to be shoving aside *the point of honor* of the *noblesse.*"[51] Under aristocratic principles of honor, "noblesse oblige" referred to the social duty of the nobility to act with generosity to those of lesser rank; the man who won his wealth through commerce often felt no such moral obligation. "England and America owe their liberty to commerce, which created a new species of power to undermine the feudal system. But let them beware of the consequence; the tyranny of wealth is still more galling and debasing than that of rank," she wrote in 1796.[52] And again: "If aristocracy of birth is leveled with the ground, only to make room for that of riches, I am afraid that the morals of the people will not be much improved by the change, or the government rendered less venal."[53] Though she could envision a commercial system that allowed for and encouraged virtue, she had not seen evidence of such an advance yet in existence. Still, the young United States gave her hope.

Like some across the Atlantic, she thought large holdings divided into small farms would encourage independence and hard work. She condemned simple charity to the poor, suggesting that the rich tended to give for appearances and, anyway, simple handouts did little to help. Rather, she suggested that the poor ought to be afforded education and dignified work that aids in the development of virtue: "It is not by squandering alms that the poor can be relieved, or improved—it is the fostering sun of kindness, the wisdom that finds them employments calculated to give them habits of virtue, that meliorates their condition."[54]

Promotion of virtue was the sole principle by which she judged relationships, institutions, and regimes. Thus, she wrote: "A truly benevolent legislator always endeavors to make it the interest of each individual to be virtuous; and thus private virtue becoming the cement of public happiness, an orderly whole is consolidated by the tendency of all the parts towards a common center."[55] But, a close corollary for Wollstonecraft was the belief that wealth, status, and power corrupted those who did not work to use their superior status, talents, and resources for the common good, and especially the weakest and most vulnerable. She did not limit her critique of power to the rich, however, even though the corruption originated there: seeking wealth and power (rather than virtue) corrupted the poor and the vulnerable just the same. Her fundamental belief remained throughout. Each person was of equal moral worth, whatever his or her status, and this provided the surest foundation for promoting each and every person's human capacity for wisdom, virtue, and thus happiness.

Following the Reign of Terror, which she was in Paris to witness, Wollstonecraft began to lose faith in achieving moral progress through political reform.[56] More still, the deep wounds she experienced at the abandonment of her first love suggested that even she, a strong, determined woman of principle, could not live a virtuous relationship under the current legal system that promoted not greatness of soul and virtue, nor even liberty, but mere power and privilege. In the final year of her increasingly melancholic life, she sought refuge from the emotional devastation of her first "marriage" in an oddly matched companionship (and ultimately marriage) with William Godwin, and in motherhood, writing not the promised treatise on laws, but rather small books of guidance. She penned the beginnings of a book on pregnancy, childbirth, and the care of infants for young mothers, and another, rife with domestic scenes, for the intellectual and moral formation of her daughter, Fanny.[57] From the beginning until the end, though her views would shift on other matters, that first affection, by which she sought to foster a rich and transformative domestic life, represented Wollstonecraft's singular devotion.

Many American women—the new country's first women's rights advocates—followed this ennobling Wollstonecraftian vision. Chapter 3 will introduce us to their aims, their shortfalls, and their gains.

CHAPTER 3

The Young Republic and
the Unequal Virtues
of the Agrarian Home

In the summer of 1793, Mary Wollstonecraft, having taken refuge with her infant daughter, Fanny, in a cottage not far outside Paris, wrote her book on the French Revolution in the very midst of the Reign of Terror. Around her, she observed the silence of Versailles, the "train of the Louises" passing by in "solemn sadness, pointing at the nothingness of grandeur, fading away on the cold canvas, which covers the nakedness of the spacious wall." She testified to the mood of those bloody summer months: "The gloominess of the atmosphere gives a deeper shade to the gigantic figures, that seem to be sinking into the embraces of death."[1] Wollstonecraft's time in Paris convinced her of the superiority of the American Revolution to its French counterpart. Inspired by what the Americans had accomplished, she had hoped to travel to the new republic with Fanny and Fanny's American father, Imlay. Sadly, the relationship with Imlay did not last long enough for her to make the trip across the Atlantic, but her books received easy passage in the newly formed United States.

John Adams, then U.S. vice president, read Wollstonecraft's *Historical and Moral View of the Origin and Progress of the French Revolution* (1794) twice, extensively marking up his copy, disputing some of its claims but noting nonetheless that its author was "a Lady of masculine masterly Understanding."[2] As though peeking into the future, Adams observed, "She seems to have half a mind to be an English woman; yet more inclined to be an American."[3] Indeed, in the wake of her death, and Godwin's notorious biography, Wollstonecraft became *persona non grata* in her homeland and remained so for decades. But with an early U.S. publication of the *Rights of Woman* in the *Ladies Home Journal* in 1792, and library copies more abundant than even Thomas Paine's *Rights of Man* by the end of the nineteenth century, it was in the United States that her thought first gained currency and, for some, the force of persuasion.[4]

Both early American purveyors of "republican motherhood" and nineteenth-century social reformers and suffragists were motivated by the quintessentially republican view, shared by Wollstonecraft too, that the political freedom promised by the new republic required personal virtue, the inculcation of which these women regarded as their most important work. John Adams himself had spoken of this American theme frequently in the early years of the republic: "Republican governments could be supported only by pure Religion or Austere Morals. Public virtue cannot exist in a Nation without private Virtue, and public Virtue is the only Foundation of Republics."[5] And in June 1778, forecasting a theme that emerged energetically in Wollstonecraft's *Rights of Woman* fourteen years later, Adams wrote:

> The foundations of national Morality must be laid in private Families. In vain are Schools, Academies, and universities instituted, if loose Principles and licentious habits are impressed upon Children in their earliest years. The Mothers are the earliest and most important Instructors of youth. . . . The Vices and Examples of the Parents cannot be concealed from the Children. How is it possible that Children can have any just Sense of the sacred Obligations of Morality or Religion if, from their earliest Infancy, they learn that their Mothers live in habitual Infidelity to their fathers, and their fathers in as constant Infidelity to their Mothers.[6]

Beginning with Abigail Adams, the self-described "pupil" of Wollstonecraft, and up through the suffragists themselves, advocates for women's political and civil rights and educational opportunities believed these to be women's American birthright. But very few at that time regarded such rights or opportunities to be disconnected from the antecedent familial and social obligations that made them necessary. In this way, early women's rights advocates followed Wollstonecraft implicitly, and often, as we'll see, quite explicitly. But, as the women's movement gained currency, a minority view among the suffragists emerged, rhetorically elevating arguments drawn instead from Enlightenment thinkers such as John Locke and John Stuart Mill. These more radical suffragists, most notably Elizabeth Cady Stanton, thus traded in Wollstonecraft's prioritization of the virtuous fulfillment of familial and social obligations—the foundation of her affirmation of civil and political rights—for Locke's more individualistic and abstract conception of rights as protective of "self-ownership." Likewise, liberty was conceived by Stanton in a Millian fashion, as an essential human capacity with no particular goal or end, rather than as a means to fulfill virtuously antecedent duties. Insofar as suffragists following Stanton held onto the concept of virtue, it was of a Rousseauian variety, with a rhetorical tendency to bifurcate the specification of virtue into masculine and feminine, with praise, in this telling, for the superior "feminine" soul. Capturing the franchise was, on this account, a means to bring women's superior soul to bear on base, male-dominated public affairs.

But even before the cause of women's suffrage would emerge victorious in the United States in the early twentieth century, the philosophical tensions between Wollstonecraft's more formative premodern/modern synthesis and an abstract Lockean view of rights grew during the Industrial Revolution, first only rhetorically, in the movement's early advocacy for joint property ownership and "voluntary motherhood," and then later, more substantively, in the internal debates over marriage and protective legislation for women workers. Each of these issues, discussed in this chapter and the two that follow, concerned the moral and political status of women, their work, and their relationships with men during a time of large-scale cultural transformation.

Agrarian Beginnings: The American Founding

The United States was founded with large-scale commercial aspirations: Alexander Hamilton especially believed economic prosperity through urban growth, innovation, and finance to be the means toward national security and independence. But until the 1840s, the country remained mostly agrarian, with deep roots in the land. Like their European counterparts, the great majority of Americans subsisted through household production, with trade at a minimum until the introduction of machines and factories in the mid-nineteenth century.[7] The U.S. Constitution, like the Declaration of Independence, was grafted onto this agrarian substructure, one in which productive family homes, an abundance of children, and deep religious faith were simply taken for granted. (In the South, this household productivity was unjustly extended by way of slave labor on Southern plantations.) Though the founding documents make no explicit mention of the colonies' reliance upon strong familial homesteads, the political independence and liberty these documents both declared and protected were possible, in large part, because of the economic security and self-sufficiency such agrarian households then assured.[8] Indeed, both the Jeffersonian and later Jacksonian approaches to American exceptionalism took their bearings from the nation's agrarian beginnings.

Married women were legally subordinate to their husbands in the founding era, as they were in all other modern states at the time. But the productivity of the homestead involved a common and collaborative family enterprise, with little leisure to discuss the propriety of gender roles or marital rights. Necessity reigned supreme. The agrarian family was constituted as a single, autonomous, and deeply interdependent unit; the husband was legal head of that unit, but his own self-interest was generally intertwined with that of his wife and his children in the family. The familial and societal influence women wielded as collaborative partners with their husbands and coeducators of their children was thus informal, a by-product of their essential contribution to the livelihood of their homes and families, and the health of the young nation. If the role of strong, agrarian families was implicit in the confidence and capacity of the Founders to erect a wholly new nation, even more so was the essential contribution of women in those families. Women's irreplaceable role in the family—and so the nation—was simply assumed.

In the months leading up to the colonies' separation from British rule, Abigail Adams challenged her husband on women's place in the new legal constellation, drawing a parallel between the arbitrary political rule the Declaration of Independence repudiated and the rule husbands had over their wives. In a March letter to her husband, Abigail wrote:

> In the new Code of Laws which I suppose it will be necessary for you to make I desire that you would Remember the Ladies, and be more generous and favorable to them than your ancestors. Do not put such unlimited power into the hands of their Husbands. Remember all Men would be tyrants if they could. If particular care and attention is not paid to the Ladies we are determined to foment a Rebellion, and will not hold ourselves bound by any Laws in which we have no voice, or Representation. That your Sex are Naturally Tyrannical is a Truth so thoroughly established as to admit of no dispute, but such of you as wish to be happy willingly give up the harsh title of Master for the more tender and endearing one of Friend. Why then, not put it out of the power of the vicious and the Lawless to use us with cruelty and indignity with impunity. Men of Sense in all Ages abhor those customs that treat us only as the vassals of your Sex. Regard us then as Beings placed by providence under your protection and in imitation of the Supreme Being make use of that power only for our happiness.[9]

The future president quipped that only in theory are husbands called masters; in truth and practice, they are subject to their wives.[10] But law is what matters, his wife retorted: "I can not say that I think you very generous to the Ladies, for while you are proclaiming peace and good will to Men, Emancipating all Nations, you insist upon retaining an absolute power over Wives. But you must remember that Arbitrary power is like most other things which are very hard, very liable to be broken."[11] The Adamses' marriage, chronicled beautifully by their letters, showcases the deep admiration and respect—indeed, friendship—they shared, and also the trust John placed in Abigail as confidant and consultant in matters of the new nation.

Abigail's plea to her husband to "Remember the Ladies" was then perhaps not so much for her own sake, though biographers do tell of her dismay in not receiving the rigorous classical education boys at the time received. Her plea was more acute for those women whose husbands were neither tender nor endearing, but rather harsh and cruel. Just as the

FIGURE 3.1. Rendering of a portrait taken of Abigail Adams at the age of twenty-one. Credit: Charles Francis Adams, 1876 (public domain).

Declaration itself suggests that the colonists would not have rebelled had King George governed them justly, so perhaps women would have had less impetus to dispute coverture—"to foment a Rebellion"—if all husbands had treated their wives with the trust, companionship, and equal dignity John had offered Abigail. But even so, Abigail still had a just complaint.

Indeed, the new republic, replete with both horizontal and vertical checks and balances, was drawn up with due regard for that irrefutable human reality that those in authority would lack constancy in virtue, even if the best among them exercised their authority with benevolence and solicitude. James Madison explained the anthropological assumptions underlying the constitutional design in 1788 in *Federalist* 51: "If men were angels, no government would be necessary. If angels were to govern men, neither external nor internal controls on government would be necessary."[12] Both Abigail and then more publicly Wollstonecraft simply observed that the domestic household existed in that same human reality, governed by the same moral logic. Virtuous regard for others often gave way to base self-regard and moral corruption; inequality of status made things far worse. This, remember, was Wollstonecraft's main complaint against monarchy and aristocracy: those in power too often used their authority badly, without a concern for the development of virtue in themselves and in others to whom they owed duties of care and concern.

In the early U.S. constitutional design, the drafters' focus was the creation of a federal government of constitutionally limited and defined powers: criminal and civil laws were left entirely in the province of states. Inculcation of virtuous regard for one's fellows, therefore, was not understood to be a project of the federal government. Importantly, the Founders assumed that the republican virtues necessary for political liberty and self-government would continue to be inculcated by self-reliant families and robust churches protected and promoted by local ordinances and state law.[13] Looking back today, with the virtues of self-government and benevolence notably lacking, perhaps we wonder if they assumed too much. But if they did, they did so with just cause. That most essential task of inculcating virtue in the citizens of the young republic was understood implicitly as the primary personal responsibility of a robust and most competent segment of society: American women.

REPUBLICAN MOTHERHOOD AND ALEXIS DE TOCQUEVILLE'S
TRIBUTE TO AMERICAN WOMEN

Even though they lacked the political rights American men had claimed for themselves and their families, the political importance of women in the young nation cannot be overestimated. Historian Linda Kerber coined the term "republican motherhood" for the exalted role women played in the new republic as the primary promoters of civic virtue in their children.[14] Indeed, the great esteem the early Americans gave women and their work was a sure advance over prior conceptions of women's lesser moral and intellectual capacity: women now had a distinctive profession informed by a high mission. "Republican motherhood" transformed women's maternity into a vital contribution to the success of the republic itself, one that, in time, was to encourage the co-education of girls as first teachers of their own children and then of the nation's pupils. "No longer to be viewed primarily as breeders who produced male heirs for families, women as mothers came to be viewed as the guardians of individual character," says historian Elizabeth Fox-Genovese.[15]

American women's distinctive and valuable contribution, though at first relegated entirely to the private sphere, came to enhance women's independence and their growing political activity. Kerber credits this early American model of "womanhood"—reconciling assumed domesticity with engaged political sensibility—as the seedling that would give rise to women's leadership in movements for the abolition of slavery, and in campaigns for social purity, workers' rights, and women's suffrage.[16] Married women in the young republic may have been legally powerless, but they were deeply influential nonetheless.

Even foreigners noticed.

In 1835, Alexis de Tocqueville, the great French observer of democracy in America, wrote in the celebrated book by that name: "And now that I come near the end of this book in which I have recorded so many considerable achievements of the Americans, if anyone asks me what I think the chief cause of the extraordinary prosperity and growing power of this nation, I should answer that it is due to the superiority of their women."[17] For Tocqueville, this was no small feat. He worried over 700 pages that individualism and materialism would threaten to undermine freedom in the new democracy, if not checked by the communitarian tendencies promoted by family and religion. As the foremost shaper of mores, Tocqueville thought, women were uniquely capable of correcting these baser impulses of democracy, especially in the growing commercial republic. "Therefore," the Frenchman argued, "everything which has a bearing on the status of women, their habits, and their thoughts is, in my view, of great political importance."[18] For Tocqueville, women were the key to the whole enterprise.

Tocqueville saw in American women an interior strength and independence that inspired them to dedicate their lives, not to their own personal aggrandizement or wealth, as American men seemed wont to do, but to the cultivation of virtue and the building of families, churches, schools, and civic associations, all of which Tocqueville viewed as essential to the survival of the new democratic enterprise. American women took republican self-governance seriously and knew the essential role they played in it, "tak[ing] pride in the free relinquishment of their will" for the sake of the new country.[19] Popular Christian authors of the time, such as Catharine Beecher, similarly extolled women's role, highlighting the character and culture-shaping work of the home and depicting women as that institution's "chief minister."[20] These women maintained networks of kinship, solidarity, and reciprocity in and through their productive family homes, thereby creating what historian Allan Carlson has aptly called "islands of antimodernity within the industrial sea."[21] Tocqueville observed in American women a deep religious sense, one he thought not present in commercially minded American men: "Religion is often powerless to restrain men in the midst of innumerable temptations which fortune offers . . . but it reigns supreme in the souls of women, and it is women who shape mores."[22] The moral norms of Christianity, mediated through women's strong moral influence over their husbands (and sons), contributed to moderating the individualism and materialism democracy naturally promoted. Christianity's moderating influence—more important for Tocqueville than its truth claims— helped guard the new republican citizens against the temptation to misuse their freedom solely for individual gain.

Women's lack of political and legal equality in the young nation was of no matter to Tocqueville: in his view, Americans had raised women "morally and intellectually" to the level of men.[23] Tocqueville notes that, by this time, American girls were educated as proficiently as boys, and at a young age, girls thought, acted, and spoke freely, trusting in their own reasoning ability rather than the authority of others:

"She is full of confidence in her own powers, and it seems that this feeling is shared by all around her."[24] Tocqueville observed that once married, these independent young women submitted freely to the dependent bonds of matrimony. They relied entirely upon the earnings of their husbands while wholeheartedly dedicating themselves to building up the domestic and communal sphere: "The Americans . . . have carefully separated the functions of man and of woman [into clearly distinct spheres of action] so that the great work of society may be better performed. . . . Both are required to keep in step, but along paths that are never the same."[25] The Frenchman regarded this social abnegation on the part of women as great evidence of their moral strength, and of the "manly habits" they received through their coequal education.

By contrast, Tocqueville wrote that European women were regarded as "seductive but incomplete beings." He suggested that, consequently, they "end up looking at themselves in the same light . . . think-[ing] it a privilege to be able to appear futile, weak, and timid."[26] In contrasting the morally strong, pioneering American women with their emotionally dependent and timid European counterparts, Tocqueville echoed Wollstonecraft's critique of aristocratic women. Both thinkers disparaged such women, who were more focused on accolades, accomplishments, and beauty than on social duty and personal virtue.[27] As Tocqueville saw it, the strict separation of public and private spheres in the United States did not lessen the respect American men had for women; rather, men saw women as worthy of great esteem, with their familial and social contributions accorded equal value to those of their male counterparts. Indeed, he remarked that American husbands showed total confidence in their wives' judgment and deeply respected their freedom: "They hold that woman's mind is just as capable as man's of discovering the naked truth, and her heart as firm to face it."[28]

Tocqueville scholar Stacey Hibbs suggests that, for Tocqueville, the capacity of Americans to maintain authentic freedom within their new democratic undertaking required a "healthy counterpoise between the public and private dimensions of human life."[29] Were the values of the political and commercial spheres to overtake entirely those of the domestic sphere, the virtues needed for freedom would give way to apathetic individualism, rampant acquisitiveness, and servile majoritarianism that threatened independence of thought and greatness of soul. These public and private dimensions, and the distinct habits they imparted, were, for Tocqueville, as for the early Americans, represented by men and women, respectively. As such, private women moderated the democratic excesses of public men. Said differently, American women represented the Old World's normative aspirations of virtue and solidarity, and American men, the New World's norms of individualism, acquisition, and enterprise. According to Hibbs,

> Either individual freedom is sacrificed to the needs of the social order, or extreme individualism leads to the denigration of social and political life. . . . Thus, liberty and order are kept in a healthy tension through the interplay of public and private. . . . [In Tocqueville's view], it is precisely because women are removed from the political sphere that they can provide a counterpoise to the excesses of democratic society. Their influence is indirect, they inform public life without being involved in the political sphere. . . . As a result, men's actions are moderated by the influence of women.[30]

From Tocqueville's perspective, without a robust, and virtuous, private sphere that shaped persons capable of exercising their freedom well, the fate of democracy, and so of the modern world, was in jeopardy. The moral strength and independence of American women, put directly in service of the young nation, gave the skeptical Frenchman a measure of hope that American democracy might indeed survive—and perhaps even flourish.

Wollstonecraft died fifty years before Tocqueville wrote his still-famous book.[31] Like Rousseau before them, Wollstonecraft and Tocqueville shared the view that the private sphere provided the moral underpinnings for virtuous public undertakings. But Wollstonecraft would have disputed Tocqueville's assumption that women were more capable of or more responsible for inculcating virtue than men were, just as she explicitly disputed the earlier view that women were less capable, or less responsible, than men for developing the whole panoply of virtues, including those virtues historically deemed "manly." Indeed, for Wollstonecraft, it was the singular duty of both men and women, as rational creatures, to grow in wisdom and virtue, through generously fulfilling their obligations to God and others.

To this day, Tocqueville's thought remains among the best correctives to modern America's turn toward a culture of acquisitiveness, atomization, and the often tyrannical social force of currently popular views. Both the political Left and Right in the Unites States still find reasons to appreciate Tocqueville's insights.[32] Still, his favorable description of women's domestic role—key to his thought—needs amending to retain his distinctive insights about the democratic project today. With women's commendable contributions to the public sphere, and fathers' increasingly active engagement in the lives of their children, Wollstonecraft's thought provides a corrective to Tocqueville's own corrective, even though her thought predated his.

For Wollstonecraft, after all, it was not women themselves who guarded against moral corruption. Rather, the *shared duties of the domestic sphere* and the development of good relationships therein properly adorned each human being with the virtues needed for upright and just public undertakings. Remember her admonitions:

> If you wish to make good citizens, you must first exercise the affections of a son and a brother. This is the only way to expand the heart; for public affections, as well as public virtue, must ever grow out of private character . . .
>
> The character of . . . a husband, and a father, forms the citizen imperceptibly, by producing a sober manliness of thought, and orderly behavior; but, from the lax morals and depraved affections of the libertine, what results?—a finical man of taste, who is only anxious to secure his own private gratifications, and to maintain his rank in society.

For Wollstonecraft, public (corruptible) men would not be saved from immoral influences by private (moral) women, as Tocqueville (and Rousseau) suggested, but *by placing their affections first and foremost in the domestic sphere*—even if their professional and social duties lay well beyond it.

A recovery of Wollstonecraft's thought today can reclaim the view, shared by Tocqueville too, that the cultivation of virtue within the life of the home serves as an essential precondition for liberty and republican government, even as she affirms something he had not: the importance of equal civil and political rights for men and women in private and public life. To reclaim this Wollstonecraftian principle in our day, what is needed is for both men and women to recognize the moral priority of the family as that institution which, at its very best, forms persons in virtue, creates bonds of solidarity, and fosters habits of both personal and republican self-government.

WOLLSTONECRAFT'S PHILOSOPHICAL INFLUENCE ON THE EARLY WOMEN'S RIGHTS MOVEMENT

Although Wollstonecraft's public reputation suffered somewhat in the United States, her philosophical influence over American women extended well beyond Abigail Adams. Indeed, University of Notre Dame political theorist Eileen Botting argues that, of the many European theorists who influenced the nineteenth-century American women's rights advocates, "none enjoyed the same iconic stature as Wollstonecraft, and most were readers of the *Rights of Woman* themselves."[33]

First among them was Lucretia Mott, a Quaker minister and powerful voice in the Garrisonian wing of the abolitionist movement. Born the second of five children, Mott had attended a Quaker boarding school in upstate New York, and she and her husband had six children of their own. A teacher by training, Mott had devoured Wollstonecraft's *Rights of Woman* in the 1820s, twenty years before she became active in the nascent women's movement.

Like Wollstonecraft, Mott believed women's enhanced opportunity in education, civic life, and the professions would redound to the benefit of their moral duties as wives and mothers. Mott similarly critiqued women's preoccupation with romantic novels and "outward adorning," along with the flattery they enjoyed receiving as "the mere plaything or toy of society."[34] Still, Mott believed, first and foremost, that moral suasion was the best means toward societal improvement and thus was not yet committed to the still more revolutionary cause of women's suffrage. Until the early twentieth century, the great majority of American women felt the same way.[35]

FIGURE 3.2. Lucretia Mott, 1842.
Credit: National Portrait Gallery (public domain).

Mott met Elizabeth Cady Stanton in 1840 at the World's Anti-Slavery Convention in London, which Stanton and her new husband, the abolitionist Henry Stanton, attended during their honeymoon. The daughter of a prominent couple in Johnstown, New York, Stanton enjoyed a rigorous liberal education at the Johnstown Academy and Emma Willard's Troy Female Seminary in New York and was fluent in ancient Greek. She also received an informal legal education from her father, Daniel Cady, a distinguished lawyer, state assemblyman, and one-term U.S. congressman. Mr. Cady engaged in discussions with Elizabeth and invited her to listen in on his conversations with colleagues and guests. Stanton recounts in her memoirs that during her time in London, when she and other women abolitionists were barred from participating in the convention, she and Mott found themselves in a lengthy discussion of "Mary Wollstonecraft, her social theories, and her demands of equality for women."[36] Though Stanton had read Wollstonecraft before, that conversation, and her ongoing relationship with Mott, inspired her deeply and served as the catalyst for Stanton to join the cause of women's rights in addition to her abolitionist work.[37]

Stanton and Mott penned the now-famous Declaration of Sentiments and Resolutions for the first Women's Rights Convention, held in Seneca Falls, New York, in 1848. The document resounded in themes Wollstonecraft herself had articulated more than a half century before. Reworking the rhetorical apparatus of the Declaration of Independence to emphasize the rights of women, Stanton and Mott, like Abigail Adams before them, analogized the common law status of married women to the injustices of King George against the colonists.

Although the Declaration of Sentiments made an initial plea for the franchise (their most controversial request even among the hundreds of people attending the convention), much of the document concerned the legal and social inequality of women, and the silencing of women's "improper" voices in public.[38] One resolution notably took issue with the prevailing double standard, and so was deeply reminiscent of a key thread in Wollstonecraft's thought: "That the same amount of virtue, delicacy, and refinement of behavior that is required of woman in the social state, should also be required of man, and the same transgressions should be visited with equal severity on both man and woman."[39] These women were not seeking to absolve themselves from cultural expectations of virtue and refinement; rather, they demanded that the same be expected of men.

Arguing that the "equality of human rights" results from the "identity of the race in capacities and responsibilities," the Declaration of Sentiments included the following lengthy resolution, expounding upon the "right and duty" of both women and men to exercise the God-given capabilities of their common rational nature. Again echoing Wollstonecraft's thought:

> That, being invested by the Creator with the same capabilities, and the same consciousness of responsibility for their exercise, it is demonstrably the right and duty of woman, equally with man, to promote every righteous cause by every righteous means; and especially in regard to the great subjects of morals and religion, it is self-evidently her right to participate with her brother in teaching them, both in private and in public, by writing and by speaking, by any instrumentalities proper to be used, and in any assemblies proper to be held; and this being a self-evident truth growing out of the divinely implanted principles of human nature, any custom or authority adverse to it, whether modern or wearing the hoary sanction of antiquity, is to be regarded as self-evident falsehood, and at war with mankind.[40]

Mott herself later sought to popularize the British philosopher's work more explicitly in her concluding speech of the National Women's Rights Convention in 1866: "Young women of America, I want you to make yourselves acquainted with the history of the Woman's Rights movement, from the days of Mary Wollstonecraft. All honor to Mary Wollstonecraft. Her name was cast out as evil, even as that of Jesus was cast out as evil, and those of the apostles were cast out as evil; but her name shall yet go forth and stand as the pioneer of this movement."[41] Mott and Stanton were not alone in studying (and valorizing) Wollstonecraft. Another prominent student, Botting suggests, was Sarah Grimké, also a Quaker and noted abolitionist. Mott had also introduced Wollstonecraft to Grimké, who read the *Rights of Woman* before penning her own influential *Letters on the Equality of the Sexes and the Condition of Woman* in 1838. Although Grimké did not expressly acknowledge her reliance on Wollstonecraft, the books share similar philosophical themes and arguments.[42] Both defend the moral and intellectual equality of the sexes as a means not of abdicating familial and social duties but fulfilling them. Botting notes: "Like Wollstonecraft, Grimké acknowledges that moral duties such as good parenting, while identical for men and women as moral universals dictated by God, are put into practice in different ways by mothers and fathers according to particular social circumstances and roles."[43] Grimké's most famous work may be remembered best for her quip: "I ask no favors for my sex. I surrender not our claim to equality. All I ask of our brethren, is that they will take their feet from off our necks, and permit us to stand upright on that ground which God destined us to occupy."[44]

Botting reports evidence of Wollstonecraft's influence on Susan B. Anthony, including an inscription in the copy of the *Rights of Woman* that Anthony donated to the Library of Congress in 1904: "Presented to the Library of Congress by a great admirer of this earliest work for woman's right to Equality of rights ever penned by a woman."[45] And in 1906, Anthony made a final tribute to Wollstonecraft at the last speech she delivered to a women's suffrage convention: "I never saw that great woman, Mary Wollstonecraft, but I have read her eloquent and unanswerable arguments in behalf of the liberty of womankind."[46] Botting writes that Anthony shared Wollstonecraft's view that the subordination of women was especially harmful because it had a "morally corrosive impact on the primary building block of society, the family."[47]

When Stanton and Anthony founded their weekly newspaper, *The Revolution*, they hung Wollstonecraft's portrait, alongside that of Lucretia Mott, on the office wall. Several Wollstonecraft-inspired philosophical articles appeared in the first year, as they also tried to restore her reputation. Throughout 1868 they reprinted *Rights of Woman* itself in the *Revolution*'s pages, so important was Wollstonecraft's thought to their early advocacy. Early claims for joint property ownership were symbolic of these efforts.

EARLY CLAIMS FOR JOINT PROPERTY:
RECOGNIZING THE PREINDUSTRIAL WORK OF THE HOME

Tocqueville had assumed that American women freely sacrificed themselves for the new nation; perhaps most did.[48] But the common law doctrine of coverture also promoted the assumed sodality, and separate spheres, of husband and wife. William Blackstone's *Commentaries on the Laws of England*, detailing the law of coverture, was appropriated by the Founders as the unquestioned common law backdrop to the national structure the U.S. Constitution had erected. According to Blackstone, "The very being or legal existence of the woman is suspended during the marriage, or at least is incorporated and consolidated into that of the husband: under whose wing, protection, and *cover*, she performs everything."[49] Thus, upon marriage, a married woman lost any property rights she had had as a *femme sole*; the husband gained full use of his wife's real property and full rights to her personal property and services. In exchange, he was bound by law to protect and provide for her. Thus, in common law jurisdictions, married women held no legal title to the common family enterprise; title was held by the husband alone, who served as legal and, assuming he owned land, political representative of the family. Were the husband to predecease his wife, she would inherit a mere third of a life interest in their shared investment. In the handful of civil law jurisdictions, such as Louisiana, however, husband and wife owned their property "in community," with the husband as head of the family legally empowered to manage the property.

Wollstonecraft, in 1792, had suggested that unjust marital laws undermined the capacity of husband and wife to share fruitfully in the collaborative duties and goods of the home; the wife's legal subservience worked against authentic marital intimacy and the development of virtue for both husband and wife—and thus domestic happiness. For nearly two hundred years, arguments against coverture were a central theme in the cause of women's rights. In the movement's very earliest legal claims, which we will discuss presently, advocates for joint property ownership maintained the very closest philosophical kinship with Wollstonecraft's original rationale. As we'll see, "joint" property rights within marriage were not urged for the separate or individualistic undertakings of each spouse; rather, these rights were advocated by Wollstonecraft's American disciples for the sake of greater union of husband and wife engaged together in their most essential task: shaping themselves and their children through the productive work they carried out in their homes.

With the cooperative and interdependent management of household duties in the young agrarian republic, the shared, if male-headed, legal status between spouses caused little public protest among American women early on. But as the industrializing American economy grew increasingly more commercial, and American men claimed their "individual rights" vis-à-vis the new republican government, more American women began to challenge the fitness and justice of applying the traditional common law approach to new economic circumstances. As work valued with wages began to command more economic power and cultural respect, women grew simultaneously more and more vulnerable to familial and social inequalities. Wollstonecraft's concerns about the ways in which married women's economic dependence upon their husbands could corrupt the essential goods of the marital relationship, and so the nation, became even more pressing as industrialization wore on. Equally relevant was her concern that the growing commercial mentality would undermine the development of virtue in a people. Was women's essential work in the private sphere—a sphere increasingly cut off from the hustle and bustle of American markets, trade, and politics—truly valued, if such work enjoyed no economic or legal status whatsoever?

The first married women's property legislation amending the common law was passed in the United States in the 1840s. Though different states enacted the law with slight differences, these new "separate property" acts allowed married women to hold in their own name property acquired separately before and even during the marriage. They often protected wives' real property from the debts of their husbands, as equitable trusts drawn up for wealthy families had for centuries before.[50] A decade later, states began to enact earnings statutes that also gave married women rights to their own wages, and often provided these women with the legal capacity to contract and sue. Although these acts amended the common law in discernible ways, their effect on the lives of most married women was not discernible at all.[51] Fewer than 5 percent of married women worked for wages during the nineteenth century; the rest, who continued to labor in their own homes, received little or no benefit from these legal amendments.[52] Something more would be needed to recognize more publicly women's work in the home.

In the 1850s, the women's movement began to focus its organizing efforts on claims for "joint" property rights, in contrast to the "separate" property acts passed a decade earlier. The movement argued not only that women's household labor was valuable "work," but that it also entitled women to an equal legal share in their families' assets. As industrialization drew more and more men out of the agrarian home to work for wages, the traditional and productive work of the home became increasingly synonymous with family life *simpliciter*. This downgrading of the economic value of the work of the home was further exacerbated by the growing cultural depiction of the private sphere as the moral and spiritual counterpoise to the often harsh realities of industrial society. Economist Nancy Folbre observes: "The moral elevation of the home was accompanied by the economic devaluation of the work performed there."[53] The great moral contributions that Tocqueville had noticed women were making to the new nation were not easily, nor desirably, counted in the new economic terminology.

And yet, the household economy remained enormously productive. Indeed, its productivity, and the industriousness, thrift, and cooperation such work required, was a good part of the reason Wollstonecraft had regarded middle-class homes, especially, as enjoying the capacity to shape the characters of both children and their parents. Although such household productivity varied by region, household capacity, and the wealth of the family, women were actively laboring to improve the economic well-being of their families, either by sale of home-produced goods and services or by their own frugality and inventiveness. But as the market economy grew more sophisticated, new economic measures of local and national productivity were developed. Such measures excluded household labor, characterizing such work as "unproductive," and women who labored in the still-productive home were uncounted among the "gainfully employed."[54] As a result, says Yale legal scholar Reva Siegel in a lengthy 1994 essay devoted to the topic, a notable rhetorical shift occurred in the depiction of marriage.[55]

Before industrialization, as we've seen, married women were "under the cover" of their husbands' protection and provision at common law, and so were regarded *legally* as "dependent." But given the interdependent communal nature of the productive agrarian home, the substantial *economic* contribution women made to the family unit was never in doubt, even if that unit was represented legally by husbands alone. If they were dependent on their husbands, so too were their husbands dependent on them. Historian Alice Clark states that women could "hardly have been regarded as mere dependents on their husbands when the clothing for the whole family was spun by their hands."[56]

But once the mechanism measuring productive labor was altered by the new wage economy, married women's legal subordination to their husbands took on an all-new economic cast. As the productive work of the home became more and more economically invisible—winning cultural esteem for its moral and spiritual qualities alone—the traditional interdependence of spouses was transformed into the image of an economically and legally *autonomous husband* and an economically and legally *dependent wife*. But the culturally powerful image was grossly inappropriate: spousal interdependence remained the economic reality in the industrial age, even if that reality was now obscured by the new accounting. Just as homebound wives were economically dependent on their husbands to bring home the new currency, wage-earning husbands were economically dependent on their wives to maintain and grow the family household. Husband and wife still built up their family assets together.

But the common law doctrine of coverture, now enlarged by the new economic visage of "productive" husband and "dependent" wife, made married women increasingly marginalized in the market-based economy, and increasingly vulnerable to their husbands' bad choices. The new stresses of factory work, more time spent away from the home, and the enhanced accessibility of urban bars and brothels made those choices all the more tempting. The Christian Temperance movement of the late nineteenth century, spearheaded by and composed mainly of women, demonstrated the growing concern. Siegel writes that although joint property advocates initially hoped to protect economically vulnerable wives from profligate husbands, the movement increasingly sought to "empower . . . economically productive women to participate equally with men in managing assets both had helped to accumulate."[57] The target of their advocacy was not yet the division of labor in the family wherein husbands left home to work for wages while women remained working in the home; rather, the focus was on the disparate value now accorded each of the separate spheres.

At the First National Woman's Rights Convention in Worcester, Massachusetts, in 1850, the following resolution was presented, modeled on the community property regime of civil (rather than common) law jurisdictions, but dropping the legal authority of husband as head of the household:

> *Resolved,* That the laws of property, as affecting married parties, demand a thorough revisal, so that all rights may be equal between them;—that the wife may have, during life, *an equal control over the property gained by their mutual toil and sacrifices,* be heir to her husband precisely to the extent that he is heir to her, and entitled, at her death, to dispose by will the same share of the joint property as he is.[58]

The women's movement sought to match better the laws of marriage and inheritance with the interdependent reality taking place in their homes.

According to Siegel, two philosophical undercurrents ran through women's advocacy for joint ownership: the first was based on age-old traditions of family autonomy and reciprocity, with emphasis given to the equal worth of work performed in each of the separate spheres; the other drew from the liberal tradition represented by Locke. The former, Siegel says, presented a "vision of equality in marriage that was rooted in values of community and sharing," and so, we would say, resonated deeply with Wollstonecraft's vision.[59] The latter appropriated the more individualist language of "self-ownership," appealing to Locke's claim that the "labor of his body and the work of his hands, we may say, are properly his."[60] These particular manifestations of important philosophical differences appeared only rhetorically in these early claims for joint property, as was true, we will see in chapter 4, in the movement for "voluntary motherhood"; they gave way to few substantive disagreements. But, in time, disagreements of substance would emerge.

Joint property statutes did not become a reality until a full century later, in the 1960s and 70s.[61] One reason for the marked delay was the shift in nineteenth-century women's rights advocacy itself. In the years following the Civil War and Reconstruction amendments, as arguments for women's suffrage began to gain more steam, these early efforts to pass joint property legislation took a back seat, even as the injustices brought to the forefront by joint property advocates had become more rhetorically effective in efforts to garner support for the vote. Husbands' vicarious representation of the family—the single most prevalent argument against married women's suffrage (as we discuss in chapter 4)—lost its resonance as women began to see their domestic industriousness culturally disregarded and their economic dependence on their husbands culturally assumed. More outspoken suffragists began to describe then extant marital law as imposing a "condition of servitude," akin to slavery, which was abolished by the Thirteenth Amendment in 1865.[62] If women were denied the equal cultural accord and legal share their essential work in the home merited, then "family" representation on the part of their husbands no longer seemed just.

In an effort to assuage suffragists' growing demands for the vote, state legislatures in the 1870s began more aggressively to pass *separate* property statutes ensuring married women's title in their own earnings.[63] Notably, John Stuart Mill was singularly responsible for the first Married Women's Property Act in England in 1870.[64] But, in an explicit knock against decades-old arguments for joint property, these statutes now often explicitly exempted wives' domestic contributions from their coverage. In excluding wives' marital service to their husbands from legal recognition, state legislators sought to preserve husbands' spousal duty of support to their wives and children, duties that the growing temperance movement suggested they often abrogated. But for joint property advocates, the spousal duty on the part of the husband ought to have justified a correlative right on the part of the wife, not to bring suit against him (which was apparently the legislators' fear), but to share fully in legal management, and justly in inheritance, should he predecease her. Instead, these separate property statutes doubled down on the common law view that the joint earnings of husband and wife together belonged properly to him alone; in the new separate property regime, she individually owned legal title only to that work she performed outside of the home. In common did they labor, but only separately did they own.

By the 1870s, some involved in the growing women's movement, now more likely than their predecessors to engage household help, began themselves to disparage the traditional, productive work of the home.[65] In step with the logic implied by the newly enacted separate property statutes, they began to argue that if married women wanted true economic independence, they ought to seek wage labor outside of the home. Some even expressly denounced the assumption inherent in decades of joint property advocacy: that both the public and private spheres were of equal value, committed interdependently to the well-being of the family. Rather, to these more radical elements, cultural efforts to extol home labor would keep women content in their subordinate position, uninterested in freeing themselves from such burdens to pursue more culturally valued opportunities in the public sphere.

With this shift came a radical transformation in discourse about women's traditional work: no longer was the work of the home so culturally essential that it defied market valuation. Now that work began to be regarded, by some in the movement, as mere "unpaid labor," with "real work" regarded as what earns a wage. The very arguments that early advocates had strongly denounced in their efforts to hold back the culturally ascendant market mentality had now become fair game. Indeed, in 1898, with the publication of *Women and Economics*, Charlotte Perkins Gilman flipped those early arguments on their head.[66]

Expressly repudiating the joint property view that husbands and wives were economically interdependent partners in marriage and so ought to be treated as such by the law, Gilman instead argued that wives were *in fact* dependents in marriage, and that only a repudiation of the family as an economic unit as such would free women from such marital inequality. Because of the increasingly dramatic split between the private and public spheres wrought by industrialization, Gilman suggested, women and men had each been overdeveloped in their respectively feminine and masculine traits. In her view, the work of the home, theoretically requiring less rigorous thought than market labor, had a stifling effect on women's authentic development. Moreover, Gilman argued, the public sphere would benefit from women's influence in it. Thus did Gilman trade traditionally (in her mind, "feminine") domestic values for modern ("masculine") economic ones. For her, no longer should the home remain an antimodern island in the industrializing sea, preserving a sphere of solidarity and kinship from market forces. She sought instead to bring the home, and the women in it, sharply in line with the modern economizing project.

FIGURE 3.3. Charlotte Perkins Gilman, 1884.
Credit: Schlesinger Library, RIAS, Harvard University (public domain).

In Gilman's view, the home should be freed from all work in order to become a pure refuge of rest and relaxation; likewise, women should be freed from home labor to seek wage labor, and thus economic autonomy, of their own. Gilman writes: "Specialization and organization are the basis of human progress, the organic methods of social life. They have been forbidden to women almost absolutely."[67] And so, the traditional work of the home ought to be contracted out as much as possible: childcare professionals should take over the most important work of caring for and educating children (since most mothers were, according to Gilman, incompetent in this regard), household cleaning ought to be conducted by professionals too, and meals ought to be shared among families in common kitchens, with professional cooks. Kitchen-less houses would be preferable since "a family unity which is only bound together with a table-cloth is of questionable value."[68] Modern efficiency, now applied to the home, was Gilman's watchword.

To be sure, Gilman was not repudiating motherhood altogether: like many at her time, she regarded motherhood as the "common duty and common glory of womanhood."[69] But she sought to decouple motherhood from the time-consuming household tasks that kept women from the kind of professional work that would ensure better personal development and so give way to more nurturing relationships with their husbands and children. Where women might find this kind of professional work during the Industrial Revolution, flexible enough to allow them valuable time with children, including a year off after each child, Gilman does not say. Perhaps hers was a theory for another time. Gilman's quest for efficiency and specialization was thus the women movement's forebearer for contemporary promotion of professional caregivers, household cleaners, and restaurant dining.[70] But it would remain, to our day, a vision that only the more well-off could afford. Gilman's theories, which gained immediate currency in the halls of newly opened women's colleges, such as Vassar, portrayed married women working in the home as economically subordinate while repudiating the robust joint property arguments that once responded to their unjust situation.

Siegel writes, "Whether or not women . . . viewed their work for the family as intrinsically degrading, they were in no position to escape it; nor, for that matter, were their prospects in the market such that wage work necessarily promised 'personal development.'"[71] More still, many women (and men) still viewed the work of the home, productive as it remained, and deeply meaningful in its educative and nurturing elements, as the more essential of the two spheres: the place where their family's flourishing was rooted and would grow strong. One notable public rebuttal to the view advanced by those like Gilman that "all work becomes oppressive that is not remunerative" was printed in *The New Northwest*: "To this idea, more than any other, may be traced the prejudice against bearing children which has become so ingrafted upon the minds of married women, that tens of thousands annually commit ante-natal murder."[72]

Although Wollstonecraft, like Gilman, believed women, the family, and the public sphere would be served by women's greater educational and professional opportunities, Wollstonecraft argued that the work of the home afforded the character development men, women, and children needed for true success in the public sphere. Without that intentional human development properly prioritized in the life of the home, persons (and markets) would do little good outside of it. As the next two chapters (and beyond) describe, these philosophical tensions, between Wollstonecraft's more virtue-centered family-oriented approach and a more market-oriented one, would reappear and influence debates over marriage and protective labor legislation. Only motherhood itself would be preserved—until the early 1970s.

CHAPTER 4

Women's Suffrage, Rational Souls, Sexed Bodies, and the Ties That Bind

In 1865, after a bitter and bloody war between the states, the Thirteenth Amendment was ratified, outlawing slavery in the Union. For some time after its passage, the still nascent women's movement, composed in large part of women who had long fought alongside men to abolish slavery, now worked with the abolitionists for universal suffrage. But when the opportunity arose to grant newly freed Black men, but not women, the right to vote with the Fifteenth Amendment, the women's movement split in two. Some were singularly intent on winning suffrage for newly freed Black men; others sought to prioritize suffrage for white women (and even succumbed to employing racist epithets in their campaign).[1]

Susan B. Anthony argued that, based on U.S. citizenship alone, women had the right to vote. She even attempted to vote in the presidential election of 1872. At her trial, after being arrested for this effort, she appealed to liberal social contract theory, the political philosophy employed by many of the abolitionists: "You have trampled under foot every vital principle of our government. My natural rights, my civil rights, my political rights, my judicial rights, are all alike ignored. Robbed of the fundamental privilege of citizenship, I am degraded from the status of a citizen to that of a subject . . . . Your denial of my citizen's right to

vote, is the denial of my right of consent as one of the governed . . . my
right of representation as one of the taxed . . . right to a trial by a jury of
my peers."[2] Equal citizenship, in this view, included both civil and political rights; women were citizens, thus civil and political rights were
justly theirs too.

Other suffragists argued for civil and political rights based on the
plain language of the new Reconstruction amendments themselves, even
though the amendments were passed in an effort to reconstitute the nation's fundamental law to include newly freed slaves after the Civil War.
Although the capacious language of the Fourteenth Amendment, ratified in 1868, one hundred years later came to protect the civil rights of
women, it was not read as such at its origins. Still, the plain meaning of
section 1 of that amendment may make it difficult, read today, to understand why women would not have been originally protected.

> Section 1: All *persons born or naturalized* in the United States and
> subject to the jurisdiction thereof, *are citizens of the United States*
> and of the State wherein they reside. No State shall make or enforce
> any law which shall abridge the privileges or immunities of *citizens*
> of the United States; nor shall any State deprive any *person* of life,
> liberty, or property, without due process of law; nor deny to any
> *person* within its jurisdiction the equal protection of the laws.[3]

Section 2 of the amendment, describing the apportionment of representatives, includes (for the first time in the Constitution) the word "male,"
but the language of section 1 speaks solely of *persons and citizens*, and
American women were both at the time the amendment was ratified.

The suffragists and other women's rights advocates argued just that.
In 1875, for instance, a leading suffragist in Missouri, Virginia Minor,
with the help of her attorney husband, argued all the way to the Supreme Court that the privileges and immunities clause of the Fourteenth Amendment had enfranchised all citizens, regardless of sex. In
Minor v. Happersett, the high court disagreed. Two years earlier in the
Slaughterhouse Cases, the Court had starkly delimited the suggestively
broad language of the privileges and immunities clause to protect only
"federal" rights of U.S. citizens, such as the right to travel. Despite the

Eng.ᵈ by G. E. Perine, & Cᵒ N.Y.

FIGURE 4.1. Susan B. Anthony, circa 1868. Credit: Courtesy of the
Susan B. Anthony Birthplace Museum, Adams, MA.

dissenting justices' view that the privileges and immunities clause had been designed to protect all the "fundamental rights" of citizens of "free governments," the Supreme Court held that the clause did no such thing. Thus, since Minor, though indeed a citizen, did not have the right to vote in her state, the Fourteenth Amendment afforded her no additional protection; voting rights, after all, were protected by states or not at all. If the language of the Fourteenth Amendment had granted anyone the right to vote, the Court reasoned, the Fifteenth Amendment would not have been necessary.

Minor helps to clarify how the Supreme Court was beginning to interpret the newly ratified Fourteenth Amendment generally, but a now-infamous concurring opinion in a case decided the day after the Slaughterhouse Cases sheds light on a commonly held view of women and their rights at the time of Reconstruction. In Bradwell v. Illinois, the Court ruled that the privileges and immunities clause did not grant Myra Bradwell the right to practice law. The Court held that, even though Bradwell's particular state permitted women to make contracts with respect to property under that state's separate property act, the statute did not give women a general right to contract. Since the Fourteenth Amendment granted citizens no new rights the states had not granted (as decided in the Slaughterhouse Cases), the Illinois Supreme Court's decision denying Bradwell admission to the bar would stand. By 1873, five states and the District of Columbia had already permitted women to obtain licenses to practice law. Following the Supreme Court decision in Bradwell, the legislature of Illinois opened the bar to women.

Justice Joseph Bradley concurred in Bradwell's judgment. Notably, Justice Bradley had dissented in the Slaughterhouse Cases a day earlier based on his view that the privileges and immunities clause protected civil rights far more broadly than the majority had held. In his Slaughterhouse dissent, he had written: "The right of any citizen to follow whatever lawful employment he chooses to adopt (submitting himself to all lawful regulations) is one of his most valuable rights, and one which the legislature of a State cannot invade, whether restrained by its own constitution or not."[4] But in Bradwell, Bradley would not defend Myra Bradwell's right to her chosen employment. Instead, he devoted his concurrence in Bradwell to articulating a disparaging view of women's capacities: "The natural and proper timidity and delicacy which belongs to the female sex evidently unfits it for many of the occupations of civil life." And then: "The paramount destiny and mission of woman are to fulfill the noble and benign offices of wife and mother. This is the law of the Creator."[5]

The initial part of *Bradwell*'s rationale—that women were too weak, timid, and delicate to engage in civil occupations and public life—is usually remembered as what formed the basis for the denial of women's suffrage too. There were, of course, those who held that view. But there were also those who argued that one's view of women's attributes was irrelevant to the question of women's suffrage entirely. Senator Pomeroy (R-KS), for instance, argued from the latter position, offering an argument much like Anthony's: "I ask the ballot for woman, not on account of her weakness or on account of her strength; not because she may be above or below a man; that has nothing to do with the question. I ask it because she is a citizen of the Republic, amenable to its laws, taxed for its support, and a sharer in its destiny. There are no reasons for giving the ballot to a man that do not apply to a woman with equal force."[6]

Senator Fowler (R-TN) argued likewise that natural rights afforded women the right to vote, and that, in his view, women would be particularly wise stewards of the ballot:

> There is no argument in favor of the suffrage of men that will not apply equally as well to women. She is equally well fitted to decide what measures are calculated to promote her own interests. If any man were asked whose advice was the wisest and truest on all matters of business and politics he would unhesitatingly answer his wife's, his mother's, or his sister's. It is all a delusion and a sham to talk of excluding women from the ballot and admitting all the civilized and uncivilized men of the world. When men base their support of suffrage upon the natural rights of man, upon the worth of the individual, and then exclude woman, they do not believe the doctrine they assert.[7]

But the view that would win the day during debates over the Reconstruction amendments was neither that women were too weak, on the one hand, nor particularly wise, on the other, nor that women's natural rights extended to the franchise. Rather, the most prevalent view, held by men and women alike, was that women's interests as citizens were not abrogated by the absence of the franchise at all: women's interests were properly represented by their husbands in a kind of vicarious, family, representation. As University of Texas law dean and legal scholar Ward Farnsworth describes the view of the day, "Politicians represent men; men represent the women and children in their families."[8]

Of course, Farnsworth well notes, the argument from vicarious representation made no sense of the denial of voting rights to unmarried women or widows. Logic aside, vicarious "family rights" accorded well with the observations Tocqueville had made of the reigning outlook in the early republic: the public obligations men undertook on behalf of their families were made possible by the private obligations women took on behalf of the same. In this way, Justice Bradley's judicial notice of the "noble office" of women—the second part of his *Bradwell* concurrence—was an accurate read of the belief at the time. Senator Bayard (D-DE) articulated this antisuffrage, complementarian view better than Bradley had, with the latter's focus on "timidity" and "delicacy." Bayard stated: "Let it not be supposed . . . in stating these objections to female suffrage, that I mean to characterize the sex as inferior to man. In their combined mental and moral organization I hold them to be quite our equals, if not our superiors. But there is a difference in the physical, mental, and moral structure of the sexes which fits them for the performance of different duties, and the pursuit of different avocations."[9] For most of the antisuffragists, then, the issue was not one of moral inequality or feminine weakness, although some held that view. Most simply regarded differences in the sexes as physically, morally, and politically complementary: public man and private woman.

Thus, women, although both *persons* and *citizens*, were first and foremost conceptualized legally as *members of families*, under the province of their husbands (just as, as children, they and their brothers were under the legal authority of their fathers). Were the federal government to grant women the franchise (or civil rights such as the right to practice law), it would be reaching too far into matters the Constitution had left to the states and localities. It was thought that such an encroachment—by a distant federal government—would threaten the

fundamental units of society that Americans most valued not only personally but also as the seedbeds for the virtues needed for republican
government. Farnsworth explains the view at the time: "Governments
exist to serve family structures rather than modify them."[10] If the Reconstruction amendments had intended to do something so radical, the
thinking was, they would have done so more explicitly, the plain language of the Fourteenth Amendment notwithstanding. Thus, if suffragists were to win the vote, they would have to change the hearts and
minds of men (and women), state by state. And so they did, capturing
the franchise in fifteen states by the time the Nineteenth Amendment
granted women in every state the federal right to vote in 1920.[11] But the
winning arguments the suffragists began to prioritize were also, by and
large, arguments that extolled the importance of the family in American life, and women's premiere role in it.

Turning from more abstract arguments for universal natural rights,
leaders of the suffragist movement, such as Susan B. Anthony, eventually
joined forces with women actively engaged in the temperance movement and other social reform movements to argue that women's powerful moral voice should not be limited to its domestic influence or the
force of moral suasion in society. Woman's Christian Temperance Union
(WCTU) president Frances Willard was finally able to persuade hundreds of thousands of her devotees: women could enhance their moral
influence in society if they engaged the political realm too. Fittingly,
Willard referred to the franchise as the "home protection ballot."[12]

The initial Lockean approach taken by Anthony and the later "maternal" approach taken by Willard are often remembered as being in opposition, as though the first focused entirely on the individual woman
as "citizen" in the abstract, and the latter focused solely on women's
social and familial role, or her maternal and especially moral voice.
Wollstonecraft, on this view, is simplistically understood as a precursor
to the natural rights view articulated early on by Anthony. And it is
true, Wollstonecraft did believe that legitimate republican government
would protect the civil and political rights of both men and women,
rights that arose from their human nature as rational creatures. But
leaving it at that would miss Wollstonecraft's view in all its complexity.
And it would oversimplify Willard's view too.

Because she rejected Locke's mythical "state of nature," Wollstonecraft did not subscribe to his particular theory of rights, even if she did believe in the "rights of man" or "natural rights." Nor did she think, as did later Enlightenment thinkers such as Mill, that such rights were to be sought for human development generally, or some ill-defined, self-chosen end. Rather, Wollstonecraft understood civil and political rights as the necessary means for each person, man or woman, to fulfill his or her antecedent duties to self, family, society, and God. Wollstonecraft prized freedom to be sure: "liberty is the mother of virtue," she would say. But she sought political and civil freedom not for mere self-ownership or self-expression, but rather for intellectual and moral excellence, the fruit of fulfilling one's various obligations virtuously.

Although her influence here is not historically explicit, it was only as the late nineteenth-century suffragist movement made the conceptual shift away from more Lockean declarations of abstract universal rights to articulating a more complete and concrete Wollstonecraftian understanding of the underlying rationale for rights that they were able to be persuasive. When the suffragists reminded the public that women were especially adept at moral leadership in the home—and that the public sphere needed their maternal, humanizing voice—the antisuffrage element, especially among women themselves, finally began to desist.

Within this winning suffrage argument there was a subtle philosophical disagreement about the nature of women and their souls, one that has important long-term implications for the way we think about sex differences and human equality. Some, implicitly following Wollstonecraft, understood both women and men to enjoy rational souls with a common *human* purpose: to develop their shared intellectual and moral capacities in and through the practice of wisdom and virtue, as an imitation of the divine wisdom and goodness. Sexual difference, for Wollstonecraft, originated at the level of men's and women's distinctive bodies, manifested in their distinctive capacities for paternity and maternity, especially, but also in differences in physical strength. Others, following Rousseau, seemed to believe, by contrast, that men and women had entirely different natures that arose from their distinctive "masculine" or "feminine" souls. Thus, for Wollstonecraft the soul was rational, but the body, sexed; for Rousseau, the soul itself was sexed.

With the ancients, and unlike Descartes, Wollstonecraft understood the rational soul and sexed body to be deeply integrated into the one unified person.[13] This understanding of deep body/soul integration is why Wollstonecraft advocated the development of self-mastery through the disciplined intake of physical exercise and food, and also of sex. She recognized a person's choices in these realms shape one's character for good or ill starting at a very young age; self-governance in more basic bodily arenas redound to the development of human maturity and true independence of mind.[14] But Wollstonecraft also thought that wisdom and virtue (and their contraries) would likely manifest themselves differently in women and men as a result of their asymmetrical reproductive roles (and the familial duties that followed). So although Wollstonecraft strongly disputed the Rousseauian idea that men's souls were more rational and women's souls more emotional, she also strongly believed that the acts of childbearing and breastfeeding, in particular, properly imparted in women a "maternal character," granting women deep and benevolent affection for their children, and others too.[15] And, as we have seen, she maintained that engaged fatherhood would shape a man's character profitably.

Bringing contemporary scientific research to bear on this complex insight, one might say that each man or woman lives out his or her body/soul union distinctively, with each person's self-development affected by physiological sex differences in different ways. For instance, no two women are exactly alike, even as they share physiological traits (at the cellular, hormonal, reproductive, and neurological levels) that differentiate them from all men.[16] And, despite these physiological differences that course through the entire body of a man or woman—affecting every cell in their bodies—these sex differences do not encompass the whole of the person. Nor do they undermine human equality. "Our differing biological matter offers to us differing *influences* for the development of our common capacities," Aristotelian philosopher Sarah Borden Sharkey has aptly put it.[17] This insight gives way to the legal view (which we discuss in chapter 7) that sex differences can be statistically significant (and thus observable across large swaths of men and women), but they ought not legally confine particular individuals to particular life choices, professionally or personally. Again, men and women are different, but no two women (or two men) are different in precisely the same ways. And all men and women, for Wollstonecraft, are rational creatures whose common human end is the development of wisdom and virtue, in whatever their given circumstances.

Wollstonecraft scholar Eileen Botting suggests that Elizabeth Cady Stanton was among the leading suffragists who expressly disagreed with Wollstonecraft's view that the soul (and thus virtue) was "unsexed."[18] Stanton seemed to believe that women were not just equal to men on a human level, but that the "feminine" souls (or natures) of women were morally superior to those of men, with essential characteristics that determined the characters of each.[19] Driven to root out the "feudal hierarchy of the saintly and moral mother subject to the authority and brute force of the father," and to teach boys "feminine" virtues and girls "masculine" virtues, Stanton elsewhere quipped, "If a difference in sex involves superiority, then we claim it for woman."[20] More to the point, thought Stanton, "the masculine and feminine elements in humanity must be in exact equilibrium" while the feminine element brings out the "diviner qualities in human nature."[21] To be sure, Stanton was not a philosopher. She simply may have been employing these contraries rhetorically, rather than seeking to render a philosophical position on the matter; she is not always consistent. Nonetheless, her rhetorical use of "feminine" element, "feminine" virtue, and especially "feminine" superiority, taken up in the next century by radical feminists, can be regarded as the very inverse of chauvinist claims of prior days (of "masculine" superiority).

In this theory of "reverse gender polarity," a term coined by philosopher Prudence Allen, women are essentially nurturant; men, aggressive.[22] Women are always and everywhere innocent victims; men, lustful perpetrators. In its most radical (and ironic) form today, reason itself is understood as "masculine" and so is not to be trusted.[23] Henry James presciently mocked this stridently dualist strand of early feminist thought in his 1886 novel *The Bostonians*. From the perspective of his protagonist, Olive, man "had trampled upon [women] from the beginning of time, and their tenderness, their abnegation, had been his opportunity." By contrast, if woman were in charge, there "would be generosity, tenderness, sympathy, where there is now only brute force and sordid rivalry."[24]

But if sex differences are understood conceptually to be at the level of the soul ("nature" or "essence"), rather than the body, arguments for the common human dignity and equality of men and women are much more difficult to ground philosophically; it is as though men and women are different species altogether. More still, in this view, one's distinctive feminine or masculine nature is understood to be so essential as to be determinative of one's actions (e.g., men always act out of lust), leaving little room for the development of human virtue and thus the shaping of one's own distinctive character. Wollstonecraft's approach—one that showcases the path of moral development for both men and women—is far more philosophically and existentially tenable.

President of the WCTU until her death in 1898, Willard echoed Wollstonecraft in her belief that it was the domestic experience of women that gave rise to the moral voice Willard and others extolled, that quality that transformed Tocqueville's "private women" into those who, wielding the vote, could morally benefit the public sphere.

Like Wollstonecraft, Willard did not think men constitutionally incapable of moral vision and profound virtue. Rather, men, like women, could develop morally if they focused their attention not first on their public ambitions or individualistic designs, but more primarily, in Willard's words, on the "creed and cult of the cradle." Engaged fatherhood, like devoted motherhood, had the potential to transform men into those with the strong moral character the culture needed, because it led them to prioritize the common good over their own self-interest. And so, *contra* Stanton, men would not need to take on "feminine virtue," or become more "feminine" or even more "maternal"; rather, men's faithful and attentive regard for their families would help them attain greater *human* virtue, transforming their baser passions toward the higher goods of wisdom and virtue. They, thereby, would become better husbands, fathers, and citizens: indeed, better men.

FIGURE 4.2. Frances Willard, circa 1890.
Credit: Library of Congress (public domain).

As Willard so beautifully writes: "*The larger participation of men in the life of the home will be the evangel* that shall add to their splendid heritage the saving grace that comes from their final coronation with what Tennyson calls 'childward care.' *It is from the creed and cult of the cradle that woman has derived those qualities most worshiped by men*, and which she in turn would worship most in them did they exist in that intellectual as well as heart fruition into which they will doubtless develop under the guidance of the future civilization in which good women shall bear an equal part."[25] Like Wollstonecraft, Willard believed that men and women, although different from one another, ought to be full companions of one other, sharing in moral and familial, and eventually societal, leadership. Willard writes,

> If a man and woman are stronger together than either can be separately in the home, by the same law of mind they are stronger together than either can be separately in literature and science, in business and professional life, in church and state. . . . [B]y the laws of being, men and women must go hand in hand if they would not go astray; . . . equally do man and woman need, not an echo, not a shadow, not a lesser nor yet a greater self, not "like with like, but like with difference," so that when these two, with their individual outlook upon destiny, shall together set their heads to any problem, or their hands to any task, they shall unite in that endeavor the full sum of power that this world holds.[26]

If men and women were collaborative partners in domestic life, they might one day, Willard envisioned, collaborate fruitfully in public and professional affairs.

A Willard-inspired corollary would recognize that "public women," like "public men," can lose the moral sense inspired by the "creed and cult of the cradle" when the goods of the home are subordinated to the individualistic temptations of professional and public life. Indeed, this was precisely the temptation wrought by industrialization and then, as we shall see, modern feminism, when men and then women respectively began to prioritize market labor over the responsibilities and solidarities of the home. But this moral vision and voice need not be lost forever: a renewed focus on the goods of home as the place where virtue and affection are first cultivated by child and parent can do much to re-orient a culture all too focused on self-satisfaction, material wealth, and consumer goods. And, as Wollstonecraft well noted, the oft-strained relationship between men and women is the first place to start.

The key nineteenth-century practice of "voluntary motherhood" sheds light on how asymmetrical reproductive differences in men and women can be harmonized by the shared human quest for virtue and by overarching moral principles that inform their collaborative union, first in marriage, but well beyond. But when such principles are jettisoned and the pursuit of virtue is traded in for power- and pleasure-seeking, those same asymmetrical sex differences can be the ground of a deep antagonism between men and women, and, worse still, violence and oppression. Indeed, when virtue-seeking is abandoned for self-seeking in individuals and then across a culture, the essentialist categories of "male-aggressor" and "female-victim" can begin to describe reality all too well.

"VOLUNTARY MOTHERHOOD": A WOLLSTONECRAFTIAN RESPONSE TO SEXUAL ASYMMETRY

Historian Linda Gordon writes that upon no other question did nineteenth-century women's rights advocates agree more universally than the concept of "voluntary motherhood."[27] From suffragists, to moral reformers, to small free-love groups, all embraced the view that, when pregnancy was not desired, periodic or permanent abstinence, by mutual decision by the couple—or unilateral decision by the woman—was the best means to both harmonize and equalize the asymmetrical sexual relationship between husband and wife and to instill moderating habits of self-mastery and intimate regard for the other.

In chapter 2, I described at length Wollstonecraft's core belief in the shared obligation of both men and women to live lives of sexual integrity. Efforts to grant women rights to coequal education, entry into the professions, and political representation were essential to achieving true social and political equality between the sexes. But it was here, in the sexual (and marital) relationship between men and women, that authentic moral equality, and harmonious companionship, would ultimately be found, or neglected. Wollstonecraft's legacy in this regard was firmly in place in the movement for "voluntary motherhood." For nineteenth-century women's rights advocates, as for Wollstonecraft before them, sexual integrity was a key precondition for authentic equality and happiness between women and men.

Recall that Wollstonecraft regarded men's lack of chastity as the "grand source" of many social ills, including women's degradation: "The little respect paid to chastity in the male world is, I am persuaded, the grand source of many of the physical and moral evils that torment mankind, as well as of the vices and follies that degrade and destroy women." Chastity was viewed as the sole "feminine virtue" in her time, and an ill-conceived virtue at that, but sexual integrity was not a widespread social expectation of men, giving way to a fierce (and deeply harmful) double standard. But sexual integrity was not to be discarded altogether, according to Wollstonecraft. Rather, it was to be expected of men too. Wollstonecraft knew this was no small request. With men tending to experience greater "libidinous" desire for sex in their bodies (which we now know is caused by massive surges of testosterone, especially in adolescence), their efforts at self-mastery are more laborious.[28] Wollstonecraft despaired: "It is the rarest thing in the world to meet with a man with sufficient delicacy of feeling to govern desire."

Thus, recall that Wollstonecraft suggested that boys especially begin the schooling of their desires at a young age, or else: "Thanks to early debauchery, [they are] scarcely men in their outward form . . . love that ought to purify the heart, and first call forth all the youthful powers, to prepare the man to discharge the benevolent duties of life, is sacrificed to premature lust." Calling forth the "youthful powers" on behalf of the "benevolent duties of life" was a serious undertaking, begun in the home through small acts of self-discipline around food and drink, and also moral education regarding the ends of sex "which the Creator has implanted in them for wise purposes." Such an effort, borne by one's parents, would bequest a young man with the self-mastery necessary to respect the dignity of women, and to allow him to enjoy the lifelong, monogamous companionship of marriage too. Given the difficulty of achieving self-mastery, and the high call of mothers and fathers to impart it while young, the noble societal effects of this virtue in men, if achieved, would be profound.

Sexual integrity was not sexual repression. The idea that it was somehow unhealthy to use one's intellect to direct one's bodily appetites to the "wise purposes" for which they were implanted would come later through Sigmund Freud, and, in the United States, Alfred Kinsey.[29] Men's and women's good and natural sexual desires, as both Wollstonecraft and the advocates of voluntary motherhood understood them, ought to be embraced within a principled view of their proper ends: procreation and marital unity. The pleasures of sex were a happy side effect. But pleasure taken as the chief end of sex would debase it, rendering it less than human. Remember Wollstonecraft's warning: "[Sexual] intemperance . . . depraves the appetite to such a degree . . . [that the] parental design of nature is forgotten." If forgotten, this most wondrous *human* act would take a degrading *animalistic* form, trading higher principles for the mere fulfillment of bodily pleasure (or worse still, the oppressive exertion of power over another). She wished instead that men and women "cherish such an habitual respect for mankind as may prevent us from disgusting a fellow-creature for the sake of a present indulgence."

Without the expectation (and practice) of sexual integrity, both men and women would fall prey to those "present indulgences." Such was an especially precarious situation for women: when a man was dominated by his bodily lust (rather than the virtuous master of it), his stronger physicality put the object of his desires directly in harm's way. Beyond the threat of physical harm, it was the woman, not the man, who might end up unwillingly pregnant as a result of his undisciplined desire. Sarah Grimké, women's rights advocate and early reader of the *Rights of Woman*, echoed this Wollstonecraftian understanding in her own advocacy of voluntary motherhood. In her provocative "Marriage" (1856), she suggests the practice would be a means for a woman to preserve her own sexual integrity in a relationship in which her husband held inordinate legal and physical power over her:

O! how many women who have entered the marriage relation in all purity and innocence, expecting to realize in it the completion of their own halfness, the rounding out of their own being, the blending of their holiest instincts with those of a kindred spirit, have too soon discovered that they were . . . chattels personal to be used and abused at the will of a master. . . . How many so called wives, rise in the morning oppressed with a sense of degradation from the fact that their chastity has been violated, their holiest instincts disregarded . . . and that, too, a thousand times harder to bear, because so called husband has been the perpetrator of the unnatural crime.[30]

As a woman was primarily responsible for "nurturing unto the fullness of life the being within her and after it is born, of nursing and tending it through helpless infancy and capricious childhood," Grimké argued, she ought to "have the right of controlling all preliminaries." If it were men who were so burdened, "common sense and common justice" would surely dictate the same.[31]

In the view of the women and men who practiced and advocated voluntary motherhood, a man's deep regard for his wife—and especially for the consequences she might endure as a result of sexual intercourse—was what inspired him to master his appetites. Monogamy and family harmony, in this view, would be promoted by working to instill in men a sense of self-governance and in women a sense of sovereignty over their bodies. Men could conform themselves to the reality of sex (as potentially procreative) rather than be ruled by their desires; in turn, their acts of self-abnegation would reveal how their marital authority and superior bodily strength could be exercised benevolently, for the good of their wives, their marriage, and their children.

Nineteenth-century voluntary motherhood advocates opposed invasive methods of birth control. They feared that, by attempting to separate sex from childbearing, these methods would embolden men to engage in infidelity, prostitution, and promiscuity, or even marital rape.[32] "Contraception . . . contradicted the systemic goals of the women's rights movement to empower women generally. While the movement sought freedom from excessive pregnancies and childbearing, it also sought respect and authority for motherhood and freedom from male sexual tyranny. . . . The solution to both the problem of unwanted pregnancies and sexual tyranny was abstinence and a single sexual moral standard restraining both women's and men's sexual impulses," states legal historian Tracy Thomas.[33]

Charlotte Perkins Gilman saw sexual integrity for the human virtue it was, to be practiced by both men and women, for the ultimate benefit to children conceived in the sexual relationship: "Chastity is a virtue because it promotes the human welfare—not because men happen to prize it in women and ignore it in themselves. The underlying reason for the whole thing is the benefit of the child; and to that end a pure and noble fatherhood is requisite, as well as such a motherhood."[34] For Gilman, as for Wollstonecraft, chastity ennobled sex, raising it from a merely animal instinct to one that, in asking both men and women to reach for higher ends, also benefited any child born of their transformed union.

The couples who practiced voluntary motherhood sought to enable women to avoid pregnancy for physical or psychological reasons. Because "they did not seek to make an infinite number of sterile sexual encounters possible," Gordon explains, "they did not believe that it was essential for women to be able to indulge in sexual intercourse under those circumstances."[35] Other forms of marital intimacy could be embraced at those times, conforming to women's desire for a more holistic sexuality rather than to men's tendency to prize sexual intercourse at all times, above all else. Some, such as physician Alice Stockham, recognized and promoted the view that abstinence would also provide aphrodisiac effects, sustaining a couple's sexual desire throughout their marriage.[36]

Although advocates at that time attempted a form of "rhythm" with the prevailing (and inaccurate) scientific theories of the day, it was not until several decades later that the ovulation cycle was understood, and several decades after that that scientists and physicians could offer effective methods of fertility regulation based on abstinence during the fertile periods of the women's ovulation cycle.[37] Making a comparison with modern methods of natural fertility regulation, Gordon writes: "The call for 'natural' birth control is reminiscent of the voluntary motherhood movement, not only in its rejection of 'artificial' contraception, but also in its emphasis on self-control within a women's reproductive culture."[38] Day by day we are learning how these nineteenth-century arguments are deeply applicable now. For perhaps the culture-wide neglect of the good of self-mastery in the sexual arena has unleashed upon women in our day the very circumstances the early women's advocates most feared: male sexual presumption and aggression.[39]

VOLUNTARY MOTHERHOOD AS A RESPONSE TO THE CRIME OF ABORTION

As abortion methods grew in sophistication and efficacy in the nineteenth century, so too did the incidence of abortion (or at least its public visibility).[40] And greater public scrutiny was not far behind.[41] Scientific advances in embryology in the nineteenth century had given rise simultaneously to a clearer picture of the process of fertilization and embryonic development.[42] In an effort to safeguard the lives of embryonic human beings, doctors in the mid-nineteenth century lobbied for and acquired the passage of state statutes prohibiting abortion at or near fertilization.[43]

Abortion in nineteenth-century America was a strongly condemned practice, and women's rights advocates offered no exception. Abortion and infanticide were referred to together as "child murder" in the pages of the women's rights newspaper *The Revolution*.[44] Victoria Woodhull, an early advocate of constitutional equality for women, a radical suffragist, and the first woman to run for president of the United States and testify before a House committee, argued that "the rights of children, then, as individuals, begin while yet they remain the fetus."[45] The 1872 presidential nominee of the Equal Rights Party, Woodhull wrote that since the same human life persists from its embryonic stage through its birth, abortion ends that "self-same life" just as much as infanticide: "Many women who would be shocked at the very thought of killing their children after birth, deliberately destroy them previously. If there is any difference in the actual crime we should be glad to have those who practice the latter, point it out. The truth of the matter is that it is just as much a murder to destroy life in its embryotic condition, as it is to destroy it after the fully developed form is attained, for it is the self-same life that is taken."[46]

Recognizing the asymmetrical consequences of sexual intercourse for women, Woodhull well articulated the concept of voluntary mother-hood: "When woman rises from sexual slavery into freedom, into the ownership and control of her sexual organs, and man is obliged to re-spect this freedom, then will this instinct become pure and holy."[47] But owning and controlling one's sexual organs did not extend, for Wood-hull and other advocates of voluntary motherhood, to owning, or con-trolling the fate of, one's unborn child. Indeed, women like Woodhull sought sovereignty over their own bodies in part because they could claim no legitimate authority to engage, in Woodhull's words, in "ante-natal murder of undesired children."[48] In like manner, Sarah Norton, who worked successfully for the admission of women to Cornell Uni-versity in 1870, wrote in Woodhull's newspaper: "Is there no remedy for all this ante-natal child murder? . . . Perhaps there will come a time when . . . the unchastity in men will be placed on an equality with the unchastity of women, and when the right of the unborn will not be de-nied or interfered with."[49] Notably, these sentiments of women's advo-cates coincided not only with the passage of state laws proscribing abor-tion but also the ratification of the Fourteenth Amendment in 1868.[50]

Unlike some leading male opponents of abortion who argued that the act was a most selfish means for women to thwart their marital du-ties, the women's rights advocates of the time maintained strongly that women were forced into the "crime" of abortion by the poor circum-stances of their lives.[51] Like Wollstonecraft before them, nineteenth-century women's advocates sought to call attention to the causes of abortion, laying the blame at the feet of "lustful" men and women's un-equal status in society.[52] According to Stanton, it was the social and legal "degradation of woman" that was causing some to "murder [their] children, either before or after birth."[53] Stanton and other women's rights advocates lamented not only the social and economic conditions that pushed some women into prostitution, and then abortion or in-fanticide. Women's advocates were repelled simultaneously by the vit-riolic antiwoman public response to the same, incredulous that women,

FIGURE 4.3. Rendering of Victoria Woodhull addressing the Judiciary Committee of the House of Representatives on women's suffrage, January 11, 1871. Credit: Library of Congress (public domain).

but not men, were blamed for the crimes. The sexual double standard tolerated male sexual misadventure, even as it blamed women for ending up unwillingly pregnant as a result. Understanding well the desperate situation women seeking abortions found themselves in—but never condoning the act itself—Stanton bemoaned abortion among other societal ills: "Do not all these things show to what a depth of degradation the women of this Republic have fallen, how false they have been to the holy instincts of their nature, to the sacred trust given them by God as the mothers of the race?"[54] To remedy such a sad state of affairs, she argued for the "education and enfranchisement of women."[55] Such a remedy included both putting women in positions of authority so the laws better reflected their experience and, importantly, "teach[ing women] how to apply the laws of science to human life."[56]

Stanton was thus an especially strong advocate of voluntary motherhood, writing in a letter that "the right to control one's body was the preeminent personal and political right."[57] Stanton's choice of Lockean rhetoric here was appropriated, a century later, by defenders of legal abortion. Yet even as radical as Stanton was, as we will explore in the next section, her meaning was never to condone abortion, but rather to advocate for voluntary motherhood. As hard as it is for modern ears to appreciate, Stanton argued for women's right to "control" their own bodies, through practicing, as desired, sexual abstinence.

To educate women about voluntary motherhood, marriage, and maternity, Stanton held separate lectures for women only. Rejecting the view (apparently inspired by then current interpretations of Genesis) that maternity was a curse, Stanton preached that "every mother in the land has it within her own [power] to be second only to God in the making of her [offspring] just what it should be. [This] is a serious responsibilit[y]; but it is one that God imposes upon every mother in the land."[58] She sought to promote "self-ownership" among women and to persuade mothers to "educate our daughters ... to regard their own lives and bodies and the laws which govern them."[59] To this end, she joined with other health advocates of the time to teach women about sex, menstruation, male and female anatomy, and reproduction; this awareness about their fertility would help women understand how abstinence could be used to prevent conceiving a new child. When asked at a lecture about "prevention by other than legitimate means," Stanton responded that these "were too degrading and disgusting to touch upon, and must be classed in the category of crime alongside infanticide."[60]

In her view, women ought not conceive children involuntarily, "as a mere machine, a tool for men's pleasure,"[61] or as an "animal,"[62] but should engage in "conscientious parenthood."[63] It was "to the mother of the race, and to her alone, [that] belonged the right to say when a new being should be brought into the world."[64] Further, voluntary motherhood would require men to be "educated up to the higher civilization as well as the women." She continued, "That same powerful force that governs the passions can be controlled and directed into the brain force, and made to result in good deeds."[65] She suggested that women could assist men by not "stimulating men's passions" through provocative dress but rather by calling men to a higher regard for the female sex.[66]

Some feminist historians in our time argue that voluntary motherhood was but a precursor—in Tracy Thomas's words, "the radical theoretical foundation"—to modern feminists' insistence on the need for widespread use of contraception and easy access to abortion. Yet, these historians also clearly demonstrate in their scholarship that the nineteenth-century advocates of voluntary motherhood, even though firmly in favor of women "controlling their own bodies" through periodic abstinence, explicitly rejected both abortion and contraception. For instance, Gordon, a leading historian of this area, reports that women's advocates at the time viewed early contraceptive methods and abortion as technological incursions into women's bodies and facilitators of male oppression of women. As Gordon also well documents (and as we discuss in chapter 8), contraception (and then, fifty years later, abortion) was first advocated by eugenics and population control movements, not by the early movement for women's rights.[67] The women's advocates of the nineteenth century—notably, *even Stanton*, who preached a radical variant of "self-ownership" for her day—stood athwart both contraception and especially abortion, practices that feminists today regard as central to the cause of women's rights.

Both Gordon and Thomas claim that any opposition to abortion in the nineteenth century among women's rights advocates was moral rather than legal or political. But women's advocates had no reason to

pursue legislative measures to protect unborn children and their mothers: fetal protective laws were already being enacted in the mid- to late
nineteenth century. These advocates thus pushed back, not on the
restrictive laws themselves, but on the ways in which women were
characterized by the most vocal doctors who lobbied for them. They
also fought judicial decisions that ignored mitigating circumstances in
women's lives.[68] For they knew that legal restrictions on abortion on
their own would not alter the desperation of those women who sought
out the dangerous procedure in the first place.[69] Women's advocates
thus focused their efforts on those educational, cultural, and legal means
that, to their mind, would so improve women's lives that need for abortion would be obviated altogether: sexual self-ownership and fertility
education, ameliorating women's educational and economic situations,
support for unwed mothers and their infants, and, eventually, enfranchisement. As the next section demonstrates, the ever-radical Stanton
added easy divorce to that list.

MARRIAGE AND THE "SOLITUDE OF SELF"

If discussing Wollstonecraft's *Rights of Woman* with Lucretia Mott
was the catalyst for Stanton's suffragist work, Stanton's own thought
was far more inspired by Locke, Rousseau, and Mill. Still, Stanton's
particular rationale for voluntary motherhood—prioritizing a kind of
Lockean self-ownership over the more Wollstonecraftian self-mastery
extolled by Grimké and many of her peers—could be viewed as a mere
rhetorical distinction that, like within the joint property issue, gave
way to few substantive differences. But her distinctive philosophical
approach reached its apex in her ardent and, for that time, radical views
on marriage and divorce. Yet even as she departed from Wollstonecraft's own philosophy of marriage in the *Rights of Woman*, Stanton
made use of Wollstonecraft's controversial personal life as an enlight-
ened example of "free love" and personal autonomy.

Although the two thinkers agreed that the social and legal reform
of the institution of marriage was vital to the social equality of men and
women, and even that the then unjust laws of marriage warranted

women's desire to remain free of them (as Wollstonecraft herself had been), the British philosopher did not herself believe in "free love."[70] Rather, Wollstonecraft envisioned a lifelong marital commitment between equals, characterized by friendship and the shared nurture and education of children, with divorce available to both spouses in cases of abuse or adultery. Whereas Stanton argued for freeing women from bonds of marriage through liberal contract theory, Wollstonecraft, by contrast, believed that familial duties, on the part of both women and men, were what enabled the development of virtue and happiness of both. Moreover, for the British philosopher, these rich familial obligations grounded philosophically the political and civil rights that women's rights advocates such as Stanton most ardently sought. One simply could not assert rights without understanding the correlative duties that made such rights necessary. Thinking of parents' duties to their children, Wollstonecraft wrote, those who "do not fulfill the duty" can "forfeit the right." As we'll see in this section, the philosophical differences between Wollstonecraft and Stanton run deep.

Most women's advocates at the time, especially the many Christian social reformers, believed in lifelong marriage as either a sacrament (among Catholics) or a covenant (among Protestants). Legally, marriage was (and still is) considered a status of social relation, a public (rather than merely individual) institution. But many also came to believe that married women required some means of legal separation (and protection) from a profligate or drunkard husband who had abdicated his own marital and parental duties. Indeed, separation from such a man, especially if he was a physical threat to his wife or their children (born or unborn), came to be understood by some to be a woman's moral duty. Once only allowed for adultery, some states began to expand grounds for divorce to include desertion, imprisonment, drunkenness, and insanity. In these cases, husbands would still be required to maintain their wives and children as much as possible.

Building upon the antislavery rhetoric of the time that made generous use of Lockean notions of the right to one's body and "free labor," Stanton extended the analogy to women's legal position in marriage, even as she admitted the actual living conditions of middle-class women did not approach the "living death colored men endure[d] everywhere."[71]

Her analogy was a legal one: "The oneness of man and woman [in marriage is] a oneness that makes woman a slave," Stanton declared.[72] Women were "slaves" to their husbands in coverture (and as disenfranchised citizens of the United States); from Stanton's perspective, they now must assert, like the newly freed slaves before them, a right to their own bodies and labor within marriage.

Having studied the law informally with her lawyer father, Stanton sought to reenvision the marital relationship as one akin to a business contract, an increasingly common legal and political concept in the growing commercial economy. As with Gilman's efforts to bring modern practices of efficiency into the home, Stanton wanted to reshape the unjust common law approach to marriage into one governed by modern commercial concepts. Indeed, Stanton wished to deregulate marriage entirely, leaving everything to the discretion of the equal and self-determining parties, with an easy exit when the terms of the bargain went bad. She advocated no-fault divorce, a radical concept in the nineteenth century (and, indeed, even for Locke, whose philosophy she employed), based entirely on the will of each party. "Why is it that all contracts, covenants, agreements, and partnerships are left wholly at the discretion of the parties, except that which, of all others, is considered most holy and important, both for the individual and the race?" asked Stanton.[73] If any aspect of the law should be strengthened, it was marital formation laws, keeping women out of marriage until they were old and mature enough to understand what it was they were getting themselves into.

Although Stanton remained married and monogamous, and bore seven children, biographers report that her advocacy for "free love" and "divorce" sprang out of her personal frustrations as a wife and mother, unsupported in her work (inside or outside the home) by her husband.[74] When we recall her tendency to essentialize masculine and feminine natures, it is not surprising that she would universalize her own poor experience to a radical theory of men: "Nearly every man feels that his wife is his property, whose first duty, under all circumstances, is to gratify his passions, without the least reference to her own health and happiness, or the welfare of their offspring."[75] Yet she knew of happily married couples in which husband and wife together practiced

Elizabeth Cady Stanton and her daughter, Harriot. from a daguerreotype 1856.

FIGURE 4.4. Elizabeth Cady Stanton with daughter, Harriot, 1856.
Credit: public domain.

voluntary motherhood, even as they shared an active commitment to women's rights, abolition, and other social causes of the day. But for Stanton, the solution to women's woes in marriage would not come through equalizing women's position in the institution or the personal transformation of men through their commitment and attentive engagement therein. Rather, she believed in "the rebellion of woman against the dynasty of sensualism, selfishness and violence, that man has inaugurated."[76] Women would be free of the oppressive marital bond only when they were free to be entirely independent of men.

Legal scholar Elizabeth Clark argues that Stanton's efforts to expand the grounds for divorce were not merely rhetorical devices to further her political aims but were shaped by modern philosophical views that diverged greatly from premodern approaches. Indeed, Stanton's philosophical approach to rights worked to upend the earlier view, held by Wollstonecraft and most of the nineteenth-century women's advocates, that civil and political rights derived from familial and social obligations. Stanton was not insisting, as Wollstonecraft had, that men fulfill their marital and familial obligations more virtuously. Rather, Stanton believed that women (and so men) should be freed from those obligations. According to Clark, advocates like Stanton "worked to destroy some of the rights formerly vested in men, but put no one under any continuing obligation, and engaged no one in any reciprocal relationship. [They sought to] lift laws that restrained and coerced, rather than [. . .] obligate or coerce others." Clark suggests that "such radical autonomy left little room for ties."[77]

Yet Stanton's view of marriage as a free contract stood up and against the bonds of maternity that she extolled. Clark writes: "The contract model of marital relations could not easily be fitted to the parent–child relationship, but in rejecting the covenant model of permanent bonds, [these advocates] sought to loosen their maternal ties by denying the aspect of demand or duty."[78] Although Stanton spoke much about the high call of motherhood (as second only to God), and even of the *duties* of maternity (a "serious responsibility . . . that God imposes upon every mother in the land"), she did not seem to worry about the effect of her commercial assumptions on the mother-child (or father-child) relationship. She thought marriage itself should be understood as primarily a "loving companionship of man and woman," seeming not to include as a primary object the nurture and education of children she disproportionately undertook in her own marriage. Unlike even Locke, who believed that parents should be free to divorce only when their children were grown, Stanton's more radical version held that the partners could exit as freely as they entered, and "as to the property and children, they must be viewed and regulated as a civil contract."[79] The deleterious effect of divorce on myriad children in our day might have made Stanton think again: unlike property, the enduring relationship of mother and father to their children is not so easily reconciled by the terms of a commercial contract.

Contemporary critics of Stanton's, such as Antoinette Brown Blackwell, America's first ordained female minister, argued that marriage was a permanent relation or covenant that, once formed, could not be destroyed. This covenant existed for the nurture and education of children and for the moral development of the spouses within the marital bond. Granting there were problems within marriage, most especially, women's lack of legal status, Blackwell suggested that Stanton's deregulating efforts would only further harm women and their children. Blackwell and others sought, like Wollstonecraft, to put the marital relationship on equal legal footing and to expect more of men. Blackwell asked, "Can the mother ever destroy the relation which exists between herself and the child? Can the father annul the relation which exists between himself and the child? Then, can the father and mother annul the relation which exists between themselves, the parents of the child?"[80]

Lucy Stone, founder of the American Women Suffrage Association, and her husband, Henry Blackwell, had personally disavowed coverture by contract. Stone also became famous for keeping her own maiden name after marriage, such that women who did so were later known as "Lucy Stoners."[81] Yet even Stone suggested that Stanton's "freedom" for a divorced mother of a large family should be called by more realistic names: "immiseration and abandonment." For these women, Stone wrote, Stanton's view of divorce meant "practically, freedom of unworthy men to leave their wives and children to starve, while it could not give similar freedom to mothers to leave their children."[82] Another critic challenged Stanton: Does not marriage bind husband to wife and wife to husband? Easy divorce would free "every vagabond husband [to] change of wives as often as he likes."[83]

Stanton claimed to believe the marital contract should require of each partner "equal and reciprocal duties," but she did not wish to pursue such equality in greater obligations for men.[84] Instead, she sought to lessen marital duties for both men and women. She wanted "freedom from all unnecessary entanglements and compulsions, freedom from binding obligations inviting impossibilities."[85] Freedom *from* constraints and duties was her vision of freedom, one starkly different from the freedom *for* excellence that Wollstonecraft extolled. Indeed, her famous 1892 address "Solitude of Self," delivered before two committees of the U.S. Congress, imagines women as "arbiter of [their] own destin[ies]," Robinson Crusoes on solitary islands, isolated in life, *by themselves.* Contrasting the law's approach to treating men as *individuals* with a woman's relational status as "mother, wife, sister, daughter," she points out that a man's rights are not decided "by his duties as a father, a husband, a brother, or a son."[86] Stanton, like the liberal feminists who followed her, thought it better to reimagine women as isolated individuals in the way the modern philosophers Locke and especially Hobbes had imagined men, rather than to recognize that these philosophers had depicted men incorrectly. Other reformers of the time thought, for instance, that a man's and woman's marital and parental duties ought to be understood as part and parcel of their respective identities, such that their development as persons would always be in the context of these constitutive relationships. This was Wollstonecraft's view too.

Showing her sharp divergence from Wollstonecraft on the proper ends of rights, Stanton pleaded in that same now-famous speech that a woman's rights as an individual "are to use all her faculties *for her own safety and happiness.*"[87] Stanton elsewhere wrote, echoing Mill far more than Wollstonecraft, that a woman had "a right to the free use, improvement, and development of all her faculties, *for her own benefit and pleasure.*"[88] But for Wollstonecraft, rights properly enabled each person's development of wisdom and virtue, especially through the exercise of his or her duties to God and others.

Stanton's "Solitude of Self" continues:

No matter how much women prefer to lean, to be protected and supported, nor how much men desire to have them do so, they must make the voyage of life alone, and for safety in an emergency they must know something of the laws of navigation. To guide our own craft, we must be captain, pilot, engineer; with chart and compass to stand at the wheel; to match the wind and waves and know when to take in the sail, and to read the signs in the firmament over all. It matters not whether the solitary voyager is man or woman. . . . The great lesson that nature seems to teach us at all ages is *self*-dependence, *self*-protection, *self*-support.[89]

Jane Croly, a popular writer in Stanton's time, provocatively challenged Stanton's pursuit of what would become understood in our time as "radical autonomy" with the (interdependent) facts of life. She suggested that Stanton's commercial conceptualization of the marital bond (and the parental bond within it) was but a legal fiction, one that grievously misunderstood the human condition and the natural duties it entails. Croly wrote:

We are tied from the moment we enter the world, and are probably the better and happier for it, though we may rebel against it. We are actual slaves to circumstances which preceded our birth, which enclosed us in a skin, which governed our height, our color, our shape, our strength or weakness, and over which we had not the least control. We are tied after birth to certain natural laws, which we very imperfectly understand, and of which we can only see the results. We are tied with cords woven by time itself to the habits and traditions which have preceded us; and more strongly still are we tied by our instincts and desires which, blind and unreasoning as they are, we are compelled to obey. . . . We see, then, there is very little of the freedom of which we boast so much in the matter. . . . As parts of one great body, we are all dependent upon and owe duties to each other.[90]

Denying the familial and marital solidarity, mutuality, and interdependence many in the women's movement had sought to highlight in its appeals for joint property ownership, suffrage, and voluntary motherhood, Stanton relied instead on newly emergent laissez-faire economic theory, free labor, and liberal concepts of the citizen as analogies for her new model of family law. Once deregulated from coercive laws, she believed, the economy, labor relations, or, in this case, marital partners would be best left to govern themselves. As Stanton put her view: "The true family needs no laws or ordinances to bind it together; the Spiritual Union no force to make it enduring; no cement but that which love and friendship ever produce."[91] Moreover, "whenever compulsion and restraint, whether of the law or of a dogmatic and oppressive public opinion, are removed," the result will be free love.[92] Hers was a philosophy, first and foremost, of absolute rights and radical autonomy, forgetting almost entirely constitutive and preexisting duties of care.

Stanton's outlying promotion of no-fault divorce was unsuccessful in her day. But reappropriated by 1970s feminists, her radical vision went a long way to creating the family law landscape we have today.[93] Indeed, as we will discuss further in chapter 9, one can draw a fairly neat line from Stanton's Lockean/Millian influence, and in particular her view of marriage, to the modern-day women's movement promotion of no-fault divorce. By the 1960s and '70s, Stanton's individualistic rhetoric served to inspire, while Wollstonecraft's ennobling moral vision of marriage and family was left behind.

It is to the Locke-inspired constitutionalism of the *Lochner* era, and women's advocacy for and against, that we now turn.

CHAPTER 5

The Industrial Revolution and the Debate between Abstract Rights and Concrete Duties

The U.S. Constitution was designed as one of limited and enumerated federal powers, authorizing the federal government to maintain the justice, tranquility, and safety of the nation as a whole. Debates over the extent of these federal powers were the main source of disagreement between the Federalists and Anti-Federalists, a debate that eventually gave way to the ratification of the Bill of Rights in 1791. Universally appreciated, however, was the far broader authority of the states to protect the health, safety, morals, and the general welfare of the people within their jurisdictions through each state's inherent "police power." The Reconstruction amendments in the 1860s and 1870s curtailed these state powers substantially. Not only did the Thirteenth and Fifteenth Amendments, respectively, prohibit Southern states from preserving slavery and require every state to guarantee voting rights to Black men, but the broadly worded Fourteenth Amendment expanded the federal judiciary's authority to review state law to ensure that the civil rights of the new Black citizens were protected. Selective incorporation of other rights vis-à-vis the states followed in due course.

With Jim Crow laws alive and well until nearly a century later, however, the Fourteenth Amendment hardly enjoyed the reach its framers intended. Still, it did import into the Constitution capacious language tailored to the philosophical resurgence of Lockean abstract rights that had emerged during the debates surrounding slavery, a philosophical resurgence that women's rights advocates such as Elizabeth Cady Stanton and Alice Paul, alongside the industrial capitalists of the time, well appropriated. The tensions between abstract (and often absolutist or "strict") Lockean views of liberty and equality and the Wollstonecraftian approach taken by female labor leaders at the time brought into stark relief the philosophical differences that emerged in the women's movement in the late nineteenth and early twentieth centuries. To be sure, Lockean principles advancing natural rights to private property, freedom of contract, and the fruit of one's labor were central to the Founders' understanding of constitutional liberty in the late 1700s. But these classically liberal principles were moderated by the view that state governments, via the police power, were authorized to specify the boundaries of rights as necessary for the common good of the community.[1] Indeed, state-based common law, infused with both premodern and modern legal principles, privately ordered legal relations of contract, property, tort, and the like, relations that remained relatively untouched by the federal Constitution, for better or worse, until Reconstruction. The common law of the states, declaring each citizen's rights and duties, served as the federal Constitution's legal backdrop.

Inherited from England but organically transposed in the new states, the common law was understood to ensure fair and just relations among individuals, with property rights and liberty of contract, for instance, providing the legal apparatus that liberated the citizens of the new nation from the feudal laws that had unjustly governed the old.[2] State legislatures existed to provide for the public welfare; state courts, to ensure that neutral laws, enacted prospectively and nonarbitrarily, treated each citizen equally under the law. Such features of law and governance were among the procedural safeguards traditionally understood by the phrase "due process of the law," first articulated in the Magna Carta in 1215.

The Industrial Revolution had in the meantime reconstituted the United States from an agrarian to a commercial economy, radically altering the world of work from rural family farms, artisan workshops, and trade guilds to city factories and coal mines. As we saw in chapter 3, interdependent couples now experienced an altogether new asymmetrical dependency relationship of homebound wives upon wage-earning husbands. The relationships between employers and employees changed almost as dramatically: once, farmhands or apprentices in the northern United States had worked alongside the farmers or master craftsmen who compensated them, but now industrialization saw class divisions grow as the roles of capitalist and skilled and unskilled labor became more pronounced and at times adversarial.

Industrial and technological innovation required massive risk of capital at the outset, but when successful it also returned massive gains: the industrial class was thus consolidated, bringing into being the socioeconomic era Mark Twain dubbed the "Gilded Age."[3] Most problematic, the industrial class all too often exerted its growing power in disputes with workers, taking advantage of the latter's weak and vulnerable position to make often harsh demands upon their time. Industrial workers organized, and unions grew, but the influence of industrial labor upon individual men, women, and children forced into the workplace by economic distress was often deleterious to their health and safety, and to the well-being of families. With the revolution in machines technology and capital accumulation, preindustrial relationships of striking social interdependence became asymmetrical power relationships of pronounced economic dominance and, increasingly, social dependence. During this time, states variously made use of their police power to protect the health and safety of workers. By and large, health and safety regulations went unchallenged legally or were upheld by the courts as pursuant to the public interest. As industrialization pressed on, however, and the wealth and power disparity between employers and employees grew more profound, states began to use their police power to place limitations upon the parties' freedom of contract, not only to protect health and safety as was more obviously in their purview, but also to prohibit the long hours industrialists expected their workers to labor.

Some state courts in the 1880s and 90s struck down these maximum hours laws, categorizing them not as licit health and safety measures designed to safeguard the public interest, but instead as illicit "class legislation," with the government illegitimately favoring one social class over another. In *Ritchie v. People* (1895), for instance, the Illinois Supreme

Court struck down an eight-hour maximum hours law for women working in factories, holding that it both violated freedom of contract and that
it "discriminate[d] against one class of employers and employees . . . in
favor of all others."[4] Other state courts upheld maximum hours legislation, at least when the state was sufficiently able to liken it to a legitimate
health and safety measure passed pursuant to its police power.

In 1897, the U.S. Supreme Court in *Allegeyer v. Louisiana* held for
the first time that the due process clause of the Fourteenth Amendment
protected not only traditional procedural rights but also economic freedoms that some had thought were the province of the privileges and
immunities clause before the high court decided the *Slaughterhouse
Cases* in 1873.[5] According to a unanimous court in *Allegeyer*:

> The "liberty" mentioned in [the Fourteenth] amendment means not
> only the right of the citizen to be free from the mere physical re-
> straint of his person, as by incarceration, but the term is deemed to
> embrace the right of the citizen to be free in the enjoyment of all his
> faculties, to be free to use them in all lawful ways, to live and work
> where he will, to earn his livelihood by any lawful calling, to pursue
> any livelihood or avocation, and for that purpose to enter into all
> contracts which may be proper, necessary, and essential to his carry-
> ing out to a successful conclusion the purposes above mentioned.[6]

Still, the very next year, the Supreme Court upheld a maximum hours
state law that prohibited workers from laboring in mines for more than
eight hours a day. Judged detrimental to the health of the employees in
the especially dangerous industry—and due in part to the Court's acknowledgment that these employees did not "stand upon an equality"
with the proprietors of establishments and so could not themselves negotiate relief from long hours—the Court in *Holden v. Hardy* ruled
that the state legislature had reasonable grounds for viewing the restriction to be necessary to public health and safety.[7]

But in 1905, the Supreme Court decided the now-infamous *Lochner
v. New York*. New York had limited the number of hours bakers could
work to ten hours a day and sixty hours a week, promoted by the state
as a health and safety measure. Holding that the state had not proved

that long hours endangered the bakers' health, the Supreme Court struck down the maximum hours law as an illicit labor law contrary to the "liberty of contract" now specially protected by the due process clause of the Fourteenth Amendment. Writing for the Court, Justice Peckham wrote that there was "no contention that bakers as a class are not . . . able to assert their rights and care for themselves without the protecting arm of the State, interfering with their independence of judgment and of action."[8] The Court thus held that statutes "limiting the hours in which grown and intelligent men may labor to earn their living, are mere meddlesome interferences with the rights of the individual."[9]

The dissenting justices suggested the majority had overstepped its reach. In the dissenters' view, the Court lacked the authority to judge the wisdom of the law; so long as the law was not an arbitrary exercise of the police power, the evaluative judgment remained in the purview of the legislative branch of the state government to whom judicial deference as to the law's reasonableness ought to be paid. Justice Oliver Wendell Holmes famously derided the majority for deciding the case upon "an economic theory which a large part of the country does not entertain," arguing that the Constitution was intended to embody neither economic "paternalism" nor "laissez-faire."[10]

Women's Rights Advocates Take Sides

Women's rights advocates were active on both sides of the debate over the Supreme Court's developing due process jurisprudence. Alice Paul, founder of the National Woman's Party, had become the leading advocate for women's suffrage guaranteed by a federal constitutional amendment. Most other suffragists were working to pass enfranchisement measures state by state. The oldest of four children and a descendent of William Penn, the Quaker founder of Pennsylvania, Paul grew up in a tradition marked by simplicity, diligence, and public service. Her Quaker parents instilled in her a belief in equality between the sexes; she even attended suffragist meetings with her mother, a member of the National American Women Suffrage Association. Growing up in a comfortable and spacious home with plenty of opportunities to engage in educational and leisurely activities, Paul went on to graduate from Swarthmore College with a bachelor's degree in biology in 1905.[11] Wielding a master's in sociology and a doctorate in economics from the University of Pennsylvania (and later several graduate law degrees), Paul believed strongly that the *Lochner* Court's emphasis on liberty of contract was a certain path toward expanding married women's legal capacity to contract.

If women were going to provide (or help to provide) for themselves and their families during these often desperate times, Paul reasoned, they would have to be free to contract with employers for the number of hours they needed to work. Should protective labor legislation limit women's hours, Paul and others argued, employers would simply hire men to work longer, and women would lose the opportunities to earn wages their families needed. For instance, maximum hours legislation, according to one of Paul's associates, "practically amounts to confiscation of whatever amount would have been earned during the forbidden hours."[12] Stanton too had unsurprisingly argued in a similar vein concerning laws protective of women to the New York legislature back in 1860: "There has been a great deal written and said about 'protection.' We as a class, are tired of one kind of protection, that which leaves us everything to do, to dare, and to suffer, and strips us of all means for its accomplishment. . . . [S]trike down all special legislation for us."[13] This repugnance of protective legislation—and support of *Lochner*'s "liberty of contract"—put equal rights advocates firmly on the side of business interests at the time. This alliance was, we should recall, an altogether new one for women's rights advocates, those who long sought to protect the family as that antimodern island in the industrial sea.

Alice Paul had a strong adversary, one coming straight out of the earlier, premodern tradition of women's advocacy. As general secretary of the National Consumers' League (NCL), Florence Kelley took a prominent lead in promoting protective legislation for women workers beginning in the late nineteenth century until her death in 1932. The daughter of a fifteen-term Republican congressman who had helped draft the Fifteenth Amendment, Kelley was educated at Cornell and studied law and government in Switzerland, later earning a degree in

FIGURE 5.1. Alice Paul, circa 1915.
Credit: Library of Congress (public domain).

law from Northwestern University and admission to the Illinois bar. Smart, strong, and dynamic, Kelley's leadership inspired many women of her time to join the cause for labor reform. In her 1905 book, *Some Ethical Gains through Legislation*, released the same year as the *Lochner* decision, Kelley argued that industrialization had forced women and children into the workforce, offering them poor wages and reprehensible working conditions, and ultimately disrupting family life among the working class. Reminiscent of Wollstonecraft's prioritization of domestic life as the seedbed of public virtue and worry that the "tyranny of wealth" in the new commercial republic would threaten the morals of the people (more even than aristocracy), Kelley argued that children's nurture, education, and other needs ought not be sacrificed at the altar of the marketplace. The future of the republic depended on self-governing citizens, and the family was the seedbed for nurturing them.

Only by affording parents, and especially mothers, time to love and cherish their young ones could the next generation become mature and independent. The very first page of *Ethical Gains* spells out Kelley's most basic proposition: "The care and nurture of childhood is . . . a vital concern of the nation."[14] Indeed, this concern was pressing at a time when family homes during industrialization were described in one book as "joyless shanties for bolting down food or snatching a little sleep."[15] An advocate of the family wage, Kelley believed that just wages for men would be the ideal means toward ensuring "the right to childhood" she enunciated, freeing both women and children from being forced to work in factories for life's necessities. In one debate, Kelley declared, "In families where the mother works for wages, the children suffer, if they do not die outright."[16] Moreover, "the presence in the market of a throng of unorganized and irregular workers . . . presses upon the wage rate of men . . . as the subsidized . . . worker must always do."[17] Far better if men would earn what was due them in natural justice, a justice "more imperious and ancient than any bargain between man and man, namely, that wages ought not to be insufficient to support a frugal and well-behaved wage-earner [and his family]," as Pope Leo XIII had written in an 1891 papal encyclical known to be quoted by Catholic workers at the time.[18]

And yet, cognizant of the current economic realities, women's lack of political power, and the low-paid, unorganized state of their menial work, Kelley expended herself not on the more theoretical hope for a "just family wage" but on seeking to protect working women from the exploits of the industrialists. Legal historian Nancy Woloch argues that Kelley had hoped that prioritizing protective legislation for women would serve as an "entering wedge" for protective laws for all workers and, one day, perhaps, for a more just economic system for the family, and so the nation.[19] Kelley had been influenced not only by her father's social advocacy on behalf of newly freed slaves, but also by her early foray into European socialism, and then later the pragmatic social outreach of Jane Addams's Hull House. While studying at the University of Zurich in the 1880s, Kelley had come under the influence of Karl Marx and Friedrich Engels, translated some of their works, married a Polish-Jewish socialist with whom she had three children, and entered briefly into socialist circles with him upon their return to New York. Kelley's own philosophy echoed what Engels had written in *Condition of the Working Class*: "If a married woman works in a factory family life is inevitably destroyed and . . . its dissolution has the most demoralizing consequences both for parents and children."[20] After suffering abuse at her husband's hands, Kelley fled with her children in 1891 to Hull House, the settlement community in Chicago founded by labor advocate (and 1931 Nobel Peace Prize winner) Jane Addams.

While living and working alongside Addams and the other women of Hull House for seven years, Kelley landed a job early on inspecting the working conditions of local factories. Her findings led to the first factory law prohibiting the employment of children under fourteen (she had found therein children as young as three and four). In 1893, Kelley drafted the eight-hour Illinois maximum hours law for women, which the Illinois Supreme Court struck down in *Ritchie v. People* two years later. Although Kelley remained inspired by Marxist critiques of capitalism for her entire life, her work in the industrial trenches and experience at Hull House seemed to have diluted her attachment to Marxism as a political program. In 1893, she wrote in a letter to Engels that she "could accomplish more for workingwomen through [her] work in Hull House than in the socialist movement."[21]

FIGURE 5.2. Florence Kelley, chief state factory inspector of
Illinois, pictured third from left, with other factory inspectors.
Credit: Library of Congress (public domain).

Kelley imbibed and shared Addams's lifelong belief in the dignity
of every man, woman, and child, regardless of socioeconomic class. With
so many vulnerable women and children landing on the doorstep at
Hull House, bereft of paternal support and forced into hazardous working conditions, Addams had sought through the enriching hospitality
and dignified solidarity of the settlement house to "bridge . . . the chasm
that industrialism had opened between social classes."[22]

In her own writing, Addams had described the profound tension
industrialization had wrought between work and home as that of the
"social claim" up and against the "family claim." According to biographer Jean Bethke Elshtain, Addams argued that "if society is to tend to
the requirements of the family claim . . . it must structure the social
claim in such a way that no child must endure such misery."[23] Like Kelley, Addams sought to ensure that the care of vulnerable children was
not sacrificed to the exploitative demands of the industrialists: "The
long hours of factory labor necessary for earning the support of a child

FIGURE 5.3. Jane Addams, 1910.
Credit: Library of Congress (public domain).

leave no time for the tender care and caressing which may enrich the life of the most piteous baby."[24] Given these influences, it is not surprising that after taking over the reins at NCL in 1899, Kelley suggested in her book that the "the judicial mind has not kept pace with the strides of industrial development."[25] Kelley argued in particular that the "liberty of contract" protected by the Supreme Court in *Lochner* (and extolled by Alice Paul) was actually a legal fiction that ignored the unequal (or even nonexistent) bargaining power between the industrial capitalists and powerless employees. Kelley suggested that women who at the time did not enjoy the protection of trade unions were especially vulnerable to maltreatment in the industrial workplace. Kelley believed the community needed to "counterbalance the excessive pressure of business interest" through use of the state's inherent police power.[26]

True liberty of contract, according to Kelley, could only be built upon a familial and communal substructure that took seriously the responsibilities parents had to their children and that employers had to their employees. Recalling an older tradition, Kelley suggested that the due process clause provided a procedural safeguard in favor of duly promulgated legislation; it did not grant the high court authority to strike down legislation passed by the community at large when it seemed unreasonable or unjust to the justices. According to legal scholar Joan Zimmerman, "Kelley emphasized the moral necessity of using legislation to preserve the commonwealth tradition and the notion of mutual obligation."[27] Kelley's insistence on the correlative nature of rights and the duties that underlie them should well remind readers of Wollstonecraft's own political theory. For Wollstonecraft, rights were not theoretical abstractions (as Locke had articulated them) but were derived from actual moral duties to others. The duties to one's family, after God, ranked highest of all. "Society is not properly organized which does not compel men and women to discharge their respective duties," wrote Wollstonecraft. If individual workers were rendered powerless at the hands of industry that did nothing to rectify the unjust burden its demands placed upon employees who sought to discharge their own familial duties, the community at large via its legislative capacity would have to step in. Zimmerman writes, "By combining the individual rights tradition with the commonwealth tradition, Kelley was theoretically restoring a balance that had been lost during the period of industrial growth."[28] This synthesis, articulated by the preindustrial-era philosopher Wollstonecraft, was put into action case by case by Kelley, one of the industrial era's leading labor advocates.

MULLER V. OREGON (1908) AND REPRODUCTIVE ASYMMETRIES BETWEEN MEN AND WOMEN

After *Lochner* had denied the constitutionality of maximum hours laws for men, Kelley and her associate Josephine Goldmark won the help of successful Boston attorney Louis Brandeis to argue on behalf of an Oregon law that restricted women from working in factories and laundries more than ten hours a day. Having lost in state court, Muller, the owner of a laundry, appealed to the U.S. Supreme Court, contending that the law was an arbitrary limitation on his liberty of contract and so contradicted the Court's decision in *Lochner*. He also claimed it was a violation of the equal protection clause of the Fourteenth Amendment, since women were "persons and citizens" and "as competent to contract with reference to their labor as men."[29] *Muller* was a perfect test case for competing views among women's rights advocates of the time.

In his effort to show that the law in question was a legitimate exercise of the state's police power, Brandeis argued the protective legislation for women was directly in the public interest. In the first of his famous "Brandeis briefs," the future Supreme Court justice argued that long hours in modern industries had been shown by numerous medical and other nonjudicial authorities to be even "more disastrous to the health of women than of men" and that the deterioration of mothers' health in particular "directly attacks the welfare of the nation."[30] Seeking to shift the burden of proof to those challenging the law, Brandeis maintained: "It cannot be said that the Legislature of Oregon had no reasonable ground for believing that the public health, safety, or welfare did not require a legal limitation on women's work . . . to ten hours in one day."[31]

The Supreme Court upheld the Oregon law unanimously, considering the woman-protective legislation to be an exception to the *Lochner* doctrine, not a repudiation of it: "[woman] is properly placed in a class by herself, and legislation designed for her protection may be sustained even when like legislation is not necessary for men, and could not be sustained."[32] Justice Brewer, on behalf of the Court, followed Brandeis's logic closely: "As healthy mothers are essential to vigorous offspring, the physical well-being of woman becomes an object of public interest and care in order to preserve the strength and vigor of the race."[33]

The legislation, albeit limiting women's contractual powers to form an agreement with their employers, was justified because of the "inherent" differences between men and women and the different "functions in life which they perform."[34] The limitation upon their working hours was not only for women's benefit, the Court surmised, but for the benefit of all. Brewer writes: "The two sexes differ in structure of body, in the functions to be performed by each, in the amount of physical strength, in the capacity for long-continued labor, particularly when done standing, the influence of vigorous health upon the future well-being of the race, the self-reliance which enables one to assert full rights, and in the capacity to maintain the struggle for subsistence. This difference justifies a difference in legislation, and upholds that which is designed to compensate for some of the burdens which rest upon her."[35]

The Court held that maternity placed women "at a disadvantage in the struggle for subsistence," suggesting that an unequal playing field existed for women in the industrial workplace because of "her physical structure and a proper discharge of her maternal functions."[36] Because of men's superior physical strength, and the dependence women have always had upon them (especially in light of the fact that education was "long denied her"), the Court recalled that courts had had to take special care to preserve women's interests. The legislation provided this compensatory effect. Responding directly to the appellant who had argued that strict equality under the law should govern the sexes and so the case at bar, the Court suggested that even if "all [statutory] restrictions on political, personal, and contractual rights were taken away [such that women stood] on an absolutely equal plane with [men]," such equality would be fictitious, because of women's disproportionate role in reproduction and caregiving. Even should she enjoy such equal legal (and eventually political) rights, Brewer wrote, woman "is so constituted that she will [always] rest upon [man] and look to him for protection." Without the legislature's protection "from the greed, as well as the passion, of man," women would not actually enjoy "a real equality of right." In summary of the Court's compensatory view: "Doubtless there are individual exceptions, and there are many respects in which she has an advantage over him; but, looking at it from the viewpoint of the effort to maintain an independent position in life, she is not upon an equality."[37]

Brewer's depiction of women as inherently "dependent" and in need of men's perpetual "protection" strikes readers today as particularly demeaning; it also struck strict equality women's right advocates such as Alice Paul and her associates this way. Brewer, after all, seemed to imply that women's and men's physical and reproductive differences rendered women socially inferior: the sheer *capacity* for motherhood made all women dependent. This was indeed the assumption of coverture too.

The appellant's attorneys in *Muller* had rhetorically posed in their brief to the Court apt responses to the mother-focused argument: What of the unmarried woman? What of a widow (or, we could add, an abandoned mother or divorcee) who was obligated to earn all the means necessary to sustain herself and her dependent children? Ought women in these situations be permitted to work as many hours as necessary to provide for themselves, and potentially their children? An astute and forward-looking response to *Muller* at the time came from suffragist Clara Colby, editor of the *Woman's Tribune* in Portland, Oregon: "The State has no right to lay any disability upon woman as an individual, and if it does as a mother, it should give her a maternity pension which would tend to even up conditions and be better for the family."[38] But Colby's suggestion of a maternity pension was overshadowed by a more popular and ultimately successful argument for elective overtime pay: any legislative restrictions upon workers' hours ought to come with the opportunity for workers to labor longer, if they so choose, at higher pay.

And yet, given all that, there is a kernel of truth in Brewer's now-controversial opinion. There *is* an inherent asymmetry between men and women *when it comes to* "the performance of maternal functions, [which] is especially true when the burdens of motherhood are upon her." This asymmetry, so clumsily depicted by Justice Brewer in 1908, does in fact exist in the case of a pregnant woman or a woman with childcare responsibilities, especially one who must both work for wages and serve as the primary (or only) caretaker of her children. Such a caregiving position places the caregiver in a position of relative vulnerability and even dependency up and against another who has no such responsibilities. These maternal vulnerabilities were the facts on the ground as Kelley knew them, as she saw them day in and day out among women at Hull House and in the tragic circumstances of mothers laboring in sweatshops while their young children went literally without care. Thus was the *Muller* decision celebrated at the time (and for the next half century) as a win for overworked mothers in the industrial era: indeed, it was regarded widely, Woloch writes, as "benevolent, humanitarian, and public-spirited."[39]

In these cases, Brewer was right then and still is today: "Looking at it from the viewpoint of *the effort to maintain an independent position in life,* [the woman in this situation] is not upon an equality."[40] If independence is the goal, broadly cast in our time as individual autonomy, then childbearing and caring responsibilities do tend to interfere with that quest. As one engaged woman aptly put it at the time in another context: "Children do add a complexity to women that they cannot add to men and I see no way of removing it entirely for the best interests of both sexes as well as for the children."[41]

Returning directly to the question of reproduction and caregiving in chapters 8, 9, and 10, we will look again at whether Brewer may have been more correct than history has allowed: "This difference justifies a difference in legislation, and upholds that which is designed to compensate for some of the burdens which rest upon her."[42]

BUNTING V. OREGON (1917): THE HAZARDS OF ALL INDUSTRIAL LABOR

Following *Muller*, nineteen states and the District of Columbia enacted hours legislation for women workers, and twenty other states enhanced the women-protective legislation they already had on the books. Under Kelley's leadership, the NCL brought about the new passage of a ten-hour restriction for women workers in Illinois. Brandeis and Goldmark, wielding a 600-page brief, then won an eventual reversal of the 1895 *Ritchie* decision by the Illinois Supreme Court.[43] Goldmark then turned her attention to the effect of industrialization upon men, publishing a lengthy investigation of men's health in 1913. Goldmark intended *Fatigue and Efficiency* to provide data to justify the extension of maximum hours laws to men, the next step of the NCL's "entering wedge" legal strategy.[44] Making a plea to industry itself, Goldmark argued that hour limitations would lead to increased productivity and profits: "Economic efficiency rises and falls with workers' physical efficiency, and whatever contributes to the latter tends to support the former."[45] Although Goldmark continued to regard women as more vulnerable to industrial hazards, she sought to show that scientific data now justified limitations for all workers.

Harvard Law professor and Brandeis protégé Felix Frankfurter replaced Brandeis as NCL's counsel when the latter joined the Supreme Court in 1916. Relying on Goldmark's findings, Frankfurter argued before the Supreme Court in favor of an Oregon law that restricted all industrial workers to ten hours a day, with a three-hour paid overtime provision. Echoing aspects of Kelley's commonwealth philosophy from 1905, Frankfurter argued in his brief in *Bunting v. Oregon*, "No nation can progress if its workers are crippled by overexertion."[46] Differentiating the needs of women and men far less than Brandeis had, Frankfurter focused his argument on the hazards of industry rather than the sex of the worker. The decision in *Lochner* was directly in his sights.

By this time, legal luminaries had begun to press the view that the Industrial Revolution had changed everything, including how government ought legitimately to function. Brandeis famously argued in his 1916 speech on the "living law" that "we [had] passed through an economic and social revolution which affected the life of the people more fundamentally than any political revolution known to history."[47] This revolution included a cultural, political, and judicial shift in the perception of the state as a mere neutral arbitrator between parties with the state's police power licitly exercised only insofar as it steered clear of privileging one class over another. For government to remain wholly neutral despite the new industrial conditions was, in the mind of many observers, to put it on the side of powerful industry up and against the far less powerful working man (and woman).

In 1908, in the wake of the *Lochner* decision, the celebrated Judge Learned Hand had also reasoned: "For the state to intervene to make more just and equal the relative strategic advantages of the two parties to the contract, of whom one is under the pressure of absolute want, while the other is not, is as proper a legislative function as that it should neutralize the relative advantages arising from fraudulent cunning or from superior physical force."[48] Similarly, William F. Willoughby, Mc-Cormick Professor of Jurisprudence at Princeton, wrote in 1914 that "liberty and law are correlative terms . . . the first can truly exist only through, and by virtue of, the second. Remove all legal restraint on the manner in which industry shall be carried on and we invite but a merciless exploitation of the weak and their subjection to a condition of dependence."[49] In 1917, the Supreme Court sided with Frankfurter, upholding the maximum hours law for all industrial workers.[50] *Bunting v. Oregon* tacitly overruled the holding in *Lochner* but left it on the books nonetheless.

MINIMUM WAGE LAWS AND THE EQUAL RIGHTS AMENDMENT

Kelley and the NCL sought to extend their success with maximum hours legislation to minimum wage laws. First introduced in 1910, twelve states had passed minimum wage laws for women by 1917. But minimum wage laws were seen by some as a bridge too far: such legislation intervened directly in labor negotiations between employers and employees and was difficult to justify as necessary for the general health and safety of workers. Still, economic conditions had deteriorated to such an extent on the eve of the Great Depression that it seemed that unorganized workers were especially unable to negotiate for wages high enough to sustain themselves and their families. (Assuming labor negotiations were a more effective lever than state legislation, male-dominated trade unions at the time favored minimum wage laws for women, but preferred union contracts for themselves.) The Supreme Court in an equally divided court in 1917 allowed a minimum wage law for women to stand, with no written opinion.[51] The lower court had relied on *Muller* to suggest that the minimum wage law was appropriate given women's inherent weakness.

Minimum wage laws had become the site of a sharp debate between Kelley and her protectionist allies and Alice Paul's antiprotectionist organization. The latter argued that minimum wage laws for women put them at a stark disadvantage when competing for jobs with men; if men could be employed at a lower hourly wage than women, men would obviously win more work. Paul was not opposed to all labor legislation, but she wanted it to apply from the outset to both women and men. She believed that women's strict equality with men, as first instantiated in the cause for suffrage, would best serve women's needs as individuals. Once the Nineteenth Amendment was ratified in 1920, Paul shifted immediately to drafting and then lobbying for an Equal Rights Amendment (ERA). The debate over the language of that amendment intersected with the movement's debate over protective legislation for women. Kelley, as we have seen, was also eager to see men eventually protected from exploitation in the workplace, but she thought the best strategy, successful to this point, was through the "entering wedge" of women-protective legislation. Kelley strongly insisted that the ERA and Paul's insistence on "theoretical equality" would bring a halt to all the gains women had made in the industrial workplace, and perhaps those of men. Kelley thought women would best be served by specific bills remedying specific inequalities ("specific bills for specific ills"), a legislative possibility that would become more likely once women won the franchise. Kelley argued that with the vote the police power would become an even more effective device for women: women would have the "right to express by statute the differences that they desire for themselves."[52] She dismissed the view that identical treatment with men would be of help to working women. "If [Paul's] ideas prevail," Kelley wrote, "the statutory working day and legal wage, the provision of seats when at work, for rest rooms, and all other special items which are more necessary for women than for men, (however much men may need them), will all be swept away."[53] Kelley was in favor of women's political equality and their ascent into all professions; indeed, she believed that women's suffrage would ensure a more humane politics and workplace, a "cooperative commonwealth."[54] In Paul's quest for formal equality, however, Kelley saw a threat of subjecting women, with men, to exploitation in the "free economy." Protective legislation for women, by contrast, compensated for their reproductive differences, and therefore was "equalizing in effect," in the words of a Kelley ally, Mary Anderson.[55]

Their debate led to an early draft of the ERA preserving protective legislation for women, written with the help of Harvard Law dean Roscoe Pound. Section 1 of the draft enunciated equal rights, but section 2 included a "savings clause" that exempted protective legislation from section 1's purview "on the basis of the physical constitution of women."[56] But this language satisfied neither side and was dropped. Paul eventually broke off discussions with the protectionists, and the ERA became the "blanket bill" for which Paul had initially hoped, articulating formal equality.

THE NINETEENTH AMENDMENT (1920) AND
ADKINS V. CHILDREN'S HOSPITAL (1923)

After some significant personnel changes, the Supreme Court in *Adkins v. Children's Hospital* struck down a DC-based minimum wage law for women that was passed by Congress in 1918. Justice George Sutherland, an ally of Paul's from the suffrage campaign, an advisor of hers on the drafting of the ERA, and prominent advocate of economic liberty, wrote the opinion for the Court. First distinguishing the licit hours legislation in *Muller* from the illicit minimum wage law at bar, Sutherland wrote that the Court could see no connection between setting wages for employees and legitimately legislating for the health and safety of the public. If the state could set a higher wage, it could also justify a lower one, he worried. Resurrecting the due process liberty of contract principles of *Lochner*, Sutherland sided with the hospital—and with Alice Paul.

Importantly, in his opinion for the Court, Sutherland addressed the relevance of the newly ratified Nineteenth Amendment on the Fourteenth Amendment liberty of contract doctrine he was championing:

"In view of the great—not to say revolutionary—changes which have taken place since [*Muller*], in the contractual, political and civil status of women, culminating in the Nineteenth Amendment, it is not unreasonable to say that these differences [between the sexes] have now come almost, if not quite, to the vanishing point." Thus, adult women are "legally as capable of contracting for themselves as men."[57] In dissent, Justice Taft argued that, not only did the Nineteenth Amendment not change the physical strength and reproductive differences upon which *Muller* rested, but, calling forth the same argument Kelley had made, Taft suggested the franchise also granted women more political power, thus giving greater assurances that any women-protective legislative restrictions would be in "accord with their interests as they see them." Taft also doubted the Court's assumption that employees and employers shared "a full level of equality of choice," suggesting that employees "are prone to accept pretty much anything that is offered" by the "overreaching of the harsh and greedy employer."[58]

Justice Holmes's separate dissent reiterated the textual concern he had expressed in his dissent in *Lochner*: the Fourteenth Amendment lacked any mention of "liberty of contract": "Contract is not specially mentioned in the text that we have to construe. It is merely an example of doing what you want to do, embodied in the word liberty. But pretty much all law consists in forbidding men to do some things that they want to do, and contract is no more exempt from law than other acts." Holmes then wrote that he could see no distinction in kind between legitimate legislation that restricts women's hours and the present wage law. Holmes finally added: "It will need more than the Nineteenth Amendment to convince me that there are no differences between men and women, or that legislation cannot take those differences into account."[59]

Paul, who had assisted the hospital's attorneys as the case moved through the federal courts, was elated with Sutherland's opinion. Her organization swiftly moved to have the ERA introduced in Congress. By this time, it read as a basic articulation of the strict equality principles she espoused: "Men and Women shall have equal rights throughout the United States and every place subject to its jurisdiction." Kelley's own response to the Court's decision in *Adkins* was equally swift. Highlighting the alliance of Paul's equal rights advocacy with commercial interests, Kelley quipped: "The women who pretend to be making heroic exertions to get 'equal rights' for all women are, in practice, the Little Sisters of the United States Chamber of Commerce [and other business organizations]."[60]

Another reaction of Kelley's was especially sharp, and historically prescient: "Under the Fifth and Fourteenth Amendments of the federal Constitution as now interpreted by the court, it is idle to seek to assure by orderly processes of legislation, to wage-earning men, women, or children, life, liberty or the pursuit of happiness. The decision fills those words with the bitterest and most cruel mockery. . . . Under the pressure of competition in American industry at this time, it establishes in the practical experience of the unorganized, the unskilled, the illiterate, the alien, and the industrially sub-normal women wage-earners, the constitutional right to starve. This is a new 'Dred Scott' decision."[61] Kelley may have been among the first to connect the substantive due process reasoning of *Lochner* and *Adkins* with the notorious *Dred Scott* decision.[62] But she would certainly not be the last.

FDR and *West Coast Hotel Co. v. Parrish* (1937)

After Franklin D. Roosevelt's landslide victory in 1936, and his court-packing proposal, the Court changed course in *West Coast Hotel Co. v. Parrish*. Reversing *Adkins* as a departure from the "true application of the principles" governing employment relations, the Court upheld a twenty-three-year-old minimum wage law for women enacted by the state of Washington.[63] Chief Justice Hughes, on behalf of the Court, maintained that freedom of contract could be curtailed when necessary to protect the health, safety, morals, and welfare of the people. Ruling in favor of Elsie Parrish, mother of six and chambermaid at a hotel owned by the West Coast Hotel Company, and echoing the reasoning of both Florence Kelley and Justice Holmes, Hughes famously wrote:

> The Constitution does not speak of freedom of contract. It speaks of liberty and prohibits the deprivation of liberty without due process of law. In prohibiting that deprivation, the Constitution does

not recognize an absolute and uncontrollable liberty. Liberty in each of its phases has its history and connotation. But the liberty safeguarded is liberty in a social organization which requires the protection of law against the evils which menace the health, safety, morals and welfare of the people. Liberty under the Constitution is thus necessarily subject to the restraints of due process, and regulation which is reasonable in relation to its subject and is adopted in the interests of the community is due process.[64]

Moving from his constitutional analysis that sounded in traditional common law reasoning to the economic conditions the nation was experiencing during the Great Depression, Hughes continued:

The exploitation of a class of workers who are in an unequal position with respect to bargaining power, and are thus relatively defenseless against the denial of a living wage, is not only detrimental to their health and wellbeing, but casts a direct burden for their support upon the community. What these workers lose in wages, the taxpayers are called upon to pay. The bare cost of living must be met. We may take judicial notice of the unparalleled demands for relief which arose during the recent period of depression and still continue to an alarming extent despite the degree of economic recovery which has been achieved. . . . The community is not bound to provide what is, in effect, a subsidy for unconscionable employers. The community may direct its lawmaking power to correct the abuse which springs from their selfish disregard of the public interest.[65]

Although Hughes did not appeal to the more controversial *Muller* "dependency" argument, nor did he even mention the still-recent passage of the Nineteenth Amendment, the Court did rule that the legislature was well within its authority to consider the situation of women in employment and how it differed, at the time, from that of men. Quoting the most compelling portion of *Muller*, Hughes maintained that "woman's physical structure and the performance of maternal functions place her at a disadvantage in the struggle for subsistence" and thus that her well-being "becomes an object of public interest and care in order to preserve the strength and vigor of the race."[66] In this case, the Washington State legislature recognized that women were the class of workers receiving the least pay and enjoying the weakest bargaining power. They were justly regarded as "ready victims" of those who would take advantage of their need. The Fourteenth Amendment, Hughes stated, "does not interfere with the state power by creating a 'fictitious equality'" between the sexes.[67]

The following year, Congress passed the Fair Labor Standards Act (FLSA) (1938), prohibiting child labor, establishing a minimum wage for large categories of workers, and requiring overtime pay for work in excess of the eight-hour day. A federal response to the economic upheavals suffered during the Great Depression, the Supreme Court upheld the FLSA as within Congress's authority pursuant to the commerce clause. The "entering wedge" strategy had given way to a labor law protective of both women and men, even as the FLSA failed to reach those industries dominated by Black workers.[68] Women close to Kelley, such as protégé Frances Perkins, took on leadership roles throughout FDR's administration. For many, the New Deal renewed the promise of the family (or "living") wage, with the new Social Security system created to undergird the family-centered economy.[69] In a dramatic about-face at the high court, the state-based police power lost much of its traditional relevance as legislation increasingly shifted to the federal level. A new era of Supreme Court jurisprudence followed, dispensing with concerns about due process "liberty" for a time in favor of strong judicial deference to both state and federal legislatures on social and economic matters.

A TIME OF ECONOMIC TRANSITION

The kind of work women took on began to change too. In 1900, more than half the country—men, women, and children—performed manufacturing work for wages, but by the end of the 1920s, the proportion of women working in office jobs had overtaken those in manufacturing.[70] Kelley, Addams, and other advocates of protective legislation for women had been concerned with the effect of menial, low-wage factory labor on vulnerable women, their children, and families at large. Paul, who remained unmarried throughout her life, touted the ERA, and had another vision of women in her ken: ambitious, high-achieving, and professional. Historian Nancy Cott writes:

> Where the [Paul-led] NWP [National Woman's Party] advocates saw before their eyes women who were eager and robust, supporters of protective legislation saw women overburdened and vulnerable. The former claimed that protective laws penalized the strong; the latter claimed that the ERA would sacrifice the weak. The NWP looked at women as individuals, and wanted to dislodge gender differentiation from the labor market. Their opponents looked at women as members of families—daughters, wives, mothers, and widows with family responsibilities—and believed that the promise of "mere equality" did not sufficiently take those responsibilities into account. The one side tacitly positing the independent professional woman as the paradigm, the other presuming the doubly-burdened mother in industry or service.[71]

Though certainly armed with different philosophies of the Constitution and the role of government, the women who took sides in the debate over protective legislation were also looking at the matter from starkly different experiences and perspectives. Kelley lived her life deep in the industrial trenches: until her death in 1932, she saw clearly the exploitative work situation for what it was and sought to protect women (and children) within it. Advocates of the ERA, on the other hand, shared a loftier, if at that time naïve, perspective with a more distant horizon; as Cott put it, they "envision[ed] the labor market as it might be, trying to insure [*sic*] women the widest opportunities in that imagined arena . . . [and they] thereby blink[ed] at existing exploitation."[72]

Historians Cott and Woloch both write that, objectively speaking, the evidence suggests protective legislation did tend to promote the well-being of women at the time, in those industries in which they predominated.[73] But in traditionally male, often unionized trades in which women were the minority of workers, maximum hours and minimum wage laws tended to curtail women's opportunity. Economist

Elizabeth Faulkner Baker wrote in an important 1925 study: "In occupations or industries where men greatly predominate, protective laws for women . . . relieve[d] men of the competition of women."[74] More recent economic studies of the era corroborate this finding.[75] First Lady Eleanor Roosevelt, a leading social reformer in her own right, spoke for many at the time when in 1933 she wrote of woman-protective legislation as, at the very least, a temporary way station during a time of profound economic turmoil and transition: "I think women have a right to demand equality as far as possible but I think they should still have the protection of special legislation regarding certain special conditions of their work and until we actually have equal pay and are assured of a living wage for both men's and women's work, I believe in minimum wage boards and regulating by law the number of hours women may work."[76]

To dismiss the dire circumstances of women at the time for but a theoretical hope in abstract "equality" was to ignore the exploitative nature of their work and the myriad social, economic, and emotional needs of their families. In the apt words of a southern academic at the time: "[Strict equality feminists] would free women from the rule of men only to make them greater slaves to the machines of industry."[77] At a time when motherhood was still regarded as the highest of callings, and the central importance of family life still dominated the imaginations of most Americans, such an exchange hardly appeared as an advance for ordinary women. Paul's vision, with the ERA at the heart of it, seemed far more like a capitulation to the commercial values that the early women's movement, in its own efforts to elevate women and their culturally essential familial work, had sought hard to resist.

After her death in 1932, Kelley's commonwealth vision lived on through the New Deal, providing compensatory relief to many working women and men who were harmed by industrialization. Paul never saw her ERA ratified. She would live, however, to experience the dramatic opening of the professions to women, and, in time, the eventual demise of the woman-protective legislation against which she had fought so spiritedly.

CHAPTER 6

The "Feminine Mystique" and Human Work

The 1950s were a period of remarkable national stability in the United States. The Great Depression and World War II were still living memory for many Americans, but the struggle—and victory—had given way to national peace, renewed patriotism, and a time of prosperity and rebuilding. To be sure, not all was right in the United States: until the Supreme Court decided *Brown v. Board of Education* in 1954, it had given a cramped reading to the Reconstruction amendments, continuing to interpret the "equal protection of the laws" in such a way that even Jim Crow segregation could be construed as constitutional. Under these fraught conditions, national peace would not endure for long.

Working- and middle-class white women in the 1950s were enjoying a different sort of postwar peace. The economic and political circumstances created by the war had compelled women who had not already entered the workforce to do so. Drawn in by either their own family situation or the patriotic duty to support the war effort, nearly 6 million women joined the workforce during the war. Hiring preferences in favor of male heads of households, wage disparities by sex, and women-protective maximum hours laws justified during the industrial era were all suspended to manage the potential shortfall of workers in defense plants and other factories; throngs of women entered industries that had been previously thought inappropriate for them. The "Lanham Act" of 1942 temporarily opened day care centers for the children of these women workers. Between 1940 and 1945, the percent-age of women in the workforce increased from 27 to 37 percent, three out of four new women workers were married women, and by the end of the war, almost one in four married women with children worked for wages.[1]

And then the baby boom started. Men and women who had post-poned marriage and childbirth to serve their country on the front lines or in the factory sought home life again. Protective labor laws for women returned, male wages rose, suburbs were built with the support of federal subsidies and tax breaks, the divorce rate dropped, and American confidence grew. Twenty percent more babies were born in 1946 than in 1945, with births growing at a pitch until 1964. The most highly educated women enjoyed the highest levels of fertility. Wives who could afford to began to forgo wage labor (at least until their chil-dren were in school) to enjoy a new material comfort with their grow-ing families, increasingly in the recently developed suburbs. Other women shifted from the traditionally male industries women had en-tered during the war to clerical jobs and "pink-collar" work in the growing service sector.

Women's rights advocates sought, and in twenty states won, equal pay laws throughout the 1950s, outlawing direct wage discrimination against women within individual firms. Still, renewed occupational segregation kept men's wages on average much higher than those of women. In fact, the "wage gap" between men's and women's work grew in the 1940s and 50s through this sort of job segregation, espe-cially because of mothers' increasing demand for part-time work.[2] The return to domesticity was viewed by many as a cultural advance brought about by greater prosperity, an elevation of the goods of the family over the often harsh demands of the industrial era. Women who had taken on work in traditionally male, blue-collar sectors dur-ing the war were now "free" to assume their proper place—the "bet-ter" place—making a home for their husbands and children. President Eisenhower's director of the Women's Bureau, Alice Leopold, stated in a press conference: "The most important function of a woman is to run a home, be a mother, and contribute to the life of her family and community."[3]

Winning and sustaining domestic peace and prosperity was celebrated in ladies' journals and depicted weekly in comedies and dramas broadcast in black and white on the new television sets now in more and more suburban homes. High school and university classes dedicated to home economics encouraged the professionalization of the work of the home, seeking to train women to be superior housewives, armed with all the efficiencies of the modern world, while making them the competent equals of their duly employed husbands. The "cult of domesticity" had reemerged with national gusto, accompanied as before with cultural expectations of separate spheres for (public) men and (private) women.

Although the return to the life of the home as an ascendant cultural value should remind us rightly of Wollstonecraft, the new postwar economy, built as it was upon manufacturing and consumption, engineered a domestic scene not like before the war. Not only were women more educated than ever before, but advances in home appliances had relieved much of the productive work of the home and saved massive amounts of time and energy. Women's role and identity were thus changed, but without the culturally salient markers—for the less religious, at least—to inform the purpose of a life well lived.

"THE PROBLEM THAT HAS NO NAME"

The tensions between the nineteenth-century's hard-won advances for working women and national hopes for blissful domesticity amid growing prosperity all paved the way for Betty Friedan's *The Feminine Mystique*.[4] Born the eldest of three children of a Russian immigrant father and Hungarian immigrant mother, Bettye Naomi Goldstein grew up in Illinois and graduated *summa cum laude* in psychology from Smith College. (She dropped the "e" from her name during her graduate fellowship at the University of California, Berkeley.) Leaving the fellowship after a year to move to New York and work as a reporter and writer, Betty met and married Carl Friedan. When their third child was born, the family moved from the city to the suburbs; Friedan quit her full-time job to tend to their children and to freelance occasionally

FIGURE 6.1. Betty Friedan in her home, 1978.
Credit: Lynn Gilbert (public domain).

for women's magazines. Growing dissatisfied with life as a housewife in the late 1950s, Friedan began her research for *The Feminine Mystique*.

Friedan's book, published in 1963, sold more than 1 million copies in the first paperback printing. Her interviews with suburban housewives, beginning with her own Smith College alumnae network, challenged the prevailing wisdom that educated, upper- and middle-class women were entirely satisfied in their role as homemakers. In those conversations, she stumbled upon "the problem that has no name," the phrase she gave the feminine malaise she was finding among many of the housewives she interviewed. Although her data revealed that a hearty minority of women were actually satisfied in their roles, the majority was enough to make her book an immediate best seller.

Reaching 1 million readers in a year is no mean feat, and Friedan's book has been credited properly as the popular start of the 1960s women's movement, the "second wave" of the women's movement. As such, it is usually interpreted by friend and foe alike as a manifesto for all women to get out to work, as though her answer to feminine malaise among the middle class was simply paid labor. Indeed, paid labor is certainly what her book and its movement seemed to inspire: at the end of World War II, only 10 percent of married women with preschool children worked outside the home; by 1985, the rates had swelled to more than 50 percent. But even as Friedan extolled the educational and professional aspirations, and market work, of middle-class women such that "find a career" was the central message that trickled down, she also declared that "a job, any job, is not the answer—in fact, it can be part of the trap."[5] She was asking, importantly, a more fundamental question, one about the nature of women's identity in an age of enhanced education, opportunity, and prosperity.

It ought to be noted from the outset that Friedan was speaking of and to an elite segment of society in her book. Many families could not afford to live in the suburbs at all, nor could they afford mothers to forgo wage labor or spend days shopping for new appliances while their children were in school. These less privileged families, especially African Americans still beset by racial prejudice in the workplace, knew nothing of a domesticity so affluent that it could be dubbed a "comfortable concentration camp."[6] Yet Friedan's investigation during this time of prosperity recalls the sort of inquiry Wollstonecraft had under-taken, even if Friedan, the budding psychologist, did not articulate as satisfactory a response as Wollstonecraft the philosopher had. Echoing Wollstonecraft and the suffragists before her, Friedan suggested that women's familial and social roles, though of central importance to their lives and to society, presupposed a prior understanding (and respect) for women *as human persons*.

In the original edition of *The Feminine Mystique*, Friedan, like Wollstonecraft and the early women's rights advocates, was in no way advocating that women abandon their children or their marriages for careers. On the contrary, Friedan suggested, "That was the mistaken choice of the feminine mystique."[7] Instead, these thinkers thought that shared domestic life would be better served when women took them-selves seriously first and foremost as persons in need of sustained human development. For both writers, it was a conceptual shift, not one intended to uproot familial obligations: no one ought to deny mar-ried women's roles as wives and mothers; women simply ought not be solely defined by these roles, as though they were not capable of (or properly interested in) anything but. According to Friedan: "Only by such a personal commitment to the future can American women . . . truly find fulfillment as wives and mothers—by fulfilling their own unique possibilities as separate human beings."[8]

Echoing Wollstonecraft's view of parenting quite closely, Friedan writes that *fully human* women would not infantilize their children by smothering them; rather, "a mature mother with a firm core of self" would imbue in her children "social conscience and strength of charac-ter."[9] As Wollstonecraft had put it, "Meek wives are, in general, foolish mothers." For Wollstonecraft, human persons flourish when they dedi-cate themselves to lives of wisdom and virtue; by so doing, women would become better mothers, better wives, and better citizens. But, for Friedan, what did it mean to be fully human, with a firm core, social conscience, and strong character? Friedan urged her readers to consider that women ought to be understood—and understand themselves—as human beings who reach self-fulfillment not by "liv[ing] through oth-ers" but by "realizing [their] full potential."[10] Relying on Abraham Maslow's newly popular theories of self-actualization, Friedan wrote that human "capacities clamor to be used," and that human beings need to express their "unique human individuality" and "to move according to a purpose."[11] Pointing to Jane Addams and Eleanor Roosevelt as female models of self-realization, Friedan wrote that "those who have most fully realized themselves . . . have done so in service of a human purpose larger than themselves," in the kind of "work that carries forward human society."[12]

Like Wollstonecraft's critique of "frivolous" aristocratic women before her, Friedan sought to call middle-class American women to focus on something greater than what could be construed as modern coquetry and pageantry. Friedan criticized the appearance-focused message imparted to women: "In the magazine image, women . . . work to keep their bodies beautiful and to get and keep a man."[13] She urged each woman to instead "realize . . . that neither her husband nor her children, nor the things in her house, nor sex, nor being like all the other women, can give her a self."[14] Both women suggested that human persons cannot be fully satisfied by fleeting pleasures, material objects, or even other people, however dear to us. For Friedan, human fulfillment, or self-actualization, was to be found in "fulfilling one's potential" and working with "higher purpose."

Friedan properly situated her critique within the new postindustrial, postwar order. She suggested that industrialization had not only transformed manufacturing work for men, but the new technologies had transformed domestic work in the home too, making that work something altogether new. The comfortable suburbs boasted homes architecturally sensitive to family life, modern time-saving devices, and burgeoning shopping malls within driving distance, all advancing the standard and ease of living. But as hard labor and productivity in the home gave way to greater leisure and increased capacity for consumption, housework became less demanding and, according to Friedan, increasingly more makeshift. If ordinary women in Florence Kelley's time were overburdened with the double shift of harsh industrial work and still difficult home labor, middle-class women in Friedan's time seemed to have become underburdened and even "bored" by the employment of those very technological advances Kelley's era had wrought.

Moreover, the serious and important social work in which women like Jane Addams had initiated and often engaged *gratis* decades before had over time become professionalized (and thus increasingly done, in the 1960s, by men), leaving part-time volunteers the more peripheral, less intellectual tasks. Thus, in Friedan's view, the most productive (and important) work had left the home, such that "occupation: housewife" was a less and less meaningful role for capable and intelligent women to play, especially as women's life expectancy now extended well beyond their childbearing and nurturing years. And yet, "the feminine mystique" had cemented itself in American culture after the war. A glorified femininity that encompassed only the life of the home appeared to Friedan unyielding, with little cultural encouragement of increasingly educated women toward aspirations outside of domestic life.

FROM PIONEER WOMAN TO THE COUNTRY'S CHIEF CONSUMER

Reminiscent of our description of the preindustrial era in chapter 3, Friedan contrasted her view of the work of the 1950s home with the distinctive contribution previous generations of women had made with their husbands in the household economy before productive work had departed from the home during the Industrial Revolution. She writes:

> Until, and even into, the last century, strong, capable women were needed to pioneer our new land; with their husbands, they ran the farms and plantations and Western homesteads. These women were respected and self-respecting members of a society whose pioneering purpose centered in the home. Strength and independence, responsibility and self-confidence, self-discipline and courage, freedom and equality were part of the American character for both men and women, in all the first generations.

Recalling Tocqueville perhaps, she continued:

> American women seemed to European travelers, long before our time, less passive, childlike, and feminine than their own wives in France or Germany or England. By an accident of history, Ameri-

can women shared in the work of society longer, and grew with the men. . . .

The identity crisis for women did not begin in America until the fire and strength and ability of the pioneer women were no longer needed, no longer used, in the middle-class homes of the Eastern and Midwestern cities, when the pioneering was done and men began to build the new society in industries and professions outside the home.[15]

Extolling the strong and independent character of this earlier generation of American women, Friedan lamented the feminine passivity she believed was born of domestic life in the 1950s suburbs. Among her most important insights, Friedan described at length the growing problem of consumerism in a more prosperous United States and the effect this was having on women's weakening sense of identity.[16]

As women's traditionally productive work in the home was displaced by new technologies (designed and manufactured predominantly by men in the industrial workplace), greater emphasis on household consumption followed. Women in the home with less intensive labor to fill their days were vulnerable to consumerist images set before them, especially as consumption was increasingly extolled as a force contributing vitally to the nation's economic boom. Calling marketeers of household conveniences "the most powerful perpetuators of the feminine mystique,"[17] Friedan wrote provocatively of the "sexual sell" that intentionally manipulated housewives to desire this or that new musthave product:

In all the talk of femininity and woman's role, one forgets that the real business of America is business. . . . [T]he growth of the feminine mystique, makes sense (and dollars) when one realizes that women are the chief customers of American business. . . .

The public image [of an American woman], in the magazines and television commercials, is designed to sell washing machines, cake mixes, deodorants, detergents, rejuvenating face creams, hair tints. But the power of that image, on which companies spend millions of dollars . . . comes from this: American women no longer know who they are.[18]

Friedan's account of the inordinate influence of consumption upon the renewed domesticity of the 1950s is especially ironic, given the cultural role domestic life had played just a century earlier. A previous generation of women's advocates, we should recall, had placed their hope in the home's capacity to serve as a communitarian counterforce to the individualist market influences in the growing commercial culture: antimodern islands in an industrial sea. Social historian Allan Carlson similarly describes how the home economists of the 1950s helped women trade domestic productivity for market consumption. As if following the suggestions of Charlotte Perkins Gilman, the home economists sought to "reorganiz[e] the home on capitalist principles: the quest for efficiency, the enthusiastic embrace of technology, and the celebration of consumerism. . . . [But] home-economics gave relatively little attention to training girls in productive activities. Instead, the focus was on educated consumption, *a complete merger of the home sphere with the industrial sphere*, and a retooling of the mother-at-home into a purchasing agent."[19] But consumerism was hardly a meaningful substitute for the great productivity of the home for previous generations of women, even as the prosperity and ease of life in postindustrial America spared women and their families the exploitative working conditions of the industrial era. Women's work had shifted substantially from the agrarian home to the industrial factory and now back to the home, but almost everything in the home had changed. In this, Friedan perceptively saw a crisis of identity.

FRIEDAN'S (ALMOST) WOLLSTONECRAFTIAN SOLUTION

The crisis of women's identity that began when most productive work moved outside the home could only be solved, according to Friedan, by "integrating a serious, lifelong commitment to society with marriage and motherhood."[20] In the book's still-revolutionary conclusion, Friedan advised modern women to forge their identities in "human work" that uses their full human capacities, that requires "initiative, leadership, and responsibility."[21] According to Friedan, "[The woman] must create, out of her own needs and abilities, a new life plan, fitting in the love and children and home that have defined femininity in the past with the work toward a greater purpose that shapes the future."[22] Their essential commitments as wives and mothers, always assumed by Friedan in the book's first edition, ought to be integrated into this fuller life vision ("life plan," "purpose," or "vocation") as one particularly important (and, at various times, all-consuming) aspect of their human work. She expressed this holistic focus as she wrote: "That sense of being complete and fully a part of the world—'no longer an island, part of the mainland'—[would] come back. . . . [That sense] did not come from the work alone, but from the whole—. . . marriage, homes, children, work, [the] changing, growing links with the community."[23]

For Friedan, then, women are individual human persons with various capacities, talents, and obligations; fulfillment would come by integrating better the various aspects of the person, in greater and lesser measure at different stages of life, depending on one's particular circumstances. Though she did assume a nine-to-five office job might provide the least distractions, Friedan argued that women's commitments should be flexible, managed around and according to family life: "Such a commitment . . . permits year-to-year variation—a full-time paid job in one community, part-time in another, exercise of the professional skill in serious volunteer work or a period of study during pregnancy or early motherhood when a full-time job is not feasible. It is a continuous thread, kept alive by work and study and contacts in the field, in any part of the country."[24]

To assist in this integration, Friedan proposed several family-centered measures to be undertaken by universities and political leaders. First, a greater "presence of women on [college] campus[es] . . . who have babies and husbands and who are still deeply committed to their own work" would enable college-age women to take their own education more seriously.[25] She recommended that universities recruit female professors who have worked part-time at various stages of their lives, and those "who have combined marriage and motherhood with the life of the mind—even if it means concessions for pregnancies."[26] She then urged a national commitment to continuing education for women who want either to continue or resume their education on a part-time basis while tending to their families, or to reenter the workplace full-time after their children have grown. Applauding the growing 1960s movement to fight discrimination against women in the workplace, she

concluded: "A woman is handicapped by her sex, and handicaps society, either by slavishly copying the pattern of man's advance in the
professions, or by refusing to compete with man at all. But with the vision to make a new life plan of her own, she can fulfill a commitment to
profession and politics, and to marriage and motherhood with equal
seriousness."[27]

Would that this sort of integration of home and work had occurred
as Friedan had imagined! Notably, the aspiration for flexibility in work,
and for respect for the prior obligations of the home, still exists unmet
today among many women (and increasingly, men) of all socioeconomic
strata, more than fifty years into the women's movement Friedan spearheaded.[28] Studies continue to show that most married women with
young children would prefer part-time (or no outside) work during
childbearing years, followed by reentry into part-time or full-time
work when children become less dependent.[29] Increasingly, a younger
generation of men report a strong desire to devote more time to their
families too.[30] But, as chapters 8 through 10 will explore in some detail,
the time women (and increasingly, men) spend away from the workforce for dedicated caregiving is disparaged, to this day, in the marketplace. Unfortunately, Friedan's own derisive rhetoric as to the seriousness of the work of the home (discussed presently)—alongside the later
fight for abortion rights she herself launched (discussed in chapter 8)—
bears a good share of the blame.

For even as Friedan held up an ennobling (and deeply adaptable)
vision of human work as the means toward a more integrated, fulfilling
life for modern women, her book has rightly been criticized for belittling the work of the home (which she considered both "dull" and
"boring"). Friedan's account underestimates the ways in which that
work, even if comparably less time- and labor-intensive than in earlier
times, and even if (to this day) devalued by an overemphasis on the
merits of paid work, can provide persons with opportunities to serve
others; forge a place of repose, solidarity, and education for family and
beyond; and grow in wisdom and human virtue. The character-shaping
work of the home, for both children and their parents, still embodies,
even under dramatically changed conditions, a person-oriented island
in a market-oriented sea.

Friedan suggests in an early chapter of *The Feminine Mystique* that she had never met a happy housewife—"one of those mystical creatures"—but her own research indicated that such women did in fact exist; of course, they still do.[31] Indeed, only 60 percent of the 200 Smith graduates she interviewed were not "totally fulfill[ed]" in their roles.[32] So what of the remaining 40 percent who were? Elsewhere in the book, she does not want to admit that such women were *truly* happy: "Surely there are many women in America who are happy at the moment as housewives, and some whose abilities are fully used in the housewife role. But happiness is not the same thing as the aliveness of being fully used."[33] She even refers to housewives as "parasites" and "parasitic."[34] But perhaps Friedan missed something important as she assumed that all housewives fit the consumerist profile she uncovered: acting as the nation's leading "thing-buyers," waxing the kitchen floor several times a day. And though there is no doubt Friedan struck a nerve with many women for whom this must have been true, what if the "happy housewives" were engaged in something far more serious and meaningful still?

Friedan summarizes early on the bombardment of cultural messaging that women in her time were receiving; she is surely correct that such messaging unjustly assumed women's only place was in the home. And yet, some of the messages she recounts quite negatively actually accord closely with the positive vision of domestic life and motherhood that Wollstonecraft and the women leaders of the nineteenth and early twentieth centuries had themselves extolled. This message is particularly apt: "The homemaker, the nurturer, the creator of children's environment is the constant recreator [*sic*] of culture, civilization, and virtue."[35] Highlighting the fruits of the "serious mother," for instance, Wollstonecraft writes: "She lives to see the virtues which she endeavored to plant on principles, fixed into habits, to see her children attain a strength of character sufficient to enable them to endure adversity without forgetting their mother's example."[36]

Further on, Friedan expresses considerable dismay when in a commencement address a well-known political figure of her day encouraged women to recognize the important political role they can play when they seek to "'inspire in [their] home a vision of the meaning of life and freedom ... to help [their] husband[s] find values that will give purpose to [their] specialized daily chores ... to teach [their] children the uniqueness of each individual human being.'"[37] That women should have access to political roles beyond this is undoubtedly Friedan's point, but that she would not consider this essential character-shaping occupation a serious commitment to society or a "human purpose larger than [oneself]" is never explored.[38]

Indeed, her relative devaluing of person-forming domestic activities—suitably shared by both mothers and fathers today—contradicts the views of Wollstonecraft and the pioneering women she otherwise admired. These women regarded these properly domestic occupations as the most important human tasks, far greater in value than the market work Friedan implicitly prefers.[39]

WORK AND THE DEVELOPMENT OF HUMAN EXCELLENCE

That Friedan disbelieved the happiness and personal fulfillment of homemakers who take seriously the formative work they do is indicative of a more fundamental misunderstanding of the person's relationship to work, and one that can be corrected by Wollstonecraft's more satisfactory account. Friedan, of course, is right that human work is a good in itself, and a prime means by which human beings grow, develop, and shape their characters. Work is constitutive of, or an essential aspect of, human flourishing. Wollstonecraft too understood work—as more broadly described as the carrying out of various obligations of state— to be most necessary for the proper development of children and the inculcation of virtue in both children as well as adults. As Wollstonecraft saw it, passivity and idleness gave way to vice and corruption of human capacities. Remember her rebuff of the idleness of the aristocracy and "frivolous" women too: "The human character has ever been formed by the employments the individual, or class, pursues; and if the faculties are not sharpened by necessity, they must remain obtuse."

As Friedan rightly explored, under nonexploitative circumstances, a person can seek to integrate the various aspects of her work, prioritizing more pressing obligations as they come. In this way, the human person is understood to exist *prior to* her work; she can transcend her work, stand above it, critique it, and find ways to improve the conditions under which she labors, or the work itself. When work is understood broadly, as the obligations one undertakes according to one's various states in life (roles or positions), this integration can come about throughout the whole panoply of a person's work: domestic, professional, and, almost always, some combination of the two, depending on one's particular obligations and family circumstances. But work can only be integrated as such when one seeks to develop her capacities according to what Wollstonecraft recognized as the ends of human personhood: wisdom and virtue. This is where Friedan's account falls short. Friedan's appreciation of self-actualization, reaching one's potential, developing one's capacities, or even working with "higher purpose" is morally inadequate without a sense of the proper goal or end of those human capacities.

For instance, my nine-year-old son, clever and inventive as he is, may have the human capacity to be an excellent thief, but by such work he would not properly be "fulfilling himself and becoming what he can be" (as Friedan expressed it), even though he would be executing a "human purpose larger than himself." Without an understanding of the human person's proper end, thought Wollstonecraft, the human quest for wisdom and virtue gives way to the relentless desire for power, and in the individual person, fleeting passions overrun firm principles.

Like Friedan, Wollstonecraft believed that the very first duty of a human person is to develop his or her capacities, *to actualize what is potential.* But according to Wollstonecraft, the human person's capacities are only authentically developed ("actualized") when directed toward his or her proper end as a rational creature. In a word, he or she must in and through his or her work aim to grow in wisdom and virtue. This arduous and daily task is accomplished through fulfilling one's particular duties in life, ensuring firm principles guide one's passions, and humbly reorienting oneself when they do not. Ultimately, for Wollstonecraft, one ought to seek to live and work with benevolence, that is, a deep concern for others. So, although Friedan is correct that one cannot live "through others," one can and should live "for others." Such benevolence is a great marker of humility, humanity, and maturity.

Thus, it is only with lived practice in the virtues (e.g., patience, self-discipline, moderation, proper regard for the good of others) and with wisdom as guide that one will be able to properly order obligations at various times of the day—and order one's life. Obligations to family, especially when children are young, ought to serve to order other obligations to professional work and service to others beyond one's family. Friedan herself saw this quite clearly, as she sought to find practical means for women to fulfill their familial obligations while also engaging in educational aspirations and professional work. Wollstonecraft also suggested about this integration that "no employment of the mind is a sufficient excuse for neglecting domestic duties, and I cannot conceive that they are incompatible."

And so, it is the acquisition, development, and practice of human excellences in and through work broadly understood, and not, properly speaking, the work itself, that can bring about human happiness. This certainly does not mean that some work is not personally satisfying and enjoyable, and other work not monotonous and repetitive, which both domestic and market labor can be. It simply means that human satisfaction is found in the growth, development, and excellence that comes about through doing well and with commitment to the work at hand, whatever it may be. To return to the present example: the work of the home is intrinsically meaningful because the human persons who inhabit (and make) the home are rational beings with inherent dignity whose growth in virtue—in whatever kind of work they do (including the work of play for children)—fosters a certain human excellence, especially when done with this human reality in mind. Though some kinds of work, notably, slave labor or work in other exploitative circumstances, are not befitting of the dignity of the person, it is not the work itself that gives dignity to the person, but the nature of the person that gives dignity to human work. To belittle the work of the home, and the little, even tedious acts that go with it (which, frankly, are found in almost all types of work), belittles the human beings who nurture and are nurtured within its walls. It also overlooks the level of freedom and autonomy a homemaker, freed from the obligations of market work, has to design her (or, sometimes, his) day and positively affect the lives of myriad others (both within and outside the walls of her home). This

compares quite well with market occupations in which the vast majority of workers have to answer to higher authorities, and often enjoy
very little autonomy themselves. The homemaker's economic dependency upon her (or, less frequently, his) spouse is what allows such autonomy, autonomy the breadwinner himself may never experience in
his market work.

Hardly "parasitic," the homemaker enjoys a certain freedom to
manage the culturally essential work that takes place in the family: to
engage in productive and cost-saving enterprises in the home; to nurture, educate, and shape the characters of her children; and to enjoy the
flexibility of part-time (paid or volunteer) work Friedan herself endorsed. Indeed, an honest account would notice instead that *the work
of the market is actually "parasitic" upon the work of the home*, resting
as all public enterprises do upon the integrity, ingenuity, and industry
of persons and the relationships of interdependence, trust, and fair play
among persons first learned therein.

Disparaging the work of the home tends also to disparage the nonmarket domestic sphere altogether, up and against the public sphere,
where productivity can be more readily calculated and therefore valued in a market economy. Friedan goes so far as to declare that the
work of the home is not "important enough to society to be paid for in
its coin," and criticizes efforts to give housewives cultural "prestige."[40]
In the final analysis, Friedan, as with Charlotte Perkins Gilman's late
nineteenth-century economizing suggestions for the home, evaluates
women's work through the economic principles from which previous
generations of women's advocates sought to immunize their families—
and the culture at large. Gilman and Friedan are not alone. This is, of
course, now the way of the postindustrial modern world. No measures
of productivity or "wealth" are counted if a mother cares for her own
children in her own home or a family cooks their own meals. Productivity is measured only when the family contracts those "transactions"
out to others. And yet, we wonder why the marketplace still does not
recognize the priority of the family and the essential work of the home.
The women's movement, then under Friedan's direction, could have
followed its predecessors' vision and worked to counteract this modern tendency. It still can.

Often the modern feminist movement is rendered, by fan and foe alike, as a movement in favor of traditionally "male" work and away from traditionally "female" work. But it would be better understood as a shift from priority given to the goods of the home to the goods of the market. This move, where modern feminism joins market forces to subordinate the family to the workplace—unintended perhaps by Friedan but accomplished nonetheless—sets second wave feminism on the wrong rail from the start, and explains much that is to come. Rather, if Friedan had followed her own vision of integrated human work more closely, she would have advocated more strongly for the Wollstonecraftian view that work both within and outside the home can ask of the person that "initiative, leadership, and responsibility" that begets human meaning, and that women and men could find fulfillment in both. Were each properly valued—with cultural priority always given to the character-shaping work that first takes place in the home and makes all work outside of it possible—the praiseworthy antidiscrimination efforts of the 1970s (discussed in chapter 7) would not have given way, in later years, to a hostility to the home and those who labor within it.

In chapter 7, I examine how such antidiscrimination efforts at the federal level and urged by the National Organization for Women, cofounded by Friedan, were undertaken to broaden the types of work women legally could do. Importantly, despite the disparaging statements found in *The Feminine Mystique* itself, these initial efforts appreciated the intrinsic value of both caregiving and homemaking and sought to organize work around these goods. Unfortunately, as we'll see in chapter 8, these original statements were undermined as the priorities of the 1970s feminist movement shifted. Abandoning the potential to disrupt the profit-oriented marketplace by calling it to a more humane, family-centered orientation, the movement had a new destination: the technological control of female reproduction.

CHAPTER 7

Sex Role Stereotypes and the Successful Quest for Equal Citizenship Status

The Universal Declaration of Human Rights was adopted by the UN General Assembly in December 1948. Under Eleanor Roosevelt's dynamic leadership, the international charter affirmed in its preamble the "equal rights of men and women." The charter also recognized the family as the "natural and fundamental group unit of society" and motherhood and childhood as "entitled to special care and assistance." It championed equal pay for equal work, including just remuneration for oneself and one's family (and, if necessary, "other means of social protection") to ensure "an existence worthy of human dignity."[1]

Nearly fifteen years later, American women more directly benefited from Roosevelt's courageous leadership. In 1961, President Kennedy established the President's Commission on the Status of Women, with Roosevelt at the helm until her death in 1962. In 1963, the very same year Betty Friedan's book was published, the Commission released its report, *American Women*, on what would have been Roosevelt's seventy-ninth birthday. The Commission, inspired by Assistant Secretary of Labor Esther Peterson, was charged with making recommendations to "overcom[e] discriminations in . . . employment on the basis of sex" and for "services which will enable women to continue their role as wives and mothers while making a maximum contribution to the world around them."[2]

Although most women's advocates in the late nineteenth century had fought for protective legislation for women workers, once the New Deal put in place higher workplace standards for all workers, their chief focus shifted to antidiscrimination measures. This shift in focus was even the case for labor advocates, such as Peterson, who still favored some sex-distinctive legislation. Significantly, the nature of work outside the home had been dramatically transformed for most women since World War II. No longer was manual labor the most prevalent work women engaged in; automation and other technology rendered the labor market increasingly centered in the growing service sectors and knowledge economy. Neither line of work specially required men's superior strength or physically threatened women's unique reproductive functions. Moreover, unions had grown to better support women's distinctive needs in contract negotiations. Still, Roosevelt, Peterson, and others sought to advance women's equality in the workplace, even while alleviating the tensions working mothers experienced and valuing the essential work of the home.

The President's Commission on the Status of Women had an immediate effect on discrimination in wages and hiring. In 1963, Congress passed the Equal Pay Act, amending the Fair Labor Standards Act to outlaw sex-based wage discrimination. The next year, Title VII of the 1964 Civil Rights Act banned discrimination in employment on the basis of race, color, religion, sex, or national origin. Ironically, "sex" had been added as an amendment to Title VII by an opponent of the civil rights legislation only two days before the bill successfully passed in the House of Representatives. Historical accounts suggest the amendment's author, Southern congressman Howard Smith, sought to quash the civil rights bill and thought adding "sex" would convince more traditionally minded representatives to scrap the whole act; others suggest that by it Smith sought to protect white women who would be competing with Black women for employment. Either way, the antidiscrimination bill passed and has reshaped employment practices vis-à-vis women ever since.

As part of the legislation, Title VII established the Equal Employment Opportunity Commission (EEOC), a five-member, bipartisan taskforce created to enforce the new law. Enforcement of the law as to sex, however, was not immediately forthcoming. Given the clause's unusual origination, this was at least partly from the lack of legislative history defining what discrimination "because of sex" was meant to encompass. The U.S. Supreme Court started to assist in that regard beginning in 1971. But, with the long-standing sex segregation in jobs (and even job postings), more political muscle first was necessary.

During a meeting of state commissions on the status of women in 1966, Friedan, along with civil rights attorney Pauli Murray, who sat on the President's Commission, and Aileen Hernandez, the first woman appointed to the EEOC, expressed profound disappointment at the lack of attention the EEOC was affording sex discrimination. Hernandez resigned from her post that year because of the agency's negligence in this regard. Together, the three founded the National Organization for Women (NOW) to exert political pressure on the EEOC. NOW's original Statement of Purpose, released in 1966, reiterated central themes Friedan had first traced in *The Feminine Mystique*, but, importantly, it included far greater affirmations of the value of caregiving and homemaking:

> NOW is dedicated to the proposition that women, first and foremost, are human beings, who, like all other people in our society, must have the chance to develop their fullest human potential. We believe that women can achieve such equality only by accepting to the full the challenges and responsibilities they share with all other people in our society, as part of the decision-making mainstream of American political, economic and social life. . . .
>
> With a life span lengthened to nearly 75 years it is no longer either necessary or possible for women to devote the greater part of their lives to child-rearing; yet childbearing and rearing which continues to be a most important part of most women's lives—still is used to justify barring women from equal professional and economic participation and advance.
>
> Today's technology has reduced most of the productive chores which women once performed in the home and in mass-production industries based upon routine unskilled labor. This same technology has virtually eliminated the quality of muscular strength

as a criterion for filling most jobs, while intensifying American industry's need for creative intelligence. In view of this new industrial revolution created by automation in the mid-twentieth century, women can and must participate in old and new fields of society in full equality—or become permanent outsiders.[3]

Industrialization and the nascent technological revolution had by then transformed both the public and private sectors well beyond their agrarian beginnings. These women sought to inspire in the public sphere respect for women as equal citizens and esteemed professionals, even as they envisioned a renewed collaboration between men and women in marriage and the family. In addition to decrying sex discrimination, the statement called for the United States to "innovate new social institutions which will enable women to enjoy the true equality of opportunity and responsibility in society, without conflict with their responsibilities as mothers and homemakers." In a Wollstonecraftian call for a "true partnership between the sexes," the statement suggested, not only that men and women share responsibilities of home and children, "and of the economic burdens of their support," but also that the "economic and social value of homemaking and child-care" be better recognized. The statement requested not only childcare centers, but also a national commitment to a GI bill–type program that would retrain women who had chosen to care for their children on a full-time basis.[4]

The NOW statement explicitly acknowledged that caring for children and making a home was of intrinsic value, as Pauli Murray herself had made clear in her celebrated 1965 law review article, "Jane Crow and the Law," discussed further below.[5] Murray's article and NOW's original statement corrected the derisive tone of Friedan's book in this regard, but major changes in NOW's platform the very next year exerted far stronger influence on the women's movement as a whole. Reading the original 1966 statement two decades into the new millennium, one may be surprised not to find a single mention of abortion rights. Abortion became a singular priority for NOW in 1967 and in decades to come (a story we relate in chapter 8), but at its origins, the organization did not claim abortion was necessary to women's legal equality or equal opportunity in the workplace. Neither, it should be noted, did the first edition of Friedan's book. Rather, Friedan wrote of the "biological oneness in the beginning between mother and [unborn] child, a wonderful and intricate process," and provocatively critiqued early sexual activity as "characteristic of underdeveloped civilizations."[6] An epilogue of an edition published ten years later includes abortion rights among her movement's new priorities, and also recounts Friedan's intervening divorce. By 1967, much had changed at NOW, but not without a fight or without ostracizing of many women who had joined the original cause.

The suggestion I make in this book (as we'll see in chapter 8) is that the quest for abortion rights as the *sine qua non* of the modern women's movement undercut dramatically the insight at NOW's founding that childbearing and child-rearing were too often what justified barring women from employment. Fifty years later, after tremendous gains in antidiscrimination law, one's status as a woman no longer disadvantages women in the workplace very often. But dedication to one's family, for mothers especially but for fathers too, most certainly does.

In this chapter, I describe the development of antidiscrimination law both in its statutory advances and, in the hands of ACLU attorney Ruth Bader Ginsburg, its constitutional successes. The next chapters will detail how pregnancy and childbearing, that most basic difference between men and women, complicates the matter exponentially. There, I will argue that the tension between the two pillars of Ginsburg's lifelong legacy, antidiscrimination and pro-abortion rights, can no longer hold.

Title VII at the Supreme Court

One of the most important aspects of the new sex discrimination regime established by Title VII was the way in which it would open doors to those more disadvantaged women who were already in the workforce but whose sex kept them relegated to lower-status, low-paid work. The first Title VII case was litigated by the Supreme Court in 1971. In *Phillips v. Martin Marietta Corporation*, and several Title VII cases to follow, the plaintiff was a working-class mother whose income was necessary to her family's financial well-being. Friedan's analysis of the "comfortable" suburban housewife seeking renewed meaning through human work was inapplicable. Indeed, the (white) middle-class assumption, on both Friedan's part and those of her detractors, that women even had the freedom to care for their children in the home, rather than go out to work for them, was an assumption that Title VII would sharply depose.

Ida Phillips, mother of seven children, age three to sixteen, worked as a waitress at the Donut Dinette when she read the job posting for entry level assembly-line work at Martin Marietta's missile factory in Orlando, Florida. Offering twice what she made at the restaurant, the job promised a pension and other benefits, including health insurance. Her husband, a mechanic, was a heavy drinker and known to be abusive to Ida and the children; when his paycheck went to booze instead of family bills, she relied on her waitressing tips to put food on the table. When Ida visited the factory to apply, she was asked if she had any preschool-age children; after acknowledging that she had a three-year-old, she was told she would not be considered for the position. The circumstances of her life, including the abundant childcare options she personally enjoyed (her mother and sister lived nearby), were irrelevant to her potential employer.

With the assistance of young civil rights attorneys associated with the NAACP, Ida sued under Title VII. The district court judge found for the factory, reasoning that "the responsibilities of men and women with small children are not the same . . . employers are entitled to recognize these different responsibilities in establishing hiring policies."[7] The U.S. Fifth Circuit Court agreed. In a unanimous opinion rendered per curiam, the Supreme Court reversed and remanded the decision to the district court. The Court held that Title VII "requires that persons of like qualifications be given employment opportunities irrespective of their sex."[8] But the Court then expounded upon the exception provided in Title VII: were an employer to show that excluding mothers with young children was reasonably necessary to the operation of the particular business, the bona fide occupational qualification (BFOQ) exception would apply. Not wanting to try their luck with the BFOQ, Martin Marietta settled with Phillips out of court.

In 1977, the Supreme Court held that the BFOQ exception would be read narrowly so as not to swallow the whole statute. Women could not be excluded outright, for instance, from hazardous jobs; they'd have to judge the hazards for themselves. Further, arbitrary weight and height requirements that had prohibited women from jobs in law enforcement were outlawed apart from reasonable necessity, opening up these traditionally male professions to women.[9] In principle, Title VII provided that individual women be treated as such, and not as members of a group ("potential mothers") with assumed characteristics or obligations.

The early 1970s saw further congressional action on behalf of women's equality under the law: in 1972, Congress extended Title VII to apply to government employers, including the federal government, and to educational institutions; the amendment also reduced the number of employees (from twenty-five to fifteen) needed for the law to cover the employer. That same year, Congress also passed Title IX of the Educational Amendments, prohibiting sexual discrimination in educational facilities that received federal funding. In 1972, the Senate also passed the Equal Rights Amendment (ERA)—introduced in every Congress since Alice Paul first authored it in 1923—following similar action on the part of the House. Sent on to the states for ratification, the amendment now read: "Equality of rights under the law shall not be denied or abridged by the United States or by any State on account of sex." The ERA was to languish in the states, but not before intense debate as to the nature of that "equality," which we discuss in chapter 8.

The 1970s had seen antidiscrimination laws not only in the United States. The United Kingdom passed the Equal Pay Act of 1970, and in 1975 the Sex Discrimination Act, outlawing "certain kinds of" sex discrimination and discrimination on the basis of marriage. That same year, the UK's Employment Protection statutorily mandated maternity pay and rendered unlawful dismissal on the grounds of pregnancy. In France, 1972 marked the year of gender equality in employment.

Interpreting the Equal Protection Clause to Protect Women

The President's Commission recommended as part of its 1963 report that test cases be brought to the Supreme Court to clarify the legal status of women under the U.S. Constitution. In a memo to the Commission, Pauli Murray, an esteemed civil rights attorney and close friend of Eleanor Roosevelt, had advocated a position akin to the early suffragist litigators: properly understood, the Fourteenth Amendment already included women.[10] Serving on the Commission from 1961 to 1963, Murray had graduated first in her class from Howard Law School (as the only woman) and received her master's of law degree from University of California, Berkeley. A pacifist, and eventually one of the first women to become an Episcopalian priest, she penned a book in 1951 that Thurgood Marshall described as the "bible" of civil rights lawyers. The President's Commission took Murray's position as its own.

Murray extended her memo's analysis further in a now-famous 1965 *George Washington Law Review* article, "Jane Roe and the Law: Sex Discrimination and Title VII." Murray argued there was no reason that women ought to be denied "the equal protection of the laws" guaranteed to "persons" by the Constitution.[11] From this perspective, the bluntly worded ERA—still contested by women's labor advocates as likely to eliminate special maternity legislation for women—might not be so necessary after all. Murray's broader (and more natural) reading of the text of the Constitution, however, stood up and against the legislative history at the time of the Fourteenth Amendment's passage, and sharply contradicted how the Supreme Court had interpreted it from the nineteenth century onward. Still, emboldened by the Court's more generous interpretation in *Brown v. Board of Education* and other recent cases, Murray argued that "the protective cover of the fourteenth amendment is broad enough to reach all arbitrary class discrimination."[12] Comparing discrimination on the basis of sex with racial discrimination, Murray wrote:

> When the law distinguishes between the "two great classes of men and women," gives men a preferred position by accepted social standards, and regulates the conduct of women in a restrictive manner *having no bearing on the maternal function*, it disregards individuality and relegates an entire class to inferior status. . . . Through unwarranted extension, it has penalized all women *for the biological function of motherhood* far in excess of precautions justified by the

FIGURE 7.1. Pauli Murray (1910–85). Credit: Carolina Digital Library and Archives at University of North Carolina at Chapel Hill (public domain).

findings of advanced medical science. . . . [I]t permits a policy originally directed toward the protection of a segment of a woman's life to dominate and inhibit her development as an individual. . . . Although the "classification by sex" doctrine was useful in sustaining the validity of progressive labor legislation in the past, perhaps it should now be shelved alongside the "separate but equal" doctrine.[13]

As with the original NOW statement, Murray clearly distinguished between discrimination against individual women and the "biological function of motherhood," even as she granted that motherhood was an experience that most women, at some point in their lives, would undertake. Classifying women *by that function*, especially when the conduct in question has "no bearing" on maternity itself, was what had become, according to Murray, legally passé. Individual women ought not be classified legally as potential mothers or mere members of a class, as they had been in the past; they ought to be regarded as equal persons under the law and thus protected by the Constitution.

Murray and a colleague had made headway comparing race and sex in 1966 in *White v. Crook*, a civil rights case in the state of Alabama.[14] There they argued that the Fourteenth Amendment prohibited the state from excluding Black men and all women from juries. No court had yet agreed that the equal protection clause prohibited sex discrimination, but the Alabama state court did just that. In the next few years, several other state and federal courts slowly followed suit. But the Supreme Court had yet to weigh in. To be sure, five years earlier, in 1961, the high court in *Hoyt v. Florida* had held that limiting jury service to only those women who had volunteered was no violation of the equal protection clause. But the women in *Hoyt* had not been *excluded* from jury service as they would be in *White*. According to a unanimous decision of the Court, states could spare women the sometimes onerous civic obligation of serving on juries because of their special place at the "center of home and family life."[15]

Enter Ruth Bader Ginsburg

In 1966, Ruth Bader Ginsburg was a young law professor at Rutgers; three years later, she became the first woman tenured on any law faculty. While in law school, she had successfully juggled schoolwork and an editorial position on law review with care of both her first child and her husband, a fellow student who was fighting cancer. Yet upon graduating at the very top of her class at Columbia Law School as one of only a handful of women, no law firm would hire her. Landing a year-long clerkship through the strong-arm persuasion of a law school mentor, she then went on to study civil procedure in Sweden, the subject she initially taught at Rutgers and then later at Columbia. But these experiences were not all that prepared her for the culture-shaping role she was to play in U.S. legal history.

Like her mother, Ginsburg was a devotee of Eleanor Roosevelt, the first lady for most of Ginsburg's childhood. Ginsburg cut her teeth on the Universal Declaration of Human Rights and the respect for the dignity of both men and women that hallowed charter enshrined. Her mother died of cervical cancer the week of Ginsburg's high school graduation, but not before encouraging her daughter to develop herself intellectually with a firm sense of independence.

FIGURE 7.2. Ruth Bader Ginsburg, 1977.
Credit: Lynn Gilbert (public domain).

Though not devoutly Jewish (and generally critical of the place of women in all the world's religions), Ginsburg's religious heritage was deeply formative in its exaltation of both learning and justice. In a newspaper column she wrote at thirteen years old, she extolled the Ten Commandments as a "code of ethics and standard of behavior."[16] Decades later, in her chambers as a Supreme Court justice, she again recalled Deuteronomy, displaying a portion of that book's celebrated passage in Hebrew letters: "Justice, justice, shalt thou pursue, that you may thrive."[17] Ginsburg took on her first *pro bono* case while teaching at Rutgers. On behalf of the ACLU's New Jersey affiliate, she represented pregnant schoolteachers who had been required by their district to take mandatory maternity leave well ahead of their due date, with neither paid leave nor the guarantee that they could return.[18] Ginsburg's own experiences of pregnancy and motherhood were not all that distant from the women she represented: the judge for whom she clerked had been unwilling to hire women with children prior to her tenure. Learning the lesson of the time well, Ginsburg concealed her second pregnancy while teaching at Rutgers for fear of reprisal.

Reed v. Reed

In 1970, while still at Rutgers, Ginsburg was called upon to coauthor, with another ACLU attorney, the Supreme Court brief for Sally Reed, on appeal from an unfavorable judgment of the Supreme Court of Idaho. The case made history and cemented Ginsburg's reputation for legal argument at the very highest level. After the death of their son, both Mrs. Reed and her estranged husband applied to administer their son's estate. Though Mrs. Reed's application was first in time, the state appointed the father in accordance with the Idaho code, which specified that in such a case, males must be preferred to females. Ginsburg saw in these facts the perfect sex discrimination test case: Mrs. Reed's sex was the only reason that she was denied the administration of her son's estate.

The equal protection clause of the Fourteenth Amendment requires that "similarly situated" individuals be treated similarly. States, and the federal government via the due process clause of the Fifth Amendment, are constitutionally required to govern with impartiality, not arbitrarily classifying individuals in a manner irrelevant to a legitimate governmental objective. The litigant claiming an abridgment of equal protection ordinarily must sustain the burden of proof; great deference is afforded the state (which duly legislates through the democratic process) that there is a "rational basis" for the law. But beginning in 1944, racial classifications became inherently suspect, shifting the burden of proof in those cases to the state, which must show the statute is narrowly tailored to achieve a compelling state interest. In this way, courts are said to "strictly scrutinize" race-based statutes.

Following Murray's successful comparison of race- and sex-based classifications in the 1966 Alabama case, Ginsburg's first play was to ask the Court to employ strict scrutiny with the sex-based statute, as the court did with racial classifications. Ginsburg's *Reed* brief reads:

> Although the legislature may distinguish between individuals on the basis of their need or ability, it is presumptively impermissible to distinguish on the basis of an unalterable identifying trait over which the individual has no control and for which he or she should not be disadvantaged by the law. Legislative discrimination grounded on sex, for purposes *unrelated to any biological difference between the sexes*, ranks with legislative discrimination based on race, another congenital, unalterable trait of birth, and merits no greater judicial deference.[19]

Ginsburg argued that since women were still lacking the adequate political representation in legislative and policymaking bodies to remedy their unequal treatment in the law (treatment that had been further aggravated by decisions of the Supreme Court), women who sought to be judged on their individual merits had little recourse. Only a few years before this case, of course, women had found political recourse in congressional action, but neither the Equal Pay Act nor Title VII could touch state laws nor areas other than employment in which actors arbitrarily discriminated on the basis of sex. "The time is ripe," Ginsburg wrote, "for this Court to repudiate the premise that, with minimum justification, the legislature may draw a 'sharp line between the sexes' just as this Court has repudiated once settled law that differential treatment of the races is constitutionally permissible."[20]

Again following Murray, Ginsburg did not deny that the biological differences between the sexes were significant; rather, she sought to show that such differences were of no consequence to the administrative role Mrs. Reed sought to perform. State convenience and expediency (among Idaho's defenses) fell short, Ginsburg wrote, "of a compelling state interest when appraised in light of the interest of the class against which the statute discriminates—an interest in treatment by the law *as full human personalities.*"[21] In other words, echoing Wollstonecraft and Friedan, Murray and Ginsburg argued that the law ought to treat women as "persons" regardless of any familial roles they may or may not perform, most notably in cases where reproductive differences were entirely irrelevant. Such differences had historically been used to denigrate women's rational capacities as a class; the Constitution required persons to be judged individually on their merits.

"Whatever differences may exist between the sexes, legislative judgments have frequently been based on inaccurate stereotypes of the capacities and sensibilities of women,"[22] Ginsburg noted, elevating to a legal argument the Wollstonecraftian principle that women enjoy with men a common rational capacity. In this case, Ginsburg argued, the Idaho statute simply assumed that men were better qualified than women to be administrators, without taking account of the respective qualifications or aptitudes of the individual persons involved. The statute's judgment, according to Ginsburg, rested on a "totally unfounded assumption . . . of differences in mental capacity."[23] Again, "when biological differences are not related to the activity in question, sex-based discrimination clashes with contemporary notions of fair and equal treatment."[24] In a footnote, Ginsburg quoted from Murray's 1965 article on this point: "To the degree women perform the function of motherhood, they differ from other special groups. But maternity legislation is not sex legislation: its benefits are geared to the performance of a special service much like veterans' legislation. When the law . . . regulates the conduct of women in a restrictive manner *having no bearing on the maternal function,* it disregards individuality and relegates an entire class to inferior status."[25] Separate restrooms and sleeping quarters in prisons or in the armed services were also in no jeopardy by a finding of invidious discrimination in this case, Ginsburg promised.

After quoting and referencing several state and federal courts that had recently struck down sex-based legislation as contrary to the Fourteenth Amendment, Ginsburg then tracked various historical sources that had contributed to the inferior legal station in which women still found themselves. From the founding era, through the long debates over women's suffrage, women (especially married women through coverture) were subjected to a subordinate legal and social status to men. Ginsburg then detailed this unequal treatment in the laws respectively in the family, property ownership, criminal law, and employment, referencing still-extant state laws in abundance. Noting that these laws were often passed to protect women from various harms in the workplace or elsewhere, she pointed out that even that putative justification was not at issue in the Idaho statute: "The law-sanctioned subordination of wife to husband, mother to father, woman to man, is not yet extinguished in this country."[26] This despite the fact that our fundamental law—the Constitution—expressly protects persons as equal under the law.

In November 1971, the Supreme Court unanimously, and for the first time in history, struck down the sex-based statute as unconstitutional. In an opinion written by Chief Justice Burger, the Court explained that although the Fourteenth Amendment did not "deny to States the power to treat different classes of persons in different ways," the sex-based statute at bar was "the very kind of arbitrary legislative choice forbidden by the Equal Protection Clause."[27] But the Court, *contra* Ginsburg's lead argument, did not employ the higher level of scrutiny used with racial classifications; the ordinary rational basis test was all that was necessary to determine the sex-based classification was "wholly unrelated to the objective of the statute."[28] Still, it was a major victory for Ginsburg.

Weeks later, the ACLU established the Women's Rights Project with Ginsburg at the helm, and in 1972, Columbia Law School hired her as their first tenured female professor. Until she became a federal judge in 1980, she authored dozens of articles on women and the law, and thus opened, with a handful of others, a whole new area of legal analysis and advocacy. And as an ACLU attorney, Ginsburg was intimately involved in twenty-four Supreme Court cases, nine on behalf of clients, and fifteen as an *amicus curiae* (friend of the court). To understand

Ginsburg's ultimately successful approach to sex discrimination, we now turn to a few of those cases.

Frontiero v. Richardson

In 1972, Ginsburg and the ACLU filed an amicus brief on behalf of the appellant in the case *Frontiero v. Richardson*. Military servicewoman Sharron Frontiero had been denied medical benefits and a supplemental housing allowance for her husband, a civilian. Under the federal statutes at issue, spouses of male members of the armed forces were automatically classified as "dependents," regardless of their dependent status; spouses of female members, on the other hand, were only classified as such if the member's husband was *in fact* dependent upon his wife for more than half of his support. Frontiero's lawyer allocated to Ginsburg part of the time he was allotted for oral argument. In the first of six cases she was to argue at the Supreme Court, Ginsburg sought to show that the sex-based classification at issue could not withstand constitutional scrutiny.

Repeating much of the same history of legal inequality that she had invoked in her *Reed* brief, Ginsburg's amicus brief in *Frontiero* turned to the ERA, at that time under review by the states. Ginsburg suggested that the Court need not await the states' ratification of the ERA to find for the servicewoman. Again, echoing Murray, she offered evidence that both Congress and the executive branch (through the President's Commission on the Status of Women) believed that the "appropriate construction and application" of the Fifth and Fourteenth Amendments on the part of the Court would render the ERA redundant. "Nonetheless [in passing the ERA]," Ginsburg suggested, "Congress wishes to provide further assurances so there would not be the slightest doubt that the right of men and women to equal treatment under the law would be recognized as a fundamental constitutional principle."[29] *Reed*, of course, had applied this rationale in a limited way, insofar as a straightforward application of equal protection to a sex-based statute was warranted without the ERA. And so too would the Court in *Frontiero*: eight of the justices voted to strike down the law as a violation of both due process and equal protection.

The justices, however, were divided on the standard of review required to make this determination. The plurality, led by Justice William Brennan, agreed with Ginsburg's arguments for strict scrutiny, supplied again in her *Frontiero* brief. But four other justices thought that a simple application of *Reed* governed the case: rational basis review was sufficient. Notably, Justice Lewis Powell in concurrence stated that the Court should await the passage of the ERA before determining whether sex was a suspect classification requiring strict scrutiny. Later revelations suggested that Justice Potter Stewart, who voted with Powell, believed the ERA would be ratified, but he also believed (like women's labor advocates opposed to the ERA's passage) that women might be better served by attacking only those laws that discriminated against them, letting stand those that seemed to favor them.[30]

Ginsburg, for her part, rejected concerns by labor advocates who still favored special "protective" legislation for women. She argued, and the *Frontiero* plurality quoted her on this point, that protective legislation was justified by a "romantic paternalism" that "put women not on a pedestal, but in a cage."[31] Pointing out that initial challenges under Title VII had come from blue-collar working women who sought to overcome a stratified employment system that kept them from attaining higher-paying traditionally male jobs, Ginsburg in several law review articles later pushed labor advocates to reject the "half a loaf" approach to labor legislation that privileged protection for women. Rather, she argued, they ought to fight for the "whole loaf": protective labor legislation for all workers. This was, of course, the very same line of argument that author of the ERA Alice Paul had taken in the late 1800s against labor advocate Florence Kelley. Whereas Kelley believed the "entering wedge" of woman-protective legislation would facilitate protective legislation for all workers, Paul thought single-sex protective legislation bad for women from the start.

During the Progressive era, Kelley's view had prevailed: recall that Kelley's "half a loaf" approach brought about *West Coast v. Parrish*, the 1937 case that upheld minimum wage laws for women; the whole loaf would be won the very next year in the Fair Labor Standards Act (putting "a floor under wages and a ceiling over hours" for all workers). Women on the ground, such as Kelley—and the labor advocates with whom Ginsburg debated—believed that working mothers would always require some kind of special protection.

Ginsburg was an outspoken advocate for the ERA. She believed that, given the race-centered legislative history that accompanied the passage of the Fourteenth Amendment, the sex-exclusive language in section 2 of that amendment, and the Court's stance toward equal protection as concerns women ever since, the ERA was the best means to ensure women's constitutional equality. Though her *Frontiero* brief articulated Murray's view that the equal protection clause, properly interpreted, would render the ERA superfluous, she did not support this view personally at the time. Ginsburg believed constitutional protection of women's equal rights under the law required a "boldly dynamic interpretation" of the Fourteenth Amendment, since its legislative history clearly did not supply this interpretation.[32] In this way, her view of the Fourteenth Amendment, as an original matter, differed little from Justice Antonin Scalia's, who rejected, as contrary to the original intent of the amendment's drafters, the constitutional propriety of the sex discrimination jurisprudence that Ginsburg, as an advocate, had helped to fashion.[33] The two just differed as to the Court's authority to interpret the Constitution in a way that contradicted the framers' original intent.

Given that the ERA was not ratified (more about this in chapter 8), originalist scholars in favor of the Court's sex discrimination jurisprudence have sought in recent years to justify that jurisprudence on originalist grounds. Law professors Steven Calabresi and Julia Rickett, for instance, suggest that the Fourteenth Amendment was intended generally to ban caste, and that, since the Nineteenth Amendment afforded women the right to vote, their status as members of a "subordinate caste" had been abrogated.[34] Echoing the sentiment of Justice Sutherland in the 1923 *Adkins* case, these scholars argue that the Nineteenth Amendment should be read back into the Fourteenth Amendment such that women—post-1920—were now under its purview.[35] But a more straightforward textual reading of section 1 of the Fourteenth Amendment—Pauli Murray's reading—is still plainly available. As law professor Michael Stokes Paulsen has argued, the text as written promises equal protection of the laws to "persons," and women, both in 1868 and today, are clearly persons.[36] Accordingly, women ought properly to be provided "equal protection of the laws."

By 1976, without the intervention of the ERA, the Court settled on a new intermediate level of scrutiny for sex-based statutes. Ginsburg's position was partially vindicated. In *Frontiero*, Ginsburg herself had suggested, as an alternative to strict scrutiny, that an "intermediate" level of scrutiny could be applied. Such a rendering shifted the burden of proof to the state, which would need to show that a sex-based classification was necessary to accomplish, in Ginsburg's words, "legitimate" governmental objectives. Although *Frontiero* was ultimately decided without reaching the appropriate level of scrutiny, in *Craig v. Boren*, the Court finally made such a determination, utilizing Ginsburg's "intermediate test" for sex-based statutes.[37]

Given the biological differences between the sexes, plainly differentiating sex from race in some cases, intermediate scrutiny seems an apt place for the Court to land. This determination theoretically keeps the Court from insisting on a strict legal equality that would strip all recognition of biological differences from the law. This allows, for instance, for legislation that compensates for past discrimination of women or that takes account of the asymmetrical conditions of men and women in pregnancy and childbearing. The Court has left, as Ginsburg put it, a legislative "corridor in which to move."[38]

RBG's Normative Approach to Sex Discrimination

Ginsburg's litigation strategy in the 1970s was not limited to securing equal protection for women. Rather, in two of the very first cases she took on (detailed below), she represented male litigants. These cases are especially illuminative of her normative (and ultimately successful) approach to sex discrimination, one that sought to eliminate "sex role stereotyping" from the law. Ginsburg well maintained that sex ought not to be used as a proxy for dependency, need, or merit, as *Reed*, *Frontiero*, and other early cases showed, but she also argued more generally that sex ought not be used to confine individuals to preordained social or familial roles. Ginsburg sought, in particular, to dislodge the legal assumption that men would necessarily be breadwinners and women caregivers. She did not suggest that spousal dependency was wrong in itself, nor did she dispute that individuals could and would continue to

make choices (such as that of homemaking) that rendered them economically dependent. Rather, she argued that government could not
constitutionally use sex-based laws to enforce such spousal dependency,
therefore ascribing social and familial roles for all individuals, regardless
of their circumstances, capacities, or preferences.

Reminiscing about these cases in 1978, Ginsburg wrote: "The
1971–1975 challengers in *Reed, Frontiero*, . . . *Wiesenfeld* [among oth-
ers] contended against gross assumptions that females are concerned
primarily with 'the home and the rearing of the family,' males, with 'the
marketplace and the world of ideas.' They did not assert that these propo-
sitions were inaccurate descriptions for the generality of cases. But
they questioned treatment of the growing numbers of men and women
who do not fit the stereotype as if they did and the fairness of gender
pigeonholing in lieu of neutral, functional description."[39] Like NOW's
original 1966 statement, Ginsburg hoped that by freeing both women
and men from legally determined familial and social roles, the law
might open the way for better collaboration between men and women
in the family and in the workplace. Quoting Susan B. Anthony in one
publication, Ginsburg echoed Wollstonecraft's hope: "The woman . . .
will be the peer of man. In education, in art, in science, in literature; in
the home, the church, the state; everywhere she will be acknowledged
equal, though not identical with him."[40]

Even as Ginsburg did not think it would apply universally, she
herself favored economic interdependence among the married couple
over assumed dependence of the wife upon the husband. This normative view of shared familial and civic obligations is the reason Ginsburg
opposed the high court's 1961 jury decision in *Hoyt*: as responsible citizens in society, Ginsburg thought women too ought to be obligated,
like men, to fulfill civic obligations such as jury service. Indeed, this argument in favor of obligating women with civic duties was one suffragists often employed, and, for both the suffragists and Ginsburg, it inspired many to question whether they supported the military draft for
women too. If men's familial roles as husbands and fathers did not keep
them from jury service, then neither should women's familial responsibilities; better to make such determinations on an individuated basis.
The Court overturned *Hoyt* in 1975.[41]

The first federal case Ginsburg brought was on behalf of a man with caregiving responsibilities. In *Moritz v. Commissioner*, Ginsburg and her tax attorney husband, Marty, brought suit together on behalf of Charles Moritz, a lifelong bachelor who was caring for his elderly mother. The Internal Revenue Code then allowed single women but not single men to claim a modest tax deduction for the cost of providing care to dependents. Although the Moritz litigation began even before Ginsburg filed her brief in *Reed*, the Court of Appeals for the Tenth Circuit decided *Moritz* months after *Reed* in 1972, striking down for the first time a sex-based provision in the U.S. tax code. Then, in 1974, Ginsburg tried what she always remembered as her favorite case, *Weinberger v. Wiesenfeld*. Her client, Stephen Wiesenfeld, was a widower whose wife, a schoolteacher, had died in childbirth. He applied for survivor benefits from his wife's Social Security, in the hopes of devoting himself to raising their newborn son. Although his wife had contributed to Social Security on the same basis as a male individual, her husband-survivor received fewer benefits than those that would have been paid out to a wife-survivor of a husband-breadwinner. Just as per the statute in *Frontiero*, a widow automatically received survivor benefits upon her husband's death, whereas a widower had to prove he was dependent on his wife's earnings. Unable to do this to the law's satisfaction, but also unable to find adequate care for his son so he could work to provide for him, Wiesenfeld sued.

A unanimous Court, once again, struck down the provision, holding that the statute could not be explained as an allowable compensatory benefit to women for past discrimination; rather, the purpose of the statute was to enable a surviving spouse to care properly for the child. Recalling the *Wiesenfeld* case, Ginsburg later said: "This is my dream for society. . . . Fathers loving and caring for and helping to raise their kids."[42] Such paternal engagement had been her own childhood experience and that within her marriage too. Her beloved husband, Marty, was not only deeply devoted to his wife and her career; he was fully engaged in the lives of their children, and was—famously—the family's talented cook.

In her brief in *Wiesenfeld*, Ginsburg quoted favorably a decision of the Commission on Railroad Retirement concerning survivorship

benefits that further illuminates her view. The *Wiesenfeld* Court included the same explanatory quote in its own footnote:

> Statistically speaking, there are, of course, significant differences
> by sex in the roles played in our society. For example, far more
> women than men are primarily involved in raising minor children.
> But if the society's aim is to further a socially desirable purpose,
> e.g., better care for growing children, it should tailor any subsidy
> directly to the end desired, not indirectly and unequally by helping
> widows with dependent children and ignoring widowers in the
> same plight. In this example, it is the economic and *functional* ca-
> pability of the surviving breadwinner to care for children which
> counts; the sex of the surviving parent is incidental.[43]

Ginsburg, like Murray before her, sought to distinguish legally the *female sex* from the caregiving *function* that women had traditionally
performed. If women's sex and the caregiving function were not inextricably linked, the law ought not pigeonhole women into this function, nor create obstacles for men to perform it too.

Said differently, though it can be affirmed that women still disproportionately engage in caregiving as mothers in their families (and in
the "care" professions too), it can also be said that the caregiving function is not exclusively tied to *womanhood* as though men are incapable
of giving care too. To push the point one step further, it is also true to
say that caregiving is not exclusively tied to *motherhood* (which *is*, as
explored briefly below and elsewhere, exclusively tied to womanhood). That is to say, men, *as fathers*, can (and should) also give care.
Murray had believed that the best way to elevate the function of caregiving, and homemaking too, was to disentangle it from the gendered
exchange made in the postwar family, an exchange that had become in
some cases undesirable and in still others financially impossible. Indeed, according to Murray, the caregiving "function" was too important to children's well-being to deem it the responsibility of only the
female sex: it is, properly, the *function of the family as a whole* (distributed as the couple sees fit), and *it should be legally and culturally protected as such*. Murray detailed this view in her recommendations to
the President's Commission, and here again in her *George Washington*

Law Review article: "What is needed to remove the present ambiguity of women's legal status is a shift of emphasis from women's class attributes (sex per se) to their functional attributes. The boundaries between *social policies that are genuinely protective of the familial and maternal functions and those that unjustly discriminate against women as individuals* must be delineated."[44]

The distinction that unfolded in Murray's view was between individual women (traditionally—and problematically—assumed by the law to be always and everywhere "potential mothers") and actual mothers (and, today, fathers) who perform the culturally essential and intrinsically valuable function of caregiving in the family. From Murray's article:

> If laws classifying persons by sex were prohibited by the Constitution, and if it were made clear that laws recognizing functions, *if performed*, are not based on sex per se, much of the confusion as to the legal status of women would be eliminated. Moreover, this may be the only way to give adequate recognition to women who are mothers and homemakers and who do not work outside the home—it recognizes the intrinsic value of child care and homemaking. The assumption that financial support of a family by the husband-father is a gift from the male sex to the female sex and, in return, the male is entitled to preference in the outside world is all too common. Underlying this assumption is the unwillingness to acknowledge any value for child care and homemaking because they have not been ascribed a dollar value.[45]

The key point here is not only that individual women ought to be protected by law as "persons" rather than only as members of families. Murray's further point is that the function of caregiving in the family is an essential one, whether performed by a mother or father—and that, as such, it deserves cultural privilege and protection.

Yet, though it is true to say, with Murray and Ginsburg, that *caregiving* and *breadwinning* can be interchangeable functions within the family, undertaken by men and women in a variety of ways today, it does not follow that *motherhood* and *fatherhood* themselves are merely *functions*, or interchangeable familial roles that women and men merely *perform* or *play*.[46] Rather, motherhood and fatherhood are exclusive and constitutive biological relations that women and men, respectively, have with their children. The reality of adoption complicates the picture, but it does not obscure the biological basis of motherhood and fatherhood. Further, maintaining this view in no way contradicts the legal approach to sex discrimination taken by Murray, Ginsburg, and, with their influence, the Supreme Court that decouples familial caregiving and breadwinning functions as legally tied to women and men, respectively.

Some have criticized Ginsburg's antistereotyping sex discrimination jurisprudence as too insistent on formal equality, and thus not disruptive enough of public or workplace institutions designed around men, who were traditionally (and sometimes today) unencumbered by caregiving. This critique is, in my view, inapt with regard to the cases reviewed thus far that do not involve reproductive differences between men and women. I will return with gusto to this critique in the next chapters, however, when our attention turns precisely to those differences. Putting aside that fraught issue for now, Ginsburg's high court advocacy in the early 1970s rightly sought, in her words, "to unsettle previously accepted conceptions of men's and women's separate spheres."[47] In her view, unsettling this highly gendered, legally restrictive relationship between market work and family work would potentially open up political efforts to advance women's position in the workplace, while also helping men to better appreciate their invaluable contribution in the family, beyond dollars and cents. As Ginsburg wrote in 1986, quoting a friend: "Human caring and concern, for home, children, and the welfare of others, ought not to be regarded as dominantly 'women's work,' it should become the work of all."[48] But, as we detail in chapter 8, Ginsburg's ardent abortion advocacy, deeply in tension with her normative goal to support women and men's shared task of caregiving, undercut these most praiseworthy aims.

GINSBURG TO THE BENCH

In 1980, President Carter nominated and the Senate confirmed Ginsburg to a seat on the DC Circuit Court of Appeals. In 1993, she became the second woman, after Justice Sandra Day O'Connor, appointed to serve on the U.S. Supreme Court. Over the course of her tenure on both the appellate and high court, she heard dozens of sex discrimination cases, often authoring opinions on the appellate court, but mostly filing dissents on the Supreme Court. Her most notable dissent, read from the bench in the 2007 case *Ledbetter v. Goodyear Tire & Rubber Co.*, garnered immediate attention from Congress, which, with President Obama, passed the Lilly Ledbetter Fair Pay Act two years later.

But no opinion would be more important in fully articulating her signature antisex stereotyping rationale than *United States v. Virginia* (1996), popularly known as the VMI case. Chief Justice Rehnquist, the lone dissenting justice in *Reed* and one who frequently voted against sex discrimination claimants, tasked Ginsburg with writing the majority opinion in VMI. (Rehnquist, for his part, wrote a separate concurrence, employing different reasoning while agreeing with the Court's outcome.) Unlike the cases we have reviewed in this chapter so far, wherein the sex-based statutes at bar did not chiefly concern reproductive differences between men and women, and unlike the pregnancy cases in which they did, VMI fell somewhere in between. Reproductive differences were not at issue, but differences of physical strength and speed were. More central though, from the Court's perspective, were what we tend now to refer to as "gender differences."

The question, as articulated in the majority opinion by Ginsburg, was whether the state of Virginia could exclude women from a state-funded military academy whose teaching methods were based on generalizations about the way men and women best learn. As we have seen, states could no longer constitutionally use sex as a proxy for need, dependency, or merit, but could the state use sex as a proxy for the kind of learner a student is? In 1990, a female high school student sought admission to VMI, a 150-year-old military academy that at that time enrolled 1,300 men as cadets each year. Virginia's only remaining single-sex public institution for higher education, VMI's distinctive mission was to produce "citizen-soldiers" prepared for leadership in either civilian life or military service. The academy boasted a successful record of national leaders and a strong alumni network. In the two years prior to the case, the academy had fielded 347 inquiries from women who sought (and had been denied) admission to the highly reputable program. The United States sued on behalf of these women.

Importantly, VMI made use of a rigorous and competitive "adversative method" meant to imbue in the male students physical and mental discipline and strong moral character. The Commonwealth of Virginia argued that the single-sex school offered diversity to the educational options available in the state; more important still, Virginia argued that the academy's unique and effective method of teaching would need to be altered if women were admitted, since the program was specially designed for men. To this end, the Commonwealth brought forth expert witnesses that offered evidence of male and female pedagogical differences: males tended to thrive in an atmosphere of physical and emotional "adversativeness," whereas most females preferred a more cooperative learning atmosphere. The Commonwealth argued that these "tendencies" were based on "important differences between men and women in learning and developmental needs." They were "real" sex differences, not mere stereotypes. Granting that "some women" may do well under the adversative model, Virginia maintained that education ought to be designed around the rule, not the exception.

Delivering the opinion for five other justices in the majority, Ginsburg explained that the Commonwealth had a demanding burden of justification for making a classification based on sex. Articulating the intermediate standard of review for sex discrimination cases with use of a term that had been used once before in a 1982 case disallowing an all-women's nursing college from excluding a duly qualified man, Ginsburg detailed that the state's proffered justification for the sex-based classification must be "exceedingly persuasive" and must not "rely on overbroad generalizations about the different talents, capacities, and preferences of males and females."[49] This most stringent articulation of the intermediate standard of review usually employed in sex discrimination cases was one of Justice Scalia's main critiques in dissent; it was also the reason Rehnquist did not join Ginsburg's majority opinion even as he agreed with the outcome.

The Court found that "neither the goal of producing citizen-soldiers nor VMI's implementing methodology is inherently unsuitable for women."[50] Ginsburg explained that although it is likely true that most women might not prefer the academy's adversative method of instruction, most men would not either; furthermore, some women might prefer the academy's teaching method to one institutionalized at a women's college. The proper distinction for the academy to make, according to Ginsburg, ought not to be based on the applicant's sex but on her physical and mental acumen, even if, by the numbers, far fewer women than men would be interested in (and capable of succeeding in) the militaristic approach. "Generalizations about 'the way women are,' estimates of what is appropriate *for most women*, no longer justify denying opportunity to women whose talent and capacity place them outside the average description," she said.[51] Ginsburg went on to write that such legal restrictions deny women "full citizenship stature," which she defined as the "equal opportunity to aspire, achieve, participate in and contribute to society based on . . . individual talents and capacities."[52]

Writing alone in dissent, Justice Scalia suggested that Ginsburg's use of the term "exceedingly persuasive" had the ill effect of transforming the standard of review in the sex discrimination case from intermediate to strict scrutiny, that standard reserved for cases concerning race. Commentators for and against the holding have suggested the same: the justice accomplished on the bench what she had failed to accomplish as an advocate. But though Ginsburg may well have adjusted the standard of review to achieve her aim, the VMI opinion does not treat sex classifications just as the Court treats racial classifications. As Ginsburg clearly states, "sex [is not] a proscribed classification," whereas race is. More still, she writes, although "supposed 'inherent differences' are no longer accepted as a ground for race or national origin classifications . . . [p]hysical differences between men and women . . . are enduring: the two sexes are not fungible."[53] She then fleshed out the difference further, and in doing so distinguished licit from illicit use of sex distinctions in the law: " 'Inherent differences' between men and women, we have come to appreciate, remain cause for celebration, but not for denigration of the members of either sex or for artificial constraints on an individual's opportunity. Sex classifications may be used to compensate women 'for particular economic disabilities [they have] suffered,' to 'promot[e] equal employment opportunity,' to advance full development of the talent and capacities of our Nation's people. But such classifications may not be used, as they once were, to create or perpetuate the legal, social, and economic inferiority of women."[54] Sex classifications may be used to *compensate* and *advance* women, but *not to denigrate* them.

Ginsburg here included a footnote in which she suggested that the mission of some single-sex schools was, indeed, to "dissipate, rather than perpetuate, traditional gender classifications."[55] Thus, the mere existence of single-sex schools was not at issue in this case. Wide-ranging research on single-sex education indicates her statement to be true: single-sex education can break down gender stereotypes in education by recognizing that boys and girls *do tend* to learn differently.[56] The problem in the VMI case was thus not the suggestion that gender differences may indeed exist, as tendencies, in learning; in fact, the United States did not challenge Virginia's expert witnesses in this regard. The problem was that the unique, state-funded program excluded those individuals "whose talent and capacity place them outside the average description"—and for whom no adequate alternatives existed.[57]

Ginsburg had explained her view of gender differences four years before during a 1992 commencement address she and her husband delivered together at Northwestern School of Law: "Theoretical discussions are ongoing today—particularly in academic circles—about differences in the voices women and men hear, or in their moral perceptions. When asked about such things, I abstain or fudge. Generalizations about the way women or men are, my life's experience bears out, cannot guide me reliably in making decisions about particular individuals."[58] Elsewhere, she asked: "Accepting the truth of the thesis generally, or 'on the average,' how should I act on it?"[59] The key for Ginsburg was that sex-based generalizations, even if statistically significant and therefore culturally salient, *ought not legally deny a particular individual* from enjoying an opportunity most in her group would or could not.

This view that applauds the distinctive talents, interests, or capacities of unique individuals even while accepting the reality of generalized gender differences across the class is reminiscent of the view of Dorothy Sayers: "What is repugnant to every human being is to be reckoned always as a member of a class and not as an individual person. A certain amount of classification is, of course, necessary for practical purposes: there is no harm in saying that women, as a class, have smaller bones than men . . . have more hair on their heads and less on their faces. . . .

What is unreasonable and irritating is to assume that *all* one's tastes and preferences have to be conditioned by the class to which one belongs."[60] Sayers continues: "'Why should women want to know about Aristotle?' The answer is NOT that *all* women would be the better for knowing about Aristotle . . . but simply: 'What women want as a class is irrelevant.' *I* want to know about Aristotle. . . . I submit that there is nothing in my shape or bodily functions which need prevent my knowing about him."[61]

Thus, this is not to argue that, if given the opportunity, all women would want to be educated in the sort of environment VMI provides; it is to argue that should an individual woman have the capacity to do so—and, crucially, no other adequate alternatives are open to her—she ought not be legally excluded from a program funded by taxpayers. If this were all this case were about, perhaps the Court's resolution of it would not have been so controversial.[62] But, in point of fact, VMI was not only about gender differences as articulated thus far. It was also about biological differences between men and women that are particularly important in the military arena: differences in physical strength and capacity. Notably, this was the difference that Wollstonecraft said gave men greater familial and social responsibilities, even as she demanded that women strengthen their bodies, alongside their minds, to allow the former "to acquire [their] full vigor."[63]

Virginia argued and the district court found that, were women admitted, the academy would have to alter the physical standards required of female cadets, in addition to making new allowances for personal privacy. Crucially, VMI also would need to change the adversative teaching method itself, which the court of appeals noted "would be materially affected by coeducation."[64] Therefore, physiological, but not reproductive, differences did play a role here. These differences were not *artificial*, nor did stating their existence itself *denigrate* women. Thus, unlike the *arbitrary* height and weight requirements the Court had struck down in 1977 as contrary to Title VII, the Court may have overstepped its constitutional authority by requiring VMI to change its own physical standards and very method of instruction in order to admit women, in light of strong justification to the contrary. Ginsburg notes in two footnotes in her opinion that these same worries were

forecasted when women were admitted to the federal military academies, and that "experience shows such adjustments are manageable."[65]
And yet, as Scalia argues in dissent, West Point, the Naval Academy,
and the Air Force Academy were not forced by the Court's interpretation of "ambiguous constitutional texts" to admit women "but because
the people, through their elected representatives, decreed a change."[66]

More than twenty years after the VMI case, women in the military
are still given different sets of physical standards for their semiannual
fitness tests, but they are otherwise expected to perform identical duties to men during training and other unit-level challenges. The army is
currently experimenting with dropping the sex-based fitness test standards and moving instead to standards based on the needs of the service member's particular job. Some training schools, such as the U.S.
Army Ranger School, already require those who attend—male or
female—to meet the preestablished physical standards. If a uniquely
strong and agile woman is capable of meeting the rigorous physical requirements (originally dictated for men), she lands the post. According
to Sarah White, assistant professor at West Point, "Even if [women] are
institutionally tested on a different standard . . . many of us still internally hold ourselves to a higher, more male-influenced standard of
physical performance."

However, there are "real" differences in the experience of men and
women in the military, well beyond the natural physical advantage most
men have over most women in fitness tests. White continues, "Having
children . . . is a much more professionally consequential decision for
women than it is for men—not because the Army isn't supportive of
pregnancy, but because pregnancy has a naturally greater impact on a
woman's ability to do physical training, go to the field, deploy, etc. . . .
[an] impact [that would] only be exacerbated in the combat arms
branches, which are necessarily averse to any type of physical limitation, and which value one's ability to 'fight' as the highest measure."[67]

It is to these reproductive differences that we now turn.

CHAPTER 8

Caring for Dependency in
the Logic of the Market

In briefs before the courts and within academic journals in the 1960s
and 70s, Pauli Murray, Ruth Bader Ginsburg, and other women's rights
advocates took pains to differentiate between women as individual
persons—to be judged on their merits as such and protected equally
under the law—and women as mothers (or, in Murray's and Ginsburg's
words, the "biological function of motherhood"). In chapter 7 we described how Murray, Ginsburg, and other women's advocates worked
to upend those laws and regulations that discriminated against women
as individuals, when reproductive differences were irrelevant to the activity in question. Those cases were the easy cases. This chapter and the
next explore the far more difficult legal task of treating women and
men equally under the law while giving due accord to their biological
and reproductive differences. On Ginsburg's account, differences between men and women need not be ignored; indeed, as she finally articulated from the bench in 1996, biological differences "remain cause
for celebration." The key legal distinction, according to *United States
v. Virginia* (1996), the VMI case (discussed in the last chapter), is that
sex classifications be used only to "compensate" for disabilities women
have suffered or to "advance" equal opportunity; they may not be employed to denigrate women, or "to create or perpetuate the legal, social,
and economic inferiority of women."

The long-standing historical responses to reproductive asymmetry, such as separate public and private spheres (discussed in chapters 3 and 4) and large-scale protective legislation for women workers (discussed in chapter 5), have been culturally, economically, and legally undermined (as chapters 6 and 7 explored). With the proper recognition of women's contribution to the public sphere and men's to the private sphere, contemporary responses to the asymmetrical nature of reproduction remain fraught. How might women be treated with equity in both the public and private spheres while doing justice to the fact that they may become pregnant, but men cannot?

The women's movement of the 1970s and 80s debated internally (and sometimes in competing briefs to the Court) how to reconcile sexual equality with reproductive difference, especially in the workplace, but also in the home. Yet, newly erected contemporaneously with this debate was an altogether novel foundation for the "second wave" of the women's movement, one that turned the previous, Wollstonecraftian foundation squarely on its head. On November 18, 1967, NOW became the first women's rights organization to advocate for the repeal of state abortion laws adopted in the nineteenth century. And abortion rights have remained the *sine qua non* of the modern-day women's movement ever since: the privileged response to the reproductive asymmetries between men and women. The story of how this came to be, in light of the nineteenth century's opposition to the practice, is the subject of this chapter. Whether this turn of events can be reconciled with the long line of women's rights advocacy before it, and with the development of sex discrimination law contemporaneous with it, is another question this chapter seeks to explore.

CONTROLLING WOMEN'S FERTILITY

Women in almost all times and places have sought to regulate their fertility. The strength of that desire, and means to do so, have differed in time and place depending on economic circumstances, social custom, moral and religious belief, and scientific and technological advances.[1] But the impetus to lessen the often burdensome (and at times physically dangerous or even fatal) effect childbearing can have on a woman and a large number of children can have upon a family has always existed. An all-too-brief history of this phenomenon will put into context the stark shift in viewpoint in the mid-twentieth century.

Infanticide, or the exposure of especially female (or otherwise imperfect) infants, was practiced legally in ancient times but grew increasingly illicit as Christianity advanced in the Western world.[2] Still, infanticide remained prevalent, especially among the poor, even as each society outlawed it.[3] Seeming to justify the practice against these prohibitions, seventeenth-century theorist Thomas Hobbes wrote that, in the state of nature, women, as equals of men in the pursuit of self-preservation, possessed an absolute dominion over their infant children, a dominion that exceeded that of men and extended to infanticide.[4] Yet other prominent Enlightenment thinkers wrote of the natural and civil duties parents had toward their offspring, vulnerable human beings whose very lives they had "[brought] into existence."[5]

Before the nineteenth century, when surgical abortion had become more widespread, abortion methods were relatively ineffective; those that were effective were often also very dangerous, or even fatal, to the mother. And early abortion was often conflated with primitive contraceptive methods (a result of errors concerning the timing of conception and the length of gestation). According to political scientist Rosalind Pollack Petchesky in *Abortion and Woman's Choice*, "Women in preindustrial Europe do not seem to have drawn any sharp distinction between 'potions' that intervened before or after conception, since conception (as opposed to 'animation') had no special meaning. In England and America prior to the mid-nineteenth century, pregnancy as a biological event was not thought to begin until 'quickening,' at which time there was a 'child.' Before that, a woman was 'irregular'; herbal potions and purgatives, hot baths, or vigorous jumping were natural, not medical, strategies to make her 'regular' again."[6]

As scientific advances in the nineteenth century better revealed the nascent human being in utero, U.S. state legislatures took greater notice of the increasingly common practice of abortion and prohibited it throughout pregnancy, except when the pregnant woman's life (or sometimes health) was at risk. Speaking for the consensus in the medical community at the time, the American Medical Association (AMA) referred to abortion in 1857 as an "unwarrantable destruction of human life."[7] Until the mid-twentieth century, women's rights advocates opposed infanticide and abortion, often speaking of the two together; most also disapproved of contraception. Remember how Mary Wollstonecraft lamented the desperate circumstances of those women who found it necessary to "destroy the embryo in the womb, or cast it off when born," scolding the irresponsible men who left women in such situations, and strongly advocated breastfeeding for the spacing of children. Recall from chapter 4 that women's rights leaders in the nineteenth century promoted "voluntary motherhood" through periodic sexual abstinence. They argued that invasive birth control methods ("washes, teas, tonics and various sorts of appliances"[8]) would facilitate the decoupling of sex and marriage, unleash men's undisciplined sexual desire, and therefore be exploitative to women.

Birth Control Pioneer, Margaret Sanger

At the start of the twentieth century, views on the merits of contraception began to change. Inspired by both the mid-to-late nineteenth and early twentieth-century "free love" and eugenics movements, Margaret Sanger became the single most successful advocate of "birth control," a term she herself helped to coin. After procuring the latest innovations in contraceptive methods in Europe—and with the financial backing of influential donors and foundations—Sanger launched the first birth control clinic in the United States in 1916, the organizational predecessor to Planned Parenthood Federation of America.

Notably, Sanger did not rely on feminist arguments for birth control as she gained traction, but they were employed at the outset of her career.[9] And although early on the wealthy were the most likely to acquire contraception from her clinics, the target clientele was not the well-off. Rather, the birth control pioneers of the early twentieth century sought specially to encourage its use among the poor and otherwise "unfit" or "defective."[10] Indeed, Sanger sought to contend with what she regarded as the scourge of "overpopulation," especially among irresponsible "breeders" both in the United States and among the underdeveloped areas of the world.[11] If Wollstonecraft saw the "grand source" of women's immiseration in vicious men's want of chastity, Sanger laid the blame squarely on women's fertility instead. In 1920, she wrote,

FIGURE 8.1. Margaret Sanger, 1922.
Credit: Library of Congress (public domain).

"As [woman] has unconsciously and ignorantly brought about so-cial disaster, so must and will she consciously and intelligently *undo* that disaster and create a new and better order. The task is hers. It cannot be avoided by excuses, nor can it be delegated."[12] Contraception was promoted as a woman's duty well before it was understood to be her right.[13]

Coercive measures were not far behind, and they grew increasingly popular among the American public.[14] Eugenics became official U.S. policy when in 1927 the Supreme Court permitted forced sterilization in *Buck v. Bell*. Never expressly overturned, *Buck v. Bell* enabled states to sterilize more than 60,000 people between 1927 and the late 1960s.[15] Over time, the birth control movement Sanger initiated increasingly became mainstream. It won acceptance among upper- and middle-class Protestants, with the Anglican Communion the first to loosen previous strictures on birth control in 1930. In 1943, 85 percent of Americans believed that married women should be able to access birth control; by 1947, 98 percent of American doctors endorsed birth control for health reasons, and 79 percent in cases of financial distress.[16]

In 1950, Sanger procured $2 million from an individual donor to fund research for the first hormonal contraceptive. In 1960 (after initial clinical trials on uninformed and nonconsenting psychiatric patients; larger studies on women in Puerto Rico and Haiti; complaints of racism, eugenic intent, and myriad side effects; and finally, adjustments to the original admixture of hormones) the FDA approved the birth control pill for sale in the United States.[17] Though the main impetus for the development of the pill lay in its potential to control population growth both at home and abroad, the demand among women in the United States fast-tracked its approval by the FDA. By late 1959, half a million American women were already using the pill, and in 1967, American women consumed more than half of the world's hormonal contraceptives.[18] Meanwhile, Sanger's eugenic efforts for population control among the poor paid off in the United States too. The U.S. government weaved funding for birth control into its War on Poverty in the mid-1960s: the federal government required state welfare agencies to provide family planning services to women receiving public aid and attached it to its overseas funding.[19] Not surprisingly, the historic connection between eugenics and birth control seems still to beset some minority communities to this day.[20]

Sanger's own advocacy for contraception, and so too the founding mission of Planned Parenthood, did not extend overtly to abortion. The clinic's first handbill read: "Do not kill, do not take life, but prevent."[21] Indeed, her early campaign among doctors eventually succeeded in part

because she argued that contraception use would reduce the need desperate women felt to procure dangerous abortions by illegal means.
By 1964, Planned Parenthood was still making the same sort of pro-
contraception, anti-abortion argument. A pamphlet from the clinic announced: "An abortion kills the life of a baby after it has begun. It is
dangerous to your life and health."[22] And yet, the contraceptive project
Sanger instigated would transform itself, within a half century, into full-
fledged advocacy for "abortion on demand," and by 2015, abortion advocates would come to "shout" their abortions.[23] Early on in her career
to promote birth control, Sanger had written: "Enforced motherhood
is the most complete denial of a woman's right to life and liberty."[24]
Sanger's early words in support of contraception but not abortion—
wholly transforming nineteenth-century advocacy for a "voluntary
motherhood" that opposed both—prepared the way for this reshaped
principle to take on a new cast altogether.

ABORTION LEGALIZED: FROM POPULATION CONTROL TO WOMEN'S RIGHTS

By the late 1950s, the Sanger-influenced, but still male-dominated,
population control movement was funded almost exclusively by elite
organizations, such as the Rockefeller Foundation. Newly inspired
by the 1954 publication of Hugh Moore's pamphlet, "The Population
Bomb," the population controllers advocated both birth control and
sterilization.[25] Most did not yet publicly advocate abortion. They too
believed that prophylactic methods would both decrease the threat
of overpopulation (especially among the poor) and make abortion unnecessary. Yet, something somewhat unanticipated happened. The
concern about overpopulation and unsafe abortion had initially inspired the research and development of the pill, but the pill's widespread usage seemed in practice to stimulate a profound change in sexual
behavior, dramatically increasing sexual activity within but even more
so outside of marriage. With this increase in nonmarital sexual activity
came a spike in the nonmarital birth rate, and thus a growing demand
for abortion.[26]

Though more effective than its contraceptive peers, the fanfare surrounding the release of the "magic pill" seemed to have promised too
much: no method of birth control (save abstinence) was 100 percent effective in preventing pregnancy. Still, according to political scientist
Petchesky, the growing confidence in the contraception revolution ac-
tivated in American women a new hope for "reproductive control." It
served as a "catalyst" for rising expectations, Petchesky says, even if the
contraceptive methods on offer did not themselves entirely meet those
expectations.[27] Reflecting on why contraception use and abortion rates
rose together in the 1970s, Petchesky offers this searching analysis: "A
uniquely effective, but not foolproof, method of contraception had
been developed, distributed, and absorbed into popular practice on an
unprecedented scale. What was the impact of the pill and the 'pill culture' on rising abortion rates? To what extent did the reality and 'aura'
of the pill . . . create changed expectations about reliable fertility control that helped also to legitimate abortion? . . . [T]o what extent did
the pill's failure to meet these expectations directly increase the need
for abortion?"[28]

With the rise in cultural expectations born of the pill, having an
unplanned pregnancy had become, in some social circles, "unthink-
able" (in Petchesky's words), even if such an expectation (given the
failure rates for typical, or even perfect, usage) was misplaced. In these
circumstances, as greater numbers of women endured single motherhood, other women began to regard abortion as the necessary response
to unplanned pregnancy, even as it still remained illegal, and sometimes
dangerous. Petchesky further suggests that with the inherent flaws and
side effects in the various contraceptive methods, abortion began to be
regarded by some, not only as a necessary response to failed or misused
contraception, but even as a better solution, in some cases. After all,
medically speaking, the more effective the hormonal contraceptive, the
more likely it was to cause both daily discomfort and long-term health
risks.[29] Linda Gordon puts the point thus: "The mid-twentieth-century gangbusters approach to technological development [of contraceptive methods]" fueled both by women's demand and the "scramble
of multinational pharmaceutical companies" looking to make a profit,
led to lack of concern among these companies to consider the consequences to women's long-term health and short-term discomfort.[30]

The often unseemly side effects caused women to use their contraceptives inconsistently or to abandon them altogether, and thus produce the very consequence the methods promised to prevent.

Initially considered a laudatory means to reduce or prevent abortions, then, the birth control pill, in actual practice, seems to have helped drive greater demand for abortion in the late 1960s and early 70s. And that increased demand inspired a growing number of doctors to suggest, as a handful had during the Great Depression as illegal abortions and maternal deaths rose, that public health demanded doctors be allowed to perform abortions without losing their licenses.[31] The force of eugenic arguments for abortion also gained more currency as the nonmarital birth rate climbed among more disadvantaged (and nonwhite) populations, also an ironic result of the overall increase in nonmarital sex inspired by the pill.[32]

Thus, though the population control movement had initially worked under the assumption that birth control would render abortion unnecessary, in the late 1960s and early 1970s, the movement began to change course. Paul Ehrlich's best-selling, if alarmist, *The Population Bomb* (1968) argued that abortion would be "a highly effective weapon in the armory of population control," and would free humanity from a "sexually repressive" society.[33] One early abortion advocacy handbook read: "The population explosion compels us to take every measure necessary to curb our growth rate" and thus "since contraception . . . seems insufficient to reduce fertility to the point of our growth, we should permit all voluntary means of birth control (including abortion)."[34]

Longtime chairman of the Population Council and founding chairman of President Nixon's Commission on Population Growth and the American Future, John D. Rockefeller III summarized the growing justification for the movement to reform abortion law in a 1968 speech. In light of the increasing illegal abortion rate, Rockefeller said, the near prohibition of abortion now threatened "disrespect for the law." Then restrictive state abortion laws ought to be reformed, he said, so that "duly licensed physicians" could best ascertain the required "mental health criteria" for "therapeutic" abortions. Finally, Rockefeller echoed a sentiment popular among abortion advocates: that the "unwanted child" should not have to live a life without "dignity and self-fulfillment"—better to have no life at all.[35]

In March 1972, just when Justice Harry Blackmun was drafting his opinion for *Roe v. Wade*, the Commission on Population Growth released the "Rockefeller Report." The report endorsed the repeal of all abortion laws as a population control, antipoverty, and public health measure. Although by then women's rights arguments for abortion had surfaced too, most population control activists were still unconvinced of either the merit or the utility of these arguments for the abortion cause.[36]

Population Controllers Meet the "Second Wave" Feminists

Concurrent with the release of the pill in the early 1960s was the growing desire among American women for higher education and market work. Industrialization and war had moved women into the workforce at greater rates than ever before, and though the postwar "baby boom" period saw these rates stall for a time among married women, their labor participation rates exploded from the 1960s through the 1980s. Granted, even as their workplace participation rose from 26 percent in 1950 to 67 percent in the mid-1980s, only a quarter of married women worked full-time.

With the arrival of the pill, many women believed they now could control their fertility with far greater efficacy than ever before, and thus reach higher in education and in the workplace. Their confidence was not unfounded: prominent studies have shown that the pill, alongside antidiscrimination policy, powered the rise of educated women in the professions.[37]

But if elite women were the "winners" of the new contraceptive revolution, more disadvantaged women seem perhaps to have been the revolution's "losers."[38] More privileged women were delaying marriage and childbearing to advance their educational and professional goals, but when these women bore children, they still did so within the marital bond. Poorer women, whose educational and work prospects were far less attractive, still saw greater hope and meaning in raising children, even if a worthy marital partner no longer could be found.[39] Underprivileged men, beset by unemployment (and underemployment), little opportunity for higher education, and, in minority communities especially, increasingly high levels of incarceration, did not seem to these women suitable fathers.[40] Better to go it alone than to miss the opportunity to raise children altogether. As a result, the sharp rise in the nonmarital birth rate, an unintended consequence of the increase in nonmarital sex born of the pill, correlates strongly with the feminization of poverty that began to take shape in the 1970s—and has not subsided to this day.[41]

As women entered the labor market in great numbers late in the last century, their demand for even more effective methods of fertility regulation grew too. But perfectly effective birth control could only be found in abstinence, or, now, in the combination of relatively effective but still fallible contraception and (illegal) abortion. Yet abstinence seemed increasingly unnecessary, with contraception now mainstream and abortion somewhat less difficult to procure.[42] If men could seemingly engage in sexual intercourse detached from the responsibilities inherent in pregnancy and childbearing (men, after all, could walk away from an unplanned pregnancy), the pill together with abortion suggested that perhaps women should now be free to do the same. Population control leader Lawrence Lader was among the first to make this suggestion explicit, and public. Though he was a friend and biographer of Sanger's, Lader quarreled with her about the merits of advocating legal abortion. In addition to its promise in the population control arena, an idea he had been proposing to state legislators for years, Lader also began to argue that legal abortion would help women gain total control over childbearing.

In his wildly influential 1966 monograph, *Abortion*, Lader wrote: "The complete legalization of abortion is the one just and inevitable answer to the quest for feminine freedom. All other solutions are compromises."[43] Abortion would allow women to better enjoy sex (with the freedom men did) and also to meet their new responsibilities in the workplace (as their male counterparts were able to do). Lader was never able to convince Sanger of the utility of abortion, but he did help to convince the leader of the newly ascendant women's movement, Betty Friedan.[44]

According to fellow population controller and abortion advocate, Dr. Bernard Nathanson, Lader regarded recruitment of Friedan's movement as the surest way to "move abortion out of the books and into the streets."[45] Nathanson was initially skeptical of Lader's strategy. They were already making headway with public health arguments, borrowing data published in the 1930s to claim that 5,000 to 10,000 women died each year from illegal abortion. Although the discovery of penicillin and other medical advances had shrunk that number markedly, even Walter Cronkite was repeating their outdated statistics in 1965.[46] But Lader continued to court the feminists anyhow. Decades later, Nathanson wrote: "I was dead wrong, of course. Larry's marriage with the feminists was a brilliant tactic."[47]

In 1967, after a fierce debate at its national meeting and the resignation of some of its members, Friedan brought NOW on board, making it the first women's organization ever to support legal abortion.[48] Two years later, Friedan joined Lader, Nathanson, and radical feminist Pat Maginnis in Chicago to speak at the First National Conference on Abortion Laws. The National Association for the Repeal of Abortion Laws (NARAL) emerged from out of that gathering. But even if Friedan's conviction to back abortion rights was strengthened by Lader's appeal, the two had wholly distinct rationales, manifest in their respective statements at the first NARAL meetings. Lader sought both to prevent increasing overpopulation and to protect the ability of (male) doctors to perform abortions without jail time. Friedan sought to promote a woman's "right to control her reproductive process" as basic to the "personhood and dignity of woman."[49] In the early years of NARAL, Lader's rationale prevailed.

After Sanger's death in 1966, Planned Parenthood officially joined the effort to reform abortion in 1967. That year Colorado and California passed the first laws relaxing prohibitions on abortion, following the model statute published by the American Law Institute (ALI) in 1962. The ALI's Model Penal Code required two doctors to certify that an abortion was necessary, permitting the procedure if there was "substantial risk" that the pregnancy would "gravely impair the physical or mental health of the mother," if "the child would be born with grave physical or mental defect," or in the cases of rape or incest.[50] Eleven other states followed the model statute by the end of the decade, with four others stipulating that the procedure be done only in the early months of pregnancy by a licensed physician. The remaining thirty-three states retained their nineteenth-century statutes, allowing abortion to save the life or, in some instances, health of the mother.[51] Numerous cases challenging these more restrictive laws were making their way through the state and federal court system, claiming in most instances that these statutory exceptions were themselves unconstitutionally vague.[52]

The AMA, which in 1857 had declared abortion an "unwarrantable destruction of human life," responded to the abortion reform movement with new recommendations in 1970. The AMA's new statement reiterated that the organization of physicians and other medical personnel was opposed to induced abortion but added certain exceptions under particular circumstances. These included evidence that the pregnancy threatened the health or life of the mother, that the infant would be born with "incapacitating physical deformity or mental deficiency," or in situations of rape and incest. "Sound medical judgment" and "the best interests of the patient" ought to govern the procedure rather than "mere acquiescence to the patient's demand."[53]

But the feminists in NOW and NARAL did not want women's access to abortion limited to those that doctors deemed "therapeutic." They sought not reform but wholesale repeal of all abortion laws, to ensure that "medical authorities could no longer be moral gatekeepers."[54] In August 1970, Friedan led the Women's Strike for Equality, with events in forty cities commemorating the fiftieth anniversary of women's suffrage. The Women's Strike added "free abortion on demand" to NOW's original appeal, apparently untroubled by (or perhaps unaware of) the sharp departure the new movement had made from the suffragists themselves.

Voluntary Motherhood Turned on Its Head

Decades later, the woman who was almost solely responsible for brokering the newfound alliance between the abortion advocates and the women's rights movement reflected upon this time. In her memoir published in 2000, Friedan writes, "Ideologically, I was never for abortion. Motherhood is a value to me, and even today abortion is not. . . . But the issue had to be confronted. You couldn't have women's equality without her own control of the reproductive process." Then, echoing the basic principle of the nineteenth century "voluntary motherhood" advocates, she continues: "The time when biology was destiny and

FIGURE 8.2. Advertisement for Women's Strike for Equality, August 26, 1970. Credit: Library of Congress (public domain).

women's lives were defined mainly by their reproductive function was over as far as the women's movement was concerned. The personhood of woman required the emergence from passivity and biology and men's laws.... I believed passionately in 1967, as I do today, that *women should have the right of chosen motherhood.*" And, finally: "For me the matter of choice has never been primarily the choice of abortion, but that you can choose to be a mother. That is as important as any right written into the Constitution."[55]

For Friedan, and so too her newly conceived women's movement, "voluntary motherhood"—achieved formerly through periodic sexual abstinence that manifested the couple's shared respect for the reproductive potential of sex and for the woman's disproportionate role in it— elided into something else entirely, even if Friedan herself hardly could see the difference. No longer did the "right of chosen motherhood" mean affirmatively choosing when to engage in that act that might make one a mother; now it meant affirmatively choosing whether to end the life of one's nascent child developing within. The original principle sought to protect against this "revolting" fate; the newly transformed version seized right onto it.[56]

In the Sanger-Friedan vision, women could now subject their reproductive capacity (and, if that didn't work, their developing unborn child) to external techno-pharmacological control, not only to cabin dreaded population growth and to enjoy the new sexual expression trumpeted in the latest women's magazines, but also to find their place in the male-dominated workforce. If (private) women were going to assume all the responsibilities of (public) men, their shared parental responsibility for children would be assumed once again by women alone, but now in the most private—and desperate—of acts. Thus was announced the new answer to the perennial question of how to respond to men's and women's reproductive asymmetry.

Once a potent cultural force against the encroaching market mentality, and always an advocate of the affirmative duties of care to the most vulnerable, the women's movement of the late twentieth century shook off its ennobling heritage and embraced the pragmatic demands of the day. Though echoing Wollstonecraft and nineteenth-century women's rights advocates in the core feminist belief that, in Stanton's words, "the right to control one's body was the preeminent personal and political right," modern-day feminists abandoned their predecessors' insights about the threats of undisciplined male desire—and the necessity of self-mastery and sexual integrity as preconditions to true equality and happiness between men and women—to turn the revolutionary appeal for "voluntary motherhood" squarely on its head.

For Wollstonecraft, we should recall, authentic rights were grounded in prior duties: it would be philosophically untenable to claim that a mother could enjoy a "right" to end the life of her own child; rather, she enjoyed rights to better discharge the special duties of care she owed to that child. And such maternal duties implied paternal duties too. Thus her core argument that women's rights depended on men taking up their responsibilities both to women and the children under their mutual care. Indeed, were men expected by law to maintain both mother and child, thought Wollstonecraft, it might well bring an end to that "abuse that has an equally fatal effect on population and morals." More still, if the mother (or father) lacked the capacity to care for their child, for want of some right or privilege, the fault lay with the society in which they lived.

Nearly a century after Wollstonecraft wrote her treatise, writer and suffrage lecturer Mattie Brinkerhoff articulated a similar sentiment in the pages of Stanton and Anthony's newspaper, *The Revolution*, in 1869: "When a man steals to satisfy hunger, we may safely conclude that there is something wrong in society—so when a woman destroys the life of her unborn child, it is an evidence that by education or circumstances she has been greatly wronged." Brinkerhoff then asks, "But the question now seems to be, how shall we prevent this destruction of life and health?" Responding to her own question, she quotes Stanton, who "has many times ably answered it—'by the true education and independence of woman.'"[57] That women, a century later, who wielded the power of the vote, greater educational opportunities, and more rights and privileges still, would find it necessary to advocate *for* abortion revealed perhaps that the women's movement had not made the advances their predecessors thought they would. Or perhaps the women's movement made a wrong turn along the way.

To be sure, Wollstonecraft and her nineteenth-century successors were not oblivious to the fact that pregnancy was not always welcome in the life of a woman, even for those who practiced "voluntary mother-hood." Yet, such trying circumstances did not transform an unwelcome pregnancy into one that was "compulsory," in the words of one 1970s abortion advocate.[58] "Forced motherhood," in the nineteenth-century view, would have been the result of forced—or unwanted—sex, not the presence of the nascent unborn child, who was rightfully due care, whatever the circumstances of her conception. Rather, the fact that sexual intercourse had the potential to create a new and dependent human being, a being who developed in a woman's body, meant that women should enjoy the "right" to demand that men, who wielded far more power over women both physically and legally, govern their sexual passions, so that the unique, and at that time uniquely dangerous, state of motherhood would be undertaken voluntarily. In the words of free-love advocate Tennessee Claflin, "No woman should ever hold sexual relations with any man from the possible consequences of which she might desire to escape."[59] This was not a condemnation of women, but *a call to arms against male sexual presumption.*

These earlier women's advocates understood a reality that goes unacknowledged by most feminists today, even after the harrowing stories of the #MeToo movement: if sexually aggressive men already tend toward sexual presumption, that presumption grows stronger still when the costs of sex are greatly reduced by easy access to abortion. Indeed, radical feminist Catharine MacKinnon was closer to the older view when in 1983 she wrote, "So long as women do not control access to our sexuality, abortion facilitates women's heterosexual availability." In the privacy of bedrooms, MacKinnon argues, "consent tends to be presumed."[60] But even MacKinnon makes one rather startling historical error. In the very same essay, she frets: "In this context [of male sexual presumption] it becomes clear why the struggle for reproductive freedom has never included a woman's right to refuse sex. In [the present] notion of sexual liberation, the equality issue has been framed as a struggle for women to have sex with men on the same terms as men: 'without consequences.'"[61] Yet, the right to refuse sex is precisely the right, and freedom, that nineteenth-century advocates of "voluntary motherhood" sought.

For the early women's rights advocates, abortion took the life of an unborn child in an act of violence that they deplored, as we saw in chapter 4. Abortion, alongside contraception, also tilted the sexual playing field further in the male direction, empowering men to prioritize sexual intercourse and their own sexual satisfaction and to ignore the asymmetrical consequences of the act.[62] If "want of male chastity" was, according to Wollstonecraft, "the grand source of many of the . . . evils that torment mankind, as well as of the vices and follies that degrade and destroy women," easy abortion, according to both Wollstonecraft and the nineteenth-century women's rights advocates, would only make things worse.

By contrast, periodic sexual abstinence, by mutual decision of the couple or unilateral decision by the woman, was the best means to harmonize and equalize the asymmetrical sexual relationship between men and women, meanwhile instilling edifying habits of self-mastery and affectionate regard for the other. Monogamy and deep companionship could be won, it was thought, when men attained a *self*-governance that freed them from seeking the mere gratification of desires and when women gained a self-respecting sense of sovereignty over their own bodies. In light of the stubborn gender imbalances in sex—in desire, satisfaction, reproduction, and early caregiving too—the voluntary motherhood movement thus expected men to conform themselves to women's sexual needs and desires rather than to their own. The movement was one championed not only by the women's advocates themselves but by men who joined the noble cause. And yet, these insights were abandoned the very next century, just at that point in history when women were gaining the kind of influence in both the private and public spheres that could have made the expectation of male sexual integrity culturally normative.

Both the early women's rights advocates and the radical pro-choice feminist Catharine MacKinnon saw clearly that a woman truly could only have "control over her body" when she had the authority to affirmatively choose when and with whom to engage in sex, ever cognizant of how very unequal women and men are when it comes to sexual intercourse and the rather serious consequences it may bring. Pro-choice University of Richmond law professor Shari Motro articulates more recently the asymmetrical realities of sex that persist despite decades of widespread contraception and legal abortion:

By trivializing the asymmetry in sexual risk—celebrating the pill as the great equalizer and framing abortion as a privilege—the current paradigm creates a cognitive dissonance of sorts in women's lived experience. The slogans tell women they are free, but they are still vomiting through their pregnancies, hemorrhaging through their abortions, losing their libido under the pill. . . .

Sex is complicated. Men and women who don't want babies choose to have sex anyway for a variety of reasons. . . . The critical difference is that when women choose sex they are choosing something fundamentally different from what men are choosing when they choose sex. Women are choosing something that, along with whatever benefits they hope to gain from it, has a much higher chance of hurting their bodies. Men and women are *un*equal in sex because for women, sex is tinged with something else, a biological difference that adds a sacrificial layer.[63]

The nineteenth-century women's advocates appreciated this stubborn inequality and sought a thoroughly woman-oriented response.

Equality of Dominion?

Put in historical and philosophical context, Friedan's approach to "chosen motherhood" as inclusive of abortion was not even countenanced by Stanton's more radical Lockean philosophy of self-ownership or her Millian approach to rights as tools of self-creation. For *self*-ownership did not extend for Stanton to doing what one willed with *the body of another*, one's unborn child growing within. Pro-life feminist Sidney Callahan warned against that alternative in 1972: "Facing [an unplanned pregnancy], we cannot give in to . . . a property rights ethic," as though women "owned" their own children.[64] To do so, in Callahan's view, would be to "identify with male sexuality, male aggression and womb-less male lifestyles."[65] In fact, only a view of maternity loosely inspired by Hobbes's absolute right of dominion—extending, without an obvious limiting principle, to infanticide—would countenance a "right" to abortion "on demand." After all, Hobbes's view of the state of nature—characterized by radically autonomous and self-interested male and female individuals, "equal" because of their capacity to engage in "war of all against all"—is not so dissimilar from the "rat race" of late capitalist societies. Women with infants are at an obvious disadvantage against those without such caregiving responsibilities; as in Hobbes's mythical state of nature, they may feel the need to discard them just to survive. Indeed, the majority of women seeking abortions in the United States today do so because of socioeconomic concerns, with three-quarters of these women at or below the poverty level.[66]

This Hobbesian philosophical posture also gives rise to the increasingly popular academic description of abortion as an act of self-defense: the unborn child as an aggressor can be expunged legitimately from his or her unwilling mother's body. The parasitic visage of the unborn child is a long way off from Friedan's description in *The Feminine Mystique* of the "biological oneness in the beginning between mother and [unborn] child, a wonderful and intricate process." But then, *even for Hobbes* (and the most cogent arguments from self-defense), only the preservation of one's very life would legitimate killing an aggressor. Abortion "on demand" was more radical still. With the concession to Lader's view of legal abortion as the linchpin for both women's sexual freedom and success in the workplace, Wollstonecraft's ennobling vision of mutuality and collaboration, brought into being for a time by the women's movement of the nineteenth century, and reenvisioned anew in NOW's founding statement, had now fully succumbed to the demands of a dog-eat-dog age.

It's no wonder that some of the founding members of NOW, who had signed onto Murray's and Friedan's original statement, quit the organization once it added abortion on demand to its official program. Those who had initially agreed that "childbearing and rearing ... continues to be a most important part of most women's lives [yet] still is used to justify barring women from equal professional and economic participation and advancement" would break off to form new organizations to fight such discrimination against women, and uphold the coherence of the nineteenth-century position.[67] Clair de Jong, founder of Feminists for Life of New Zealand, wrote in 1978: "The demand for abortion is a sell out to male values and a capitulation to male lifestyles rather than a radical attempt to renegotiate the terms by which women

and men can live in the world as people with equal rights and equal opportunities. . . . Accepting the 'necessity' of abortion is accepting that
pregnant women and mothers are unable to function as persons in this
society. It indicates a willingness to adjust to the *status quo* which is a be-
trayal of the feminist cause, a loss of the revolutionary vision of a world
fit for people to live in."[68] And yet, the capitulation to a Hobbesian
kind of sexual equality, an equality of autonomy and dominion, would
only grow as the abortion rights movement wore on.

A Putative Right in Search of
a Constitutional Justification

In 1973, the U.S. Supreme Court decision *Roe v. Wade* struck down
every nineteenth-century abortion law, and also those reform laws of
more recent vintage. *Roe* was born of the new consensus among the
population control movement, the family planners, and the medical
community that illegal abortion had to be brought out of the shadows
and under the supervision of medically trained personnel.[69] But *Roe's*
actual reach extended far beyond the most liberal of state reform laws
for the full repeal that NOW and NARAL had sought, even if the *Roe*
opinion itself was not to the feminists' liking.

For the eugenic rationale that initially brought the pill into being
haunted the abortion cause too. In the years before *Roe* was decided,
the Black liberation movement voiced strong concerns about the abortion reform measures taking place in several states, suspicious that the
birth control movement's eugenic cast extended to abortion too.
Petchesky writes: "Given the racist policies of government-funded
[birth control] clinics and family planners—targeting minority neighborhoods for family planning services; providing birth control devices
and 'follow-up' in abundance, but not jobs, decent housing, basic health
care, maternity care or child care; sterilizing poor black, Hispanic, and
Native American women without their informed consent—these sus-
picions grew out of a stark reality."[70] Thus, when in 1971, Rutgers law
professor Ginsburg gave a presentation about her views on sex discrimination at a conference on women and law, she was peppered with

"heated" questions about abortion from Black men, even though she had not mentioned the issue at all. Later she wrote: "[They] noted the coincidence of rising population [in their communities] with the liberalization of abortion laws, and sometimes were strongly suspicious of the implications. . . . The strong word 'genocide' was uttered more than once."[71]

Ginsburg, like the Black men who questioned her, was not blind to the prevailing view, found in the law journals and popular press of the day, that the leading justification for the liberalization of abortion laws, alongside public health, was population control.[72] Since birth control by that time received state funding for such a purpose, she assumed abortion would too, especially since abortion "was always a far less expensive course, in the short and long run."[73] "Frankly," Ginsburg stated in a 2009 interview, "I had thought that at the time *Roe* was decided, there was concern about population growth and particularly growth in populations that we don't want to have too many of. So that *Roe* was going to be then set up for Medicaid funding for abortion. Which some people felt would risk coercing women into having abortions when they didn't really want them. But when the court [did not require abortion funding in *Harris v. McRae* (1979)] then I realized that my perception of it had been altogether wrong."[74]

But as much as pro-choice feminist lawyers like Ginsburg wanted to see public funding for abortion, the assumed association with eugenics was not in keeping with the growing feminist rationale, even if prominent population control figure Larry Lader had been among the first to suggest abortion's merits for the feminist cause. The embarrassing lineage was not all that clouded the new abortion right for the feminists, however; it was the constitutional rationale behind the 1973 decision itself. For even as *Roe v. Wade*, when read together with its companion case, *Doe v. Bolton*, bestowed upon women a constitutional right to abortion throughout the course of their pregnancies, the new women's movement bickered with the Court's "privacy" reasoning.[75] The "privacy right," after all, merely kept the state from regulating abortion, at least before viability: the negative right would not be robust enough to affirmatively require abortion funding, nor would such a right require state funding for childbirth or childcare. Others worried that the "privacy" precedent may work to countenance violence against women in their "private" homes.[76] Privacy, for these feminists, was simply an inadequate constitutional foundation for the new right.

But it was not only feminists who disliked the Court's opinion in *Roe*: so too did nearly every constitutional law professor on record.[77] Pro-choice constitutional law scholar John Hart Ely excoriated the decision the very year it was rendered in the *Yale Law Journal*, famously writing: "[*Roe*] is bad because it is bad constitutional law, or rather because it is *not* constitutional law and gives almost no sense of an obligation to try to be."[78] To Ely, the Court in *Roe* had simply extended the inventive "right to privacy" rationale it had employed creatively in the contraception cases several years earlier, but without offering any justification for doing so.[79]

It was, after all, one thing to hold that the state has no legitimate governmental authority to intervene in "the sacred precincts of marital bedrooms," as the Supreme Court had in *Griswold v. Connecticut*, when it struck down one of the only remaining statutes against the sale of contraceptives in 1965.[80] It was an innovative and decidedly consequential interpretation for the Court to then declare in *Eisenstadt v. Baird* seven years later that since *Griswold* protected the capacity of *married* people to purchase contraception without state interference, the equal protection clause of the Fourteenth Amendment bestowed upon an *unmarried individual* a constitutional *right* to enjoy the same.[81] But it was another thing altogether for the Court to decide that a woman enjoys a constitutional right to end the life of her own dependent unborn child, to whom she (and the child's father) would otherwise legally owe special affirmative duties of care. And yet, inexplicably to Ely (and many others), the Court in *Roe* treated all these acts, different though they are in kind, under the same new banner of "privacy."[82]

For Ely, and *contra* the Court's reasoning in *Roe*, the legal question at issue in the abortion case was not first and foremost whether the unborn child had a Fourteenth Amendment "right to life" as a constitutional "person." Compelling legal and constitutional arguments of this kind had resurfaced in the 1960s and 70s, building on the international movement for human rights and the civil rights movement in the United States, and calling for Fourteenth Amendment protection of unborn

human beings.[83] But the constitutional question properly at issue in
Roe, according to Ely, was a step before even this. The question ought
simply to have been whether the nascent child's mother (and her physician) now had the legal authority to engage in private killing or whether
the state enjoyed its usual authority to prevent such an act. Ely critiqued
the *Roe* Court thus: "The argument that fetuses lack constitutional
rights is simply irrelevant. For it has never been held or even asserted
that the state interest needed to justify forcing a person to refrain from
an activity, *whether or not that activity is constitutionally protected,*
must implicate either the life or the constitutional rights of another person. Dogs are not 'persons in the whole sense' nor have they constitutional rights, but that does not mean the state cannot prohibit killing
them.... That the life plans of the mother must, not simply may, prevail
over the state's desire to protect the fetus simply does not follow from
the judgment that the fetus is not a person."[84] The question of "personhood" that *Roe* seemed to prioritize was, for Ely, a strawman.

In striking down laws in all fifty states, *Roe v. Wade* energized the
decades-old pro-life movement—a movement that had made recent
gains against liberalization in numerous states—to grow in size and influence, even as the abortion rate soared in the decades that followed.[85]
But the poorly reasoned decision also inspirited an effort within the
pro-choice legal community in search of an alternative constitutional
foundation for the beleaguered new right. With almost unanimity, that
alternative was "equality" or, in constitutional cadence, "the equal protection of the laws."

Abortion Rights as Equal Rights

While Jane Roe's case was malingering, with other abortion cases,
through the federal court system in the early 1970s, so too was Alice
Paul's ERA making its way through state legislatures. Passed by the
two houses of Congress by wide majorities in 1971 and 1972, by 1973 it
had won easy ratification in thirty state legislatures. But after *Roe* came
down the very same year, the amendment quickly became associated
with abortion rights in the public mind, and not only because NOW
was both the leading sponsor of the ERA and a foremost defender of

abortion on demand.[86] In the early 1970s, feminist lawyers had begun to articulate an equality rationale for abortion rights, seeking to steal association of the procedure away from eugenics, population control, and, after *Roe*, "privacy." They wanted to justify the procedure as Lader and Friedan had, as necessary to women's control of their own bodies, and lives.[87] Sarah Weddington, attorney for Jane Roe in the 1973 case, put the putative connection between the two succinctly in a NARAL meeting: "Women cannot take advantage of opportunities . . . under the ERA if they cannot control their fertility."[88]

Though anti-ERA forces brought other concerns to the public's attention, the proposed amendment's association with the new abortion right was among the chief causes of the ERA's downfall.[89] Pro-life feminists, and others who had been backers of the ERA but opposed abortion, read the tea leaves: were abortion increasingly understood as an equality right for women, it might not only mean taxpayer funding for the procedure, but would also suggest that maternity itself was an encumbrance to women's equality. This was an ill-conceived assumption the pro-life feminists were working hard to resist. The new association between the ERA and abortion rights intensified the growing cleavage between the pro- and anti-abortion feminists, marginalizing the latter along with New Deal Catholics in the ERA-backing Democratic Party.[90] It also enabled the GOP to erect the uneasy alliance with pro-lifers that exists to this very day.

The irony was not lost on the original author of the ERA and long-time advocate of its passage, Alice Paul. For even as the octogenarian Paul rejoiced in the progress the women's movement had made since her time fighting against protective legislation for women workers fifty years before, she still also held onto the views of abortion common to the women's rights advocates of her day. Indeed, her close colleague Evelyn Judge recalled that Paul said abortion was nothing less than "the ultimate in the exploitation of women." More still, "how can one protect and help women by killing them as babies?"[91]

The equality arguments legal advocates began to offer in favor of abortion rights themselves revealed just how much further the women's movement still had to go to gain cultural and legal respect for women's contributions, both at home and in the workplace. These advocates properly called attention to the reproductive and social asymmetries between men and women, asymmetries to which women's rights advocates had always sought to respond. But whereas previous generations regarded abortion as evidence that a woman had been "greatly wronged" by both a particular man and society at large, the 1970s feminists now regarded legal abortion as a means to right those wrongs.

For instance, in *Abramowicz v. Lefkowitz*, a 1970 case challenging the New York abortion law, the attorneys on behalf of more than 100 women argued, in the first of its kind legal brief, that since the burdens of carrying and bearing children were borne exclusively by women—even though both men and women had "equal responsibility for the act of sexual intercourse"—legal abortion was necessary to equalize the sexes. Since, the brief states, "the man who shares responsibility for her pregnancy can and often does just walk away," legal equality demanded that the woman ought to enjoy the same freedom, through abortion.[92] As Harvard Law professor Laurence Tribe articulated the concept two decades later, "while men retain the right to sexual and reproductive autonomy, restrictions on abortion deny that autonomy to women."[93] But it is not abortion restrictions that deny sexual and reproductive autonomy to women: the state of pregnancy itself exhibits the embodied reality that, when pregnant, a woman is not physically autonomous. She is carrying a new, albeit dependent and vulnerable, human being within her. Thus, unlike a man who has fathered a child, a pregnant woman cannot simply walk away: to approach the desired autonomy of the child-abandoning man, a pregnant woman must engage in a life-destroying act.

Sexual equality then, in this new view, was found not in calling men to meet women at a high standard of mutual responsibility and care, as Wollstonecraft and the nineteenth-century women's rights advocates had argued. Rather, as men had wielded the common law right of dominion over their wives, women would now seek a similar right to the ultimate sort of dominion over their unborn children. It was a new (and peculiar) breed of women's rights advocacy that sought to rely on the subordination of and violence against another class of human beings, vulnerable children no less, in its efforts to elevate women.

In a 1995 article reporting on the origins of Feminists for Life, the author describes the parallel between the historic treatment of women and the new arguments for legal abortion: "Having known oppression, we cannot stand by and allow the oppression of an entire class of weaker human beings. Having once been owned by our husbands, we cannot condone a position that says the unborn are owned by their mothers. Remembering a time when our value was determined by whether a man wanted us, we refuse to bow to the patriarchal attitude that says the unborn child's value is determined by whether a woman wants her."[94] The earlier women's rights advocates sought to enable women to have the political means to work toward a more humane society, one that would be more hospitable to both women and vulnerable children (both born and, as they themselves said, those still developing in their mothers' wombs).[95] There may have been utilitarian arguments for abortion in the 1970s, but they were not arguments that shared a close affinity with the historical cause of women's rights.

The attorneys in the 1970 *Abramowicz* case in New York rightly described the many ways in which modern-day society was still inhospitable to women and children, fifty years on from women's suffrage. Society had clearly failed women, not only because women were putting their lives and health at risk when they sought out illegal abortions. If they carried the child to term, the brief argued, the status of motherhood itself, especially unwed motherhood, subjected them to "a whole range of de facto types of discrimination."[96] The brief offered a plethora of examples of very real discrimination against pregnant women and working mothers: young women might be expelled from school or robbed of the opportunity for education; they could be fired from employment, denied a job, or forced to live on welfare. Women were also solely responsible for the expenses of the child in utero, and for the next eighteen years, and should that child become a juvenile delinquent, women were regarded as responsible for that too. In a word, children were still unjustly regarded as women's sole responsibility. And so, in a rather poignant leap in logic, their child's very existence became their mother's "choice."

The historic *Abramowicz* brief concludes its section on equality with this legal claim, a claim that was also offered by the same attorney in an amicus brief in *Roe*: "As long as she is forced to bear such an extraordinarily disproportionate share of the pains and burdens of child-rearing (including, of course, pregnancy and childbirth), then, to deprive her of the ultimate choice as to whether she will in fact bear those burdens violates the most basic aspects of 'our American idea of fairness' guaranteed and enshrined in the Fourteenth Amendment."[97]

In the decades since, this argument has become perhaps the single most popular argument for abortion rights.

Abortion Rights as Equal Citizenship Rights

After *Reed v. Reed* and the other antidiscrimination decisions of the early 1970s had come down from the Supreme Court, and *Roe* had been decided too, UCLA constitutional law professor Kenneth Karst wrote a law review article that received much attention in the legal academy. Perhaps inspired by the earlier equality arguments of feminist attorneys, Karst sought in 1977 to connect theoretically the sex discrimination cases with the contraception and abortion cases of the same time frame. Bundling these cases together and describing them at a high level of generality, he suggested the new constellation of rights were necessary for women's "equal citizenship":

> Cases such as . . . *Eisenstadt, Roe v. Wade, and LaFleur* [a 1974 pregnancy-discrimination case]—all these can be seen as "woman's role" cases. So viewed, they implicate the principle of equal citizenship, for they involve some of the most important aspects of a woman's independence, her control over her own destiny. . . . The abortion question was not merely a "women versus fetuses" issue; it was also a feminist issue, an issue going to women's position in society in relation to men. The focus of equal citizenship here is not a right of access to contraceptives, or a right to an abortion, but a right to take responsibility for choosing one's own future.[98]

Karst suggested further that the twin rights to contraception and abortion would remedy the situation in which society "places a greater stigma on unmarried women who become pregnant than on the men who father their children," and the social expectation that women continue to take the major responsibility for children.[99] Equal citizenship, for Karst, was defined principally by "autonomy": "To be a person is to respect one's own ability to make responsible choices in controlling one's own destiny, to be an active participant in society rather than an object."[100] Dependency, by contrast, was its antithesis. Thus, in addition to Lader's argument that abortion would both allow women to enjoy sex free of encumbrances like men did and make their way in the male-dominated workplace, Karst suggested that abortion rights would enable women to frustrate the sexual double standard and to manage the social reality that fathers do not take responsibility for their children.

Neither man seemed to reckon with the fact that abortion as a response to the failures of men places the burden for children and the management of fertility squarely on the shoulders (or, better, bodies) of women, just as they have always been. Abortion further alleviates men of their shared duties of care. Rather than making significant demands upon men and society at large, the child-abandoning man—or the ideal (male) worker with no caregiving responsibilities—remains, in this paradigm, the model for a "responsible" life in the American workforce and, in Karst's view, for equal citizenship. If women want to ascend to men's position in society, women would have to mimic this duly independent and autonomous version of the "citizen," caregiving responsibilities be damned.

Enter Ruth Bader Ginsburg

The same year Karst published his article, in a lecture that would become the 1978 article, "Sex Equality and the Constitution," Ginsburg, now of Columbia Law School, employed Karst's "equal citizenship" approach. After reviewing the long history of women in U.S. law from the Declaration of Independence through the nineteenth and early twentieth centuries and up to the recent wins in sex discrimination cases in the early 1970s, she turned explicitly to Karst's argument. "Not only the sex discrimination cases, but the cases on contraception, abortion, and illegitimacy as well," she paraphrased, "[these] present various facets of a single issue—the roles women are to play in society."

She then asked rhetorically, "Are [women] to have the opportunity to participate in full partnership with men in the nation's social, political, and economic life?"[101] Or, she implied, will vulnerable children, and the dependency they represented and caregiving they required, continue to impede them? She concluded with a judgment she repeated time and again: "Eventually, the Court may take [all these cases] out of the separate cubbyholes in which they now rest, acknowledge the practical interrelationships, and treat these matters as part and parcel of a single, large, sex equality issue."[102]

Ginsburg was more critic than defender of the Court's decision in *Roe*. As she would argue in both articles and speeches over the next few decades, the *Roe* Court had not only gone too far, too fast, but, just as importantly, it also had decided the case on the wrong constitutional basis. The Court, in the first place, had acted too swiftly in striking down every other state statute when it could have acted, she would say, "by slow degrees."[103] The Court, in her view, might have invalidated only the strict Texas abortion statute then before the Court, thus opening a "dialogue" with the political branches of government as the cases she litigated in the sex discrimination realm had.[104] She seemed to agree too with Harvard Law professor Archibald Cox that the trimester approach in *Roe* "read like a set of hospital rules and regulations," and with Justice Sandra Day O'Connor, who in a 1983 abortion case described *Roe*'s approach as, in light of medical advances, "on a collision course with itself."[105] And though she did not want to suggest that Karst's equality approach would have fully mitigated the strong negative reaction *Roe* caused, she thought it a far more compelling constitutional argument than the erroneous view assumed in the Court's "privacy" reasoning that abortion "be described as nothing more than birth control delayed."[106] Rather, Ginsburg wrote, citing Karst, "a woman's autonomous control of her full life's course, . . . her ability to stand in relation to man, society, and the state as an independent, self-sustaining, equal citizen" was at stake in the abortion question.[107]

Once on the Supreme Court, Justice Ginsburg took the occasion of her dissent in the 2007 case *Gonzales v. Carhart* to announce officially her distaste for *Roe*'s "privacy" rationale and to articulate Karst's approach: "Legal challenges to undue restrictions on abortion procedures do not seek to vindicate some generalized notion of privacy; rather, they center on a woman's autonomy to determine her life's course, and thus to enjoy equal citizenship stature."[108] But Karst's approach to equal citizenship, adopted by the highest-ranking women's advocate in the country, departs not at all from the troubling Enlightenment accounts of citizenship, or even from Aristotle's much earlier account. In each of the liberal myths of origin—by Hobbes, Locke, or Rousseau—self-interested, autonomous individuals contract with one another to form a government that in turn secures their rights. Women and children exist in each theorist's "state of nature," but when civil society comes into being, only male individuals are counted as "citizens." Women disappear into the newly erected private sphere: their traditional duties of nurture and caregiving render them as dependent as their children, just the contrary of the autonomy necessary for full citizenship. Aristotle himself regarded participation in political life as the key to citizenship; those who lack full independence—children, slaves, women—cannot possibly participate. As Carole Pateman writes in her insightful book *The Sexual Contract*, among historic political theorists, Wollstonecraft was the first to recognize the "complex interdependence of the [public and private] spheres," understanding the priority, for virtuous public participation, of the domestic sphere.[109]

In Karst's and Ginsburg's view, women can now be full and independent citizens too, if they but become "autonomous," that is, leave their children behind. Indeed, Ginsburg's view of "equal citizenship" as necessitating a right to abortion would seem to be in much tension with the definition of "full citizenship" she offered in the opinion for the Court in the 1996 VMI sex discrimination case. There, she wrote that full citizens ought to have "the equal opportunity to aspire, achieve, participate in, and contribute to society based on . . . individual talents and capacities." But men and women are not free-floating, autonomous minds. They are embodied individuals who enjoy distinctive capacities when it comes to sex and reproduction. If citizenship is understood along the traditional, male model—one that assumes the capacity to remain both physically autonomous from the reproductive consequences of sexual intercourse and unencumbered by the demands of caregiving—the affirmative attachment and nurturing required of young children, and those who care for them, become symbols of dependence, anathema in Karst's view of citizenship. Those whose "autonomy" is constrained by their caregiving responsibilities are defined on the outside of citizenship, just as they always have been.

It is no wonder that Georgetown law professor Robin West has written that such a model of citizenship might "legitimat[e], and with a vengeance, the [supposed] inconsistency of motherhood and citizenship itself."[110] Although Ginsburg herself wrote that "disadvantaged treatment based on [women's] unique childbearing capacity" was at the very top of those "arbitrary barriers that have plagued women seeking equal opportunity"—and would shape the law to affirm caregiving on the part of fathers, as we saw in chapter 7—she seems to underappreciate how her praise of autonomy as the defining characteristic of citizenship undervalues those with caregiving responsibilities, especially when those responsibilities impede one's capacity *to work like an autonomous, unencumbered man.*[111]

The bias then is set against those who seek to work fewer or more flexible hours when they have children, take months (or even years) away from the workplace with the hope of reengaging when their caregiving duties subside, or, because of their commitments in the home or communities, choose not to enter the paid workforce at all. As it is, the market, ever prizing efficiency and profits, already carries an inherent bias against the time-consuming and often unpredictable task of caregiving. Given the prevalence of Ginsburg's view in the women's rights movement, it's no wonder discrimination against caregiving persists, for mothers especially, but also for fathers. This path is not one of "advancing" equal opportunity, to harken back to Ginsburg's formula in the VMI case, but rather of "denigrating" caregiving, perpetuating the "social and economic inferiority" of caregivers, who remain, out of cultural convention, necessity, and so often choice, disproportionately women.

Previous generations of women's rights advocates sought to protect the culturally essential work of caregiving from the erosion of an ever-encroaching market and its materialist economic principles. A women's movement that regards abortion rights *as equal citizenship rights* has surrendered, once and for all, to the logic of that market.[112]

"Relying" on Abortion for Women's Equality

Despite the attention given to equality arguments for abortion rights in the years before and decades since *Roe*, the U.S. Supreme Court has never held that abortion restrictions violate the equal protection clause.[113] Still, when the high court upheld *Roe* in its 1992 *Planned Parenthood v. Casey* decision, the new and prevailing equality rationale for abortion rights seemed foremost on several of the justices' minds.[114] In their plurality opinion for the Court in *Casey*, Justices O'Connor, Kennedy, and Souter wrote that although they could not affirm that *Roe* was rightly decided as an original matter, its "precedential force" required them to uphold the decision, albeit with substantial changes.[115] The justices deemed that the country, over the intervening nineteen years, had come to "rely" on the right bestowed in *Roe* as a centerpiece of women's liberty and equality, whatever the Constitution said (or did not say) about the matter. This "reliance interest" is what gave *Roe*, according to the plurality, its "precedential force": "For two decades of economic and social developments, people have organized intimate relationships and made choices that define their views of themselves and their places in society, *in reliance* on the availability of abortion in the event that contraception should fail. The ability of women to participate equally in the economic and social life of the Nation has been facilitated by their ability to control their reproductive lives."[116]

Casey too was weakly reasoned as a constitutional matter. Not only did the Court make use of "reliance interests" as more metaphor than legal claim: such legal interests are generally employed in commercial or property disputes, not to describe sociological patterns. But even assuming the Court's societal reliance claim were true, such a sociological fact does not ensure the integrity of the constitutional decision. As law professor Michael Stokes Paulsen observes in a 2000 *Yale Law Journal* article, "For 'decades of economic and social developments,' in vast regions of the nation, people organized personal relationships and defined their views of themselves" *in reliance* on the legal regime of segregation.[117] So too with slavery: the entire Southern economic system had "relied upon" slaveowners putative "property rights" for its economic and social development. That they did so rely does not transform their (deplorable) legal claims into constitutional trumps, as we have so grievously learned. On its own, reliance is hardly a solid foundation for a constitutional claim.

Casey's substantive claim as to women's equality also lacks merit. Abundant evidence does exist that there is a correlation between lower fertility rates and higher rates of education and labor force participation among women, but no evidence exists that abortion itself, rather than fertility regulation of various kinds, is specifically correlated with these (imperfect) markers of women's equality.[118] Indeed, the historical account offered earlier in this chapter would suggest that societal reliance on widespread contraceptive use with abortion as a "backup" may actually have had distortive, detrimental effects upon women and women's equality, most notably among the poor.

Rather than merely offer a fail-safe in individual cases "in the event that contraception should fail," the easy abortion access granted in *Roe* seemed instead to have inspired a large-scale, societal-wide increase in sexual risk-taking on the part of sexual actors.[119] Dr. Alan Guttmacher, then president of Planned Parenthood, was prescient in this regard when in 1968 he said: "When an abortion is easily obtainable, contraception is neither actively nor diligently used."[120] But easy abortion access does not only tend to disincentivize contraceptive use.[121] By offering sexual partners the false confidence that their acts will be definitively sterile, the abortion-backed contraceptive revolution ushered in an unprecedented mentality of risk-taking that is often unwarranted by the couple's level of commitment and their ability to assume parental duties in the case of unexpected pregnancy. Over time, increases in such risk-taking, coupled with contraceptive failure, misuse, or nonuse have led to dramatic increases in abortion and nonmarital childbearing overall.

Richard Posner in 1994 described the unintended consequences the United States experienced in the decades after *Roe* like this: "If abortion is cheap, . . . intercourse will be more frequent and . . . may generate more unwanted pregnancies, not all of which will be aborted. This should help us to understand the combination of cheap contraceptives, frequent abortions, and yet a high rate of unwanted births in our society."[122] Were abortion *less* readily available, economists suggest, contraceptive use (and greater avoidance of sexual intercourse) would increase and the rate of unintended pregnancy, abortion, and even single motherhood would likely decrease (though never to a vanishing point, of course).[123]

In practice, then, the 1970s sexual insurance policy, putatively taken out to insure both sexes against childbearing, in reality seems to insure primarily men. Not only were the new abortion-backed contraceptive provisions the chief catalysts in erecting casual norms around sex, norms that are increasingly disfavored by most women,[124] but the still-high rates of unintentional pregnancy, nonmarital births, and abortion that accompany the new sexual insurance scheme disproportionately affect women, especially those who are poor. The now-common mentality that sex has no consequences and thus entails no responsibilities too often leaves women alone with their pregnancies—to procure abortions or rear their children on their own.

Just as Wollstonecraft and the nineteenth-century women's advocates anticipated then, relatively easy abortion access has relieved men of the mutual responsibilities that accompany sex, and so has upended the duties of care for dependent children that fathers ought equally to share. Sexual intercourse and potential motherhood remains an unshakable biological reality, but the connection between sexual intercourse *and potential fatherhood*—the connection that irresponsible men have always sought to avoid—has withered even further since *Roe*.[125] Here again, Planned Parenthood's Guttmacher saw the consequences all too clearly in the years before the high court's fateful decision in 1973: "Abortion on demand relieves the [man] of all possible responsibility; he simply becomes a coital animal."[126]

Indeed, if the institutionalized male sexual prerogative was finally undone by legal reforms to marriage and criminal law in the last century, relatively easy abortion access has emboldened men to reclaim that prerogative once again. As the #MeToo movement has revealed in spades, the new "coital animal"—lacking the formative schooling of desire expected of an aspiring gentleman—will not so readily heed the word "no."[127]

The New Rebels?

Increasingly reliable methods of natural fertility regulation now exist that better enable women to "take charge" of their fertility and the conditions under which they engage in sexual intercourse.[128] These methods, as birth control scholar Linda Gordon rightly observes, "are reminiscent" of the nineteenth-century movement for voluntary motherhood. Rather than turning to "washes, teas, tonics and various sorts of appliances," or more sophisticated external techno-pharmacological controls of recent vintage, natural methods employ modern scientific and technological know-how *to inform and enhance the interior practice of self-mastery instead*, just as Wollstonecraft and her successors had envisioned.

Noticing that the decades-long orientation toward a "magic-bullet technological solution" has both underappreciated the asymmetrical power differentials between men and women and also discouraged personal responsibility in sex, Gordon insightfully suggests:

> Sexual freedom and smaller families have sometimes become new standards to which individuals are pressured to conform. They are imposed on us through a highly sexualized commercial sphere and the pressure for consumption. Perhaps these new standards will in turn become objects of rebellion. But such rebels should not expect to return us to an earlier set of gender and reproductive relations. . . . [T]he need for abortion is unlikely to decline without an increase in contraceptive quality, access, and education. [Relying on abstinence] is unlikely to alter sexual activity significantly *unless there is a corresponding development in women's autonomy and confidence and men's egalitarianism.*[129]

But perhaps such a development is within our grasp. If we took seriously the insights of an earlier generation of women rebels, we might leverage women's heightened influence in all sectors of society today and reorient our approach to fertility regulation to better align with women's (rather magnificent) bodies and their rightful sense of sovereignty over them.

Instead of allowing men's often relentless appetites to dictate cultural norms around sex, a new expectation of sexual integrity could take its cue instead from the cyclical nature and organic signs of women's fertility, about which we are learning more every day. Not only would scientifically informed periodic abstinence within a high-commitment relationship demand far more emotional engagement, patience, self-possession, and cooperation from men, encouraging them to better understand (with their bodies, as women do) the asymmetrical consequences of sex. It would also offer women, well before they become unintentionally pregnant, far more self-knowledge, confidence, and reproductive agency than they have yet known, entrusting the management of their fertility not to pills or other external controls, *but to themselves*. And Elizabeth Cady Stanton, who more than a century ago urged women to grow in reproductive self-sovereignty by educating themselves and their daughters to regard "their bodies and the laws which govern them," would be most well pleased.

Contemplating the Counterfactual

The 1960s and 70s were decades awash in new questions that emerged with the revolutionary release of the birth control pill alongside women's increased social status and the unprecedented entry of mothers of young children into the workforce. As the distinctive women's movement moved apace, alongside both the population control movement and the emerging sexual revolution, but not yet together, Americans had before them a new set of yet unforeseen and entangled questions: first, how to enable women to participate more fully in the public sphere; second, how to manage the significant "technology shock" created by the advent of the pill (far more effective than its predecessors, but importantly not 100 percent so); and third, how to maintain utmost societal concern for the perennial need to nurture dependent children who heretofore had been the primary responsibility of their mothers.

The Supreme Court in 1973 chose one definitive route, short-circuiting the impassioned debates going on across the country in state after state, and thereby frustrating not only a better compromise among contending perspectives. It also thwarted more humane and creative cultural responses to the asymmetries that naturally exist, and socially persist, because of women's disproportionate role in human reproduction. The Court in 1992 then doubled down on this particular response, explicitly acknowledging that over the course of nearly two decades, the country and its actors had come to "rely" upon abortion for women's equal participation in public life.

It may be that when the justices in *Casey* maintained that "an entire generation has come of age free to assume *Roe*'s concept of liberty in defining the capacity of women to act in society," it was an altogether accurate description.[130] When *Casey* reaffirmed the "right to choose" abortion, employers and other public institutions remained "free" to be unchanged by women's participation in them.[131] In the words of pro-choice law professor Deborah Dinner: "The discourse of reproductive choice continues to legitimate workplace structures modeled on the masculine ideal [with no caregiving responsibilities] as well as social policies that provide inadequate public support for families."[132] That is, relatively easy abortion access has made it unnecessary for businesses and other institutions in the United States to acknowledge an essential cultural reality: most working persons are (or ought to be) deeply encumbered by their obligations to their families. In the end, it may just be that an unmitigated right to abortion serves a profit-driven market above all else.[133] But caring for dependents and participating in the economic and social life of the nation need not be a zero-sum game: only our lack of imagination, and our culture-wide capitulation to the now-reigning logic of the market, has made it so.

Given the centrality of abortion rights in the feminist movement today, it is no surprise that work-family balance remains such a pressing issue and that it is women's status as mothers, not their status as women, that causes the greatest inequities socially and professionally, even as women have made remarkable gains overall. If the "gender revolution" has stalled—elevating women in the workplace without a concomitant elevation for the work mothers and fathers do in the home—constitutionalizing the right to abortion shares a good deal of the blame. Without the Court's intervention, but with Ginsburg's commendable wins in sex discrimination cases in the early 1970s and the pregnancy discrimination laws that followed, workplaces would have had to adjust much more quickly to encumbered women, and duly encumbered men, and so to the demands of the child-rearing family more generally. The country would have been then one broad step closer to acknowledging that ennobling Wollstonecraftian vision: individuals and societies flourish best when the work of families is culturally acknowledged, publicly supported, and given the utmost priority. As chapter 9 explores further, however, the United States has chosen a different path altogether.

In the same period that Ruth Bader Ginsburg rose to prominence, only to depart ultimately from Wollstonecraft, the latter's vision found a vigorous and eloquent proponent in New England. It is to her work that we now turn.

CHAPTER 9

Sexual Asymmetry,
American Law, and the Call for
a Renewed Family Ecology

On August 28, 1963, the Reverend Martin Luther King Jr. delivered his masterful "I Have a Dream" speech before hundreds of thousands of supporters at the Lincoln Memorial, with millions more viewing the televised March on Washington from home. Recalling the "architects of our republic," the "magnificent" words of the Constitution and Declaration of Independence, and the "great" emancipator Lincoln himself, King demanded that "the unalienable rights of life, liberty, and the pursuit of happiness" finally be fully shared by American citizens of color. His dream—"deeply rooted in the American dream"—was that the nation would one day be true to its founding creed, the moral proposition that "all men are created equal." Echoing the indictment of the abolitionists the century before, King declared that the nation was still not living up to its founding ideals.

Among the throngs of people gathered in the nation's capital that late summer day was a young Irish-Catholic attorney named Mary Ann, who had traveled by bus from Berkshire County, Massachusetts, with her sister and others. Mary Ann and Julia were the daughters of Martin and Sarah (Pomeroy) Glendon. Martin, a staunch Catholic Democrat, was a newspaper reporter with the *Berkshire Eagle* and had served as chairman of the local board of selectmen in Dalton. Sarah hailed from a Congregationalist family with deep roots in the local Republican Party and a strong attachment to conservationism. When Mary Ann was ten, the Glendons had taken her on a driving trip to North Carolina where they witnessed firsthand the racial segregation that persisted in the South. Now nearly twenty-five-years old, Glendon was a card-carrying member of the Democratic Party who had happily cast her first ballot in the 1960 presidential election in favor of her own U.S. senator, John F. Kennedy, who became the nation's first Catholic president.

Beginning her first year of college at Mount Holyoke at sixteen, Glendon was awarded a full scholarship to attend the University of Chicago and transferred there for her sophomore year. At Chicago, she immersed herself in the Western canon, and was beckoned to continue to law school by a law professor's lecture on Plato. One of only four women in the class of 1961 at the University of Chicago Law School, she became an editor of the school's prestigious law review, and upon graduation began a master's of comparative law to continue studies with the great comparativist Max Rheinstein. Glendon had only just returned from a year and a half of graduate legal studies in Brussels when she boarded the bus to DC.

Glendon found in King a civil rights leader who preached a legal and political philosophy that resonated deeply with her own. Here was a preacher-scholar-advocate who grounded his political activism and righteous claim for legal change in a robust understanding of the foundations of Western law. His now-famous "Letter from Birmingham Jail," written in April 1963, invoked an ancient Christian tradition that distinguished just from unjust laws by the former's compatibility with a higher or "eternal" law. King quoted St. Augustine in his letter: "An unjust law is no law at all." But Augustine himself was indebted for this insight to Cicero, the great philosopher of even more ancient origin, perhaps Glendon's favorite among the ancients. King preached an uncompromising nonviolence that entailed a "process of self-purification," seeking political and economic power not for its own sake but for a more noble end: "a truly brotherly society, the creation of the beloved community."[1]

The same month of King's extraordinary letter, Pope John XXIII published (and the *New York Times* printed in full) the papal encyclical

FIGURE 9.1. The Board of Editors of the *University of Chicago Law Review* for 1960–61. Mary Ann Glendon, seated on right. Credit: Courtesy of University of Chicago Law School and the American Catholic History Research Center and University Archives at the Catholic University of America.

Pacem in terris (Peace on Earth). The pope's historic letter, addressed to all people of good will, emphasized the moral imperative to respect the equal human dignity of all persons, and the rights and duties that flowed from their nature as creatures with intelligence and free will. Calling for women's rights, just wages, religious and associational freedom, nuclear disarmament, and an end to racial discrimination, the pope urged governments to pursue "the common good of the entire human family," one that "favor[s] the full development of human personality."[2] Glendon felt a keen sense of pride that her church was "in the vanguard of historic changes."[3]

Inspired by her moral convictions, her legal training, and King's words that late August day, Glendon took a short leave from her new job as a first-year associate at a long-established white-shoe Chicago firm to join lawyers from across the country to assist Blacks as they asserted their voting rights and to defend jailed civil rights workers in Jackson, Mississippi, in "Freedom Summer" 1964. The bodies of three civil rights workers had been pulled out of a swamp that summer, and Glendon, like so many other young Americans in those turbulent years, knew she needed to join the cause. That very year, Congress had passed the Civil Rights Act (1964), and would a year later pass the Voting Rights Act (1965).

After a few weeks in Mississippi assisting those who had dedicated their lives to this great work, Glendon returned to Chicago to carry on her more conventional occupation at Mayer, Brown and Platt. But her work in Mississippi had not only invigorated her lawyerly spirit and cemented in her a lifelong pursuit in service of the disenfranchised. She also had met a young African American civil rights attorney during the trip, and in 1965, the two were married in a civil ceremony. The relationship was short-lived. In late May 1966, when Glendon gave birth to their daughter in the local hospital's de facto segregated ward, just weeks after her own father's passing, the child's father did not visit them and disappeared from their lives. After using as maternity leave the four weeks of vacation her firm dispensed to all its associates, Glendon returned to work and set about fashioning a life consumed by a challenge that she had not anticipated just weeks before: single motherhood.

Glendon would one day become known as one of the great legal thinkers of her time, combining a stunningly broad knowledge of the law and its historical and philosophical foundations with penetrating insight into the cultural conditions that animate it. Her rich family life in small-town New England and exceptional education in political theory and law, knit together with her uniquely measured but indomitable spirit, developed in Glendon a deeply gifted legal mind. Yet nothing was more formative for Glendon than her experience of single motherhood. It gave rise to an unfailing recognition of the dependency and vulnerability at the very heart of the human condition. This insight was to enliven Glendon's scholarship and public service for decades to come.

In 1968, Glendon became the first woman hired to teach at Boston College Law School, and in 1987, she joined the law faculty at Harvard University where, as the Learned Hand Professor of Law, she taught with rave student reviews for more than three decades.

In 1970, Glendon married a Jewish labor lawyer who adopted her daughter as his own. Mary Ann and Edward Lev went on to have their own daughter in 1971, and then, "in gratitude for their many blessings," adopted a third daughter from Korea the following year. In a 2017 award ceremony celebrating her internationally acclaimed work in comparative law, a colleague described the family of Glendon, her husband of forty-three years, and their daughters as "a daily celebration of diversity: a multi-cultural, multi-ethnic and multi-religious environment."[4] A kind of beloved community of her very own.

The American legal scholar Glendon and the British philosopher Wollstonecraft are separated by two centuries and much else. They both rose to the very pinnacle of their professions (posthumously for Wollstonecraft) and endured the onerous trials of single motherhood. Otherwise, their biographical details are fairly dissimilar. Yet these two women articulated, in their respective disciplines, a strikingly similar approach to marriage, family, and work, and to law, government, and rights. In their own ways, they both sewed together the modern quest for political liberty and legal equality with an older appreciation of the essential goods of family and community, and of the intellectual and moral excellence for which all human beings properly strive. Glendon fittingly has been described as "a feminist and a radical, but not a radical feminist."[5] Just so, the principles that emerge from her distinguished legal scholarship provide a profitable lens through which to begin to rehabilitate a renewed Wollstonecraftian vision for our day.

FIGURE 9.2. Official Harvard Law School portrait of
Mary Ann Glendon upon joining the HLS faculty (1986–87).
Credit: American Catholic History Research Center and
University Archives at the Catholic University of America.

SEXUAL ASYMMETRY AND THE POSTINDUSTRIAL
TRANSFORMATION OF THE LAW

In 1977, Glendon published *State, Law & Family*, and in 1981, *The New Family and the New Property*. The earlier book was revised and republished more than a decade later as *The Transformation of Family Law*, winning the legal academy's highest honor, the Order of the Coif Triennial Book Award. In 1987, also winning a prestigious legal book award, came *Abortion and Divorce in Western Law*. And in 1991, her most widely read book, *Rights Talk*. During this early stage of her academic career, the significance of Glendon's scholarly work made an immediate impression that echoed from the hallowed halls of academia all the way to the Oval Office. Her alma mater invited her to serve as dean of the University of Chicago Law School, and both the Carter and Reagan administrations considered her for judgeships. Yet neither role suited her; her heroes, she says, have always been the great scholars. And emulate those heroes she did.

Glendon's early books draw deeply from her singular expertise in comparative law, demarking carefully and crisply the cultural and legal shifts that have taken place in marriage and the family in modern times throughout the Western world. Read as all of a piece, the corpus of her early work offers tremendous insights into the decline of the status-conferring, patriarchal family and its traditional ties to property and inheritance law with the rise of industrialization, women's rights, and the modern centralized state. As such, her analysis can serve to heighten our understanding of the seismic legal, economic, and cultural shifts described in the foregoing chapters, the significance of these changes for men, women, and children, and the relationship between work and family too.

Much of what makes the work-family dilemma so thorny today, Glendon writes, is that it is virtually unprecedented. Recall from chapter 1 Wollstonecraft's hope-filled assumption that married women's intellectual pursuits and professional occupations would not be "incompatible" with their "domestic duties." So long as women (and the men who loved them) prioritized the domestic sphere—and the great good of human formation that takes place there—they would not vainly "value accomplishments more than virtues." "An active mind embraces the whole circle of its duties, and finds time enough for all," wrote Wollstonecraft. Wollstonecraft's guiding principle remains the central theme of this book. Domestic affections ought to take priority over professional responsibilities in the lives of both women and men, for their own flourishing, their children's, and that of the society at large. Society is properly ordered only when it enables, and encourages, such a prioritization.

Yet Wollstonecraft could not anticipate, no one could, how the enormous dislocation wrought by the Industrial Revolution (moving work for men first, and then increasingly for women, out of the home and into the city) made work and family geographically incompatible like no era before. More distressing still, however, was the new economic vulnerability women experienced in marriage after this time. As we explored in chapters 3 and 4, industrialization undermined the economic interdependence and collaboration the agrarian home required, putting the homemaking wife at the mercy of the wage-earning husband, rendering her far more economically dependent upon him, Glendon emphasizes, just as he had grown far less dependent upon her.

The movement for joint property rights, the first among other legal rights women sought in response to industrialization, followed with just cause. But that movement—advocating an equal legal share of the family assets, given the culturally essential and economically productive work of the home—was abandoned for nearly a century as state legislatures instead passed separate property statutes, allowing married women to hold title in their own earnings. Married women began to seek remunerative labor outside the home in due course. Glendon reveals in her early work how the transformation that took shape in Anglo-American law regarding marriage, family, and dependency exacerbated the difficult economic transitions that beset the new postindustrial family. Together with the economic gains and losses of industrialization came a profound unsettling of former familial and communal assumptions. The premodern, patriarchal, marriage-centered family had not only (inequitably) conferred status and rank for much of human history. It also had been the locus of support, economic security, and solidarity for its members, prioritizing the needs of the whole over the personal aspirations of each person within it.

With the revolutionary rise of the social and legal status of the "individual," in the United States most notably, "self-sufficiency" became the new mid-twentieth-century presumption in U.S. family law, as the next section details further. Glendon describes in her early scholarship how social status and wealth increasingly were no longer determined by marriage but by one's labor force participation or, so often for the poor, one's dependence upon the newly emergent welfare state. This new legal presumption in U.S. law became a double-edged sword for women. The very philosophical and legal revolution that had inspired women's enhanced legal status in the family and in society—recognizing women as "individuals" with civil and political rights of their own—also tended to upend age-old support structures that traditionally had provided women the solidarity they needed to undertake their familial and communal responsibilities. The expectation of lifelong marriage in tandem with the day-to-day support of multigenerational families and close-knit communities softened the ever-present trials of caregiving, while providing the joys and close bonds of friendship, too.

Glendon thus makes the case that at nearly the same moment in history when the law was beginning to protect women's *abstract rights* and to promote their opportunities to engage in professional work as never before, it was simultaneously devaluing the *concrete caregiving work* women had provided in the home, gratis, throughout the centuries. And so early on in her scholarly career, Glendon saw the need to, in her words, "work out an understanding of sexual equality that takes account of women's roles in procreation and child raising without perpetuating their subordination."[6] But recognizing sexual equality within the analytical categories of "sameness" or "difference," as was debated in much feminist scholarship in the 1980s, was not enough: women's distinctive reproductive capacities gave way not only to "difference" *but to a deep sexual asymmetry*. And yet, modern law had rendered the roles of mother and caregiver *even riskier still*. Concerning women's postindustrial situation, Glendon writes, "[In modern times, women] have adapted to that situation as best they can by hedging their bets in two ways. They are having fewer children, and they are maintaining at least a foothold in the labor force even when their children are very young. But that strategy still does not protect mothers very well against the risk of the four deadly Ds: disrespect for non-market work; divorce; disadvantages in the workplace for anyone who takes time out; and the destitution that afflicts so many female-headed households."[7] Glendon saw too that hedging against this asymmetrical risk through increased commitment to market work, in order to protect oneself and one's children from abandonment or impoverishment, in turn had deleteriously affected the lives of young children, the elderly and infirm, and others who had relied for centuries on women's dedicated nurture and care.

Women's equal legal status in the family and increased participation in the labor force and in public life are surely signs of great progress—and for more privileged and educated couples they have encouraged the reestablishment of a kind of spousal interdependence—but for many, these gains have been accompanied by a "caregiving crisis" that we still have yet to resolve. No society, Glendon emphasizes, has figured out how to replace, replicate, or revalue the nurture and care women have disproportionately provided in their own families, which men had supported traditionally through the strong economic ties of marriage. It is surely an advance that marriage is increasingly entered into for love rather than for money, but the modern arrangement has weakened the spousal bonds that children and elderly family members, and their caregivers too, had relied on traditionally for their emotional needs and financial support.

For women who are not mothers, and for those mothers whose professional or family situations allow them the means to engage outside help and the flexibility to juggle family and work with relative ease, the antidiscrimination gains we detailed in chapter 7 have been an unmitigated boon. Indeed, for women who have made the same kinds of life decisions as their male counterparts, their earnings no longer substantially trail those of men.[8] But for the great majority of women who are mothers, antidiscrimination law is but a start. Taken to its limit philosophically as a kind of strict or absolute equality in all things, the antidiscrimination principle can be detrimental. Mill's ideal, raised up by Stanton and often quoted by Ginsburg, advocating a "perfect equality, admitting no power or privilege on the one side, nor disability on the other," can at best ignore, and at worst exacerbate, the sexual asymmetries that tend to accompany childbearing and child-rearing, as chapter 5 explored in the industrial age and chapter 8 began to treat in our own.[9] It does childbearing women and child-rearing parents no good to be likened to those without such responsibilities or to define equality of citizenship by a standard of autonomy that few caregivers can reach.

Wollstonecraft and Glendon alike appreciate both the burden and the gift these asymmetries present in the lives of childbearing women and caregiving parents. They advocate not a "perfect equality" between women and men but rather an equal dignity that admits the special "power" and "privilege," and "disability" too, of childbearing and child-rearing, seeking not erasure of these facts of life, but a reconciliation of them within reciprocal relationships of mutual respect, interdependence, and collaboration in all realms of life. Yet, as the next section further details, modern American ways of thinking about equality and liberty have tended to exacerbate rather than allay the asymmetries that accompany childbearing and child-rearing, both substantively and, perhaps just as importantly, in the messages the law conveys about dependency and caregiving. This Millian tendency, most prevalent within modern women's rights advocacy itself, has been to the detriment of the familial and social bonds that might have made men and women's more equitable sharing in the public and private goods of life more readily possible.

A QUINTESSENTIALLY AMERICAN RIGHTS DIALECT

Among Glendon's most notable scholarly achievements is her thoroughgoing analysis of the ways in which the West's distinctive legal traditions of Anglo-American common law, on the one hand, and the Romano-Germanic civil law system, on the other, influenced the transformation of family law, and much else in the modern world. She describes a strikingly "libertarian" model in the United States (and, to a lesser extent, in the Nordic countries) up and against a "dignitarian" model in those European countries with canon and civil law roots. In the peculiar rights dialect of the United States, Glendon quips, "'liberty' . . . and 'equality' did not rub shoulders with 'fraternity.'"[10] But it is fraternity, solidarity, and collaboration that make personal liberty and sexual equality truly possible.

U.S. common law, we recall from earlier chapters, drew heavily from Blackstone's *Commentaries on the Laws of England*. Synthesizing the old English common law traditions with the eighteenth-century political philosophy of Locke, Blackstone was the most widely read legal thinker among both the American Founders and the young republic's judges and lawyers. Importing the Lockean emphasis on property rights as both protected by government and free of governmental interference, U.S. common law, and the judges that interpreted it, tended toward "noninterference" in family life too: the family home was a man's private castle, a protected sphere into which the state or anyone else ought not to enter. In addition to the legal principle of coverture, by which the common law sparsely defined the unity of the couple and dominion of the husband, was also the husband's right to the "society and service" of his wife through the legal principle of consortium.[11] The early fault-based laws governing separation and divorce, which delineated the manner in which affirmative marital duties could go unmet, provided the only other legal guidance regarding the respective duties of the spouses. Marriage was defined simply: patriarchal, lifelong, and only terminable for serious cause. The absence of any mention of the family in the U.S. Constitution, according to Glendon, further reveals the particularly Lockean legal assumptions of the Founders. Because the primary purpose of government was to secure the (male) individual's "absolute" rights to property and other civil and political rights, both localities and civic, religious, and charitable organizations were left to meet the myriad social needs of families and communities. The Founders well knew that personal and civic virtue would be especially needed for the new republican form of government, but they made few affirmative provisions to sustain it.

Importantly, Glendon argues, the Founders took for granted the robust, local, self-governing communities and tight-knit religious families that inculcated the myriad virtues needed to pursue self-government and maintain stable families and communities. To be sure, lifelong marriage was highly valued, as many state laws and local ordinances attest.[12] But in the main, the Founders relied on each man's and woman's duties to God, spouse, and country to preserve the goods of the family. The Constitution would meanwhile uphold the family's rights, via the individual rights of the (white, male, propertied) head of the household, and keep the distant federal government at bay.

As the Married Women's Property Acts of the mid- to late nineteenth century were passed in U.S. states, followed by suffrage and then greater civil rights for women into the mid-twentieth, the common law principles of coverture and consortium were very slowly traded in for more equal status for women. But, Glendon explains, rather than extend the duties (of service and support, for instance) to husbands that had previously only been expected of wives, thus matching equal dignity and unity in the couple with high expectations for both spouses, the marriage law reforms of the early 1970s especially tended instead to drain marriage of legal content and consequently cultural expectation altogether. Glendon brings attention to the consequential choice reformers made, and the alternative: "While equality theoretically can be implemented by extending legal rights and duties connected with marriage to whichever sex previously lacked them, the equality principle [in the U.S.] more often . . . result[ed] in diminished rights and duties for both."[13]

The deregulating shift in U.S. family law that was promoted in statute and, by the early 1970s, constitutional adjudication, thus rendered in the American imagination a new idea of marriage as "an association of separate individuals."[14] Rather than expect spouses to be equally encumbered by their reciprocal duties to one another and to their children, U.S. law, with its antidiscrimination cast, made husbands and wives instead equally rights-bearing, and thus equally capable of terminating what had become effectively, in many jurisdictions, an at-will relationship. Rather than prioritize the shared, culturally essential work of child-rearing, U.S. law emphasized "individual privacy" and adult self-fulfillment. "When applied to the family," Glendon laments, the quintessentially American "right to be let alone often turns out in practice to be the right to leave others alone."[15]

The once autonomous American family imagined in the common law and at the founding was thus traded in for the autonomous American individual: self-determining, unencumbered, "a being connected to others only by choice," Glendon writes. She continues: "The lone rights-bearer of American political discourse is an admirable figure in many ways. Yet he possesses little resemblance to any living man, and even less to most women."[16] Recalling the thought of Max Weber, Glendon describes the risks that accompanied the deregulating trends in the law of the family, especially for women. She writes, "Deregulation in the name of freedom . . . means leaving the realm abandoned by the law to be governed by the play of private power relations." Though this deracinating reality has been more widely recognized in the realm of the increasingly global marketplace, the effect of the deregulation of the family is still far less appreciated. She continues: "In the areas of procreation and the family, where women and children have generally been the weaker parties, withdrawal of regulation thus may operate to shore up the traditionally dominant position of men, despite the new legal rhetoric of equality. Underneath the mantle of privacy that has been draped over the ongoing family, the state of nature flourishes. . . . Stamped on the reverse side of the coinage of individual liberty, family privacy, and sex equality, are alienation, powerlessness, and dependency."[17] The American aspiration of equality between spouses is surely to be commended, writes Glendon, but the discrepancy between the visage of the law and the actual circumstances of women is often yawning, especially in the majority of households where children are being raised.

The unintended consequences of no-fault divorce were immediate and have scarcely subsided in the decades since: a half century after California first liberalized its marriage law in 1969, fathers' standard of living still tends to rise after divorce, while the standard of living of women, and the children who generally remain in their custody, declines, and for some, quite substantially.[18] No-fault, unilateral divorce also disempowers the spouse who would seek to contest the divorce, whose only leverage in negotiations is to assent. In a 2006 *New York Times* op-ed, Marcia Pappas, president of the New York chapter of NOW, explains the financial issues involved: "The problem with unilateral no-fault divorce is that it hurts women by removing the incentive for the moneyed spouse (who is usually the husband) to make a settlement. Instead of negotiating with a dependent spouse—whose only leverage for avoiding an impoverished post-divorce life for herself and her children may be her assent, or lack of it, to divorce—the husband can simply go to court and obtain an uncontested divorce."[19]

Thus, Glendon argues, in attempting to correct for issues that had arisen in a nation already beset by high levels of divorce relative to other nations, the no-fault reforms radically uprooted the most essential societal purpose of the centuries-old institution: to provide nurture to dependents and support to those who care for them.

No-fault divorce coupled with new legal expectations of "spousal self-sufficiency" ushered in the ideal of autonomy Stanton had envisioned in her *Solitude of Self*, undoubtedly to the satisfaction of those feminists who, in following the Millian-Stanton line, had fought for the 1970s reforms. But as Stanton's interlocutors had warned the mother of seven in her day, self-sufficiency was an especially difficult ask for the vast majority of women who had forgone paid labor to prioritize care for their children when they were young. Echoing the very response women's advocates at the time had made of Stanton's then radical pleas for the deregulation of marriage, Glendon suggested that the new 1970s approach to marriage and divorce spoke volumes for the dim cultural value we accord dependency and caregiving. Glendon writes, "[As] the law holds self-sufficiency up as an ideal, [it suggests] that dependency is somehow degrading, and implicitly den[ies] the importance of human intersubjectivity."[20] In a word, it denigrates the culturally essential work of the family.

The European Civil Law Alternative

But Stanton's Millian vision of "perfect equality" in marriage (and its dissolution) was not the only one on offer. Indeed, Glendon reports that the American path of deregulation was not the one taken by the revisers of the civil code in continental Europe. The civil law in many European countries characteristically had enunciated spousal rights and duties in far more comprehensive detail than the Anglo-American legal regime had. Prior to modern reforms, these laws expressed cultural aspirations about the nature of the marital bond as a community of persons for the nurture of children, even as it detailed wives' traditionally subordinate status. But, as women won equal status in various countries throughout the twentieth century, marriage law was not emptied of content as it was in the United States. Nor did European reforms presume the self-sufficiency of the spouses. Rather, the law continued to recognize the need for familial interdependence, even as it was infused with a thoroughly modern aspirational message of spousal equality. Thus, reforms highlighted the still-essential communal and interdependent bonds between the now legally equal spouses and suggested that each couple work out their shared duties to one another and their dependent children in a framework of cooperation.

The substantive differences between the two legal regimes were manifest in the specifics. For instance, a hearty number of U.S. states opted for unilateral no-fault divorce "on demand." Meanwhile, the great majority of European countries protected the contesting spouse and encouraged marital reconciliation by requiring significant waiting periods in unilateral divorce (of several years, not, as in the case of some U.S. jurisdictions, a few months). But even more noteworthy were the economic burdens that accompanied divorce in the civil law reforms. There, fault remained a significant factor when courts determined the postdivorce financial settlement. In addition, the financial expectations for the noncustodial parent were more substantial and robustly enforced than in U.S. jurisdictions. The European reforms thus better acknowledged the perspective of the contesting spouse and prioritized care for dependents. According to Glendon, the European reforms "did not entirely relinquish the notion of the common good when they accepted the idea of individual liberty."[21]

Unlike in the United States, then, the reformed marriage law on the European continent tended to envision the newly recognized "individual" as a human person who was always and everywhere embedded in interdependent familial and social relations. Indeed, the basic social institution of the family (and often the status of motherhood) was specially protected in most modern European constitutions, as it had been in the 1948 UN Universal Declaration of Human Rights. Among the abundant evidence Glendon offers of this European tendency to balance individual rights and human interdependence is a 1970 statement of the Federal Constitutional Court in West Germany interpreting its constitution ("Basic Law"): "The concept of man in the Basic Law is not that of an isolated sovereign individual; rather the Basic Law has decided in favor of a relationship between individual and community in the sense of a person's dependence on and commitment to the community, without infringing upon a person's individual value."[22] The codes also tended to pair newly named rights together with correlative responsibilities: as Wollstonecraft had envisioned, new rights for women still assumed familial duties, but the joint project of child-rearing was now undertaken by spouses with equal social and legal status.

Indeed, for Wollstonecraft, this was the very purpose of civil and political rights: for men and women to mutually, and virtuously, fulfill their familial and social responsibilities. Women's new rights ought not upend paternal or maternal duties, even as they expanded the capacity for women to take on new professional responsibilities outside the home and improved their legal status within it. In Wollstonecraft's vision, rights ought to make the whole range of women's, and men's, duties more attainable. Remember her injunction: "I mean, therefore, to infer that the society is not properly organized which does not compel men and women to discharge their respective duties." Laws and cultural norms ought to be organized in such a way that men and women are enabled, and encouraged, to give their familial relationships the pride of place they deserve.

For Wollstonecraft, as for Glendon, these formative relationships, and the institution of marriage that underlies them, were foundational to the flourishing of persons and of societies as a whole. Marriage had the potential to bring harmony between the sexes, thought Wollstonecraft, or to sow corruption in the same. And getting it wrong would affect human happiness across the board. The corruption of the institution that "draw[s] man from the brutal herd" was, to the British philosopher, "more universally injurious to morality than all the other vices of mankind collectively considered."

The Law as Teacher

In her work, Glendon, the legal scholar, underscores the essential pedagogical role of the law that the nonlawyer Wollstonecraft had noticed, a classical understanding that European continental jurists appreciated far more than their American counterparts. The European drafters of the civil codes recognized the law as a "carrier of meaning" that is intimately bound up with the flourishing of families and personal relationships. As a result, they intentionally articulated their aspirations for familial interdependence and collaboration in marriage into the prefaces of their revised statutes, even as their constitutions gave voice to these foundational social institutions too.

Neglecting the law's role as an important teacher is both naïve and ironic, Glendon suggests, especially for Americans. What Tocqueville noticed of the young republic is ever truer today, in the world's most litigious society: the power of the law in the United States, the Frenchman wrote, "enwraps the whole of society, penetrating each component class and constantly working in secret upon its unconscious patient, till in the end it has molded it to its desire."[23] The laws we make inevitably tell a story about the kind of people we want to be, Glendon writes, and over time, for better or worse, we tend to become that people.[24] U.S. law, in its libertarian cast, has "foster[ed] a climate," Glendon laments, "that systematically disadvantages caretakers and dependents," prioritizing individual autonomy and material success over the needs of children, the aged and infirm, and all those who care for them.[25] It is no wonder that most parents and other caregivers in the United States feel overburdened, both financially and emotionally, and underappreciated too.[26]

Since Glendon's early scholarship on the family in the 1980s and 90s, some important things have changed. A few U.S. jurisdictions, as Glendon had suggested, now differentiate between couples with children from those without when considering division of property upon divorce. Notably, divorce rates have fallen in the United States from their highest rates in the 1980s, especially among the college-educated. But the rates of cohabitation and the tendency to raise children within its loose bonds have skyrocketed in the United States, and in much of Europe.[27] Indeed, the quintessentially American value of "individual autonomy" has pushed its way into the modern European moral imagination too. Thus, even Europe's aspirational communal laws have not been enough to safeguard against a "liquid modernity" that cautions against the thick bonds of commitment and besets every Western society today.[28] As the ancients taught, and Wollstonecraft, Tocqueville, and Glendon appreciated, laws rightly teach a culture's aspirations, but once that culture no longer aspires to the good that laws teach, those laws will become an empty shell and are soon discarded. Ultimately, mores, habits, and beliefs are more durable.

In a recent interview, Glendon took stock of the changes over the last few decades: "When I wrote [my early books], I was hoping that the hyper-individualism of U.S. rights discourse could be tempered as it then was in many continental European societies. But instead there has been more convergence, legally and culturally, with European rights discourse moving in, and in some cases, ahead, of [the United States]."[29] Glendon found this convergence especially pronounced during her time in Beijing representing the Holy See at the Fourth World Conference on Women in 1995. Despite the fact that Europeans' own national constitutions—and the UN Declaration of Human Rights itself—took pains to uphold both motherhood and childhood as entitled to "special care and assistance," the European delegations, no less than the U.S. contingent, were especially hostile to including the words "marriage," "motherhood," and "family" in the conference documents, "except negatively as impediments to 'women's self-realization' (and as associated with violence and oppression)."[30] And yet, to this day, these are the very principles that underlie those nations' generous family-assistance programs.

But even as American tendencies toward "self-sufficiency" and "autonomy" have made their way across the West, manifesting themselves in the substantial portion of adults who are now childless and live on their own,[31] one particular feature in the current demographics of marriage and child-rearing stands out in sharp relief: college-educated white women in the United States are just as likely to be married today as they were in 1950. Indeed, educated women remain today the single most likely demographic group to marry in the United States. Brookings scholars Richard Reeves, Isabel Sawhill, and Eleanor Krause write that these findings suggest that women who have reached a significant education level (and, implicitly, economic independence) are using their newfound influence "to renegotiate the terms of marriage in a more egalitarian direction."[32] These women apparently intuit what reams of data on the matter report: raising their children within the marital bond is not only most likely to offer their children the familial stability that correlates with strong outcomes both personally and academically, but marriage also makes it far more likely that these women will have a partner in the demanding task of raising those children, too.[33]

The Brookings scholars conclude their analysis of the data with a thought Wollstonecraft would have liked: "The 'new' American marriage, and its promise that both partners will contribute equally to the many demands of raising a family, might in fact be an institution that furthers rather than inhibits the feminist agenda."[34] If so, it will be the kind of feminism that Glendon called for decades ago: a feminism in which "women and men [are viewed] as partners, rather than antagonists, in the quest for better ways to love and work [and one that] recognize[s] that the fates of men, women, and children, privileged and poor alike, are inextricably intertwined."[35] But if today in the United States more privileged and educated women and men are enjoying the cultural benefits of living within a social milieu that once again values the bonds of marriage—and the goods of mothers together with fathers for raising children—the poor have yet to benefit.[36]

CULTURAL MESSAGES ABOUT PREGNANCY, DEPENDENCY, AND CAREGIVING

The negative cultural messages about dependency and caregiving that were conveyed by the divorce reforms of the 1970s were not at all dissimilar from those conveyed by the nation's laws governing abortion, wrote Glendon in the late 1980s and early 1990s. Like other women's advocates who immediately recognized the problem with *Roe*'s "right to privacy," offering a negative, if vast, sphere of liberty against state regulation of abortion, Glendon, for her part, noticed how the new privacy right would tend to leave a pregnant woman "alone with her rights," with little regard for how she might actually fulfill her maternal responsibilities should she hope to undertake them.[37] The new "right to privacy," Glendon explains, was "pulled from the hat of property" and shared its exaggerated Lockean attributes: absolutist, radically individualistic, insular, and with little regard for the complex interplay of correlative responsibilities.[38] Like the more traditional American fixation with property as "marking off a sphere around the individual which no one could enter without permission," the right to privacy proclaimed an absolute sovereignty in the individual, so long as, as Mill had famously written, his or her actions did not obviously harm another.[39] The new privacy rights, Glendon argues in a particularly Wollstonecraftian moment, were proclaimed "without much consideration of the ends to which they are oriented, their relationship to one another, to corresponding responsibilities, or to the general welfare. [They] encourage[d] our all-too-human tendency to place the self at the center of our moral universe."[40]

Ever relying on the comparative approach, Glendon in 1987 brought attention to the cultural message the *Roe* Court conveyed, up and against those messages European counterparts were hearing on the contentious issue. Whereas *Roe* treated abortion as, in Glendon's telling, a "conflict involving a woman's individual liberty or privacy" with that of a "nonperson," the 1975 reform law of France, for instance, more honestly "named" the issue as one involving dependent human life, and duly recognized the state's proper role in protecting that life.[41] Indeed, as we described in chapter 8, in striking down even compromise statutes that had been passed in many states, *Roe* (alongside *Doe*) erected steep hurdles against the protection of dependent unborn children even late in pregnancy. Meanwhile, most Western European countries *required* regulations to safeguard the life of the fetus after the tenth or twelfth week (or at the Swedish extreme, eighteenth week) of pregnancy.

Furthermore, nowhere did the laws of European countries at that time refer to abortion as a women's "fundamental right," as the U.S. Supreme Court did. Nor did these jurisdictions remove the contentious issue from the legislature entirely, as *Roe* did. Rather, in the words of Simone Veil, the chief promoter of the French reforms in the mid-1970s, "abortion should remain an exception, the last resort for hopeless situations."[42] But, even more important than the particulars of the various European abortion laws of the 1970s, in Glendon's view, was the distinct role the state was called to play in these jurisdictions. The varied European abortion laws all expected the government to take an active and positive role in promoting respect for unborn life, motherhood, and familial relationships in general. Abortion was regarded as a serious matter in these jurisdictions, but so too was motherhood and fatherhood. The dignity, needs, and interests of both the mother and her unborn child were considered as of a piece, rather than through the antagonistic lens of "rights talk," with mother and child pitted against each other, as has been the case in the United States.

Thus, the French, for instance, knew that should they put extensive restrictions on abortion, they ought also to provide serious assistance with parenting. The 1975 French law thus stated that "education toward responsibility, the acceptance of the child in society, and family-oriented policy are national obligations."[43] Though the details of the laws varied in each jurisdiction, this communal response was the general approach throughout Europe. This was true even, or especially, in Germany, where the country's high court rendered a 1975 ruling that was the mirror image of *Roe*. The West German Constitutional Court held that, given the country's recent anguish of having allowed innocent life to be taken in the "final solution," the state could not neglect its constitutional duty to protect "human dignity," including the unborn child at its very earliest stages.[44] Exceptions were to be permitted by the legislature only for the most serious reasons, and provisions were made to promote the needs of the pregnant woman, her child, and the family as a whole. Glendon sums up the two legal regimes' distinctive messages: "[Whereas U.S.] law stresses autonomy, separation, and isolation in the war of all against all. . . . European laws not only tell pregnant women that abortion is a serious matter, they tell fathers that producing a child is serious too, and communicate to both that the welfare of each child is a matter in which the entire society is vitally interested."[45]

The laws of most European countries have shifted since Glendon wrote these words in 1987, with European jurisdictions loosening their abortion restrictions somewhat, and many increasingly referring to abortion as a "women's right." For its part, U.S. abortion jurisprudence has changed somewhat since 1992, permitting, for instance, states to dissuade women from choosing abortion, as European countries required much earlier on.[46] But the "constitutional right" in the United States remains virtually absolute, given the privileged status of the "health" exception in U.S. abortion jurisprudence. Broadly rendered "well-being" in 1973, "women's health" continues to work as an absolute trump on even most late-term prohibitions.[47] In the United States, nothing in the Supreme Court's jurisprudence affirmatively protects the life of the unborn child as European jurisdictions had, nor does it prohibit individual states from providing even more expansive abortion access.[48]

Despite the various changes in the law since Glendon wrote her comparative treatise, the essential analytical point remains: the message women and men receive in the United States is that caring for dependency is a private, lonely matter. Constitutionally speaking, women are still given great latitude in exercising their "right to choose" abortion or, should they carry their unborn children to term, motherhood. But should they choose the latter, especially if they are poor, they ought not expect the support they need, beyond minimal welfare benefits. "In the United States today," Glendon wrote in 1991, "pregnant women . . . have their constitutional right to privacy and little else." She continues, "By making abortion a woman's prerogative, the Court has made it easier to treat it as a woman's problem [and] her responsibility. [It then seems] legitimate, not only for taxpayers but also for the fathers of unborn children, to leave the freely choosing right-bearer alone."[49] In the United States, then, both abortion and childbearing are rendered *privately* chosen acts with *privately* borne consequences.

Echoing the arguments Glendon made two decades before, pro-choice constitutional law scholar Robin West suggested in 2009 that the "rhetoric of choice" in the context of abortion "exists in considerable tension" with public support for motherhood:

> Constitutionalizing this particular right to choose simultaneously legitimates . . . the lack of public support given parents in fulfilling their caregiving obligations. By giving pregnant women the choice to opt *out* of parenting by purchasing an abortion, we render parenting a market commodity. . . . The choice-based arguments for abortion rights strengthen the impulse to simply leave her with the consequences of her bargain. She has chosen this route, so it is hers to travel alone. . . .

The right to an abortion gives women a right not to be a caregiver, but at the cost of rhetorically making the difficulties of caregiving all the harder to publicly share, should she opt for it. For
privileged women, this is not such a terrible trade off. . . . The
woman only marginally capable of supporting even herself, however, faces a choice between parenting and severe impoverishment,
on the one hand, and forgoing children on the other.[50]

For Glendon, and presumably West too, childbearing and child-rearing are *public* goods with very *public* consequences, and thus ought to
enjoy affirmative *public* support.

But how U.S. law manages abortion and divorce are not the only
ways the law today conveys negative messages about dependency and
caregiving. Significant federal legislation protecting pregnant women
against workplace discrimination in 1978 and winning unpaid family
leave in 1993 merit important consideration too. As we review these
victories below, Glendon's central point, and indeed the chief argument of this book, remains salient: the culturally essential and unpaid
work of the family is still undervalued up and against the paid work of
the postindustrial workplace, and *it is poor women and their children
who suffer the most*. As Glendon herself put it, "Something is wrong
when we frame laws and policies as though human beings existed to
serve the economy, rather than the other way around."[51]

Pregnancy and Women's Labor

In the wake of *Roe*, state officials and employers who sought to exclude pregnancy from health insurance or disability coverage found
themselves with an additional argument for their position: pregnancy
after *Roe* could now be understood as a condition affirmatively chosen
by a woman and so not quite comparable with medical or other disabling conditions that might befall a man. So, when Sally Armendariz,
for instance, could not work for three weeks after suffering a miscarriage when her car was rear-ended, the state insurance program, into
which she had paid for ten years, denied her disability claim because
her injury arose "in connection with pregnancy." She was similarly de-

nied unemployment insurance benefits because the state now treated her pregnancy-related disability as "voluntary." Ironically, for Armendariz, her pregnancy loss was a result of miscarriage, not abortion.

Armendariz sued, claiming that California had contravened the equal protection clause. In their brief defending against Armendariz's claim, the attorneys for California took full advantage of newly emergent equality arguments in favor of abortion: "[A] large part of woman's struggle for equality involves gaining social acceptance for roles alternative to childbearing and childrearing." The brief continued, citing *Roe*, pregnancy is now "voluntary and subject to planning."[52] In 1974, the U.S. Supreme Court ruled against Armendariz and in favor of the state of California. *Geduldig v. Aiello* held that the Fourteenth Amendment did not require the state to include coverage for pregnancy in its disability insurance programs. Two years later, in *Gilbert v. General Electric*, the Court ruled that neither did Title VII require such coverage.

The business lobby received the Court's message loud and clear. In 1971, three years before *Geduldig* and five years before *Gilbert*, the EEOC had issued a departmental ruling stating that the exclusion of pregnancy from disability coverage violated Title VII. By 1973, the same year as *Roe*, 75 percent of 929 companies surveyed reported that they offered maternity leave, up from 40 percent in 1965. But after *Roe*, *Geduldig*, and *Gilbert*, this trend slowed substantially.[53] In *Roe*'s wake, however, corporations, especially those with large numbers of female employees, made sure that (far cheaper) abortions were covered in their medical plans.

Early in 1977, the pro-life feminist organization American Citizens Concerned for Life (ACCL) issued a press release in response to the 1976 *Gilbert* decision, explicitly suggesting that *Roe* "set the precedent" for General Electric to intimate in their briefs before the Supreme Court that "women employees should be willing to end the lives of their unborn children if they were financially unable to withstand a period of wage loss."[54] ACCL alongside 200 other pro-life, pro-choice, labor, and civil rights organizations formed the Campaign to End Discrimination Against Pregnant Workers to lobby Congress to pass the Pregnancy Discrimination Act (PDA) and thereby overturn the high court's decision in *Gilbert*.

In testimony before Congress in favor of the PDA, special counsel for ACCL, Jacqueline Nolan-Haley, argued that the *Gilbert* decision elevated the logic of the market over the value of unborn children, thereby treating them as "'affordable' or 'non-affordable' commodities," whose very worth ought to be determined by a "cost/benefit analysis." When taken together, *Roe*'s new privacy right alongside *Gilbert*'s denial of pregnancy coverage amounted to, in Nolan-Haley's words, "economic coercion" in favor of abortion.[55] Poor and single mothers were clearly most harmed by this sort of "choice." U.S. senator Joe Biden argued as much in a 1977 statement: "In a very real-world-sense what this denial of freedom [because of discrimination] means is that many women, especially low income women, may be discouraged from carrying their pregnancy to term. To put it bluntly they will be encouraged to choose abortion as a means of surviving economically."[56]

Other feminists, otherwise in favor of "reproductive choice," offered critiques of *Gilbert* that also borrowed from an earlier era of women's rights advocacy. They suggested that women's childbearing labor was a public good whose benefits were shared by all. In making this sort of argument, an attorney for the New York Civil Liberties Union wrote, "Because women serve the biological function of continuing the species, society should share the disabilities and costs instead of penalizing her for her necessary physiological role."[57] The old alliance was thus revived among diverse groups of women's rights advocates, echoing the shared goals of the original NOW platform. Affirming both women's economic opportunity and the value of motherhood, their efforts culminated in the passage of the Pregnancy Discrimination Act in 1978.

Pregnancy as *Dis*-ability?

After the passage of the PDA, which had amended Title VII to ensure that employers could not discriminate against pregnancy or maternity, a few state legislatures went about requiring more generous maternity benefits. The PDA had only required that pregnant workers or new mothers were given the "same treatment" as nonpregnant workers who were otherwise "similar in their ability or inability to work."

Pregnant women could not be discriminated against in the workplace, but the federal statute required no affirmative allowances for pregnancy or maternity. Judge Richard Posner memorably interpreted the statute: "Employers can treat pregnant women as badly as they treat similarly affected but nonpregnant employees."[58] To fit Title VII's antidiscrimination paradigm, pregnancy had been analogized in the legislation to male disability.[59]

The legal question quickly arose as to whether the PDA prohibited greater allowances for pregnant women and mothers when states elected to make them. Thus, when California in 1979 passed the Pregnancy Disability Leave law, which required employers to allocate four months unpaid leave to women upon the birth of their child and reinstate them in a same or comparable position when they returned, California Federal Savings and Loan (CalFed) and two business groups brought suit in federal court. The businesses alleged that the state law violated the PDA by requiring that pregnant workers be treated better than others. In a word, they claimed the California law discriminated against men.

Just as women's advocates during the Industrial Revolution and *Lochner* era took opposite sides concerning protective legislation for women, so too did feminist attorneys in the 1970s advocate on both sides of the new pregnancy-related issue. Was job-protected maternity leave just another form of illicit protective legislation? Some of the main proponents of the PDA agreed with CalFed: by singling out pregnancy for "special treatment," California would make women costlier than men to employ and therefore create disincentives to hiring them. The pregnancy leave statute also reinforced, in these feminists' minds, the antiquated view that *women were mothers first and employees second*. This assumption, they argued, controverted the antistereotyping rationale of sex discrimination law. The solution, according to Georgetown law professor and the PDA's chief architect Wendy Williams, was to enhance leave policies and fringe benefits for *all* workers rather than to focus legislative attention and assistance on pregnancy and maternity in particular. Like Alice Paul in the *Lochner* era, Williams thought that even benefits putatively favoring women would harm rather than help them: privileging pregnancy would stigmatize women, bringing unnecessary attention to their reproductive differences from men.

On the other side sat labor advocates who matched Florence Kelley's early twentieth-century concern for the concrete situation of women on the ground. Kelley had argued that Paul's strict version of equality abstracted from and thus tended to ignore the actual lived experiences of women, leaving disadvantaged mothers especially bereft of any assistance during childbirth and thereafter. Likewise, members of the Coalition for Reproductive Equality in the Workplace (CREW) suggested that although the PDA would ensure that these women did not lose their jobs, without greater protection and support they were guaranteed no time to recover from childbirth or to provide nurture and care for their infant children. Unless, of course, their employers happen to offer significant leave for men.

For CREW and those defending the California maternity law, such women-specific benefits did not prefer women to men. The law simply took into account the asymmetrical facts of human reproduction (that women are affected more by childbirth than men are) and thus acted as "an equalizer."[60] In this way, they echoed, even while modernizing, Justice Brewer's more patronizing appreciation of reproductive asymmetry in the 1908 case *Muller v. Oregon*: "This difference justifies a difference in legislation, and upholds that which is designed to compensate for some of the burdens which rest upon her." Even more important for our purposes, though, was that the antidiscrimination framing of Williams's PDA sent a powerful cultural message about pregnancy, childbirth, and maternity when it analogized pregnancy to male disability. CREW attorney Christine Littleton suggested as much in 1986, while *CalFed* was making its way through the federal courts: "What makes pregnancy a *dis*ability rather than, say, an additional ability, is the structure of work, not reproduction. Normal pregnancy may make a woman unable to 'work' for days, weeks or months, but it also makes her able to reproduce. From whose viewpoint is the work that she cannot do 'work,' and the work that she is doing *not* work? Certainly not from hers."[61]

One might say that Littleton sought to call attention not to the "disability" that accompanies childbearing for women but to the "privilege" and "power" that remain theirs alone. She sought to shift the guiding paradigm from one which looked upon the issue from the perspective of the modern-day workplace to one which put postindustrial views of "work" and the norms of the workplace themselves into question. Littleton states, "It is not impossible to imagine a definition of 'work' that includes the 'labor' of childbirth; nor is it impossible to imagine a workplace setting in which pregnancy would not be disabling."[62]

The California maternity leave statute for which Littleton's organization advocated prevailed at the U.S. Supreme Court in 1987. The high court ruled in *California Federal v. Guerra* that the PDA did not preempt more generous state law; rather, quoting approvingly from the lower court decision, the Court held that the PDA established "a floor beneath which pregnancy disability benefits may not drop—not a ceiling above which they may not rise."[63] Writing for the majority, Justice Marshall explained: "Unlike protective labor legislation prevalent earlier in this century, [the California law] does not reflect archaic or stereotypical notions about pregnancy and the ability of pregnant workers."[64] CREW's interpretation of the PDA had won, but only a few states had opted to pass supplementary legislation. More was needed.

In 1993, President Clinton signed into law the Family and Medical Leave Act (FMLA), which provided the remedy Williams and others had sought for at least a decade: the creation of a federal program that secured temporary leave for both male and female workers who needed time to recover from their own serious health condition, or to care for a newborn, adopted child, or a seriously ill family member. A modest first step in a cultural landscape otherwise bereft of affirmative supports for child-raising families, the FMLA also conveyed an important message about men and caregiving whose time had come. As Chief Justice Rehnquist wrote in the 2003 case upholding the family-leave portion of the FMLA, the statute properly worked to uproot "the pervasive sex-role stereotype that caring for family members is women's work."[65]

But even as the FMLA, like the PDA before it, was a crucial advance, to this day the law remains wholly inadequate for the needs of most child-rearing families. For although twelve weeks is likely enough for a woman to recover from normal childbirth, it is hardly enough to offer nurture and care to one's infant or to assimilate an adopted child into one's family. Moreover, the statute is irrelevant for those disadvantaged mothers who cannot afford to take unpaid leave. Harrowing stories of poor women returning to work days after childbirth recall the situation to which Florence Kelley and Jane Addams were responding in the late industrial era.[66] No wonder that both sides of the political aisle are now seeking ways to fund paid leave, especially for the nation's most disadvantaged families.

THE NEED FOR A COMMUNITARIAN RESPONSE

The very same winter that Clinton had signed the FMLA, Glendon and other scholars of various political persuasions published a lengthy and substantive statement entitled "The Communitarian Position Paper on the Family." Three years earlier, Glendon had helped the sociologist Amitai Etzioni and Democratic strategist William Galston draft the Responsive Communitarian Platform, the founding statement of the nascent bipartisan political movement. In a speech at the Second National Communitarian Teach-In in 1992, Glendon defined the movement as "an effort to knit the two halves of [the nation's] divided soul together": love of individual liberty with "our sense of an inclusive community for which we accept a common responsibility."[67] The platform's signatories were an impressive array of academics and social thinkers: even Betty Friedan had signed on.

In 1993, a subset of scholars within the movement sought to use their influence to renew public support for the basic social institution of the family, a pressing issue that had received substantial, if contentious, attention during the 1992 presidential election. The "Position Paper on the Family" sought to "promote the common good by supporting families in the vital work they do" and thus to articulate a "coherent pro-family agenda."[68] The paper named a variety of worthy recommendations for policymakers and society at large, many of which were taken up by the Clinton administration and other state and federal governmental bodies in due course.[69] The foremost recommendation of the paper, however, has gone virtually unheeded to this day. After recognizing ninety days of unpaid leave (i.e., FLMA) as a "good first step," and calling for public resources to improve childcare for older children (and infants in special circumstances), the paper gave utmost priority to a more radical and urgent ask: the need for society to support infant-parent bonding in the home until the age of one year.[70]

To enable such bonding, the paper recommended "at least six-months of publicly-provided paid leave" (as fiscal and economic circumstances allow) and an additional six months unpaid leave for those who work at larger companies.[71] In addition to advocating flex-time and home work arrangements, the paper called for a generous European-style child allowance: "Parents should be able to choose between working at home and outside the home, but government tax policies should not be used to favor families who earn more because both parents work outside the home when there are young children in the family."[72] But such public policies and workplace reforms were still not enough: a "culture of familialism" was needed to shore up the culturally essential work parents do in the family. "Children are bearing the brunt of a profound cultural shift toward excessive individualism," the authors declared. The paper called for the culture to reaffirm the value of children over "excessive careerism or acquisitiveness" so that parents might "recommit themselves to their work as nurturers and stewards of the next generation and put their children first."

The communitarian vision at its core sought to put into question the capitalistic view that tended to regard market work as of primary importance and economics as the choice framework of analysis. So, for instance, although the position paper repudiated discrimination against women and "the notion that parenting is only a mother's job," the communitarians would not have understood the fundamental problem in the terms the "equality feminists" did, that is, that women were too often regarded illicitly as "mothers first and employees second." Rather, the more fundamental trouble, according to the communitarians, was that *all people* in the workplace were presumed to be *employees first and caregivers second*. The capitalistic paradigm missed the more basic Wollstonecraftian insight: stable, just, and flourishing political and economic systems rest upon the integrity, ingenuity, and industry of persons, and the relationships of interdependence, trust, and fair play among persons, virtues first learned in families, or not at all. "If you wish to make good citizens," the eighteenth-century philosopher wrote, "you must first exercise the affections of a son and a brother. This is the only way to expand the heart; for public affections, as well as public virtue, must ever grow out of private character."

This character-shaping work of parents, although unpaid and often undervalued, was thought by the communitarians to be just as important as any other work, or perhaps more so. And though some economists, social thinkers, and even international bodies have tried since then to put an economic value on such care work in order to reveal its abundant (and too often invisible) worth to nations, even these worthwhile attempts at "valuing" care still operate from within the capitalistic framework; they do not challenge it.[73] The communitarians at their best recognized that only a higher viewpoint, one that sees the *economy in service of families* and its members (and not the other way around), would provide the underlying rationale for a humane "work-family" agenda. As Glendon put it elsewhere, "Think of it: human values ahead of economic values; the dignity of all types of work. That is a radical program. It goes to the root of the materialism of capitalist and socialist societies as we have known them."[74]

Indeed, the communitarian position paper named this crucial character-shaping work in the family as the chief reason "public" policy needed to support "private" families. Children in their families "learn or fail to learn what it means to give and take; to trust or to mistrust; to practice self-restraint or self-indulgence; to be unreliable or reliable." The work of the family is not merely a private affair; it has consequences for us all. Glendon memorably had put the same point years before in her celebrated book *Rights Talk*: "If history teaches us anything, . . . it is that a liberal democracy is not just a given; that there seem to be conditions that are more, or less, favorable to its maintenance, and that these conditions importantly involve character—the character of individual citizens, and the character of those who serve the public in legislative, executive, judicial, or administrative capacities. Character, too, has conditions—residing in no small degree in nurture and education. Thus one can hardly escape from acknowledging the political importance of the family."[75]

And in a later publication, speaking perhaps to those who most especially prize the free market and presume that private families and the women within them can manage quite well without public support, Glendon writes:

Let us stipulate the free market is the greatest device that human beings have discovered for unleashing economic energy and creativity,
for utilizing resources, and for responding to human needs. . . .
Nevertheless, those who do not want to see any interference with
market forces in the form of family policy or labor policy need to
think again. . . . The market, like our democratic experiment, requires a certain kind of citizen, with certain skills and certain virtues. . . . In short, it depends on culture, which in turn depends
on nurture and education, which in turn depends on families.
Capitalism, like liberalism, long took civil society, the family, and
women's roles in nurture and education for granted. Now, capitalism, like liberalism, needs to worry about whether it is eroding its
own supports in civil society. . . . Today we need to attend to social
capital, to consider how to replenish it, and to reflect on how to
keep from destroying it.[76]

Although one can discern Glendon's fingerprints on much of the
"Communitarian Position Paper on the Family," this line especially
bears her voice: "Being a mother or father isn't just another 'life-style
choice,' but rather an ethical vocation of the weightiest sort. A responsive community must act to smooth the path for parents so that joys of
family life might be more easily felt and its burdens more fairly borne."[77]

For the communitarians, supporting child-raising families required not
only material aid and workplace flexibility—though these were essential goods the state was in the best position to offer. The communitarians also recognized that families—properly the first community for
both children and their parents—also needed other, broader communities of support to carry out their profound task. Child-rearing is too
important—and just too difficult—to expect parents (never mind
single parents) to go it alone.

The "Position Paper on the Family" articulated the point this way:
"As Americans, we rightly cherish our individual freedom. But we cannot live without communitarian roots: families, communities, religious
and secular associations, and various social movements. Children growing up outside a richly textured, interconnected network of human

272   THE RIGHTS OF WOMEN

relations are deprived of a most precious gift: society itself." Communities of "memory and mutual aid," as Glendon often referred to them, provide something the state cannot: emotional, social, and in many cases, religious support for children and their parents, and also meaning and purpose in their lives.

But these supportive communities play more than an essential role in meeting basic human needs for sociality and solidarity. The communitarians, like their intellectual predecessor Tocqueville, believed that they simultaneously act as buffers between families and the overweening power of both the market economy and the bureaucratic state. At their best, families, and the communities that support them, provide the surest protection against the ever-encroaching market mentality, helping persons, in Glendon's words, "to develop an internalized willingness to view others with genuine respect and concern, rather than as objects, means, or obstacles."[78] The preamble to the Responsive Communitarian Platform that Glendon had helped to craft reads: "The preservation of individual liberty depends on the active maintenance of the institutions of civil society where citizens learn respect for others as well as self-respect; where we acquire a lively sense of our personal and civic responsibilities, along with an appreciation of our own rights and the rights of others; where we develop the skills of self-government as well as the habit of governing ourselves, and learn to serve others—not just self."[79]

Mediating institutions, Glendon writes elsewhere, "sustain the democratic order, by relativizing the power of both the market and the state, and by helping to counter both consumerist and totalitarian tendencies. . . . When individual rights are permitted to undermine the communities that are the sources of such practices, they thus destroy their own surest underpinning."[80] The institutions of civil society, Glendon and the communitarians believed, provide the very bulwark for the preservation of liberty itself. This was no small feat and, at a time when both families and their supportive communities had progressively weakened, it would require intentionality to succeed.

CULTIVATING RENEWED ECOSYSTEMS IN SUPPORT OF FAMILIES

Glendon parted ways with the communitarians soon after the "Position Paper on the Family" was published. The movement had begun to focus its energies not on proposals for shoring up support for families and local communities, but on welfare, public schools, and crime. Glendon viewed these areas as important too (even as she disagreed with several of the communitarians' specific recommendations). But to her, no single issue mattered more to the future of the country and the flourishing of persons than the support of families. If the Founders had taken the essential work of families for granted in shaping the foundational law of the new republic, today family policy had to become a national priority. At a time when families were overburdened, mothers' tireless work undervalued, fathers' essential contribution ignored or undermined, and the value of children getting short shrift, she recalled by way of analogy the affirmative vision of Martin Luther King's "Beloved Community." We ought to work, Glendon said in a speech on that theme, for "a society that holds out its arms to children, that supports and honors motherhood, that encourages families engaged in the all-important task of raising children because it knows that good parents are not just doing something for themselves but for all of us."[81] In a published conversation among scholars around the same time, she suggested language for a hypothetical constitutional amendment modeled after those of modern European constitutions: "The nation has a special responsibility for the protection and welfare of children and their families."[82]

But Glendon did not just wish to see an affirmative family policy in order to counter the kinds of negative messages U.S. law was conveying both subtly and not so subtly about dependency and caregiving. "A nation without a conscious family policy has a family policy made by chance, by the operation of policies and programs in other areas that have an impact on families," she observed.[83] She also sought to draw attention to the way in which the growing cultural attitude enamored of "rights" had worked alongside those laws and policies to undermine the very structures individuals and families needed to flourish. "Family members may need nurturing environments as much as they need rights," Glendon argued in 1989.[84] But the absolutist focus on rights pervasive in U.S. legal and political discourse tended to act as a corrosive agent upon both families and the community environments upon which they depended. "Ideas that had been useful for the purposes of establishing limited government," Glendon argues, "began to pervade social discourse, to the detriment of the cultural supports on which a liberal democratic regime depends."[85]

As the foregoing sections of this chapter have described, U.S. law had increasingly protected abstract rights with little regard for the concrete familial and social responsibilities that underlie them, leaving the dependent and those who care for them especially vulnerable. The consequences had become evident: "The image of the free, self-determining individual exerts such a powerful attraction for modern imaginations that we tend to relegate obvious facts about human dependency to the margins of consciousness."[86] In a word, caregiving families and the communities that support them were suffering from neglect. Drawing a line from the education her conservationist relatives had given her concerning the complexity and fragility of natural environments, Glendon, with other thinkers, had begun to employ an "ecological" analogy in an effort to describe the fragile and interconnected networks of relationships and associations that provided support to individuals and families. Just as natural ecosystems needed protection, sustenance, and cultivation for their flourishing, so too did the social ecosystem. Glendon explained in 1991: "Our legal and political vocabularies deal handily with rights-bearing individuals, market actors, and the state, but they do not afford us a ready way for bringing into focus smaller groups and systems where the values and practices that sustain our republic are shaped, practiced, transformed, and transmitted from one generation to the next. In short, we have a serious and largely overlooked ecological problem, yet our ability to address it lags even behind our halting progress on problems relating to natural environments."[87]

By the mid-1990s, the ecological analogy was helping a diverse group of thinkers bring attention to the growing deterioration of once-stable families and communities, the deleterious effect that was having on the nation's children and the nation's poor, and the consequences of this cultural, or ecological, disintegration on American institutions. Robert Putnam famously reported in *Bowling Alone* (1995) that the civic engagement that had long characterized small-town America had given way to mass political movements and individualized leisure activities (including, by then, videogames and the Internet). Neither of these, in Putnam's view, tended to meet human needs of sociality, nor maintain the civic fabric upon which our republican form of government depends.[88] While social ecology, or in Putnam's phase "social capital," was deteriorating, converging economic and social trends had conspired to further weaken both marriage and family and their traditional supports: real wages in manufacturing jobs had declined, religious attendance waned, unions receded, and corporations had gone global. Decades after Glendon, Putnam, and others had sought to call attention to the importance of mediating structures for families, a number of significant books reveal more recently the ways in which these seismic cultural shifts have left underprivileged neighborhoods virtually bereft of communal supports, giving way to fatherlessness, joblessness, and addiction, or, as one book title has put it, an "alienated America."[89]

The Path to Solidarity within a Structural Constitutionalism

A chief trouble, according to Glendon, is that political thinkers on both the Left and Right tend only to see the individual, the market, and the state. They seem to forget that individuals grow up in families and that families live and move within small networks and communities. And so the respective market- and state-based political solutions tend to ignore, crowd out, or even do significant damage to the families and intermediary institutions that have the greatest influence on people's concrete lives. "The basic flaw in current state-based, market-based, and mixed approaches," she writes, "is that they neglect the family—either by treating society as a collection of individuals in competition with one another for scarce resources, or by treating the family as a public instrument to remedy failures of state and market. In doing so, they undercut the very solidarity that would be needed to remedy those failures."[90] Thus, just as important as direct state support, governments should assist families, she suggests, indirectly by shoring up the vitality of their local communal supports or, at the very least, by being mindful not to undermine them where they organically occur. Glendon writes, "It may well be that an active government acts best by strengthening the rights and responsibilities of other institutions [by] aim[ing] at setting conditions and establishing frameworks, rather than directing outcomes."[91]

In Glendon's view, the U.S. Constitution expressly favors such solutions when understood properly as a "design for self-government, not merely a charter of rights." The Constitution pushes political responses closer to the people themselves, where true democracy, civic engagement, and solidarity among people can take root. This deliberate constitutional structure merits renewed attention in every generation, but especially today, even as those who designed it took for granted the critical work of families and local communities for the flourishing of both individuals and the wider society.[92] As an important affirmative step in this direction, she praises the state's cooperation with community, nonprofit, and religious organizations that carry out human welfare and educational goals. These efforts to support nongovernmental initiatives not only channel wealth and power away from rich lobbyists, special interest groups, distant bureaucracies, and multinational corporations to needy local communities (that have often been harmed by the former's policies in the first place).[93] They also have the potential to rebuild the kinds of local networks of concrete care and concern required for authentic solidarity among persons and families. In particular, the work of religious groups and others that care for the poor and needy, and support the flourishing of families of every social class, ought to be celebrated and encouraged in a properly ecological approach to family and work-family policy.

Crucially, in her view, and in keeping with proper First Amendment constitutional protections for religious and associational rights, government must not seek in implementing its policies or distributing its funds to make every local group or charity into its own image. She writes, "Democratic states and free markets may need to refrain from imposing their own values indiscriminately on all the institutions of civil society. They may even need, for their own good, to be actively solicitous of groups and structures whose main loyalty is not to the state and whose highest values are not efficiency, productivity, or individualism."[94] For persons and families in need to receive the communal supports that assist them far beyond their material needs, government must allow civic and especially religious organizations to do their important work without undue interference.

Courts too have a responsibility not to damage the fragile familial and cultural ecosystems upon which all human flourishing depends, even as they properly protect the rights of individuals. She advises humility and self-restraint on the part of both policymakers, and especially judges who properly defer to the legislature in these delicate matters: "Recognizing the primitive state of our knowledge about the likely long-term effects of changes in these areas, an ecological approach to family policy would proceed modestly, encouraging local experiments, and avoiding the court-imposed uniformity that would follow from excessive constitutionalization of family issues."[95] Imposing a one-size-fits-all approach to family issues, especially by the highest court in the land (whose decisions, when couched in constitutional terms, are not easily overturned), ignores the diversity of family situations and circumstances and the myriad unintended consequences of top-down solutions.

More still, each time the Court intervenes without clear constitutional warrant, Glendon writes, it eats away at the habits and practices of self-government, "depriv[ing] citizens of the opportunity to have a say in setting the conditions under which we live, work, and raise our children."[96] The right of self-government is, after all, Glendon notes, as important a right as any other guaranteed by the Constitution. Local and legislative efforts also tend to afford a far better means to resolve (and compromise) on complex and deeply contentious issues than courts do. In this vein, Glendon often reminds her readers of landmark national achievements, such as the New Deal and the Civil Rights Act of 1964, that were won not through high court decisions but through ordinary politics. For Glendon, the art of politics, law, and government is best approached in an Aristotelian posture: as a deeply human practice of "ordering our lives together."

At this point, one is right to be reminded of Florence Kelley, that Wollstonecraftian advocate of the industrial age. Kelley argued that the Supreme Court in the *Lochner* era had elevated constitutional "liberty of contract" to the detriment of duly promulgated legislation that safeguarded the health, safety, and well-being of workers, and the crucial practice, she wrote, "of mutual obligation." Maintaining, as do Wollstonecraft and Glendon, that the "care and nurture of children is . . . a vital concern of the nation," Kelley sought to preserve the essential work of the family from the industrializing forces that engulfed the lives of the working class especially. "Liberty of contract," Kelley argued, was at that time a legal fiction that ignored the asymmetries between employer and employee, rendering the latter vulnerable to industrial exploits and ultimately undermining the capacity for poor workers to care for their families.

Just so, the corpus of Glendon's work puts into question yet another legal fiction: the "autonomous individual" that guides much personal liberty jurisprudence today. If "property" and "contract" rights of an earlier era were absolutized to the detriment of familial duties and social relations, so too have "personal liberty" rights been eclipsed from the duties of care that underlie them. Today's legal fiction, for its part, ignores, and in many cases exacerbates, the asymmetries inherent in childbearing and caregiving, asymmetries that disproportionately affect women and especially those who are poor. As in the industrial era, the balance, and important interconnection, between rights and duties must be restored.

Thus, as Kelley does, Glendon suggests that liberty is not always best safeguarded by high court decree (though sometimes judicial intervention is necessary).[97] It is more readily secured by protecting and promoting the complex and interconnected web of familial and communal supports that nurture and educate individuals in the habits, practices, and relationships necessary for both personal and political self-government and independence and for mutual obligation and solidarity among people. "Rather than aiming at the common good," Glendon writes, echoing both the late eighteenth-century philosopher and the late nineteenth-century labor advocate, freedom today "tends to become an end in itself."[98] In so "exalting choice for its own sake," we can neglect "responsibility for its ends."[99]

With the great corpus of Glendon's work as an anchor to our contemporary situation, we are now prepared to look again at Wollstonecraft's vision of freedom and how it might reshape the women's movement today. And so, let us conclude by reimagining feminism anew: a feminism in search of human excellence.

CHAPTER 10

Reimagining Feminism Today in Search of Human Excellence

In her opening statement to the Senate Judiciary Committee as President Clinton's nominee for the U.S. Supreme Court in 1993, Judge Ruth Bader Ginsburg recalled Judge Learned Hand's "Spirit of Liberty" speech, paraphrasing a portion of Hand's now-famous words: "Liberty lies in the hearts of men and women; when it dies there, no constitution, no law, no court can save it."[1] Hand's 1944 speech, delivered in Central Park before an audience of 150,000 newly naturalized U.S. citizens, captures elegantly the subtle realities of the human longing for freedom. He respects its elusive nature, recognizing it as a dynamic principle that itself judges each era in history and that no particular era can hold.

The speech is also one to which Mary Ann Glendon, whose academic chair at Harvard Law School bore the great judge's name, also makes frequent reference. For Hand takes pains to describe the fragile preconditions of liberty, that theme to which Glendon's own scholarship consistently attests. Asking rhetorically, "What is this liberty which must lie in the hearts of men and women?" Hand answers, "It is not the ruthless, the unbridled will; it is not freedom to do as one likes. That is the denial of liberty, and leads straight to its overthrow. A society in which men recognize no check upon their freedom soon becomes a society where freedom is the possession of only a savage few—as we have learned to our sorrow."[2] Freedom, as both Hand and Glendon describe

279

it then, is not only an abstract principle to be protected and promoted. It is also a concrete practice "in the hearts of men and women" that requires a certain personal and societal discipline, some "check" on our desires and preferences. Lacking such self-restraint and concern for the basic dignity of others, freedom retains its name but becomes a kind of savagery, a weapon wielded by the powerful against the powerless instead. True freedom, and its political variant, self-government, presupposes self-government of the personal variety, or as the ancients called it, virtue or human excellence. As Wollstonecraft aptly put it: "Society can only be happy and free in proportion as it is virtuous."[3]

Hand was right to remind the new citizens of our constitutional republic of this ancient view of freedom, extolled too by many of our founders (even as they excluded many from its universal appeal).[4] Without internal checks on freedom, as Hand well notes, our free constitution becomes an empty shell or, worse, a refuge for those who would refuse to impose upon themselves this ennobling ethic of self-restraint. Since Hand's time, U.S. culture has become more and more defined by an enormous degree of consumer choice, and this has seemed to shape our view of "choice" in other areas too. It might well be said that the ancient view of freedom that Hand, Glendon, and Wollstonecraft articulated has been traded in increasingly for the kind of freedom ostensibly delivered by the market: the freedom to choose among one's preferences. A real woman with myriad needs and desires, a pornographic image, or a sex doll: which will do?[5] The market seems not to take a position: the putatively autonomous consumer is now "free to choose."[6] Scarcely contemplated in this new consumerist approach to freedom is its proper use or end, that most important question of a prior age.[7] Wollstonecraft minced no words for such a view: to extol a freedom without virtue was to reduce men to beasts. Such an approach fortified power in the hands of the strong and offered no authentic path to true human progress or personal and societal happiness.

In its inception in the nineteenth century, the early American women's movement worked hard to resist the powerful draw of market values in the personal lives of men, women, and children. These women recognized early on that the most good, true, and beautiful things in life would never be counted in the growing commercial economy nor valued by a wage. Indeed, they foresaw clearly that the character-shaping, solidarity-building work they did with their husbands, raising up new generations of Americans in the virtues of collaboration, reciprocity, trust, and concern for others, could be undermined by the materialistic tendencies of the new commercial economy, even as these virtues make such an economy viable and sustainable in the first place. Through their political advocacy for joint property ownership, suffrage, and more, these women sought to elevate legally and politically the essential work of the home: that person-oriented island in a market-driven sea.

In the last half century, that traditional resistance to the encroaching logic of the consumeristic market has withered, and more often than not feminism too has ceded to its worldview. Today, the women's movement on the whole promotes a view of freedom as autonomous choice, manifest most plainly in the popular abortion rights slogan "right to choose." In this dominant choice framework, parenthood is increasingly viewed as one lifestyle choice among many, and for mothers an "opportunity cost" at that. The value of children (and other dependents) are too often subject, like other "trade-offs" in the marketplace, to individual (or social) "cost-benefit" analysis.

As this book has celebrated, the women's movement of the last fifty years has made extraordinary gains, not the least of which is the recognition of women as individual persons equal under the law. The myriad and diverse capacities, interests, and abilities of women, especially as opportunities have become increasingly available to them, know no end. The modern-day women's movement can be credited with at last putting to rest the ways in which women's unequal legal status in the family and in society had subordinated women unjustly for too long. But the women's movement today has been slower to recognize that abstract rights only take women so far. Taken to their limit as the freedom of the autonomous will, or the mere power to choose, abstract rights tend to eat away at the very conditions that make their exercise worthwhile—and humane. Other evaluative considerations, especially our shared responsibilities to the vulnerable and dependent, are subordinated to the duly unencumbered, autonomous self so prized in the "good life" of our late modern capitalist society. And that consuming, choosing, disembodied self makes no room for the concrete asymmetries inherent in sexual intercourse and reproduction, and in caregiving too. The deck is stacked today against pregnant women and caregiving families: the very people to whom future generations will owe their existence and well-being.

Feminist historian Linda Gordon recognizes the price that has been paid in the midst of authentic advances: "Feminists have conducted a close scrutiny of the family in the last years and seen how oppressive it can be for women. But undermining the family has costs, for women as well as men, in the form of isolation and further deterioration of child raising, general unhappiness, social distrust, and solipsism; and sensitivity to these problems is also part of the feminist heritage."[8] The very purpose of this book has been to uncover that heritage and to rediscover its wisdom. Authentic liberty and equality remain proper objectives for the women's movement today. Yet these tend toward mere abstraction, and to isolation, distrust, and unhappiness, without a recognition of their proper ends and the concrete conditions needed for their achievement.

As Wollstonecraft taught, authentic liberty of both the personal and political variety requires self-governance and independence of mind. True equality meanwhile flourishes in relationships of solidarity, mutual respect, trust, and collaboration. But these virtues are not easily learned or practiced; indeed, they scarcely emerge in individuals without the guidance, care, and nurture of many others, beginning in our families and family-supporting communities. Indeed, as the corpus of Glendon's work attests, the true achievement of rightly cherished independence in the next generation requires great care, nurture, time, and attention from us all, but especially our nation's parents and those who support their vital work.

If much historical injustice and prejudice against women has been corrected in our time, the culturally essential work of families and family-supporting communities—practiced and handed down over the ages—has been sorely neglected. Without a substantive account of human freedom, and its proper end, human excellence, the essential human goods of children, family, and community, so necessary for authentic human flourishing, are subordinated to the dominant value of choice dictated by the logic of the market. We're left with a culture that aggrandizes consumerism, workaholism, and the relentless quest for power, wealth, and pleasure. And though this new American way of life *may appear* to benefit the rich, well-educated, and otherwise privileged, none of this bodes well for children and other vulnerable populations.

Women's rights are no different: without an account of *what freedom is for*, feminism ends up appropriating a market orientation too. Individual choice is to be maximized without an obvious limiting principle and without due consideration of the apparent goods that are being chosen. As a consequence, the modern-day women's movement on the whole has difficulty condemning epidemic pornography and other forms of sexual exploitation (from "sex work" to now-normative casual sex).[9] It insists on retaining "consent" as the highest value in the sexual context, even as asymmetrical power disparities rightly put this concept into question in other areas, and as increasing numbers of ordinary women lament today's male-oriented sexual norms.[10] More still, the movement possesses little means beyond the econometric of articulating *why* caregivers ought to enjoy public support or *why* workplaces should be "family-friendly." In the now-dominant logic of the market, marriage, children, and caregiving, human goods that have been affirmed and celebrated throughout human history, are treated as merely individual preferences with substantial financial consequences.[11] Rendered private goods mediated by private choices, the inherently public nature of these goods, and the communal and political responsibilities they entail, is widely forgotten. The wealthy are scarcely affected by such cultural amnesia, as the majority persist in living out relatively family-centered lives, but the poor are shorn of that essential familial and communal substructure upon which they might find their own footing and rise above their circumstances.[12]

As a result, the women's movement, like modern culture as a whole, is bereft of a language with which to celebrate beautiful marriages (like the Ginsburgs') or to offer those relationships as worthy of emulation, by rich and poor alike. If we dare call sexual integrity, faithful marriage, or devoted parenting what they are—*manifestations of human excellence that cohere with human flourishing*—we render a moral judgment we moderns are no longer supposed to make. And yet, we happily make such evaluative assessments on less consequential human

activities all the time: in our celebration of talented athletes and musi-
cians, scientists and entrepreneurs, we are *affirming human excellence*
and, implicitly, *the self-discipline needed to achieve it*. So why not affirm
such excellence in what matters far more to our children and our future: in the tireless work we do in our marriages and our families? And
why not demand that our workplaces—the epicenter of the capitalistic
ethic—affirm these human goods too?

Wollstonecraft argued more than two hundred years ago that civil
and political rights would enable women (and men) to strive for human
excellence. Such excellence would be achieved, she thought, by fulfilling the day-to-day responsibilities one had to God, self, family, and society, whatever one's current station (or we might now say, season) in
life. Wollstonecraft was very clear about this: human beings' daily progress in virtue, not their attainment of property, wealth, or status, would
bring about human happiness. The late eighteenth-century philosopher believed that if every person's equal dignity and human potential was recognized and their liberal education and moral formation
promoted, each person could make moral progress and all of society
would benefit.

To affirm the highest good in human endeavors is not to disparage
those who do not reach its ideals. To be sure, Wollstonecraft noticed
that we human beings fall short of this or that ideal all the time; such a
human diversity of excellences and shortcomings ought not give way to
a sense of entitlement, or worse, social castes. Rather, such an honest accounting of our fragile and flawed humanity ought to inspire to a personal humility shared by all.[13] A true love of humanity holds up the
highest ideals for emulation while recognizing the propensity of human
beings to fall short, and thus to need assistance, understanding, and,
often, a fresh start to begin again. For Wollstonecraft, it was precisely
the *shared human capacity to strive for excellence, whatever one's starting point*, that gave human beings their equal human dignity amidst
manifold diversity in natural talents, individual responsibilities, and
human achievement.[14]

Feminism can be reimagined today with this ennobling moral vision
in mind. Such a feminism—a dignitarian feminism, to employ Glendon's term—would first defend, as she and Wollstonecraft saw it, the

"native" or basic dignity of every human being whose very nature, *qua human being*, provides the surest foundation for human rights.[15] But it would also promote a second, higher sense of dignity, borrowed from the ancients and extolled by Wollstonecraft and Glendon too: *dignitas*, or the honor and nobility found, not in high social status, but *in living human life excellently*.

For Wollstonecraft and Glendon alike, human beings elevate their given nature and perfect their human dignity as they live virtuously, fulfilling their responsibilities in the family, in the workplace, and in the public square. If basic dignity is the recognition of that which Cicero, Glendon reminds us, saw as the "divine spark" in each of us, aspirational dignity is achieved as we work to ignite that divine spark through the practice of virtue, imitating, as Wollstonecraft would say, the excellences of the divine.[16] And such excellence, according to these great women scholars, is what makes for a flourishing life.

The Work of the Family

As this book's early chapters on Wollstonecraft explored, this conception of human excellence as achieved through virtuously carrying out one's "duties of station" is deeply Aristotelian. Clearly, Aristotle got some things wrong. Working from a wrong-headed understanding of biology, his view of females as "deformed males" is foremost among those errors, casting misogynist ripples throughout the course of Western civilization.[17] But Aristotle's view of happiness as the ultimate end or goal of every human being has withstood the test of time. Happiness, for the Greek philosopher, was not a subjective feeling, or something achieved through external rewards. Aristotle taught that happiness— *eudaimonia* or "full human flourishing"—was found in a life lived in accordance with the highest human principles (e.g., justice, courage, temperance, practical wisdom). A life practiced in virtue or "self-government" enabled a person to deliberate and choose the just or courageous course of action freely and with earned independence of mind rather than as a slave to the then popular views of the crowd or one's fears or desires, as fleeting (and irrational) as each may be.

For Aristotle and Wollstonecraft, too, virtue was learned little by little, practiced in the daily obligations and circumstances of life through the nurture and guidance of a community that seeks to encourage each person's development and, ultimately, flourishing.[18] For both thinkers, the first essential community for human development was the family.[19] But, of course, Wollstonecraft's conception of the family was not characterized by the hierarchy inherent in Aristotle's account. Wollstonecraft instead envisioned a reciprocity among persons of equal dignity whose particular family and professional duties might differ day to day (and certainly over the course of their lives) but who were engaged in a common, collaborative goal: each person's development in virtue and thus personal, familial, and, ultimately, societal happiness.

In Wollstonecraft's account of human flourishing, the work of human formation and education—"preparing young people to encounter the evils of life with dignity, and to acquire wisdom and virtue by the exercise of their own faculties"—was among the most important work there was.[20] Undertaken with intentionality and the seriousness it deserves, the formative work of the family (later, in collaboration with the children's teachers) could well be a manifestation of human excellence itself, giving "dignity," Wollstonecraft writes, to a common duty: "The parent who sedulously endeavors to form the heart and enlarge the understanding of his child, has given that dignity to the discharge of a duty, common to the whole animal world."[21]

More still, the work of parenting, of instructing and inspiring children to act in accordance with the highest human principles, had the potential, Wollstonecraft believed, to be deeply transformative of mothers and fathers too. That work, properly shaping and enlivening the culture of the home, building character, nurturing trust and solidarity, and instilling lifelong virtues, incarnated a commitment to society of the very greatest sort. For the habits learned and practiced in the home, for good or ill, and in both children and parents, carried well beyond the home, into the broader community, the workplace, and the public square.

Ennobling Duties of Care

Parental duties thus require, as Wollstonecraft put it, "exertion and self-denial" and "a serious kind of perseverance that requires more firm support than emotions." Indeed, according to Wollstonecraft, good parenting requires "a plan of conduct." So too in our time. As the foregoing chapters have explored, for a good portion of recent history, this self-denying plan has manifested itself in the caregiving of mothers and the breadwinning of fathers. As Wollstonecraft would have appreciated, this gendered division of labor, though still the happy norm for many in the West (especially when children are very young), no longer holds sway for others.

Today, we increasingly see a multiplicity of familial arrangements as both women and men engage in the public and private spheres of life.[22] Economic necessity (especially as manufacturing jobs wane and service industry jobs grow); individual aptitudes, talents, and opportunities; women's just desire to contribute professionally and to enjoy a greater measure of financial security; and increasingly, men's praiseworthy desire to be active in the daily lives of their children have all engendered a modern flexibility in the family that properly elevates the circumstances of each above preordained gender norms. This flexibility presupposes a shared sense of collaboration and mutual reciprocity—an elevation of the common good of the family above predetermined individualistic plans—that well reminds us of the kind of cooperation required of men and women in the agrarian home.

But even as the traditional "roles" or, as Murray and Ginsburg referred to them, "functions" of *caregiver* and *provider* have been decoupled from their respective association with women and men in a significant number of families, the embodied reality of human dependency and human development persists. Children need not only "caregivers" and "providers," however these relatively interchangeable functions are shared in their families. They also need, for their full human development, *deep and abiding relationships* with each of their parents, to as far an extent as is possible.[23] Though unfortunate circumstances do not always allow these most formative relationships to form or grow, parents do well by their children to recognize, in justice, their responsibilities to them.

According to Aristotle, the virtue of justice asks that we give each person his or her due. Justice is the rightful end or purpose of any political regime, today often rendered "social justice." But it is a personal virtue too: political and social justice presuppose that individuals act justly in their personal and professional relations (e.g., judges carry out their duties with impartiality; employers offer just wages; spouses treat each other with the equal dignity each is due). A just regime cannot come into being without an abundance of just individuals. And like the other virtues, justice is learned and experienced first in the family, or only with great difficulty later in life.

Indeed, justice is the primary virtue that governs relationships between parents and children: parents owe duties of care to their dependent children precisely because of the existential dependency relationship that exists between them.[24] (When parents age, children, in justice, owe their now-dependent parents a reciprocal duty of care.) Young children depend upon their parents not only for meeting their material needs but also to provide the nurturing and loving environment, moral guidance, and good example by which they can develop the virtues needed to become mature, independent, benevolent, and happy adults. In parent-child relations, vulnerability begets responsibility. More still, the more vulnerable the child, the more, in justice, that child is "due." As Wollstonecraft well understood, individual rights thus flow from these preexisting duties: children have a right in justice to that which is due them; parents likewise enjoy the right to carry out their duties to their children. Good societies, ordered to the full flourishing of human beings, properly recognize and protect both.

Sexual Asymmetry and Authentic Reproductive Justice

The affirmative duty of parental care is first shared by biological mothers and fathers, because in ordinary circumstances they are uniquely situated to meet the needs of their vulnerable children.[25] And in exercising these duties well, with the daily perseverance, patience, and ingenuity parenting requires, biological (and adoptive) mothers and fathers exhibit a human excellence that is worthy of social praise and emulation. However, the duties of care that mothers and fathers respectively undertake differ, albeit in ways that are not altogether obvious. Wollstonecraft herself gave little detail in discussing such differences. Still, she aptly (and presciently) highlighted the embodied states of pregnancy and breast-feeding for mothers and engagement and attentiveness for fathers, suggesting that though distinctive, these *gendered* duties ought to be undertaken with the same *human* virtues. Since fathers' contributions to their children's development are less evident as bodily realities, conventional approaches to the family have tended sometimes to undervalue fathers' active and engaged presence in their children's lives.

Today, as more than a third of children in the United States live without their fathers in their homes, social science has begun to isolate the essential contributions these men make to their children's development.[26] Leading research has found that fathers' active and engaged presence seems to be a determining factor in their daughters' and (especially) their sons' capacity to exercise self-control, a strong indicator of overall emotional and social well-being.[27] The absence of fathers is sometimes profound: boys without fathers show higher levels of aggressive behavior and are more likely to commit crimes; girls are more likely to engage in sexual activity sooner and become pregnant as adolescents.[28] And in communities in which fathers are generally absent, children are much less likely to achieve economic mobility as adults.[29]

Meanwhile, research has also found that a leading determinant of a mother's happiness is the father's commitment to and emotional investment in her well-being and that of their children.[30] Studies show that paternal attentiveness is especially essential to a new mother's needs early on: the capacity of new fathers to take intermittent leave from work to care for both mother and child leads unsurprisingly to substantial decreases in physical and psychological ailments in mothers following childbirth.[31] Wollstonecraft sagely saw "the affection of [a woman's] husband as one of the comforts that render her task less difficult and her life happier."[32] Although marital rates have declined substantially in recent decades, marriage remains that arrangement in which fathers are most likely to stay connected to their children, and in which mothers are most likely to enjoy the emotional and financial support they need.[33] And happier mothers tend to make for happier children and long-standing marriages, too.[34]

Of course, the most obvious and asymmetrical sex difference in parenting is the extensive time and laborious exertion mothers undertake in pregnancy and, for those who pursue it, breastfeeding. This nine-plus-month embodied exertion is often rendered colloquially as a burden, or as comparatively akin in the law to (male) disability, as previous chapters have observed. And it is true: for most women, pregnancy is accompanied by sustained discomfort and fatigue, and for some more serious conditions still. Yet the wondrous capacity to bear another human being in one's body and to suckle that child at one's breast too often goes unspoken today, as though to call attention to it would be to treat women as mere instruments, forgetting the subject who possesses this unique privilege, or devaluing those who do not undertake it.

Considering the instrumentality to which women's bodies have been put historically, this reticence is eminently understandable. Indeed, contrary to notions of earlier times, women's reproductive capacity does not impose upon each woman a general duty to bear children; nor does bearing children mean women are unable to do anything but, as though reproductive activities and intellectual or professional ones are mutually exclusive. This is the egregious mistake rightly corrected by antidiscrimination law today: women, including those who are pregnant or are otherwise caring for children, must not be assumed to be less competent or committed to their work than their peers.[35] But in shoring up respect for women as rational individuals and agents of their own lives, we best not make the contrary error: it's not sexist (or, in legal parlance, "sex role stereotyping") to recognize the life-giving power women uniquely possess, or to notice that sexual intercourse has the potential to transform intimate (or casual) partners into a biological mother and father. Given the stubborn sexual asymmetries that persist (despite decades of widely available contraception and abortion), it would be sexist indeed were we not to take due notice.

Opening our eyes to the realities of sex for women, an intimate and embodied source of connectivity and so not just for sport, also helps us to see better the reality of pregnancy: the most intimate, embodied experience of connection, nurturance, and solidarity that human beings are capable of, and one that is enjoyed by women alone. When we culturally and legally belittle the moral status of the embryo or fetus (an unrepeatable human being just like us though rudimentary in size and form), treating the young one as something foreign, nonhuman, or parasitic upon a pregnant woman, *we are also belittling the state of pregnancy itself, and so too each and every pregnant woman.*

If pregnancy continues to be likened to any other lifestyle choice or medical condition—or worse, a disability in a Hobbesian contest with wombless men—pregnant women will never receive the cultural esteem and support they, in justice, are due. Their affirmative "choice," or voluntary "consent," to continue their pregnancies will be regarded as akin to all other choices in the now-hegemonic market frame of reference: a private assumption of a burden that is theirs alone to carry (and a benefit that they alone might enjoy).[36] Of course we ordinarily do not think of dependent children and their developmental needs as choices to which we must consent; nor do we regard human beings as private goods we may choose to enjoy. Rather, human beings are endowed with a certain intrinsic dignity that cannot, indeed, ought not, be degraded by cost-benefit analysis nor affirmed existentially by another's choice. Indeed, our formative relationships, in the family especially, involve obligations of an involuntary sort all the time. The family, after all, as Allan Carlson writes, is "necessarily organized on nonmarket principles. . . . [The family] alone can successfully embody the socialist principle: 'from each according to his ability, to each according to his need.'"[37] Respecting the nonmarket norms and values of these most intimate human relationships, and the duties of mutual care and concern they imply, provides the surest defense against a complete commercialization of all of human life, and assures too the kind of life that is worth living at all.

Only by reestablishing the inherent dignity and value of each human being, the moral proposition to which our country has ever been called, will pregnant women and caregiving families receive the public support and commendation they, in justice, deserve. For the cultural value of their caregiving depends unavoidably upon recognizing the incalculable value of the vulnerable and dependent human beings in their care. An authentic reproductive justice then would not only ask expectant mothers, in ordinary circumstances, to offer their developing unborn children due care. For pregnant and childbearing mothers to receive in justice the abundant care and support they need, fathers must take up their shared duties of care toward both mother and child too.

For as Wollstonecraft foresaw in the late eighteenth century, the single best response to the sexual asymmetries in both human reproduction and caregiving is an emotionally engaged and deeply attentive fatherhood. Such a fatherhood is, most essentially, one in which men who sire children recognize the distinctive and irreplaceable bonds they enjoy with them. But even more than that, it is the embrace of fatherhood as a core, constitutive, primary identity for men with children, one that prioritizes the collaborative, character-shaping, solidarity-building work of the home and deeply respects the distinctive burdens women experience in childbearing and child-rearing, just as good men in generations past and present have always done. As Wollstonecraft argued, the well-being of women and children depends upon the capacity of men to take up their responsibilities to both, *a responsibility that extends backward to learning to live lives of sexual integrity from their youth.* For we ought not forget that sexual integrity, for Wollstonecraft and her nineteenth-century successors, was at the very core of their ennobling vision of happiness between men and women in the home, and beyond. Indeed, sexual integrity was a full flourishing of the habits of self-mastery first learned and practiced in the home. A dignitarian feminism would thus part ways sharply from a modern feminism that merely views consensual sex as good sex, and adhere rather to Wollstonecraft's noble ethic: "Cherish such an habitual respect for mankind as may prevent us from disgusting a fellow-creature for the sake of a present indulgence."

But for authentic reproductive justice to prevail in our time, more than that is needed still. It is high time the work of the family be given the cultural respect, attention, and assistance it deserves. A dignitarian feminism would promote the historic view that the culturally essential duties undertaken in the home properly underlie civil and political rights and privileges, and thereby provide the preconditions for our economic, political, and civil life together. Only when we fully acknowledge this reality will it be possible to cogently and powerfully challenge the dominant marketplace mentality that disfavors family obligation, for both women and men.

THE FAMILY THAT WORKS

More than two hundred years after Wollstonecraft penned the *Vindication of the Rights of Woman*, and one hundred years after American women won the right to vote, explicit sex discrimination in education and the workplace is almost entirely a thing of the past. Describing the narrowing gender gap in college majors, education, occupations, labor force participation, paid hours of work, earnings, labor force experience over a lifetime, and hours of work at home, Harvard economist Claudia Goldin writes that the "grand gender convergence" is among the greatest advances of the last century.[38]

The antidiscrimination focus of U.S. law and policy has been a marked success, at least for those women who need only equal opportunity to "prove their mettle."[39] But American mothers and increasingly fathers find it difficult to fulfill well their responsibilities to their children (and other loved ones) and the responsibilities in their jobs. For the working class, declining real wages and unpredictable "just-in-time" scheduling—not to mention the millions of men out of work entirely, even before the COVID-19-driven recession—have compounded the pressures of providing both resources and time to one's children, scarce as each has become.[40] Two full-time incomes are often needed to make ends meet, leaving little time or energy to nurture the necessary bonds with one's children and one's spouse, too.

As social thinker Oren Cass laments in *The Once and Future Worker* (2018), rising economic pressures on middle- and lower-income families arrived in the midst of decades of enormous economic growth in the United States. It does not add up. "If, historically," Cass writes, "two-parent families could support themselves with only one parent working outside the home, then something is wrong with 'growth' that imposes a de facto need for two incomes."[41] It is no wonder that blue-collar men, in particular, many of whom remain shaped by their capacity to be "good providers," have shown in recent years rising disaffection with American institutions.[42] For the more educationally and economically elite, another story has emerged over the last decade or two. Not too little work or too little pay but rather what has been dubbed "overwork," "workism," or "work devotion."[43] Greater workplace demands in the global technological economy, coupled with a growing white-collar tendency to locate one's identity in work, has led to a kind of quasi-religious worship among many professionals.[44] Referring to the new alluring promise of "identity, transcendence, and community" in one's work, an author in the *Atlantic* remarked: "The economists of the early 20th century did not foresee that work might evolve from a means of material production to a means of identity production."[45] In the most highly remunerated sectors of the labor market, moreover, American "overwork" not only tends to secure one's identity and provide "moral credentialing" within one's social class.[46] It also pays a steep premium.[47]

So just as more educated women have been making enormous strides in the workplace, the workplace has become far more demanding of workers' time, especially as they rise to the top.[48] Diving deep into one's professional work may exhilarate the college-educated twenty-five-year-old, but that same professional is more likely than not to want to reduce her hours or find more flexible work when a new baby arrives.[49] In both wage labor and salaried work, such flexibility comes at a profound cost.

Across the economy, sex discrimination and gaps in pay that remain are almost entirely due to motherhood.[50] Leading researchers in the field report that "the wage gap between mothers and others is now larger than that between men and women, and motherhood accounts for much of the pay gap between men and women."[51] Those who work part-time or merely seek flexibility in their hours to care for dependents tend to be paid disproportionately less and are assumed to be less competent or committed to their work than those without caregiving responsibilities.[52] More still, when women seek to return to work after caring for children for even a short time, their labor market absence is more greatly penalized by prospective employers *than had they been simply unemployed.*[53] When they do return to work, women can feel they need to hide that they are parents.[54] For fathers who seek to have more flexible hours or to take time off to care for their children, the penalties are just as serious, if not more so.[55]

For those with low-paid work, the economic penalty associated with motherhood is especially harsh, and not only because their wages barely cover childcare costs.[56] Discrimination against mothers remains a potent force, and yet mothers' income is often needed just to make ends meet. Indeed, a mother's income might be the only income that the family enjoys. In this environment, some have argued that because of the greater demands upon workers' time, the inflexibility of American workplaces, and the inadequate work-family policies in the United States, women who leave the workforce to care for their children do not "opt out," as some have argued, but are "forced out."[57] And it is true: the Organisation for Economic Co-operation and Development (OECD), providing cross-cultural data from thirty-four democracies with market economies, reports that, on average, U.S. employees work the longest hours while enjoying the weakest work-family reconciliation policies.[58]

But both the liberal Left and libertarian Right, beholden to the market frame of reference, tend to misunderstand the nature of the burden on caregivers. Many on the Left, most notably leading feminist organizations, assume universal institutional day care would fix parental ills, providing infants and very young children with the care they need and getting mothers back to work. The rationale they offer is primarily economic: the politically progressive Center for American Progress suggests that annual GDP would increase by 5 percent "if women's labor participation matched that of men's." Indeed, expanding labor force participation for women could yield "an additional 5 million women in the labor force and $500 billion in increased GDP."[59] Equality would advance, on this view, were women and men more equal winners of their family's bread. But universalizing institutional day care for very young children is fixing the wrong problem. The most salient issue for most families is not how to fund institutional care for infants and toddlers; rather it is how better to support the majority of parents who seek to find the resources so that they (or their parents, other relatives, or close friends) might care for their young children in their own homes.[60]

Economic libertarians also tend to miss the point. Because they recognize the disparity in earnings for mothers as the result of individual women's choices to step out of the workplace to care for their families, this private "choice" is thought to be borne properly by women (and their families) alone. In a word, both the Left and the Right seem to agree that any allowances for parental leave and more family-friendly workplaces ought to incentivize not better care in the home for young children but a quicker return to the workforce for their mothers. Once regarded respectively as breadwinners and caregivers, both men and women are now assumed to be breadwinners first and foremost.[61] The essential work of mothers and fathers in their homes is not taken seriously as "work," nor is the caregiving they do there understood as providing the necessary preconditions for our economic, political, and civil life together. We have forgotten the great truth that Glendon taught throughout her esteemed career: nurturing our families and local communities requires much time and attention if they are to provide the bedrock for every kind of human excellence that individual persons and human societies might achieve.

Most mothers and fathers do not want to be displaced in their caregiving roles in the family; on the contrary, they see the caregiving they do—and the deep, intimate, and irreplaceable relationships it fosters—as affording them a great "power" and "privilege" (to return to chapter 9's Millian framework), even as their active presence in their children's young lives redounds to their children's lifelong advantage.[62] These parents instead seek support in lessening the "disability" that caregiving imposes upon their families financially. Whereas women once demanded the right to equal opportunities to work, some now request "the right to care"—without unjust penalty.[63]

The European experience attests to this fact: policies seeking to ease the tensions between work and family responsibilities are more widely available than in the United States, but the majority of European women believe part-time work is best for women when their children are very young.[64] Even in the Nordic countries, where generous leave and childcare options enable new mothers to return to full-time work at high numbers, most women regard part-time work as preferable for mothers of young children; indeed, some enjoy it as a right.[65] But in the United States, despite the desire of most mothers of young children to work part-time, less than a quarter do so.[66]

Leading work-family expert Joan Williams reports that decades of offering "the business case" for increased workplace flexibility in the United States has only moved the needle so far. Even when flexibility policies exist, many workers, especially fathers, do not use them out of fear of appearing less committed to their work. And Williams notes that their intuitions are all too correct: flexibility policies are often offered for show, with employees who use them meeting stigma, slow wage growth, fewer promotions, and lower performance reviews.[67] In response to the intractability of workplace norms, Williams suggests that perhaps it is now time to make a moral case: "Just as we do not argue against child labor or slavery with a business case, but consider these practices to violate incontrovertible human values, perhaps we should also not rely on a business case to argue against inhumane and discriminatory work norms that hurt employees and their families."[68]

A women's movement that relied on the wisdom of its predecessors would help.

Toward Policies That Prioritize the "Family Claim" over the "Social Claim"

The women who argued for joint property ownership in the mid-nineteenth century and better working conditions into the twentieth century may not be obvious exemplars for our current situation. Their lives were structured by cultural, legal, and economic norms that no longer govern the modern world. But the older women's movement understood what today more and more young parents have come to appreciate: The life of the home can be enjoyed as a deeply collaborative task, shared by both mothers and fathers. Indeed, it is a joint project that many women and men today regard as the most important work they do, and one they take very seriously.[69]

Parents today, like all individuals, have varied talents and aspirations, capacities and opportunities. So, when they engage in the common work of building a home together and raising their children, how they organize who-does-what-when depends upon the couple itself, their children's needs, and their own capacities and constraints. The duties of care they owe in justice to their children, and to each other, are universal, but how they undertake those responsibilities requires a practical wisdom that they alone must employ. In the end, the flourishing of the persons within the family, attained through doing whatever work they do well, is the common aim. But it requires a deep regard for each member of the family, and his or her varied contributions, within an abiding commitment to the good of the whole. And it requires a society that respects the work of the family as foundational to the success of the market and all else, and thus respects the autonomy of each family to best organize itself according to its own concrete needs. As Jane Addams put it, what is required is a culture-wide prioritization of the "family claim" over the "social claim."

Although culture, that is, the way families and communities choose to organize themselves over time, is always the best mover of social norms, the state, the workplace, and other institutions play key roles too. After all, incentives exist throughout society, in the tax code, in corporate policies, and in public accommodations, that tend to influence the decisions mothers and fathers make, and are able to make, for the well-being of their families. Some social and economic realities forestall family formation altogether or make family life far more difficult than it need be. The state and the workplace certainly cannot grant every family a smooth path, nor can either compel parents themselves to prioritize the "family claim" over the "social claim," but these institutions can remove some of the boulders along their way. Though the state, acting on behalf of the community at large, must today take the lead in family-supportive policies—renewing once more the nation's hospitality to family life—employers and other local institutions have an essential role to play too. The Glendon-led communitarians of the 1990s put it well: "A responsive community must act to smooth the path for parents so that joys of family life might be more easily felt and its burdens more fairly borne."

Employers: Ensure Workplace Flexibility for All

Flexibility in the workplace is the watchword for working parents, whether they are professionals drawing salaries or employees earning an hourly wage. Workplaces that promote flexible work options, with schedules released well in advance, are especially good environments for mothers and fathers to work.[70] Where flexibility is not the workplace norm, however, caregivers can tend to stand out as especially needy or lacking in commitment. Offering flexible schedules to those employees who have children is a laudable response to their evident needs, but research shows that such targeted policies tend to incur resentment and subpar treatment from childless co-workers and supervisors.[71] Thus, experts who have long studied discrimination against caregivers in the workplace suggest that workplaces be redesigned with enhanced flexibility for *all employees*.[72] Not only would parents benefit from institutional restructuring that promoted flexibility, but such corporate-wide policies could serve potentially to rewire the world of work such that persons were attended to as a matter of priority, as the subjects of their work but also in the broader decision-making of an enterprise such that the drive for efficiency and profits does not overtake the more human quest to serve persons (and their families) above all else. Unsurprisingly, flexible workplaces tend to boost workplace morale substantially.[73] Family policy ought then to better encourage, through tax incentives or other means, flexible work options (e.g., flex-time, part-time, job sharing, telecommuting, results-based reviews, paid leave, etc.) in all sectors of the economy.[74] And for those workplaces that are unable to offer adequate flexibility for their employees, on-site child care would be of great help.[75]

Government: Protect Parents on the Job and Promote Their Work in the Home

But working parents need not only flexible workplaces as they juggle their responsibilities to both their families and their jobs; as the corpus of Glendon's work shows, they need laws and policies that protect and promote their important contributions in both the home and the workplace. First, state legislatures should pass laws and courts should recognize discrimination on the basis of caregiving responsibilities, including within that ambit discrimination on the basis of labor market absence alone.[76] Employees should be judged and promoted on their own merits and their capacity to fulfill the requirements of the job, not on the false assumption that being a parent (or reducing one's time at work to engage in caregiving) makes them a less competent or committed employee. In the same vein, part-time pay equity is a point of justice: assuming employees are doing half the work, they are due half the pay, not some measure less than their full-time peers.[77]

After all, mothers (and fathers too) are increasingly cognizant of a lived reality that employers should find ways to better acknowledge: time away from market work may decrease some skills, but it grows others, and these latter ("softer") skills are needed more than ever in the workplace today. Rather than incur a "care penalty" for the care work they do with their children (and other family members), the workplace ought to better reward the transferability of the skills—and virtues—they acquire, and the "care advantage" they bring.[78] As Betty

Friedan, Pauli Murray, Ruth Bader Ginsburg, Mary Ann Glendon, and other thinkers have argued for decades, the service parents provide to the country, albeit usually not putting them in harm's way, is deeply analogous to the service military personnel offer; we ought to treat them analogously.[79] Thus, just as veterans enjoy preferences in hiring and retraining programs, so too should primary caregivers enjoy a similar privilege. Reviewing the panoply of veterans' benefits for their transferability as caregiver benefits would also make sense.

The government can also help to compensate for some of the asymmetrical burdens child-raising families bear: mothers and fathers should not be economically disadvantaged by their efforts to raise the next generation. Indeed, Americans increasingly report that they are not having the number of children they would like to, and they cite economic anxieties at the very top of their concerns.[80] The community at large has a social duty to share in parents' child-rearing responsibilities by finding creative ways to alleviate some of their costs. In recent years, a handful of states have begun to offer paid maternity (or family) leave, a policy especially important to those many mothers (and fathers) on the lower end of the economic spectrum who do not receive paid leave as a benefit of employment.[81] Congressional Democrats and more recently Republicans have federal family leave bills on the table too.[82]

Yet, as essential as it is to find ways to ensure that mothers and possibly fathers too receive paid leave, such proposals do not reach those mothers or fathers who care for their families full-time in the home (or engage in market labor on a part-time basis); nor would these monies assist with caregiving needs beyond the allocated time off. Like the separate property laws that went into effect in the late nineteenth century, paid family leave assists only those women and men who are already engaged in market work and prioritize a quick return. To enable families with small children to determine the best means of caring for them, it is time to adopt a far more generous child tax credit, or perhaps even a European-style family allowance. Diverse versions of proposals in this regard—relieving the economic burdens families take on as they do this most important work—have been proposed by thinkers from across the political spectrum for decades.[83] Putting aside the differences in these proposals, and there are many, the key principle that must be affirmed is this: government ought not discriminate against parents who seek to care for their own children in their own homes. Such a policy would finally fully affirm the truth that joint property advocates had urged centuries ago: the work of the home is serious work, worthy of value and recognition.

The government is also in a privileged position to bear some of the expense of the market-based "opportunity cost" borne by a mother (or father) who leaves the workforce to care for children. Although the gap in wages between one who has prioritized work in the home and one who has passed those same years in the workplace full-time could never be entirely closed (nor ought it), creative solutions might be found to lessen the marked disadvantage that attends caregivers who seek to reenter the workplace on a more regular basis as their children grow more independent.[84] In 2019, for instance, in an effort to boost fertility and promote support for families, the Hungarian government enacted a measure that waived personal income tax for married women who had raised at least four children.[85] Repurposed as a means to requite caregivers who have dedicated substantial time to their families, such a measure should be studied for its application in the United States. Efforts could also be made to ensure that Social Security benefits would accrue for those caring for children in the home, akin to a pension for their labors; such benefits could be saved or withdrawn, according to the family's needs.[86] Policies such as these might also help to reduce the asymmetrical dependency caregivers have on breadwinners, a dependency that can put a caregiver in an unjust financial situation in the case of separation or divorce.

Finally, if the Industrial Revolution is the proper cause of today's sharp cleavage between wage labor and family life, why not insist that today's technological revolution find ways to reintegrate the same? Just as government supported technology to put a man on the moon, so too should it encourage technological innovations that would better integrate the whole panoply of adult responsibilities—to families, jobs, and the broader community. Indeed, by forcing widespread "social distancing" during the 2020 coronavirus pandemic, it inadvertently already has.[87] Though clearly all paid work cannot be done remotely, technology can enable this reintegration to take shape in many sectors, bringing more economically productive work back into the home.[88] Less commuting (by car and plane) would also translate into less tax on the natural environment, and more home-cooked family dinners and other shared labors and traditions, reestablishing that privileged time to instill basic habits of self-mastery and respect for others and domestic affections too.[89] A nation that sought to elevate the "family claim" over the "social claim" would make this more of a priority still.

Family-Supporting Communities:
Intentionally Advance Their Vital Work

As we explored in chapter 9, the needs of individual persons and families can never be fully met by the market or the state. Rather, as Glendon argues, individuals' and families' needs are best viewed through a more "ecological" lens, one which sees clearly the myriad ways in which neighborhoods, schools, houses of worship, and worker and other associations encourage and support familial and professional responsibilities.[90] Just as environmental impact studies are often required before new projects are undertaken, Glendon suggests that lawmakers assess the effect of their programs upon this vital social ecology.[91]

Mothers and fathers, especially, need communities to help them form their children in the virtues they need to use their freedom responsibly, and to offer families assistance and encouragement when time or money is tight, or marital or parental difficulties arise. Successful individuals from humble origins consistently relay with gratitude the ways in which broader communities shored up support for their families and challenged them as persons. Schools, and the communities that often form around them, are especially important in this regard. When education is understood not simply as preparation for the workplace but more broadly as the means to instill in children the intellectual and moral virtues that will make them independent and self-governing adults, schools stand as crucial bulwarks against the prevailing consumerist mindset. They properly teach children those lifelong habits of mind and heart that will also guide them in their relationships as they mature and form families of their very own. More still, at their very best, schools offer opportunities for mothers, fathers, and families alike to build up lasting communities, imperceptibly forging vital networks of trust, interdependence, and mutual help and concern. In this way, they manifest, grow, and sustain bonds of solidarity and citizenship too, enabling individuals, families, and communities to order their lives together, practicing the very habits, Glendon frequently reminds us, required for republican self-governance.

Finding ways to strengthen formal and informal institutions like these, especially in our poorest communities where they no longer tend to emerge organically, would also go a long way toward recognizing the human reality at the very center of our story: women and men, and girls and boys, flourish best when they enjoy the nurture, formation, and support of families and family-supporting communities.

It is no surprise that as law and policy over the past several decades have elevated the rights of the isolated, unencumbered, autonomous individual above our common and shared responsibilities to the dependent, weak, and vulnerable, our workplaces have not grown much more hospitable to those who care for such persons. Nor has the community at large found ways to support this most essential work. The feminists of the 1970s believed free and easy access to abortion would empower women to achieve unsurpassed levels of autonomy, enabling them to take full advantage of the new freedoms and opportunities available to them. But perhaps easy abortion access in the United States has allowed *women to be taken advantage of* more fully in the workplace and in the bedroom instead. Rather than making room for dependents and the asymmetrical duties of care that inhere in both sex and caregiving, we have sought to remake women (and men) in the exalted image of the ever-competitive, rights-bearing, unencumbered, pleasure-maximizing, autonomous individual of Thomas Hobbes's imaginings. And we now see in concrete, especially among the most disadvantaged among us, what this vaunted abstraction tends to deliver: mothers and other caregivers who must fend for themselves, and sex that is reduced to sport.

Of course, it is possible that a real advance occurred around the mid-1970s, and that earlier ways of thinking about freedom and its responsibilities should be relegated to the dustbin of history. Women are obviously better off today—pussy hats and all. All that remains lacking is their greater access to power. It's more likely, in my view, that older conceptions of freedom have simply been forgotten or have been discarded unfairly along with contemporaneous historical ideas and practices that modern-day feminists rightly have judged unjust. But historical insights need not be appropriated with all the coincident conditions that accompanied them historically. Wisdom can transcend time and place, and serve as a course correction, if we allow it to do so.

It would surely be difficult for feminist advocates of the 1970s to reimagine a women's movement without abortion rights at its very center. Those feminists remember a time when women were regarded as designed solely for domestic life, when women's opinions were undervalued, and when mothers were seen as more capable and essential to their children's upbringing than were fathers. For 1970s feminists, restrictions upon abortion seem to betray precisely that vision of women, one that unfairly confines women solely to maternity, with no respect for their contributions beyond. But for those of us who grew up with the antidiscrimination gains of the 1970s securely in place, there is no question that women are as capable of educational and professional achievement as men. The questions have now become why the essential work of caring for dependents—still undertaken disproportionately by women—is not as valued and supported as it should be, and why poor women, especially, continue to be bereft of the paternal support both they and their children so heartily need. These are the questions a renewed women's movement must work to address. And rethinking the country's reliance on abortion as a privileged response to sexual asymmetry would be a good place to start.

At this time in our nation's history, when the consumerist approach to freedom tends to dominate our cultural sensibilities, when the quest for autonomy is elevated over the familial and communal preconditions of every freedom we might enjoy, when our capacity to raise up moral leaders has been compromised, it is time once again to remind our nation of its most basic moral proposition. All human beings are created with equal dignity and worth. But such dignity finds its true nobility when, as Mary Wollstonecraft taught more than two hundred years ago, each of us is encouraged and empowered by our families, our communities, and society at large to seek excellence in all we do.

Today, perhaps more than ever before, Wollstonecraft's noble vision recommends itself to us anew.

NOTES

INTRODUCTION

For all quotes, British (and early American) spellings have been changed to modern American spellings.

1. Janet Beer and Katherine Joslin, eds., *American Feminism: Key Source Documents, 1848–1920* (London: Routledge, 2003), 372.

2. Quoted in Sheridan Harvey, "Marching for the Vote: Remembering the Woman Suffrage Parade of 1913," *Library of Congress Information Bulletin*, https://guides.loc.gov/american-women-essays/marching-for-the-vote#note_12.

3. Betty Friedan and Pauli Murray, "The National Organization for Women's 1966 Statement of Purpose," National Organization for Women, October 29, 1966, https://now.org/about/history/statement-of-purpose/.

4. Betty Friedan, *Second Stage* (Cambridge, MA: Harvard University Press, 1988). The publisher's description of the book reads, in part: "Friedan argues that once past the initial phases of describing and working against political and economic injustices, the women's movement should focus on working with men to remake private and public arrangements that work against full lives with children for women and men both."

5. Christine de Pisan, *The Treasure of the City of Ladies* (1405); Mary Astell, *A Serious Proposal to the Ladies* (1694); John Stuart Mill, *The Subjection of Women* (1869).

6. Anne-Marie Slaughter, *Unfinished Business: Women Men Work Family* (New York: Penguin Random House, 2016), 79.

7. Richard V. Reeves, "How to Save Marriage in America," *The Atlantic*, February 13, 2014, https://www.theatlantic.com/business/archive/2014/02/how-to-save-marriage-in-america/283732/.

CHAPTER 1. MARY WOLLSTONECRAFT'S MORAL VISION

1. Richard Price, *Observations on the Importance of the American Revolution* (1784), quoted in Lyndall Gordon, *Vindication: A Life of Mary Wollstonecraft* (New York: HarperCollins Publishers, 2005), 48; see also Carl B. Cone, "Richard Price and the Constitution of the United States," *The American Historical Review* 53, no. 4 (1948): 726–47.

2. Quoted in Gordon, *Vindication*, 56.

3. Price, Correspondence to John Jay (July 9, 1785), quoted in Gordon, *Vindication*, 57.

4. Abigail Adams, Adams Family Correspondence (June 26, 1785), vi, 196, quoted in Gordon, *Vindication*, 53.

5. Abigail Adams, "Letter to John Adams, 2 February 1794," The Adams Family Papers: An Electronic Archive (Boston: Massachusetts Historical Society, 2002), http://www.masshist.org/digitaladams/.

6. See Eileen Hunt Botting, "Thomas Paine amidst the Early Feminists," in *The Selected Writings of Thomas Paine*, ed. Jane Calvert and Ian Shapiro (New Haven, NH: Yale University Press, 2014), 645: "*Memoirs of the Author of a Vindication of the Rights of Woman* (1798)—William Godwin's posthumous biography of his wife, who died after giving birth to their daughter, Mary Shelley, in 1797—was too open in disclosing the details of Wollstonecraft's early fascination with the married Henry Fuseli, the breakdown of her first marriage to Gilbert Imlay, and her premarital sexual relationships with each of her two husbands. In the context of British and American anti-Jacobinism, Wollstonecraft's life quickly became a morality tale for how revolutionary ideas such as the 'rights of woman' caused the breakdown of sexual morality and femininity. This backlash against her was strongest in her homeland of Britain, driving engagement of her ideas underground for the bulk of the Victorian era." See also Christopher Lasch, *Women and the Common Life: Love, Marriage, and Feminism* (New York: W. W. Norton, 1997), 71: "Godwin's memoir of his wife, written shortly after her death in childbirth, did her a disservice by dwelling on her disappointments in love at the expense of her writings."

7. For instance, here is Wollstonecraft writing to Imlay: "I have been playing and laughing with the little girl so long, that I cannot take up my pen to address you without emotion. Pressing her to my bosom, she looked so like you (*entre nous*, your best looks, for I do not admire your commercial face) every nerve seemed to vibrate to the touch, and I began to think that there was something in the assertion of man and wife being one—for you seemed to pervade my whole frame, quickening the beat of my heart, and lending me the sympathetic tears you excited"; Letter XXIV, September 23, 1794, in *Complete*

Works of Mary Wollstonecraft, Delphi Classics, loc. 21376 of 27946, Kindle. Hereafter cited as *CWMW*.

8. Wollstonecraft, Letter XLII, May 27, 1795, in *CWMW*, loc. 21737 of 27946.

9. In this chapter, I rely gratefully upon the scholarship and publications of Virginia Sapiro, Lyndall Gordon, Eileen Hunt Botting, Alan Coffee, Nancy Kendrick, Barbara Taylor, and many others. Full references can be found in the bibliography.

10. Aristotle, *Generation of Animals*, trans. A. L. Peck, Loeb Classical Library 366 (Cambridge, MA: Harvard University Press, 1942), 2.3, p. 175 (sometimes translated "mutilated" or "defective").

11. See, for instance, Mary Astell's *A Serious Proposal to the Ladies* (1694) and the letters of eighteenth-century English author Lady Mary Wortley Montagu.

12. Wollstonecraft, *Rights of Woman*, 198.

13. Ibid., 13.

14. Ibid., 7.

15. Mary Wollstonecraft, *Vindication of the Rights of Men, in a Letter to the Right Honourable Edmund Burke, occasioned by his Reflections on the Revolution in France, Second Edition* (London: J. Johnson, 1790), 131.

16. Ibid., 71, 29.

17. Ibid.

18. Marcus Tullius Cicero, *De Legibus* (*On the Laws*), trans. David Fott (Ithaca, NY: Cornell University Press, 2014), 1.45, https://www.nlnrac.org /classical/cicero/documents/de-legibus.

19. Wollstonecraft, *Thoughts on the Education of Daughters*, in *CWMW*, loc. 4789.

20. Wollstonecraft, *Rights of Men*, 72–73.

21. Aristotle, *Nicomachean Ethics*, 1098a.1, bk. 1.

22. Marcus Tullius Cicero. *De Officiis* (*On Duties*), trans. Walter Miller, Loeb Library (Cambridge, MA: Harvard University Press, 1913), 1.102, p. 49, n. 102.

23. See, for instance, Angela Duckworth and James J. Gross, "Self-Control and Grit: Related but Separable Determinants of Success," *Current Directions in Psychological Science* 23, no. 5 (2014): 319–25.

24. David Hume, *A Treatise on Human Nature* (London: Longmans, Green, and Co., 1874), 2:195.

25. Wollstonecraft, *Rights of Men*, 70–71.

26. Wollstonecraft, "Letter on the Present Character of the French Nation" (February 15, 1793), in *CWMW*, loc. 20465 of 27946: "I am not become

an Atheist, I assure you, by residing in Paris: yet I begin to fear that vice, or, if you will, evil, is the grand mobile of action."

27. Ibid., 135.

28. "Mary Wollstonecraft to George Blood, Newington Green, May 22nd, 1787," in *William Godwin: His Friends and Contemporaries*, ed. Charles Kegan Paul (London: Henry S. King and Company, 1876), 1:184.

29. Wollstonecraft, *Rights of Woman*, 53. In a note accompanying the word "perfection" here, she writes: "This word is not strictly just, but I cannot find a better."

30. Ibid., 117.

31. Wollstonecraft, *Original Stories*, in *CWMW*, loc. 4281 of 27946.

32. Wollstonecraft, *Rights of Woman*, 14.

33. Wollstonecraft, *Mary: A Fiction*, in *CWMW*, loc. 712 of 27946.

34. Wollstonecraft, *Rights of Woman*, 45.

35. Ibid., 139–40.

36. Wollstonecraft, *Rights of Men*, 78.

37. Wollstonecraft, *Rights of Woman*, 139.

38. Ibid., 50.

39. Ibid., 63.

40. Ibid., 21.

41. Ibid., 50 (emphasis in original).

42. Ibid., 50.

43. Ibid., 149.

44. Ibid., 152.

45. Ibid., 157.

46. Ibid.

47. Ibid., 168.

48. Ibid., 198.

49. Ibid., 180.

50. Ibid., 64.

51. Ibid.

52. Wollstonecraft, *Thoughts on the Education of Daughters*, in *CWMW*, loc. 5012 of 27946.

53. Wollstonecraft, *Rights of Woman*, 145–46.

54. Ibid., 156–57.

55. Ibid., 196.

56. Wollstonecraft, *Thoughts on the Education*, in *CWMW*, loc. 5053 of 27946.

57. Wollstonecraft, *Rights of Woman*, 173.

58. Ibid., 146.

59. Ibid., 68.

60. Ibid., 68–69.

61. Wollstonecraft, *Rights of Men*, 47.

62. See, for instance, George A. Akerlof, "Men without Children," *The Economic Journal* 108 (March 1998): 298. See also Linda J. Waite and Maggie Gallagher, *The Case for Marriage: Why Married People Are Happier, Healthier, and Better Off Financially* (New York: Doubleday, 2000).

63. See Bradford Wilcox and Jeffrey Dew, "If Momma Ain't Happy: Explaining Declines in Marital Satisfaction among New Mothers," *Journal of Marriage and Family* 73, no. 1 (2011): 1–12.

64. Wollstonecraft, *Rights of Woman*, 27.

65. Ibid., 4.

CHAPTER 2. MEN, MARRIAGE, LAW, AND GOVERNMENT

1. Wollstonecraft, *Rights of Woman*, 143.

2. Ibid., 50.

3. Ibid., 141.

4. Ibid., 143.

5. Jean-Jacques Rousseau, *The Discourses and Other Early Political Writings*, ed. and trans. Victor Gourevitch (Cambridge: Cambridge University Press, 2018), 148.

6. Wollstonecraft, *Rights of Woman*, 63.

7. Mary Wollstonecraft, *Hints*, in *CWMW*, loc. 20872 of 27946. *Hints* was a posthumous publication of Wollstonecraft's notes, apparently intended to be incorporated into a second part of *A Vindication of the Rights of Woman*, a book never written.

8. Wollstonecraft, *Rights of Woman*, 142 (emphasis mine).

9. Ibid., 170 (emphasis mine).

10. Ibid., 6: "A profound conviction that the neglected education of my fellow-creatures is the grand source of the misery I deplore; and that women, in particular, are rendered weak and wretched by a variety of concurring causes, originating from one hasty conclusion. . . . One cause of this barren blooming [of women] I attribute to the false system of education, gathered from the books written on this subject by men who, considering females rather as women than human creatures, have been more anxious to make them alluring mistresses than affectionate wives and rational mothers; and the understanding of the sex has been so bubbled by this specious homage, that the civilized women of the present century, with a few exceptions, are only anxious to inspire love, when they ought to cherish a nobler ambitions, and by their abilities and virtues exact respect."

11. See, generally, Cora Kaplan, "Mary Wollstonecraft's Reception and Legacies," in *The Cambridge Companion to Mary Wollstonecraft*, ed. Claudia L. Johnson (Cambridge: Cambridge University Press, 2002), 246–70.

12. Wollstonecraft, *Rights of Woman*, 21.

13. Wollstonecraft, Letter XXXI, December 30, 1794, in *CWMW*, loc. 21542 of 27946.

14. Ibid., 170–71.

15. Ibid., 133.

16. Ibid., 142.

17. Christian Gotthilf Salzmann, *Elements of Morality, for the Use of Children; with an introductory address to parents* (translated by Mary Wollstonecraft) (J. Crowder, 1792), xiv.

18. Ibid. "Children very early see cats with their kittens, birds with their young ones, etc. Why then are they not to be told that their mothers carry and nourish them in the same way?" (Wollstonecraft, *Rights of Woman*, 130).

19. Wollstonecraft, *Rights of Woman*, 133.

20. Ibid., 143.

21. Ibid.

22. Ibid.

23. Ibid.

24. Ibid., 133.

25. Ibid., 147.

26. Ibid., 13.

27. Ibid., 142.

28. Ibid., 122.

29. Ibid., 66.

30. Ibid., 147.

31. Ibid., 9.

32. Ibid., 199.

33. Ibid. (emphasis mine).

34. Paul H. Due, "Origin and Historical Development of the Community Property System," *Louisiana Law Review* 23 (1964): 82–83: "The 'general community of goods,' by which all the spouses' property was included in the collective estate, resulted by operation of the marriage itself." Also see Alice Clark, *Working Life of Women in the Seventeenth Century* (London: Frank Cass, 1968).

35. Eileen Power, "The Position of Women," in *The Legacy of the Middle Ages*, ed. C. G. Crump and E. F. Jacob (Oxford: Clarendon, 1926), 432–33.

36. At common law, *consortium* was a legally protected interest a husband had in the services and society of his wife, including his exclusive right to

engage in sexual relations with her, a right that was not reciprocal. See Evans Holbrook, "The Change in the Meaning of Consortium," *Michigan Law Review* 22, no. 1 (1923): 1–9.

37. Wollstonecraft, *Rights of Woman*, 184.

38. Ibid., 182.

39. Ibid., 47.

40. Wollstonecraft, Letter XLIV, June 12, 1795, in *CWMW*, loc. 21760 of 27946.

41. Wollstonecraft, *Hints*, in *CWMW*, loc. 20882 of 27946.

42. Wollstonecraft, *Rights of Woman*, 161.

43. Ibid., 146.

44. Quoted in Virginia Sapiro, *A Vindication of Political Virtue: The Political Theory of Mary Wollstonecraft* (Chicago: University of Chicago, 1992), 179.

45. Edmund Burke, *Appeal from the New to the Old Whigs* (1791), in *The Works of the Right Honourable Edmund Burke* (Boston: John West and O. C. Greenleaf, 1807), 3:392.

46. Wollstonecraft, *Rights of Woman*, 158–59.

47. Ibid., 15.

48. Wollstonecraft, *An Historical and Moral View of the Origin and Progress of the French Revolution; and the Effect it has Produced in Europe* (1794), in *CWMW*, loc. 17878.

49. Wollstonecraft, *Rights of Men*, 49–50.

50. Richard Price, *The Correspondence of Richard Price: March 1778–February 1786* (Durham, NC: Duke University Press, 1983), 268.

51. Wollstonecraft, "Letter on the Present Character of the French Nation," February 15, 1793, in *CWMW*, loc. 20479 (emphasis in original).

52. Wollstonecraft, *Letters Written during a Short Residence in Sweden, Norway and Demark* (1796), in *CWMW*, loc. 19616 of 27946.

53. Wollstonecraft, "Character of the French Nation," in *CWMW*, loc. 20455 of 27946.

54. Wollstonecraft, *Rights of Men*, 146.

55. Wollstonecraft, *Rights of Woman*, 149.

56. Wollstonecraft, *A Historical and Moral View of the Origin and Progress of the French Revolution*, in *CWMW*, location 16691 of 27946: "But, from the commencement of the revolution, the misery of France has originated from the folly or art of men, who have spurred the people on too fast; tearing up prejudices by the root, which they should have permitted to die gradually away."

57. Wollstonecraft, *Fragment of Letters on the Management of Infants and Lessons*, in *CWMW*, loc. 20495 of 27946; *Lessons*, in *CWMW*, loc. 20712 of 27946.

CHAPTER 3. THE YOUNG REPUBLIC AND
THE UNEQUAL VIRTUES OF THE AGRARIAN HOME

1. Wollstonecraft, *An Historical and Moral View of the French Revolution*, in *CWMW*, loc. 15315 of 27946.

2. Richard Brookhiser, "John Adams Talks to His Books," *New York Times*, September 3, 2006, http://www.nytimes.com.

3. Daniel I. O'Neill, "John Adams versus Mary Wollstonecraft on the French Revolution and Democracy," *Journal of the History of Ideas* 68, no. 3 (2007): 468–69.

4. Eileen Hunt Botting, *Wollstonecraft, Mill, and Women's Human Rights* (New Haven, CT: Yale University Press, 2016), 44.

5. "From John Adams to Mercy Otis Warren, 16 April 1776," last modified November 26, 2017, Founders Online, National Archives, http://founders.archives.gov/documents/Adams/06-04-02-0044.

6. "John Adams Autobiography, Part 2, 'Travels, and Negotiations,' 1777–1778, Sheet 27 of 37, 30 May–3 June 1778," Adams Family Papers: An Electronic Archive, Massachusetts Historical Society, http://www.masshist.org.

7. Allan C. Carlson, *From Cottage to Work Station* (San Francisco: Ignatius, 1993), 10.

8. Ibid.

9. "Abigail Adams to John Adams, Braintree, March 31, 1776," in *Political Thought in the United States: A Documentary History*," ed. Lyman Tower Sargent (New York: New York University Press, 1997), 66.

10. "John Adams to Abigail Adams, April 14, 1776," in Sargent, ed., *Political Thought*, 66.

11. "Abigail Adams to John Adams, Braintree, May 7, 1776," in Sargent, ed., *Political Thought*, 67.

12. James Madison, "The Federalist Papers: No. 51," Yale Law School Lillian Goldman Law Library, http://avalon.law.yale.edu/18th_century/fed51.asp.

13. See Thomas G. West, *The Political Theory of the American Founding* (Cambridge: Cambridge University Press, 2017), 165–306.

14. Linda K. Kerber, *Women of the Republic: Intellect & Ideology in Revolutionary America* (Chapel Hill: University of North Carolina, 1980), 36.

15. Elizabeth Fox-Genovese, *Feminism without Illusions: A Critique of Individualism* (Chapel Hill: University of North Carolina, 1991), 125.

16. Kerber, *Women of the Republic*.

17. Alexis de Tocqueville, *Democracy in America*, trans. George Lawrence and ed. J. P. Mayer (New York: Harper Perennial Modern Classics, 1969), 603.

18. Ibid., 590.

19. Ibid., 602.

20. Catharine E. Beecher and Harriet Beecher Stowe, *The American Woman's Home, or, Principles of domestic science: being a guide to the formation and maintenance of economical, healthful, beautiful, and Christian homes* (New York: J. B. Ford and Company, 1869), 19, https://archive.org/details /americanwomansho00beecrich.

21. Carlson, *From Cottage to Work Station*, 34.

22. Tocqueville, *Democracy in America*, 291.

23. Ibid., 603.

24. Ibid., 590.

25. Ibid., 601.

26. Ibid., 602.

27. Ibid.

28. Ibid.

29. Stacey Hibbs, "Liberty without License, Authority without Oppression: Women in *Democracy in America*" (PhD diss., Boston College, 1999), 168.

30. Ibid., 168, 191–92.

31. See Eileen Hunt Botting, "A Family Resemblance: Tocqueville and Wollstonecraftian Protofeminism," in *Feminist Interpretations of Alexis de Tocqueville*, ed. Jill Locke and Eileen Hunt Botting (University Park: Pennsylvania State University Press, 2010), 100, arguing that though there is no evidence Tocqueville had read Wollstonecraft, "it is all but impossible that Tocqueville did not encounter her ideas and their impact at home and abroad (even if he would not have been able to attribute them to her)."

32. See, for instance, the work of conservatives Patrick Deneen and Yuval Levin and left-leaning scholars Leo Damrosch and Amitai Etzioni.

33. Eileen Hunt Botting and Christine Carey, "Wollstonecraft's Philosophical Impact on Nineteenth-Century American Women's Rights Advocates," *American Journal of Political Science* 48, no. 4 (2004): 709. Botting and Carey list other prominent but lesser influences as Germaine de Stael, Frances Wright, Harriet Martineau, George Eliot, George Sand, Harriet Taylor, and John Stuart Mill.

34. Lucretia Mott, "Discourse on Woman" (December 17, 1849), in *Lucretia Mott: Her Complete Speeches and Sermons*, ed. Dana Greene (New York: The Edwin and Mellen Press, 1980), 148.

35. Mott and other Garrisonian abolitionists believed that moral suasion affected culture change more than politics did, and so did not publicly advocate for women's suffrage at this time. Notably, even by 1914, the National Association Opposed to Woman Suffrage claimed 105,033 members across 17 states and the District of Columbia. Beyond formal membership numbers, antisuffrage

sentiment among women extended to many unenrolled in such associations; see U.S. Congress, House Committee on the Judiciary, Hearings, 63rd Cong., 2nd sess., March 3, 1914, 75; referenced in Thomas James Jablonsky, "Duty, Nature and Stability: The Female Anti-Suffragists in the United States, 1894–1920" (PhD diss., University of Southern California, 1978), 177–78.

36. Elizabeth Cady Stanton, Susan B. Anthony, and Matilda Joslyn Gage, eds., *History of Woman Suffrage*, vol. 1, *1848–1861*, The Project Gutenberg eBook 421, https://www.gutenberg.org. Notably, this volume itself is "affectionately inscribed to the memory of Mary Wollstonecraft," listed first among a host of other women's rights advocates.

37. Elizabeth Cady Stanton, *Eighty Years and More (1815–1897): Reminiscences of Elizabeth Cady Stanton* (London: T. Fisher Unwin, 1898), 79–83.

38. Stanton, Anthony, and Gage, eds., *History of Woman Suffrage*, 72.

39. Ibid.

40. Ibid.

41. Mott, speech given at the National Women's Rights Convention in New York City (May 10, 1866), in *Lucretia Mott: Her Complete Speeches and Sermons*, 270.

42. Botting and Carey, "Wollstonecraft's Philosophical Impact," 714.

43. Ibid.

44. Sarah Grimké, "Letter II: Woman Subject Only to God, Newburyport, 7th mo. 17, 1837," in *Letters on the Equality of the Sexes*, http://www.worldculture.org/articles/12-Grimke%20Letters,%201-3.pdf. She continues: "If he has not given us the rights which have, as I conceive, been wrested from us, we shall soon give evidence of our inferiority, and shrink back into that obscurity, which the high souled magnanimity of man has assigned us as our appropriate sphere."

45. Susan B. Anthony, "1904 Inscription in Mary Wollstonecraft's *A Vindication of the Rights of Woman*" (Boston: Thomas & Andrews, 1792), The Susan B. Anthony Special Collection, Rare Book/Special Collections, Library of Congress, Washington, DC.

46. Susan B. Anthony, "Speech at National American Convention of 1906," in *History of Woman Suffrage*, ed. Ida Harper (Salem, NH: Ayers, 1985), 5:185.

47. Botting and Carey, "Wollstonecraft's Philosophical Impact," 718.

48. Tocqueville, *Democracy in America*, 593.

49. William Blackstone, *Commentaries on the Laws of England in Four Books. Notes selected from the editions of Archibold, Christian, Coleridge, Chitty, Stewart, Kerr, and others, Barron Field's Analysis, and Additional Notes, and a Life of the Author by George Sharswood. In Two Volumes*

(Philadelphia: J. B. Lippincott Co., 1893), 1:430, http://www.gutenberg.org (emphasis in original). By committing to paper in 1765 what was heretofore unwritten law, Blackstone in some sense effectuated "coverture" in a way that it had not been fully before. See, for instance, Mary Beard, *Woman as Force in History: A Study in Traditions and Realities* (New York: Macmillan, 1946).

50. As far back as the thirteenth century, courts of equity had allowed lawyers to create separate estates, by way of trust, for married women to en-sure the family property they brought into the marriage would be kept in their family of origin's bloodline, protecting that property from their husbands' creditors. These marital trusts, created for wealthy families, provided the legal mechanism to, centuries later, extend the "separate" marital property concept to all families, regardless of their capacity to hire an attorney.

51. Mary Ann Glendon, *The Transformation of Family Law: State, Law, and Family in the United States and Western Europe* (Chicago: University of Chicago Press, 1989), 111.

52. Reva B. Siegel, "Home as Work: The First Woman's Rights Claims Concerning Wives' Household Labor, 1850–1880," *The Yale Law Journal* 103 (1994): 1084.

53. Nancy Folbre, "The Unproductive Housewife: Her Evolution in Nineteenth-Century Economic Thought," *Signs: Journal of Women in Culture and Society* 16, no. 3 (1991): 465.

54. Siegel, "Home as Work," 1092.

55. Ibid., 1093.

56. Clark, *Working Life of Women in the Seventeenth Century*, 145.

57. Siegel, "Home as Work," 1116.

58. *The Proceedings of the Woman's Rights Convention, Held at Worces-ter, October 23d and 24th, 1850* (Boston: Prentiss and Sawyer, 1851), 15, https://babel.hathitrust.org (emphasis mine).

59. Siegel, "Home as Work," 1125.

60. John Locke, "An Essay Concerning the True Original, Extent and End of Civil Government," in *Social Contract: Essays by Locke, Hume, and Rousseau* (Oxford: Oxford University Press, 1947), 17.

61. Siegel, "Home as Work," 1115, citing Glendon, *Transformation of Family Law*, 123.

62. Ibid., 1148.

63. Siegel, "Home as Work," 1168.

64. "[Working women's] complaints were brought to the attention of the public and Parliament largely through the influence of one man, *John Stuart Mill*, who was then at the height of his power. According to Dicey's *Lectures on Law and Opinion in England*, published in 1905, 'his [Mill's] authority

among the educated youth of England was greater than may appear credible to the present generation. . . . To no cause was he more ardently devoted than to the emancipation of women"; quoting Albert Venn Dicey, *Lectures on the Relation between Law and Public Opinion in England during the Nineteenth Century*, 384, in Max Rheinstein and Mary Ann Glendon, "Interspousal Relations," in *International Encyclopedia of Comparative Law, Persons and Family* (Tubingen: J. C. B. Mohr, 1980), 4:41.

65. Siegel, "Home as Work," 1189–90.

66. Ibid., 1203.

67. Charlotte Perkins Gilman, *Women and Economics: A Study of the Economic Relation between Men and Women as a Factor in Social Evolution* (Boston: Small, Maynard and Company, 1898), 67, https://archive.org/details /womeneconomicsst00gilmuoft.

68. Ibid., 244.

69. Ibid., 246.

70. Allan C. Carlson, "The Productive Home vs. the Consuming Home," in *Localism in the Mass Age*, ed. Mark T. Mitchell and Jason Peters (Eugene, OR: Cascade, 2018), 116.

71. Siegel, "Home as Work," 1208.

72. Ibid., 1166.

CHAPTER 4. WOMEN'S SUFFRAGE, RATIONAL SOULS, SEXED BODIES, AND THE TIES THAT BIND

1. For instance, on the eve of congressional passage of the Fifteenth Amendment, at the National Woman Suffrage Convention in January 1869, Elizabeth Cady Stanton said, "I urge a Sixteenth Amendment because, when 'manhood suffrage' is established from Maine to California, woman has reached the lowest depths of political degradation. So long as there is a disfranchised class in this country, and that class its women, a man's government is worse than a white man's government with suffrage limited by property and educational qualifications, because in proportion as you multiply the rulers, the condition of the politically ostracised is more hopeless and degraded. John Stuart Mill, in his work on 'Liberty,' shows that the condition of one disfranchised man in a nation is worse than when the whole nation is under one man, because in the latter case, if the one man is despotic, the nation can easily throw him off, but what can one man do with a nation of tyrants over him? If American women find it hard to bear the oppressions of their own Saxon fathers, the best orders of manhood, what may they not be called to endure when all the lower orders of foreigners

now crowding our shores legislate for them and their daughters? Think of Patrick and Sambo and Hans and Yung Tung, who do not know the difference between a monarchy and a republic, who can not read the Declaration of Independence or Webster's spelling-book, making laws for Lucretia Mott." Stanton, Anthony, and Gage, eds., *History of Woman Suffrage*, 2:353.

2. Ida Husted Harper, *The Life and Work of Susan B. Anthony* (Indianapolis and Kansas City: Bowen-Merrill Company, 1899), 439.

3. U.S. Const. amend. XIV, §1 (emphasis mine).

4. *Slaughterhouse Cases*, 83 U.S. 36 (1873), 113–14.

5. *Bradwell v. Illinois*, 83 U.S. 130 (1872), 141.

6. Marion Mills Miller, ed., *Great Debate in American History: Civil Rights, Part Two* (New York: Current Literature Publishing Company, 1913), 111.

7. Ibid., 139.

8. Ward Farnsworth, "Women under Reconstruction: The Congressional Understanding," *Northwestern University Law Review* 94, no. 4 (2000): 1237.

9. Miller, ed., *Great Debate*, 134.

10. Farnsworth, "Women under Reconstruction," 1239.

11. See "Map: States Grant Women the Right to Vote," Centuries of Citizenship: A Constitutional Timeline, from National Constitution Center, https://constitutioncenter.org. Twelve additional states allowed women the right to vote for president before passage of the Nineteenth Amendment.

12. Christina Hoff Sommers, *Freedom Feminism: Its Surprising History and Why It Matters Today* (Washington, DC: American Enterprise Institute, 2013), 33.

13. Philosopher W. Norris Clarke articulates a view of the rational but sexless soul, which he attributes to Thomas Aquinas: "St. Thomas speaks of each soul being 'commensurated' or adapted actively by God to its own particular body. . . . Thus the soul itself becomes differentiated in itself from every other, not because it is a different kind of soul, but because it is joined with this particular body as a permanent instrument of self-expression. . . . The differences are deep, running all the way through its personality and mode of self-expression, but they are not because it is a different kind of soul, but because the human soul in each case has to operate and express itself through this particular body, which allows some of its potentialities to develop, others not, or some more than others"; W. Norris Clarke, *The One and the Many: A Contemporary Thomistic Metaphysics* (Notre Dame, IN: University of Notre Dame Press, 2015), 103. It is unknown whether Wollstonecraft, or even her mentor Richard Price, read Aquinas, but both were deeply literate intellectuals, and had read Aristotle, Aquinas's philosophical forebearer. Still, although both Price and

318 Notes to Page 101

Wollstonecraft assumed something akin to Aristotle's hylomorphism—that the body and soul are deeply integrated, with the soul the form of the body—they would have disputed Aristotle's false biological assumption that the female body was an imperfect version of the male.

14. In an early work of fiction, Wollstonecraft's main character, Mrs. Mason, advises: "Families meet at meals, and there giving up to each other, learn in the most easy, pleasant way to govern their appetites. Pigs, you see, devour what they can get; but men, if they have any affections, love their fellow-creatures." Testing a young apprentice in this vein, Mrs. Mason describes: "As Mary had before convinced me that she could regulate her appetites, I gave her leave to pluck as much fruit as she wished; and she did not abuse my indulgence. On the contrary, she spent most part of the time in gathering some for me, and her attention made it sweeter. Coming home I called her my friend, and she deserved the name, for she was no longer a child; a reasonable affection had conquered her appetite; her understanding took the lead, and she had practiced a virtue" (Mary Wollstonecraft, *Original Stories from Real Life*, in *CWMW*, loc. 4115–33 of 27946).

With this example of earned self-mastery, Mrs. Mason confirmed that the youth had achieved true independence; she was no longer a child, needing an outside authority to help her govern her appetites but had matured into one whose mind, now firmly governed by immutable principles of virtue, could look beyond self-satisfaction to the good of others. Indeed, Mrs. Mason remarks that such a girl had become an equal, a friend.

15. Wollstonecraft, *Rights of Woman*, 184. For similar arguments in contemporary feminist writing, see Sara Ruddick's *Maternal Thinking* and Eva Feder Kittay's *Love's Labor.*

16. See, for instance, Louanne Brizendine, *The Female Brain* (New York: Broadway Books, 2006); Theresa M. Wizemann and Mary-Lou Pardue, eds., *Exploring the Biological Contributions to Human Health: Does Sex Matter?*, Committee on Understanding the Biology of Sex and Gender Differences, Board on Health Sciences Policy (Washington, DC: The National Academies Press, 2001), https://www.nap.edu; Stuart J. Ritchie et al., "Sex Differences in the Adult Human Brain: Evidence from 5,216 UK Biobank Participants," *Cerebral Cortex* 28, no. 8 (2018): 2959–75; Donald W. Pfaff and Yves Christen, eds., *Multiple Origins of Sex Differences in the Brain* (Berlin: Springer-Verlag Berlin Heidelberg, 2013). To understand how mismatches at the chromosomal, hormonal, or anatomical levels in a very small minority of the population have served to confuse the basic biological reality of sexual dimorphism, see Deborah Soh, *The End of Gender: Debunking the Myths about Sex and Identity in Our Society* (New York: Simon & Schuster, 2020).

17. Sarah Borden Sharkey, *An Aristotelean Feminism* (New York: Springer, 2016), 52.

18. Botting and Carey, "Wollstonecraft's Philosophical Impact," 720: "Stanton was partly a student of the Romantic tradition and shared its skepticism of the Wollstonecraftian view that the only significant differences between the sexes were the greater physical strength of males and the female capacities for childbirth and nursing. Yet Stanton insists that her belief in the existence of masculine and feminine souls does not justify the belief that there are natural differences between the sexes that are reflected in their unequal social and political status. Stanton holds that while the souls of men and women are different, their complementary natures equally contribute to a kind of cosmic balance and equilibrium in the universe."

19. Tracy A. Thomas, *Elizabeth Cady Stanton and the Feminist Foundations of Family Law* (New York: New York University Press, 2016), 39, quoting Stanton in an 1854 address to the legislature of New York: "The rights of every human being are the same and identical." Jean Bethke Elshtain, *Public Man, Private Woman* (Princeton, NJ: Princeton University Press, 1981), 232.

20. Quoted in Thomas, *Elizabeth Cady Stanton*, 198 and 25.

21. Quoted in Thomas, *Elizabeth Cady Stanton*, 25; quoted in Elshtain, *Public Man, Private Woman*, 232.

22. Prudence Allen, *Concept of Woman* (Grand Rapids, MI: Eerdmans, 1997), 1:3.

23. Sarah Borden and Christopher Manzer, "Feminism and Metaphysics," *eJournal of Personalist Feminism* 2 (2015): 1–30.

24. Henry James, *The Bostonians*, 163, cited in Jean Bethke Elshtain, *Jane Addams and the Dream of American Democracy* (New York: Basic Books, 2002), 81.

25. Anna Gordon, ed., *What Frances E. Willard Said* (Grand Rapids, MI: Fleming H. Revell Company, 1905), 154 (emphasis mine).

26. Frances E. Willard, "Individuality in Woman," in *You and I: Or, Living Thoughts for Our Moral, Intellectual and Physical Advancement, by Leading Thinkers of To-day* (Detroit: F. B. Dickerson & Company, 1887), 453.

27. Linda Gordon, *The Moral Property of Women* (Chicago: University of Illinois Press, 2007), 55–71.

28. S. M. van Anders, "Testosterone and Sexual Desire in Healthy Women and Men," *Archives of Sexual Behavior* 41 (2012): 1471–84.

29. Gordon, *Moral Property*, 125–35.

30. Sarah Grimké, "Marriage," in *The Grimké Sisters from South Carolina: Pioneers for Women's Rights and Abolition*, ed. Gerda Lerner (Chapel Hill: University of North Carolina Press, 2004), 308.

31. Ibid., 34.

32. "Perhaps most passionately, voluntary motherhood advocates feared contraception as a means by which men could exploit, even rape, women with impunity" (Gordon, *Moral Property*, 57).

33. Thomas, *Elizabeth Cady Stanton*, 174. See also Jane Farrell Brodie, *Contraception and Abortion in Nineteenth-Century America* (Ithaca, NY: Cornell University Press, 1994), 262, 280.

34. Charlotte Perkins Gilman, *The Man-Made World: Or, Our Andro-centric Culture* (New York: Charlton Company, 1914), 134.

35. Gordon, *Moral Property*, 59.

36. Ibid., 58.

37. The development of the rhythm method began in the nineteenth century, when doctors recommended sexual intercourse only during the "safe period" when a woman was not ovulating. However, these doctors misidentified the time of ovulation; the "safe period" they identified was, in fact, the time when women were most likely to conceive. See Brodie, *Contraception and Abortion*, 79–86.

In the 1920s and 30s, gynecologists Kyusaku Ogino and Hermann Knaus developed a more accurate understanding of the "safe period." Their work led to American doctor Leo J. Latz's publication of *The Rhythm of Sterility and Fertility in Women* (1932). He recommended that to avoid pregnancy, women should abstain from intercourse for eight days (for women with a regular, twenty-eight-day cycle, this meant avoiding intercourse five days before ovulation, "with an extra three days tacked on for safety's sake").

As more sophisticated and scientific methods for tracking a woman's ovulation period developed, so did the natural methods of fertility regulation. See, for instance, the best-selling Toni Weschler, *Taking Charge of Your Fertility* (New York: William Morrow and Company, 2015); and the website Facts about Fertility, https://www.factsaboutfertility.org/.

38. Gordon, *Moral Property*, 339.

39. Katie Rife, "An Incomplete, Depressingly Long List of Celebrities' Sexual Assault and Harassment Stories [updated]," AV Club, November 22, 2017, https://www.avclub.com/an-incomplete-depressingly-long-list-of-celebrities-se-1819628519; Ronan Farrow, "From Aggressive Overtures to Sexual Assault: Harvey Weinstein's Accusers Tell Their Stories," *The New Yorker*, October 10, 2017; Jessica Bennett, "The #MeToo Moment," stories compiled online at the *New York Times*, http://www.nytimes.com/series/metoo-moment.

40. Although Linda Gordon and others argue that rudimentary methods of abortion (e.g., plant- or herb-based portions) had been around in all cultures and times, these methods were not well publicized or commercialized until the

nineteenth century, when developments in surgical technique also made abortion more available and effective. See, generally, Gordon, *Moral Property*, and Brodie, *Contraception and Abortion*.

41. In 1871, the *New York Times* referred to abortion as the "The Evil of the Age" and reported that there were an estimated two hundred full-time abortionists in New York City alone; see Gordon, *Moral Property*, 25.

42. Aristotle began the rudimentary and theoretical study of embryos, with the science developing in fits and starts (and errors) over the millennia. By late in the seventeenth century, scientists had theorized the existence of the sperm and egg as the key components of fertilization. In 1677, Antonie van Leeuwenhoek engineered a microscope with which to study human semen; in 1827, Karl Ernest von Baer observed the mammalian ovum, the date that marks the beginning of modern embryology. Oscar Hertwig then observed the nuclei of sperm and egg fuse during fertilization in 1876, thus conclusively "settling the long standing debate over the role of the egg and sperm in the generation of new life"; see Dean Clift and Melina Schuh, "Restarting Life: Fertilization and the Transition from Meiosis to Mitosis," *Nature Reviews Molecular Cell Biology* 14, no. 9 (2013): 549–62.

43. James C. Mohr, *Abortion in America* (Oxford: Oxford University Press, 1979), 147–70, 200; see also Joseph Dellapenna, *Dispelling the Myths of Abortion History* (Durham, NC: Carolina Academic Press, 2006), 315–16: "By 1868, when the Fourteenth Amendment was ratified, thirty of the thirty-seven states had abortion statutes on the books. Just three of these states prohibited abortion only after quickening. Twenty states punished all abortion equally regardless the stage of pregnancy." The American Medical Association in 1857 called abortion "an unwarrantable destruction of human life"; see *The Transactions of the American Medical Association* (Philadelphia: Collins, Printer, 1859), 12:27: "The following resolutions . . . were unanimously adopted: 'Resolved, That while physicians have long been united in condemning the act of producing abortion, at every period of gestation, except as necessary for preserving the life of either mother or child, it has become the duty of this Association, in view of the prevalence and increasing frequency of the crime, publicly to enter an earnest and solemn protest against such unwarrantable destruction of human life."

Although male doctors led the lobbying efforts for the nineteenth-century abortion statutes, well-known female doctors were also against abortion. For instance, Elizabeth Blackwell, the first woman in the United States licensed to practice medicine, was deeply opposed to the practice and despised the cultural association of female physicians with abortion. Referring to Madame Restell, a well-known abortionist in New York, she wrote: "She was known distinctively as a 'female physician,' a term exclusively applied at that time to those women who carried on her vile occupation. . . . That [this] honorable term should be exclusively applied to those women who carried on this shocking trade seemed to me a horror. It was an utter degradation of what might and should become a noble position for women"; Elizabeth Blackwell, *Pioneer Work in Opening the Medical Profession to Women* (London: Longmans, Green, and Company, 1895), 30. See also Brodie, *Contraception and Abortion*, 34, 228. *The Revolution* also published accounts of the antiabortion sentiments of female doctors at the time. For instance, in the editorial "Restellism Exposed," the unsigned editor recounts the story of Dr. Charlotte Lozier, who caused the arrest of a man seeking to procure an abortion from her for the young woman who accompanied him to her office. "The Dr. assured him that he had come to the wrong place for any such shameful, revolting, unnatural and unlawful purpose. She proffered to the young woman any assistance in her power to render, at the proper time, and cautioned and counseled her against the fearful act which she and her attendant . . . proposed. The man becoming quite abusive, instead of appreciating and accepting the counsel in the spirit in which it was proffered, Dr. Lozier caused his arrest under the laws of New York for his inhuman proposition." The editorial then excerpts from two other newspaper accounts of the incident, one of which, the Springfield *Republican*, concludes: "May we not hope that the action of Mrs. Lozier in this case is an earnest of what may be the more general practice of physicians if called upon to commit this crime, when women have got a firmer foothold and influence in the medical profession? Some bad women as well as bad men may possibly become doctors, who will do anything for money: but we are sure most women physicians will lend their influence and their aid to shield their sex from the foulest wrong committed against it. It will be a good thing for the community when more women like Mrs. Lozier belong to the profession" (Editorial, "Restellism Exposed," *The Revolution*, December 2, 1869, 346).

44. See, for instance, note 51.

45. Victoria Woodhull, "Children—Their Rights, Privileges and True Relation to Society," *Woodhull & Claflin's Weekly*, December 24, 1870, 4. "[Women] are appointed to the holy position of motherhood, and who, by this position, are directly charged with the care of the embryonic life, upon which so much of future ill or good to its future depends" (ibid.).

46. Victoria Woodhull, "When Is It Not Murder to Take a Life?," *Woodhull & Claflin's Weekly*, October 8, 1870, 11.

47. Victoria Woodhull, *Tried as by Fire: or, The True and The False, Socially, an Oration delivered by Victoria C. Woodhull, in all the principal cities and towns of the country during an engagement of one hundred and fifty consecutive nights* (New York: Woodhull & Claflin, 1874), pamphlets from the

Irvin Dept. of Rare Books and Special Collections, 40, http://digital.tcl.sc.edu
/digital/collection/vcw/id/39.

48. Victoria Woodhull, "*Times*, October 17th, 1875. Chicago (Ill.)," in
Victoria Woodhull, "A Speech on the Principles of Social Freedom, Delivered
in Steinway Hall, Monday, November 20, 1871 and Music Hall, Boston,
Wednesday, January 3, 1872" (Blackfriar Printers, 1894).

49. Sarah Norton, "Tragedy, Social and Domestic," *Woodhull & Claflin's
Weekly*, November 19, 1870, 11. "Scores of persons advertise their willingness
to commit this form of murder, and with unblushing effrontery announce their
names and residences in the daily papers. . . . Circulars are distributed broadcast, recommending certain pills and potions for the very purpose, and by
these means the names of these slayers of infants, and the methods by which
they practice their life-destroying trade, have become 'familiar in our mouths
as household words'" (ibid.).

50. For a recent argument that appeals to this nineteenth-century history,
see Josh Craddock, "Protecting Prenatal Persons: Does the Fourteenth
Amendment Prohibit Abortion?," *Harvard Journal of Law and Public Policy*
40, no. 2 (2017): 539–71.

51. For instance, the AMA 1871 *Report of Criminal Abortion* states, "She
becomes unmindful of the course marked out for her by Providence, she overlooks the duties imposed on her by the marriage contract. She yields to the
pleasures—but shirks from the pains and responsibilities of maternity"; quoted
in Thomas, *Elizabeth Cady Stanton*, 177. Horatio Storer, one of the first male
gynecologists and the leading anti-abortion advocate for the AMA wrote that
"the true wife" does not seek "undue power in public life, . . . undue control in
domestic affairs, . . . or privileges not her own" (Thomas, *Elizabeth Cady Stanton*, 177). See also Reva Siegel, "Reasoning from the Body," *Stanford Law Review* 44 (1992): 302–14.

52. "Enforced motherhood is a crime against the body of the mother and
the soul of the child. . . . I hesitate not to assert that most of this crime of 'child
murder,' 'abortion,' 'infanticide,' lies at the door of the male sex" (Matilda E. J.
Gage, "Is Woman Her Own?" *The Revolution*, April 9, 1868). And from an
1869 *Revolution* editorial, "Marriage and Maternity" (quoted at length): "Much
as I deplore the horrible crime of child-murder, I cannot believe . . . that such a
law [restricting abortion] would have the desired effect. It seems to me to be
only mowing off the top of the noxious weed, while the root remains. We
want *prevention*, not merely punishment. We must reach the *root* of the evil,
and destroy it. To my certain knowledge this crime is not confined to those
whose love of ease, amusement and fashionable life leads them to desire im-
munity from the cares of children; but is practiced by those whose inmost

souls revolt from the dreadful deed, and in whose hearts the maternal feeling is pure and undying. What then, has driven these women to the desperation necessary to force them to commit such a deed? . . . The wife has . . . no right over her own body. . . . No matter what her condition, physical or mental, no matter how ill-prepared she may feel herself for maternity, the demands of his passion must never be refused. He thinks, or cares nothing, for the possible result of his gratification. . . . It is clear to my mind that this evil wholly arises from the false position which woman occupies in civilized society. . . . Guilty? Yes, no matter what the motive, love of ease, or a desire to save from suffering the unborn innocent, the woman is awfully guilty who commits the deed. It will burden her conscience in life, it will burden her soul in death; but oh! thrice guilty is he who, for selfish gratification, heedless of her prayers, indifferent to her fate, drove her to the desperation which impelled her to the crime. . . . No, I say, yield to woman her God-given right of individuality. Make her feel that to God alone is she responsible for her deeds; teach her that submission to any man without love and desire is prostitution. . . . let maternity come to her from a desire to cherish love and train for high purposes an immortal soul, then you will begin to eradicate this most monstrous crime. Teach man to respect womanhood whether in the person of his own wife or the wife of another; teach him that as often as he outrages his wife he outrages Nature and disobeys the Divine Law, then you will have accomplished still more" (Editorial, "Marriage and Maternity," *The Revolution*, July 8, 1869).

53. Stanton, "Editorial: Infanticide and Prostitution," *The Revolution*, February 5, 1868, first, quoting the *Tribune*, "The murder of children, either before or after birth, has become so frightfully prevalent," and then her analysis: "For a quarter of a century sober, thinking women have warned this nation of these thick coming dangers, and pointed to the only remedy, *the education and enfranchisement of woman*; but men have laughed them to scorn. . . . We ask our editors who pen those startling statistics to give us *their* views of the remedy. We believe the cause of all these abuses lies in the degradation of woman."

54. Stanton, Anthony, and Gage, eds., *History of Woman Suffrage*, 1:861.

55. Stanton, "Editorial: Infanticide and Prostitution," *The Revolution*, February 5, 1868.

56. Stanton, Anthony, and Gage, eds., *History of Woman Suffrage*, 1:861.

57. Quoted in Thomas, *Elizabeth Cady Stanton*, 163.

58. Noelle A. Baker, ed., *Stanton in Her Own Time: A Biographical Chronicle of Her Life, Drawn from Recollections, Interviews, and Memoirs by Family, Friends, and Associates* (Iowa City: University of Iowa Press, 2016), 113 (emphasis omitted).

59. Ibid., 111.

60. Ibid., 116.
61. Quoted in Thomas, *Elizabeth Cady Stanton*, 163.
62. Ibid., 165.
63. Ibid., 168.
64. Ibid., 163.
65. Baker, *Stanton in Her Own Time*, 116.
66. Ibid.
67. See, generally, Gordon, *Moral Property*; see also Brodie, *Contraception and Abortion*, 280: "Organized feminists did not speak out against the Comstock laws, in large part, because many disliked contraception, viewing it as a threat to their demands for 'voluntary motherhood'. . . . Stanton spoke . . . on women's need for 'self-sovereignty' over their bodies and their sexual lives. But she and others did not officially oppose Comstockery."
68. See, for instance, Elizabeth Cady Stanton, "Hester Vaughn," *The Revolution*, November 9, 1868, 312, deploring the legal treatment of a destitute young woman whose infant child was found dead at her side; rather than recognize the mitigating circumstances of her desperate situation, the justice system tried and convicted the woman; she was pardoned and deported to England before her scheduled execution.
69. See, for instance, note 51.
70. "Free love" was a concept used pejoratively by opponents of the women's rights movement. However, it was a more nuanced concept than that used by the media and activists at the time. Opponents attempted to show a link between "free love" and sexual promiscuity, something Stanton emphatically rejected. Stanton herself described "free love" as "nothing short of unlimited freedom of divorce, freedom to initiate at the option of the parties new amatory relationships, love put above marriage" (quoted in Thomas, *Elizabeth Cady Stanton*, 94). She continues in her speech on free love: "If by 'free love' you mean woman's right to give her body to the man she loves and no other, to become a mother or not as her desire, judgment, and convenience may dictate, in fine, to be the absolute sovereign of herself, then I do believe in freedom of love" (quoted in ibid., 90).
71. Quoted in Thomas, *Elizabeth Cady Stanton*, 77.
72. Elizabeth Cady Stanton, "The Antagonism of Sex," quoted in Elisabeth Griffith, *In Her Own Right: The Life of Elizabeth Cady Stanton* (Oxford: Oxford University Press, 1984), 164.
73. Quoted in Thomas, *Elizabeth Cady Stanton*, 98.
74. Ibid., 3, 6–7.
75. Ibid., 87.
76. Ibid., 89.

77. Elizabeth Clark, "Matrimonial Bonds: Slavery and Divorce in Nineteenth-Century America," *Law and History Review* 8, no. 1 (1990): 35–36.

78. Ibid., 39.

79. Ibid., 35.

80. Clark, "Matrimonial Bonds," 41.

81. Thomas, *Elizabeth Cady Stanton*, 84.

82. Clark, "Matrimonial Bonds," 47.

83. Thomas, *Elizabeth Cady Stanton*, 143.

84. Ibid., 98.

85. Ibid., 93–94.

86. Elizabeth Cady Stanton, "Solitude of Self," address delivered before the Committee of the Judiciary of the United States Congress, January 18, 1892, 1, Library of Congress, http://loc.gov/item/93838358.

87. Ibid. (emphasis mine).

88. Elizabeth Cady Stanton, "Letter from Mrs. Stanton. National Woman's Rights Convention, Cooper Institute, 1856," Seneca Falls, NY, November 24, 1856 (emphasis mine), in *History of Woman Suffrage*, ed. Elizabeth Cady Stanton, Susan Brownell Anthony, Matilda Joslyn Gage (Rochester, NY: Charles Mann), 1:860.

89. Stanton, "Solitude of Self," 2 (emphasis mine).

90. Jane Cunningham Croly, *For Better or Worse: A Book for Some Men and All Women* (Boston, 1875), 4–5, 221.

91. Thomas, *Elizabeth Cady Stanton*, 98–99.

92. Ibid., 74.

93. See, generally, Thomas, *Elizabeth Cady Stanton*.

Chapter 5. The Industrial Revolution and the Debate between Abstract Rights and Concrete Duties

1. According to Blackstone: "By the public police and economy I mean the due regulation and domestic order of the kingdom, whereby the individuals of the state, like members of a well-governed family, are bound to conform their general behavior to the rules of propriety, good neighborhood, and good manners, and to be decent, industrious, and inoffensive in their respective stations. . . . Common nuisances are a species of offense against the public order and economical regimen of the state, being either the doing of a thing to the annoyance of all the king's subjects, or the neglecting to do a thing which the common good requires" (Blackstone, *Commentaries*, 2:161, 373; emphasis omitted).

2. The common law obviously did not ensure property rights for all, notably married women, but also for others thought too dependent. Slaves, however, were not protected as property in the common law; just to the contrary. Blackstone in 1765: "This spirit of liberty is so deeply implanted in our constitution, and rooted in our very soil, that a slave or a negro, the moment he lands in England, falls under the protection of the laws, and with regard to all natural rights becomes *eo instanti* a freeman" (Blackstone, *Commentaries*, 1:123).

3. Census data from 1890 revealed that 9 percent of the nation's families controlled 81 percent of the nation's wealth; and according to the U.S. Industrial Commission report in 1900, 60 to 88 percent of Americans could be considered poor or very poor. See Howard Gillman, *The Constitution Besieged: The Rise and Demise of Lochner Era Police Powers Jurisprudence* (Durham, NC: Duke University Press, 1993), 77.

4. *Ritchie v. People*, 155 Ill. 98 (1895).

5. Recall from chapter 4 that the *Slaughterhouse Cases* limited the privileges and immunities clause to the protection of "federal" rights of U.S. citizens, such as the right to travel.

6. *Allegeyer v. Louisiana*, 165 U.S. 578, 589 (1897).

7. *Holden v. Hardy*, 169 U.S. 366, 397 (1898).

8. *Lochner v. New York*, 198 U.S. 45, 57 (1905)

9. Ibid., 61.

10. *Lochner v. New York*, 75. Modern revisionist accounts of *Lochner*, such as Gillman's *The Constitution Besieged*, put into question Holmes's interpretation of the Court's action here. Rather than promoting laissez-faire economics, Gillman argues, the *Lochner* Court was observing a long-standing constitutional prohibition against "class legislation."

11. Ibid.

12. Nancy Woloch, *A Class by Herself: Protective Law for Women Workers, 1890s–1990s* (Princeton, NJ: Princeton University Press, 2015), 24.

13. Thomas, *Elizabeth Cady Stanton*, 59.

14. Florence Kelley, *Some Ethical Gains through Legislation* (New York: Macmillan, 1905), 3.

15. Edwin Markham, Ben Barr Lindsey, and George Creel, *Children in Bondage* (Arno, 1914), 71.

16. Woloch, *A Class by Herself*, 23.

17. Ibid.

18. Pope Leo XIII, *Rerum novarum* (1891), nos. 45–46. The natural law arguments of *Rerum novarum* were popularized by Fr. John Ryan. See, for instance, John Augustine Ryan, *A Living Wage: Its Ethical and Economic Aspects* (New York: Macmillan, 1906), 118: "The laborer has a right to a family Living

Wage because this is the only way in which he can exercise his right to the means of maintaining a family, and he has a right to these means because they are an essential condition of normal life."

19. Woloch, *A Class by Herself*, 20–21.

20. Quoted in Susan G. Bell and Karen M. Offen, *Women, the Family, and Freedom 1750–1880* (Stanford, CA: Stanford University Press, 1983), 215–16.

21. Quoted in Michael Reisch and Janice Andrews, *The Road Not Taken: A History of Radical Social Work in the United States* (Philadelphia: Routledge, 2014), 18.

22. Christopher Lasch, ed., *The Social Thought of Jane Addams* (Indianapolis: Bobbs-Merrill, 1965), xiii–xiv.

23. Elshtain, *Jane Addams*, 107.

24. Quoted in Elshtain, *Jane Addams*, 105.

25. Kelley, *Some Ethical Gains*, 142.

26. Ibid., 184.

27. Joan Zimmerman, "The Jurisprudence of Equality: The Women's Minimum Wage, the First Equal Rights Amendment, and *Adkins v. Children's Hospital*, 1905–1923," *Journal of American History* 78, no. 1 (1991): 197.

28. Ibid.

29. Quoted in Woloch, *A Class by Herself*, 70. The law of Oregon at the time provided equal contractual and personal rights of women, married or single.

30. Ibid., 65, 236.

31. Ibid., 67.

32. *Muller v. Oregon*, 208 U.S. 412, 422 (1908).

33. Ibid., 421.

34. Ibid., 423.

35. Ibid., 422–23.

36. Ibid., 421–22.

37. Ibid., 422.

38. Quoted in Woloch, *A Class by Herself*, 76.

39. Ibid.

40. *Muller v. Oregon*, 422 (emphasis mine).

41. Woloch, *A Class by Herself*, 133.

42. *Muller v. Oregon*, 423.

43. *Ritchie v. Wayman*, 244 Ill. 509 (1910).

44. Josephine Goldmark, *Fatigue and Efficiency: A Study in Industry* (New York: Survey Associates, Inc., 1913).

45. Ibid., 169.

46. Quoted in Woloch, *A Class by Herself*, 101.

47. Louis D. Brandeis, "The Living Law: An Address Delivered before the Chicago Bar Association" (Jan. 3, 1916), Louis D. Brandeis School of

Law Library, http://louisville.edu/law/library/special-collections/the-louis-d
.-brandeis-collection/business-a-profession-chapter-21.

48. Learned Hand, "Due Process of Law and the Eight-Hour Day," *Harvard Law Review* 21, no. 7 (1908): 506.

49. William F. Willoughby, "The Philosophy of Labor Legislation," *American Political Science Review* 4, no. 1 (1914): 19.

50. *Bunting v. Oregon*, 243 U.S. 426 (1917)

51. *Stettler v. O'Hara*, 243 U.S. 629 (1917).

52. Zimmerman, "The Jurisprudence of Equality," 219.

53. Ibid., 207.

54. "All modern-minded people desire, of course, that women should have full political equality and also be free from the old exclusion from the bench, the bar, the pulpit, the highest ranges of the teachers' profession, and of the civil service"; Florence Kelley, *Twenty Questions about the Federal Amendment Proposed by the National Woman's Party* (New York: National Consumers' League, 1922), quoted in Josephine Clara Goldmark, *Impatient Crusader* (Lexington, MA: Plunkett Lake Press, 2020), 15.

55. Woloch, *A Class by Herself*, 131. Single-sex protective legislation, according to Women's Bureau head Anderson, "obtain[s] for women certain economic rights and benefits which men have already in large measure attained. . . . The worker prefers industrial equality, which is in this case *defeated* by legal equality" (ibid., emphasis in original).

56. Zimmerman, "The Jurisprudence of Equality," 207.

57. *Adkins v. Children's Hospital*, 261 U.S. 525 (1923), 553–54.

58. Ibid., 567, 562.

59. Ibid., 569–70 (J. Holmes, dissenting).

60. Woloch, *A Class by Herself*, 128.

61. Zimmerman, "The Jurisprudence of Equality," 222–23.

62. In *Dred Scott v. Sanford*, 60 U.S. 393 (1856), the Supreme Court infamously relied on the due process clause of the Fifth Amendment to protect the property rights of slaveowners.

63. *West Coast Hotel Co. v. Parrish*, 300 U.S. 379, 397 (1937).

64. Ibid., 391.

65. Ibid., 399–400.

66. Ibid., 394, quoting *Muller v. Oregon*.

67. Ibid., 398, 395.

68. See Ira Katznelson, *When Affirmative Action Was White* (New York: W. W. Norton, 2005).

69. Women's Bureau head Mary Anderson wrote: "I think the whole thing could be taken care of if the provider for the family got sufficient wages. Then married women would not be obliged to go to work to supplement an

inadequate income for their families and could make their own choice as to what they should do"; Mary Anderson and Mary N. Winslow, *Woman at Work: The Autobiography of Mary Anderson as Told to Mary N. Winslow* (Minneapolis: University of Minnesota Press, 1951), 157. The Social Security system offered child allowances for widowed and abandoned mothers and spouse and survivor benefits for homemakers.

70. Valerie Kincade Oppenheimer, *The Female Labor Force in the United States: Demographic and Economic Factors Governing Its Growth and Changing Composition* (Westport, CT: Greenwood Press, 1976), 3, 149.

71. Nancy F. Cott, "Historical Perspectives: The Equal Rights Amendment Conflict in the 1920s," in *Conflicts in Feminism*, ed. Marianne Hirsch and Evelyn Fox Keller (New York: Routledge, 1990), 50.

72. Ibid., 52.

73. Woloch, *A Class by Herself*, 139.

74. Quoted in Woloch, *A Class by Herself*, 139.

75. Claudia Golden, *Understanding the Gender Gap: An Economic History of American Women* (New York: Oxford University Press, 1990).

76. Eleanor Roosevelt, *It's Up to the Women* (New York: Nation Books, 2017), 198.

77. Quoted in Cott, "Historical Perspectives," 53.

CHAPTER 6. THE "FEMININE MYSTIQUE" AND HUMAN WORK

1. "Women in the Workforce," National Archives at Atlanta: An Archival Facility of the National Archives, https://www.archives.gov/atlanta /exhibits/women.html.

2. In 1939, median female earnings were 59.29 percent of males'; by 1966, female earnings had fallen to 53.66 percent; see Peter J. Sloane, *Women and Low Pay* (London: Macmillan, 1980), 238. In 1950, 64.4 percent of women working were employed 35 or more hours a week; by 1965, the number of full-time women workers shrunk to 58.9 percent; cited in Carlson, *From Cottage to Work Station*, 55.

3. Quoted in Carlson, *From Cottage to Work Station*, 56.

4. Betty Friedan, *The Feminine Mystique: 50th Anniversary Edition* (New York: W. W. Norton, 2013), Kindle edition.

5. Friedan, *The Feminine Mystique*, Kindle loc. 5628 of 8353.

6. Ibid., 5018.

7. Ibid., 5583.

8. Ibid., 5508.

9. Ibid., 4844.

10. Ibid., 626, 940.

11. Ibid., 5165, 5154, 5101.

12. Ibid., 5456, 5466.

13. Ibid., 528.

14. Ibid., 408.

15. Ibid., 5471.

16. Ibid. See also Anna Quindlen, ed., afterword to *The Feminine Mystique*, loc. 6432 of 8353; Lasch, *Women and the Common Life*, 105–20.

17. Friedan, *The Feminine Mystique*, loc. 3708.

18. Ibid., 3347, 1104.

19. Carlson, "The Productive Home vs. the Consuming Home," 119 (emphasis mine).

20. Friedan, *The Feminine Mystique*, loc. 6009.

21. Ibid., 5665, 6002.

22. Ibid., 5519.

23. Ibid., 5820.

24. Ibid., 5685.

25. Ibid., 5994.

26. Ibid., 5998.

27. Ibid., 6129.

28. Alan Kohll, "What Employees Really Want at Work," *Forbes*, July 10, 2018, citing Brie Weiler Reynolds, "Survey: Parents Rank Work Flexibility Ahead of Salary," Flexjobs, August 12, 2016 (84 percent of working parents ranked flexibility as the most important factor in a job). According to one study: "Almost 80% of employees that lacked such options would like to have more flexible work options and would use them if they felt it would not place them in jeopardy at work. Similarly, 80% of working parents regarded flexible scheduling as an important and sought after condition of work or coping mechanism. An additional 70% regarded this for working at home. Women tended to attach somewhat more importance to it than men. About 15% of women rated more flexible work hours and schedules as one of the top factors that would make their life better"; Lonnie Golden, "Limited Access: Disparities in Flexible Work Schedules and Work-at-Home," *Journal of Family and Economic Issues* 29, no. 1 (2008): 88 (internal citations omitted). See also Amber Lapp and David Lapp, "Work-Family Policy in Trump's America: Insights from a Focus Group of Working-Class Millennial Parents in Ohio," *Institute for Family Studies* (December 2016), https://ifstudies.org/blog/work-family -policy-in-trumps-america-part-1.

29. According to a 2016 Gallup poll report: "More than half of women (54%) who do not work and who have a child younger than 18 say their desire to stay home with their children is a 'major reason' why they are not working.

Other factors are considerably less relevant, including the need to earn money, the cost of childcare and the ability to find a good job. . . . Among women who are employed and do not have a child under the age of 18, 70% would prefer to work outside the home. That number falls to 40% among women who are employed and do have a child under the age of 18"; "Women in America: Work and Life Well-Lived," Gallup, Inc., 2016, https://www.gallup.com/workplace /238070/women-america-work-life-lived-insights-business-leaders.aspx. See also Sylvia Ann Hewlett, *On and Off Ramps* (Boston: Harvard Business Review Press, 2007).

30. Brad Harrington, Jennifer Sabatini Fraone, and Jegoo Lee, "The New Dad: The Career-Caregiving Conflict," Report of the Boston College Center for Work & Family, 2017.

31. Friedan, *The Feminine Mystique*, loc. 3787.

32. Ibid., 5849.

33. Ibid., 4141.

34. Ibid., 4450: "This male outrage is the result, surely, of an implacable hatred for the parasitic women who keep their husbands and sons from growing up, who keep them immersed at that sickly level of sexual phantasy."

35. Ibid., 633.

36. Wollstonecraft, *Rights of Woman*, 50.

37. Friedan, *The Feminine Mystique*, loc. 933.

38. Ibid., 5457.

39. For instance, Addams's biographer writes that Addams and her ilk "stressed the importance of women's ties to the wellsprings of tradition and extolled the centrality of family and children in women's lives; but the domestic arena was seen as a springboard into wider civil life rather than an inhibition to matters civic" (Elshtain, *Jane Addams*, 77).

40. Friedan, *The Feminine Mystique*, loc. 4022, 4136.

CHAPTER 7. SEX ROLE STEREOTYPES AND
THE SUCCESSFUL QUEST FOR EQUAL CITIZENSHIP STATUS

1. UN General Assembly, Universal Declaration of Human Rights, December 10, 1948, 217 A (III).

2. United States Department of Labor, *American Women: Report of the U.S. President's Commission on the Status of Women*, October 28, 1963.

3. "The National Organization for Women's 1966 Statement of Purpose," adopted by the National Organization of Women, October 29, 1966, https://now.org/about/history/statement-of-purpose/.

4. Ibid.

5. Pauli Murray and Mary O. Eastwood, "Jane Crow and the Law: Sex Discrimination and Title VII," *George Washington Law Review* 34, no. 2 (1965): 232–56.

6. Friedan, *The Feminine Mystique*, Kindle loc. 4688, 4497: "'Symbiosis' is a biological term; it refers to the process by which, to put it simply, two organisms live as one. With human beings, when the fetus is in the womb, the mother's blood supports its life; the food she eats makes it grow, its oxygen comes from the air she breathes, and she discharges its wastes. There is a biological oneness in the beginning between mother and child, a wonderful intricate process. But this relationship ends with the severing of the umbilical cord and the birth of the baby into the world as a separate human being" (loc. 4685).

7. *Phillips v. Martin Marietta Corp.*, No. 67-290-ORL-Civil, 1968 U.S. Dist. LEXIS 8595 (M. D. Fla. July 9, 1968), 2.

8. *Phillips v. Martin Marietta Corporation*, 400 U.S. 542, 544 (1971).

9. *Dothard v. Rawlingson*, 433 U.S. 347 (1977).

10. Recall from chapter 4 how Virginia Minor and her attorney husband argued in 1875 before the Supreme Court that the privileges and immunities clause had enfranchised all citizens, regardless of sex.

11. Murray and Eastwood, "Jane Crow and the Law."

12. Ibid., 238.

13. Ibid., 239–40 (emphasis mine).

14. *White v. Crook*, 251 F. Supp. 401 (1966).

15. *Hoyt v. Florida*, 368 U.S. 57, 62 (1961).

16. Ruth Bader Ginsburg, *My Own Words* (New York: Simon and Schuster, 2018), 10.

17. Ibid., 85.

18. David Von Drehle, "Redefining Fair with a Simple Careful Assault," *The Washington Post*, July 19, 1993.

19. Appellant's Brief, *Reed v. Reed*, 404 U.S. 71 (1971), no. 430, on file with the Library of Congress, Ginsburg Collection, Accession 1, ACLU File, Box 6, at 5 (emphasis mine).

20. Ibid., at 6.

21. Ibid., at 7 (emphasis mine).

22. Ibid., at 17.

23. Ibid., at 7.

24. Ibid., at 19.

25. Ibid., at 20, no. 13 (emphasis mine).

26. Ibid., at 48.

27. *Reed v. Reed*, 404 U.S. 71, 75–76 (1971).

28. Ibid.

29. Amicus Brief of the ACLU, *Frontiero v. Richardson*, 411 U.S. 677 (1973), on file with the Library of Congress, Ginsburg Collection, Accession 1, ACLU File, Box 3, at 19.

30. Amy Leigh Campbell, *Raising the Bar* (Printed by the author: Xlibris, 2003), 59. This was still the position of labor leaders. For instance, in her closing arguments during congressional hearings on the ERA, Myra Wolfgang, vice president of the Union of Hotel Employees and Restaurant Employees, defended the view that women-protective labor laws were still necessary. As her predecessors before her, she accused pro-ERA feminists of being elitist "white, middle-class and college-oriented." "Thousands of women, because of economic necessity, will submit to excessive hours without a law to protect them in order to obtain or hold a job. . . . They accede to this excessive overtime or quit the job. In the first instance, the children become the victims, in the second instance, the entire family suffers from the loss of that income. . . . Don't talk theory to me, tell me the practice." She went on: "Laws that treat women differently than men are not necessarily 'discriminatory' or 'unfair'"; "Statement of Mrs. Myra Wolfgang," Equal Rights 1970: Hearings before the Committee on the Judiciary, 91st Cong., 2nd Sess., S. J. Res 61 and S. J. Res 231, September 9, 10, 11, and 15, 1970 (Washington, DC: Government Printing Office, 1970), 28–45; quoted in Woloch, *A Class by Herself*, 222.

31. *Frontiero v. Richardson*, 411 U.S. 677, 684 (1973). This now-famous language was actually first employed by the California Supreme Court in *Sail'er Inn v. Kirby*, 5 Cal. 3d 1 (1971). That decision had been drafted by Justice Raymond Peers's law clerk, now law professor Wendy W. Williams. Woloch, *A Class by Herself*, 215.

32. Ruth Bader Ginsburg, "Sexual Equality under the Fourteenth and Equal Rights Amendments," *Washington University Law Review* (January 1979): 161.

33. Steven G. Calabresi and Julia T. Rickert, "Originalism and Sex Discrimination," *Texas Law Review* 90 (2011): 1, 2: "It is a truism of modern constitutional law scholarship that originalism . . . cannot justify the Supreme Court's sex discrimination cases of the last forty years. Justice Scalia confidently announced in a speech at Hastings College of Law recently that the Fourteenth Amendment does not ban sex discrimination because '[n]obody thought it was directed against sex discrimination.'"

34. Ibid., 50.

35. Ibid., 67. See also Reva Siegel, "She the People: The Nineteenth Amendment, Sex Equality, Federalism, and the Family," *Harvard Law Review* 115, no. 4 (2002): 1012–19. Siegel argues that the Nineteenth Amendment

imports into the Constitution a "sex equality norm" that ought to be synthetically read back into the equal protection clause, and as such ought to free women from historic forms of subordination in the family.

36. Michael Stokes Paulsen, *The Constitution: An Introduction* (New York: Basic Books, 2015), 194: "The Equal Protection Clause's language simply does not countenance discrimination against women solely because of their sex. While the drafts*men* of the Fourteenth Amendment may have had racial discrimination most centrally *in mind* when they wrote the Fourteenth Amendment, what they said *in words* was that no 'person' should be deprived of the equal protection of the laws. Women are persons—obviously. It should be equally obvious that state laws that discriminate against women with respect to civil rights, privileges, and benefits for which there is no true difference between the sexes—or that rest on current social views, stereotypes, or generalizations— deny women the equal protection of the laws" (emphasis in original).

37. *Craig v. Boren*, 429 U.S. 190 (1976).

38. Ruth Bader Ginsburg, "Remarks on Women Becoming Part of the Constitution," *Law & Inequality* 6 (1988): 23.

39. Ruth Bader Ginsburg, "Sex Equality and the Constitution," *Tulane Law Review* 52, no. 3 (1978): 451, 467.

40. Lynn Sherr, *Failure Is Impossible: Susan B. Anthony in Her Own Words* (New York: Crown, 1995), 305, quoted in the foreword by Ruth Bader Ginsburg to *Supreme Court Decisions and Women's Rights*, ed. Clare Cushman (Washington, DC: CQ Press, 2010), xii.

41. *Taylor v. Louisiana*, 419 U.S. 522 (1975).

42. Quoted in Scott Dobson, ed., *The Legacy of Ruth Bader Ginsburg* (Cambridge: Cambridge University Press, 2015), 63.

43. *Weinberger v. Wiesenfeld*, 420 U.S. 636, 654 (1975), no. 19 (emphasis mine).

44. Murray and Eastwood, "Jane Crow and the Law," 239 (emphasis mine); see also Pauli Murray, "A Proposal to Reexamine the Applicability of the Fourteenth Amendment to State Laws and Practices Which Discriminate on the Basis of Sex Per Se," December 1962, PCSW Papers, Doc. 11-20, Box 8, Folder 62, on file with the Schlesinger Library, Radcliffe Institute, Harvard University, at 8–9.

45. Murray and Eastwood, "Jane Crow and the Law," 241 (emphasis in original).

46. In 1974, Ginsburg coauthored a report in which she troublingly suggested replacing "Mother's Day" and "Father's Day" with a "Parents' Day" so as to "minimiz[e] traditional sex-based differences in parental roles"; see Ruth Bader Ginsburg and Brenda Feigen Fasteau, "The Legal Status of Women

under Federal Law," *Report of Columbia Law School Equal Rights Advocacy Project* (1974), 133. But *Bostock v. Clayton County*, a 2020 U.S. Supreme Court case that extended Title VII protections to gay and trans-identifying individuals, takes the functional analysis well beyond even this. The Court held in *Bostock* that an employer illicitly discriminates on the basis of sex when it fires a person "for traits or actions it would not have questioned in members of a different sex" (590 U.S. ___ [2020]). Though the Court claimed not to put into question the assumption that "sex" in the statute refers "only to biological distinctions between male and female," its holding (i.e., that trans-identifying individuals be considered, for Title VII purposes, as their preferred, not biological, sex) betrays this claim. For while dressing "as a woman" may well appear as a mere "trait" or "action" (and a stereotypical one at that), other "real" sex differences— pregnancy and motherhood most obviously—will not profitably be regarded as mere "functions," "traits," or "actions" that women may perform or play. Nor will female athletes, promised equality of opportunity in Title IX, benefit in a world in which trans-identifying males ("trans women") are legally required to compete against them in sports or share their locker rooms. Though the Court claimed not to have reached these questions, it is difficult to see how the relevant text from Title VII could be interpreted differently in Title IX, or how the logic of *Bostock* will not negatively influence how the law treats pregnancy and motherhood.

47. Ruth Bader Ginsburg and Barbara Flagg, "Some Reflections on the Feminist Legal Thought of the 1970's," *University of Chicago Legal Forum* (1989): 17.

48. Ruth Bader Ginsburg, "Some Thoughts on the 1980's Debate over Special versus Equal Treatment for Women," *Law & Inequality* 4, no. 143 (1986): 150, quoting friend Cynthia Epstein.

49. *Mississippi University for Women v. Hogan*, 458 U.S. 718 (1982).

50. *United States v. Virginia*, 518 U.S. 515, 520 (1996).

51. Ibid., 517.

52. Ibid., 532.

53. Ibid., 533.

54. Ibid.

55. Ibid., 534.

56. Single-sex education expert Dr. Leonard Sax: "The teacher's lack of awareness of sex differences has the unintended consequence of *reinforcing* gender stereotypes. Conversely, teachers who understand these differences can break down gender stereotypes: they can enable more girls to excel in and to *enjoy* math and computer science, and they can inspire more boys to get excited about creative writing, poetry, and Spanish language"; Leonard Sax, "Why Gender Matters for Teachers" (emphasis in original), https://www

.leonardsax.com/workshops/teachers-and-administrators/why-gender-matters
-for-teachers/.

57. *United States v. Virginia*, 550.

58. Ruth Bader Ginsburg, "A Grand Ideal for the Future," *Oregon State Bar Bulletin* 53, no. 19 (1993).

59. Ginsburg, "Some Thoughts," 148.

60. Dorothy L. Sayers, *Are Women Human? Astute and Witty Essays on the Role of Women in Society* (Grand Rapids, MI: Eerdmans, 2005), 24–25 (emphasis in original).

61. Ibid., 26–27.

62. Scalia makes many important points in dissent, one of which is especially important for our purposes. At the end of his opinion, he reports that VMI traditionally provided its first-year students with a signature booklet that contained, among other items, "The Code of a Gentleman." The "Code" makes clear the expectation that an honorable man treats women with dignity and respect, never, for instance, "discuss[ing] the merits or demerits of a lady," nor going into a lady's house if "affected by alcohol," nor "so much as lay[ing] a finger on [her]." Scalia observes, "I do not know whether the men of VMI lived by this Code; perhaps not. But it is powerfully impressive that a public institution of higher education still in existence sought to have them do so. I do not think any of us, women included, will be better off for its destruction"; *United States v. Virginia*, 602 (Scalia, J., dissenting opinion).

63. Wollstonecraft, *Rights of Woman*, 49.

64. *United States v. Virginia*, 588.

65. Ibid., 551.

66. Ibid., 568–69.

67. Email correspondence, May 6, 2018, on file with author. The views expressed are those of Sarah White, and do not reflect the official position of the U.S. Military Academy, the Department of the Army, or the Department of Defense.

CHAPTER 8. CARING FOR DEPENDENCY
IN THE LOGIC OF THE MARKET

1. See generally, Brodie, *Contraception and Abortion*; Gordon, *Moral Property*.

2. G. van N. Viljoen, "Plato and Aristotle on the Exposure of Infants at Athens," *Acta Classica*, 1959, http://www.casa-kvsa.org.za/1959/AC02-06 -Viljoen.pdf; see also Gordon, *Moral Property*, 15: "Infanticide was . . . frequently a direct expression of male supremacy. Not only have male babies been

more valued, but female children were sometimes so valueless, despised, and even burdensome that a portion of them were systematically killed." See also Rodney Stark, *The Rise of Christianity* (New York: HarperOne, 1997), 95–128. "Thou shalt not murder a child by abortion nor kill them when born" (*The Didache*, 50 AD–150 AD).

3. The English Parliament enacted laws regulating midwives in 1512, apparently to address the problem of infanticide; see Dellapenna, *Dispelling the Myths of Abortion History*, 99.

4. Thomas Hobbes, *Leviathan* (1651) (Indianapolis: Hackett, 1994), 128–30: "The right of dominion by generation is that which the parent hath over his children, and is called Paternal. . . . Again, seeing the infant is first in the power of the mother, so as she may either nourish or expose it."

5. In his *Second Treatise on Government*, Locke argues that both mothers and fathers share a duty to care for and educate children while they are incapable of fending for themselves. He writes: "All parents were, by the law of Nature, under an obligation to preserve, nourish and educate the children they had begotten. . . . The power, then, that parents have over their children arises from that duty which is incumbent on them, to take care of their offspring during the imperfect state of childhood" (2.6.56 and 58). Similarly, John Stuart Mill wrote in *On Liberty*: "Hardly any one indeed will deny that it is one of the most sacred duties of the parents (or, as law and usage now stand, the father), after summoning a human being into the world, to give to that being an education fitting him to perform his part well in life towards others and towards himself. . . . It still remains unrecognized, that to bring a child into existence without a fair prospect of being able, not only to provide food for its body, but instruction and training for its mind, is a moral crime, both against the unfortunate offspring and against society" (5.12). And in Blackstone's *Commentaries*, he writes that the "most universal relation in nature, is . . . that between parent and child. . . . The duty of parents to provide for the *maintenance* of their children is a principle of natural law; an obligation . . . laid on them not only by nature herself, but by their own proper act, in bringing them into the world: for they would be in the highest manner injurious to their issue, if they only gave the children life, that they might afterwards see them perish. By begetting them therefore they have entered into a voluntary obligation . . . and thus the children will have a perfect *right* of receiving maintenance from their parents" (1:434–35; emphasis original).

6. Rosalind Pollack Petchesky, *Abortion and Woman's Choice* (Boston: Northeastern University Press, 1990), 29–30.

7. American Medical Association, *The Transactions of the American Medical Association* (Philadelphia: Collins, Printer, 1859), 12:27.

8. Gordon, *Moral Property*, 57, quoting Tennessee Claflin.

9. Ibid., 196: Gordon notes that "as time progressed, [Sanger] gave less attention to feminist arguments and more to eugenic ones."

10. Margaret Sanger, *Woman and the New Race* (New York: Blue Ribbon Books, 1920), 3–4: "Birth control itself, often denounced as a violation of natural law, is nothing more or less than the facilitation of the process of weeding out the unfit, of preventing the birth of defectives or of those who will become defectives."

11. Ibid., 4, 203: "The creators of over-population are the women.... [She] is plunged blindly into married life . . . an unfit breeder of the unfit" (203).

12. Ibid., 5–6 (emphasis in original). "By her failure to withhold the multitudes of children who have made inevitable the most flagrant of our social evils, she incurred a debt to society. Regardless of her own wrongs, regardless of her own lack of opportunity and regardless of all other considerations, *she* must pay that debt. . . . She cannot pay it with palliatives—with child-labor laws, prohibition, regulation of prostitution and agitation against war. . . . They do not touch the source of the social disease" (6; emphasis in original).

Linda Gordon laments how the often imperialist motives among Sanger and other twentieth-century population controllers in the United States contravened the nineteenth-century arguments for voluntary motherhood. According to Gordon: "[The] common denominator [of the U.S. population control programs in the early twentieth century] was the treatment of birth control as a weapon in the arsenal of economic planners. It was almost a full reversal of the nineteenth-century conception of birth control—voluntary motherhood—in which technology followed the human and especially female desire for self-determination; now technology was leading and individual will was being molded, planners hoped, by powerful persuasive techniques" (Gordon, *Moral Property*, 239–40).

13. See generally Matthew Connelly, *Fatal Misconception* (Cambridge, MA: Harvard University Press, 2008).

14. According to Mary Ziegler, a 1937 Gallup poll reported that 70 percent approved of compulsory sterilization of "the feebleminded and insane"; see Ziegler, "The Framing of a Right to Choose: *Roe v. Wade* and the Changing Debate on Abortion Law," *Law and History Review* 27 (2009): 286; see generally Melissa J. Wilde, *Birth Control Battles: How Race and Class Divided American Religion* (Berkeley: University of California Press, 2019).

15. *Buck v. Bell*, 274 U.S. 200 (1927). See also Alexandra Minna Stern, "Sterilized in the Name of Public Health," *American Journal of Public Health* 95, no. 7 (2005): 1128–38, analyzing the eugenic arguments that led to the sterilization of 20,000 patients in state institutions between 1909 and 1979 in the state of California.

16. Daniel K. Williams, *Defenders of the Unborn: The Pro-Life Movement before* Roe v. Wade (Oxford: Oxford University Press, 2016), 14.

17. Jonathan Eig, *Birth of the Pill: How Four Crusaders Reinvented Sex and Launched a Revolution* (New York: W. W. Norton, 2015); see also Petchesky, *Abortion and Woman's Choice*; Gordon, *Moral Property*.

18. Gordon, *Moral Property*, 288.

19. Ibid., 289. See also Williams, *Defenders of the Unborn*, 61 and 101.

20. In 2019, for instance, two researchers at the University of California, San Francisco warned in the *New York Times* that employing long-acting reversible contraceptives in efforts to decrease maternal poverty were at risk of sharing in the country's "long and shameful" eugenic heritage; see Christine Dehlendorf and Kelsey Holt, "The Dangerous Rise of the IUD as Poverty Cure," *New York Times*, January 2, 2019: "Promoting [IUDs] from a poverty-reduction perspective still targets the reproduction of certain women based on a problematic and simplistic understanding of the causes of societal ills. . . . This idea distracts from the structural factors—like the availability of social services and racial discrimination—that determine economic opportunities." The researchers suggested that such arguments may also harm the quality of reproductive care offered to the "very women they are intended to help," with studies showing that low-income Black and Latina women often feel pressured to use contraceptive devices they do not want. A 2012 study showed that 40 percent of Black and Latina women think the government encourages people of color to use birth control to limit children born in their communities. The authors also cite Corinne H. Rocca and Cynthia C. Harper, "Do Racial and Ethnic Differences in Contraceptive Attitudes and Knowledge Explain Disparities in Method Use?," *Perspectives on Sexual and Reproductive Health* 44, no. 3 (2012): 150–58.

21. Ellen Chesler, *Woman of Valor: Margaret Sanger and the Birth Control Movement in America* (New York: Simon & Schuster, 1992), fig. 15, cited in Angela Franks, *Margaret Sanger's Eugenic Legacy* (Jefferson, NC: McFarland, 2005). Franks reports that clinics sometimes privately referred clients for abortion.

22. Birth Control Federation of America, Inc., "Pamphlet, 'Plan Your Family for Health and Happiness,' undated," Smith Libraries Exhibits, https://libex.smith.edu/omeka/items/show/440.

23. Vauhini Vara, "Can #ShoutYourAbortion Turn Hashtag Activism into a Movement?," *The New Yorker*, November 10, 2015, reporting that one of the creators of the campaign "likes to describe herself, pointedly, as not only pro-choice but *pro-abortion*" (emphasis in original).

24. Margaret Sanger, "Suppression," *The Woman Rebel* 1, no. 4 (1914): 25. "Our fight is for the personal liberty of the women who work. A woman's

body belongs to herself alone. . . . The first step toward getting life, liberty and the pursuit of happiness for any woman is her decision whether or not she shall become a mother" (ibid.)

25. Hugh Moore, "The Population Bomb" (December 1959), 14, in the Hugh Moore Papers, MC 153, Box 20, Folder 5. Moore became the president of the Association for Voluntary Sterilization in 1964.

26. George A. Akerlof, Janet L. Yellen, and Michael L. Katz, "An Analysis of Out-of-Wedlock Childbearing in the United States," *The Quarterly Journal of Economics* 111, no. 2 (1996): 277–317, theorizing that the sudden increase in the availability of contraception and then abortion in the late 1960s and early 1970s produced a "reproductive technology shock" that led to a dramatic increase in out-of-wedlock births, especially among poor women. Andrew Beauchamp and Catherine R. Pakaluk, "The Paradox of the Pill: Heterogeneous Effects of Oral Contraceptive Access," *Economic Inquiry* 57, no. 2 (2019): 813–31. "Exploiting exogenous variation in laws governing access to the pill, we find that changes in marital access to the pill increased the nonmarital birthrate by between 15% and 18%, accounting for about one-third of the overall increase in nonmarital births. These effects are concentrated almost entirely among women whose fathers did not graduate high school and among minority women" (813). Catherine R. Pakaluk, "Essays in Applied Microeconomics" (PhD diss., Harvard University, 2010): "Increased contraceptive efficacy increases demand for sex across both married and unmarried households," which "yields more children among unmarried households and fewer children among married ones, generating both an increase in non-marital births and a plausible decrease in the overall fertility rate" (66–67).

27. Petchesky, *Abortion and Woman's Choice*, 169, referring also to the work of Susan Scrimshaw, "Women and the Pill: From Panacea to Catalyst," *Family Planning Perspectives* 13 (November/December 1981): 260.

28. Petchesky, *Abortion and Woman's Choice*, 169. Similarly, Gordon writes: "From a historical perspective, contraception at first may have increased the clientele for abortion because it accustoms people to planning reproduction and makes them unlikely to accept loss of control." She suggests it is inaccurate to see contraception and abortion as alternatives since "no method of contraception yet developed can eliminate the need for abortion" (Gordon, *Moral Property*, 340).

29. Petchesky, *Abortion and Woman's Choice*, 186; Gordon, *Moral Property*, 341. Such risks have not subsided a half century later. See, for instance, Sarah Hill, *This Is Your Brain on Birth Control* (New York: Avery, 2019), finding that the hormonal birth control pill affects cells in the brain that regulate attraction, sexual motivation, stress, hunger, eating patterns, emotion regulation, friendships, aggression, mood, learning, and more. For instance, women

on the pill have a dampened cortisol spike in response to stress, which can negatively affect learning, memory, and mood.

30. Gordon, *Moral Property*, 342.

31. Williams, *Defenders of the Unborn*, 20, citing Frederick J. Taussig, *Abortion: Spontaneous and Induced, Medical and Social Aspects* (St. Louis: C. V. Mosby, 1936), 26. Williams reports that the Great Depression saw hundreds of thousands of abortions each year, with thousands of women dying from complications related to the illegal procedure.

32. Beauchamp and Pakaluk, "The Paradox of the Pill."

33. Paul Ehrlich, *The Population Bomb* (San Francisco: Sierra Club/Ballantine Books, 1968), 88, 141.

34. Ziegler, "The Framing of a Right to Choose," 314–15, quoting NARAL, *Speaker and Debater's Handbook* (circa 1972).

35. Quoted in Petchesky, *Abortion and Woman's Choice*, 123.

36. Ziegler, "The Framing of a Right to Choose," 319. Ziegler reports that Wilma Scott Heide, president of NOW in 1970, represented the women's organization before the Rockefeller Commission, offering a case that women's rights and population control shared a common goal. Heide argued: "First we must affirmatively change the [role of women] (not merely note the slowly changing role of women passively); then family size will change. . . . On the question of overpopulation . . . , no matter how safe, effective, and universally available is any contraceptive method for women or men, women will continue to be the producers of excess children . . . unless they have viable significant alternatives to motherhood. . . . If you opt for quality population, you must adopt this human liberation movement."

37. Lawrence Katz and Claudia Goldin, "The Power of the Pill: Oral Contraceptives and Women's Career and Marriage Decisions," *Journal of Political Economy* 110, no. 4 (2002): 730–70.

38. Akerlof, Yellen, and Katz, "An Analysis of Out-of-Wedlock Childbearing in the United States"; Beauchamp and Pakaluk, "The Paradox of the Pill"; Sara McLanahan, "Diverging Destinies: How Children Are Faring under the Second Demographic Transition," *Demography* 41, no. 4 (2004): "To sum up, different forces were driving the behavior of women in the top and bottom strata. For women from the most-advantaged backgrounds, feminism was providing a new identity, advances in birth control technology were providing the capacity, and increases in economic opportunities were providing the incentives to delay marriage and childbearing and to invest in careers. The promise of a new identity and the new birth control technologies, however, were of much less value to women in the bottom strata, who had little incentive to delay motherhood and pursue a career. At the same time, changes in the labor

market conditions of low-skilled men were making the potential partners of these women less 'marriageable,' while changes in norms, bargaining power, and welfare benefits were making it easier for men to shirk their fatherhood responsibilities" (619).

39. Kathryn Edin and Maria Kefalas, *Promises I Can Keep: Why Poor Women Put Motherhood before Marriage* (Berkeley: University of California Press, 2005); Kay Hymowitz, *Marriage and Caste in America: Separate and Unequal Families in a Post-Marital Age* (Chicago: Ivan R. Dee, 2006).

40. Ibid. See also Nicholas Eberstadt, *Men without Work: America's Invisible Crisis* (West Conshohocken, PA: Templeton, 2016); Bruce Drake, "Incarceration Gap Widens between Whites and Blacks," Pew Research Center, September 6, 2013, https://www.pewresearch.org/fact-tank/2013/09 /06/incarceration-gap-between-whites-and-blacks-widens/; Adam Looney and Nicholas Turner, "Work and Opportunity before and after Incarceration," Brookings, March 14, 2018, https://www.brookings.edu.

41. Isabel Sawhill, "Non-Marital Births and Child Poverty in the United States," testimony, Brookings, June 29, 1999, https://www.brookings.edu /testimonies/non-marital-births-and-child-poverty-in-the-united-states/, arguing that the surge in single parenting accounts for "virtually all of the increase in child poverty since the 1970s."

42. Laura Kaplan, *The Story of Jane* (Chicago: University of Chicago Press, 1997).

43. Lawrence Lader, *Abortion* (Indianapolis: Bobbs-Merrill, 1966), 169. See also Williams, *Defenders of the Unborn*, 169. Williams writes that this became the mantra of the abortion rights movement. Quoting an advocate who gave testimony before the California State Assembly in 1970: "Every contraception method, no matter how faithfully practiced, has an inherent failure rate. . . . Compulsory pregnancy [was a] bizarre punishment for mechanical failure" (61–62).

44. Lawrence Lader, *Abortion II* (Boston: Beacon Press, 1973), 20: Lader writes: "Ironically, I would eventually split with Margaret over abortion. . . . Margaret had always opposed abortion. In her work as a nurse on Manhattan's Lower East Side around 1910, she would watch in horror the long lines of immigrant women, worn out by poverty and constant childbearing, waiting outside the offices of nonlicensed abortionists with five dollars clutched in their hands. The rate of injury, and even death, from this crude, underground surgery was frighteningly high. Margaret detested the waste and degradation of human life, and pleaded for contraception as a rational and humanitarian alternative."

45. Bernard Nathanson with Richard Ostling, *Aborting America* (Garden City, NY: Doubleday, 1979), 32: Nathanson, quoting Lader: "If we're going to

move abortion out of the books and into the streets, we're going to have to recruit the feminists. Friedan has got to put her troops into this thing—while she still has control of them."

46. Williams, *Defenders of the Unborn*, 63–64, reporting that fewer than 300 women died from abortion in 1965.

47. Nathanson with Ostling, *Aborting America*, 33.

48. In 1967, NOW published a Bill of Rights that included similar demands to its original statement, but its eighth point read: "The right of women to control their own reproductive lives by removing from penal codes the laws limiting access to contraceptive information and devices and laws governing abortion"; see National Organization for Women, "Bill of Rights," https://350fem.blogs.brynmawr.edu/about/1968-bill-of-rights/. Those opposed to NOW's new advocacy for abortion rights established the Women's Equity Action League in 1968 to fight discrimination in the workplace and to lobby for the ERA.

Graciela Olivarez, original member of NOW's national board, wrote the following words in her 1972 statement as vice chair of the President's Commission on Population and the American Future: "With the recent advances in contraceptive technology, any woman who so desires is better able to control her fertility in a more effective way than has ever been before available. . . . [But] personal and contraceptive failures do not give women the 'right' to correct or eliminate the so-called 'accident' by destroying the fetus. Advocacy by women for legalized abortion on a national scale is so anti-women's liberation that it flies in the face of what some of us are trying to accomplish through the women's movement, namely, equality—equality means an equal sharing of responsibilities by and as men and women"; "Separate Statement of Graciela Olivarez," in *Report of the President's Commission on Population and the American Future* (U.S. Government Printing Office, 1972).

49. Betty Friedan, *Life So Far: A Memoir* (New York: Simon & Schuster, 2006; orig. 2000), 214. Siegel and Greenhouse, *Before* Roe v. Wade, 40.

50. American Law Institute, "Moral Penal Code" (1951–1985), https://www.ali.org/publications/show/model-penal-code/.

51. Siegel and Greenhouse, *Before* Roe v. Wade, 121–22.

52. Ibid., 123.

53. Ibid., 27–28.

54. Petchesky, *Abortion and Woman's Rights*, 167.

55. Friedan, *Life So Far*, 200–201 (emphasis mine).

56. Editorial, "Restellism Exposed," *The Revolution*, December 2, 1867.

57. Mattie H. Brinkerhoff, "Women and Motherhood," *The Revolution*, September 2, 1869, 138.

58. Williams, *Defenders of the Unborn*, 61.

59. Tennessee Claflin, "The Ethics of Sexual Equality," April 6, 1872, quoted in Gordon, *Moral Property*, 57.

60. Catharine MacKinnon, *Feminism Unmodified* (Cambridge, MA: Harvard University Press, 1987), 99–100. Pointing to the tendency of both the Left and Right in the abortion debate to focus on who controls reproduction rather than who controls sex, MacKinnon writes:

> Liberals have supported the availability of the abortion choice as if the woman just happened upon the fetus. The political right, imagining that the intercourse preceding conception is usually voluntary, urges abstinence, as if sex were up to women, while defending male authority, specifically including a wife's duty to submit to sex. [These] share a tacit assumption that women significantly do control sex.
>
> [But apart from stopping to employ the contraceptive, do] you think [the woman] would stop the man for any other reason, such as, for instance, the real taboo—lack of desire? If she would not, how is sex, hence its consequences, meaningfully voluntary for women? . . . Sex doesn't look a whole lot like freedom when it appears normatively less costly for women to risk an undesired, often painful, traumatic, dangerous, sometimes illegal, and potentially life-threatening procedure than to protect themselves in advance [by resisting the sex]. (MacKinnon, *Feminism Unmodified*, 94–95)

Building on MacKinnon's insights, Robin West writes: "[The *Roe* approach] shifts the focus away from addressing the social and sexual imbalances that result in unwanted pregnancies to the unwanted pregnancy itself, and strongly suggests that the appropriate social and individual response to unwanted sex is to protect the decision to end the pregnancy"; Robin West, "From Choice to Reproductive Justice: De-Constitutionalizing Abortion Rights," *Yale Law Journal* 118 (2009): 1409. She continues: "The focus on the abortion right has diverted resources not only from political and legal possibilities for promoting reproductive justice, but also from other forms of social persuasion, including moral argument, that might reduce the number of unwanted pregnancies women experience, whether they result in live births or not. Bluntly, if women and men were encouraged to be more sexually responsible, there would be fewer unintended pregnancies and less need for abortions or abortion rights" (ibid., 1428–29), and she argues that opposite sex partners have a "moral duty" to use birth control if they do not intend to conceive and that a girl or young woman has a moral duty "to her future self not to engage in sex she does not want," and a boy or man a similar duty "not to engage in sex undesired by his partner."

Today, advocates of long-acting reversible contraception (LARC) argue that LARCs provide a foolproof means to curtail the still-high rate of unintentional pregnancies, and thus reduce the abortion and nonmarital childbearing rates by helping women affirmatively choose when to become mothers. A 2016 article suggests that intrauterine devices and implants "change the default from drifting into parenthood to planned conception"; Caitlin Parks and Jeffrey F. Peipert, "Eliminating Health Disparities in Unintended Pregnancy with Long-Acting Reversible Contraception (LARC)," *American Journal of Obstetrics and Gynecology* 214, no. 6 (2016): 681–88. This language borrows from Isabel Sawhill, *Generation Unbound: Drifting into Sex and Parenthood without Marriage* (Washington, DC: Brookings Institution Press, 2014), in which Sawhill argues that LARCs will help those who tend to "drift" into parenthood become "planners" instead, and thus put marriage ahead of childbearing. But those who advocate for LARCs would do well to heed MacKinnon's warning. As MacKinnon (and West) help us to see, it is not parenthood (or pregnancy) into which sexual actors initially drift: it is often the sex itself. And altering the "default" setting of a woman's body from fertile to infertile will only further signal that she is presumptively available for sex. "When the default [is] yes," as Angela Franks recasts MacKinnon's insight, "what begins as a right [to sex] often turns into a duty"; see Franks, "Consent Is Not Enough: Harvey Weinstein, Sex, and Human Flourishing," *Public Discourse*, November 26, 2017. Young women and girls often feel the need to relent to "unwanted" sex, and then are left to manage the consequences on their own. The underlying assumption guiding the advocacy for LARC is that, in the words of Richard Reeves, while "casual sex may be fine, casual childbearing is not"; Reeves, "Where's the Glue? Policies to Close the Gender Gap," in *Unequal Family Lives*, ed. Naomi R. Cahn, June Carbone, Laurie Fields DeRose, and W. Bradford Wilcox (Cambridge: Cambridge University Press, 2018), 227. But many teenage girls and young women today are not satisfied with casual sex either—and LARCs increase the likelihood of engaging in it. See also note 124, below.

61. MacKinnon, *Feminism Unmodified*, 98.

62. Gordon, *Moral Property*, 272–73, 276–77: "Since modern contraception was designed to make unlimited intercourse possible, it was not at all odd that [the birth control–advocating doctors] focused on intercourse itself as the center of sexual normality. The development of mechanical contraception had made the twentieth-century birth controllers less aware than the nineteenth-century voluntary motherhood advocates of the importance of other forms of sexual expression, both genital and nongenital. . . . [From the 1870s to the 1940s] there was a progression toward greater frankness about sex and greater acceptance of women's sex drivers. Yet the earlier sex reformers were more radical in

the breadth of their understanding of their task. The voluntary motherhood advocates challenged male tyranny in sexual and family life."

63. Shari Motro, "The Price of Pleasure," *Northwestern University Law Review* 104, no. 3 (2010): 969–70 (emphasis in original). See also Shari Motro, "Scholarship against Desire," *Yale Journal of Law & the Humanities* 27, no. 1 (2015): 129: "The sad truth is that stories about asymmetry in desire and satisfaction are utterly banal."

64. Sidney Callahan, "Feminist as Anti-Abortionist," *National Catholic Reporter*, April 7, 1972, reprinted in Siegel and Greenhouse, *Before* Roe v. Wade, 49.

65. Ibid., 48.

66. Sophia Chae et al., "Reasons Why Women Have Induced Abortions," *Contraception* 96, no. 4 (2017): 233–41; Jenna Jerman et al., "Characteristics of U.S. Abortion Patients in 2014 and Changes since 2008," Guttmacher Institute May 2016 Report, https://www.guttmacher.org/report/characteristics -us-abortion-patients-2014.

67. These include Women's Equity Action League in 1968 and Feminists for Life in 1972.

68. Daphne Clair de Jong, "The Feminist Sell-Out," *New Zealand Listener*, January 14, 1978, republished in Mary Krane Derr, Rachel MacNair, and Linda Naranjo-Huebl , *Prolife Feminism: Yesterday and Today* (Bloomington: Xlibris Corporation, 2005; orig. 1995), 232, 234. Also republished in that volume, Daphne Clair de Jong writes: "[All arguments in favor of abortion rights] bear an alarming resemblance to the arguments used by men to justify discrimination against women. Principally, the arguments are that the fetus is not human, or is human only in some rudimentary way; that it is a part of its mother and has no rights of its own. . . . A fetus, while dependent on its mother, is no more a part of its mother than she is a part of her husband. . . . The fetus lives its own life, develops according to its own genetic program, sleeps, wakes, moves, according to its own inclinations"; de Jong, "Feminism and Abortion: The Great Inconsistency" (ibid., 228, 230).

69. "The attending physician, in consultation with his patient, is free to determine, without regulation by the State, that, in his medical judgment, the patient's pregnancy should be terminated"; *Roe v. Wade*, 410 U.S. 113, 163 (1973). Notably, the Court in *Roe* quoted Lader's book eight times.

70. Petchesky, *Abortion and Woman's Rights*, 130.

71. Ruth Bader Ginsburg, "Some Thoughts on Autonomy and Equality in Relation to *Roe v. Wade*," *North Carolina Law Review* 63 (1985): 376, n. 6; 376–77.

72. Ibid., citing "City Blacks Get Most Abortions," *New York Times*, December 6, 1973, 94. Ziegler writes that "African-American leaders like Jesse

Jackson and civil rights advocates like Ted Kennedy were also suspicious of abortion reform when it was characterized as a form of population control legislation" (Ziegler, "The Framing of a Right to Choose," 323). Once the abortion rights movement shifted to prioritize women's rights arguments, Jackson and Kennedy came aboard.

73. Ginsburg, "Some Thoughts," 384.

74. Ginsburg quoted in Emily Bazelon, "The Place of Women on the Court," *The New York Times Magazine*, July 7, 2009. *Harris v. McRae*, 448 U.S. 297, 322 (1979), upheld the Hyde Amendment, which prohibits federal funding of abortion; states can (and do) fund abortion through their own welfare systems.

75. *Doe v. Bolton*, the companion case to Roe decided the same day, defined "health" broadly as "well-being": "Whether, in the words of the Georgia statute, 'an abortion is necessary' is a professional judgment that the Georgia physician will be called upon to make routinely. We agree with the District Court that the medical judgment may be exercised in the light of all factors— physical, emotional, psychological, familial, and the woman's age—relevant to the well-being of the patient. All these factors may relate to health"; *Doe v. Bolton*, 410 U.S. 179 (1973), 192.

76. Catharine MacKinnon noticed early on that abortion as a "privacy right" amounted to a "sword in men's hands presented as a shield in women's"; see MacKinnon, *Toward a Feminist Theory of the State* (Cambridge, MA: Harvard University Press, 1989), 191.

77. See, for instance, Archibald Cox, *The Role of the Supreme Court in American Government* (Oxford: Oxford University Press, 1976); Paul Freund, "Storms over the Supreme Court," *American Bar Association Journal* 69, no. 10 (1983):1474–80 (adapted from inaugural Harold Leventhal Lecture at Columbia Law School); and Ruth Bader Ginsburg, "Some Thoughts on Autonomy and Equality in Relation to *Roe v. Wade*."

78. John Hart Ely, "The Wages of Crying Wolf," *The Yale Law Journal* 82, no. 5 (1973): 947 (emphasis in original).

79. Ibid., 931–32; 931–32, n. 79: "The Court provides neither an alternative definition nor an account of why *it* thinks privacy is involved. It simply announces that the right to privacy 'is broad enough to encompass a woman's decision whether or not to terminate her pregnancy.' . . . Even reading the cases cited 'for all that they are worth,' it is difficult to isolate the 'privacy' factor (or any other factor that seems constitutionally relevant) that unites them with each other and with *Roe*."

80. *Griswold v. Connecticut*, 381 U.S. 497, 485 (1965). The Supreme Court in *Griswold* objected specifically to the state's lack of authority to enter the

privacy of the marital bed; even as it controversially innovated a constitutional basis for its decision (i.e., "guarantees in the Bill of Rights have penumbras, formed in emanations"), it did not enshrine a constitutional right to contraception in the individual or even in the married couple. Such an affirmative right would come seven years later, in *Eisenstadt v. Baird* (ibid., 483).

81. *Eisenstadt v. Baird*, 405 U.S. 438 (1972). *Eisenstadt* declared that an individual—whether married or unmarried—had a right "to be free from unwarranted governmental intrusion into matters so fundamentally affecting a person as the decision whether to bear or beget a child." *Eisenstadt*, far more than *Griswold*, set the stage for extending the newly created right to privacy to abortion (ibid., 453).

82. Justice Blackmun in the *Roe* opinion admits as much: "[The pregnant woman] carries an embryo and, later, a fetus, if one accepts the medical definitions of the developing young in the human uterus. *See* Dorland's Illustrated Medical Dictionary, 478-479, 547 (24th ed.1965). The situation therefore is inherently different from marital intimacy, or bedroom possession of obscene material, or marriage, or procreation, or education, with which *Eisenstadt* and *Griswold, Stanley, Loving, Skinner,* and *Pierce* and *Meyer* were respectively concerned" (*Roe v. Wade*, at 159).

83. See Craddock, "Protecting Prenatal Persons," for a recent article arguing for Fourteenth Amendment protection.

84. Ely, "The Wages of Crying Wolf," 926 (emphasis in original).

85. See, generally, Williams, *Defenders of the Unborn*.

86. Jane J. Mansbridge, *Why We Lost the ERA* (Chicago: University of Chicago Press, 1986), 13: "Unable to overturn the *Roe* decision directly, many conservatives sought to turn the ERA into a referendum on that decision. To a significant degree, they succeeded. The opponents began to organize and convinced the first of several states to rescind ratification—a move that had no legal force but certainly made a political difference in unratified states."

87. Mansbridge explains how the pro-ERA, abortion rights feminists sought to keep the ERA and abortion separate. Yet in their efforts to repel the passage of laws restricting abortions (and especially its public funding), they made appeals to the equal protection clause of the Fourteenth Amendment, comparable guarantees in state constitutions, and to state ERAs. This litigation seemed to prove the ERA-abortion connection; see Mansbridge, *Why We Lost the ERA*, 124.

88. Quoted in Ziegler, "The Framing of a Right to Choose," 315.

89. Mansbridge, *Why We Lost the ERA* (other arguments included that the ERA would force women into combat roles and disallow separate public restrooms).

90. Ziegler says that, as NARAL's president in the mid-1970s, Sarah Weddington pushed the view that pro-lifers were not interested in protecting the unborn but rather keeping women "barefoot and pregnant." Similarly, Larry Lader worked to portray the pro-life movement as a minor, sectarian position; see Mary Ziegler, "Women's Rights on the Right: The History and Stakes of Modern Pro-Life Feminism," *Berkeley Journal of Gender, Law & Justice* 28, no. 2 (2013): 232–303, 251.

91. Letter from Evelyn K. Samras Judge to Mary Krane Derr, September 12, 1989, quoted in Derr, MacNair, and Naranjo-Huebl, *Prolife Feminism*, 172; letter archived at Feminists for Life of America, Alexandria, Virginia; copy of original letter on file with author.

92. Siegel and Greenhouse, *Before* Roe v. Wade, 143, 144, excerpting plaintiffs' brief, *Abramowicz v. Lefkowitz*, No. 69 Civ. 4469, S. D. N. Y, March 9, 1970.

93. Laurence Tribe, *Abortion: The Clash of Absolutes* (New York: W. W. Norton, 1992), 105.

94. Cindy Osborne, "Pat Goltz, Catherine Callaghan, and the Founding of Feminists for Life," in Derr, MacNair, and Naranjo-Huebl, *Prolife Feminism*, 222–23.

95. "Sweeter even than to have had the joy of caring for children of my own has it been to me to help bring about a better state of things for mothers generally, so that their unborn little ones could not be willed away from them"; Susan B. Anthony, quoted in Frances Willard, *Glimpses of Fifty Years: The Autobiography of an American Woman* (Chicago: Woman's Temperance Publishing Association, 1889), 598.

96. Siegel and Greenhouse, *Before* Roe v. Wade, 144, quoting from plaintiffs' brief.

97. Ibid., 145. Nancy Stearns of the Center for Constitutional Rights wrote both briefs (ibid., 328).

98. Kenneth L. Karst, "Foreword: Equal Citizenship under the Fourteenth Amendment," *Harvard Law Review* 91, no. 1 (1977): 57–58.

99. Ibid., 57.

100. Ibid., 58.

101. Ruth Bader Ginsburg, "Sex Equality and the Constitution," *Tulane Law Review* 52, no. 3 (1978): 459.

102. Ibid., 462.

103. Colleen Walsh, "Ginsburg Holds Court," *The Harvard Gazette*, February 6, 2013 (reporting on Ginsburg presentation at Harvard Law School).

104. Ruth Bader Ginsburg, "Speaking in a Judicial Voice," *New York University Law Review* 67, no. 6 (1992): 1205.

105. Cox, *The Role of the Supreme Court in American Government*, 113; *City of Akron v. Akron Center for Reproductive Health, Inc.*, 103 S. Ct. 2481, 2507 (1983). Both referenced in Ginsburg, "Some Thoughts," 381.

106. Ginsburg, "Some Thoughts," 383.

107. Ibid.

108. *Gonzales v. Carhart*, 550 U.S. 124, 172 (2007) (Ginsburg, J., dissenting).

109. Carole Pateman, *The Sexual Contract* (Redwood City, CA: Stanford University Press, 1988), 12. Elsewhere, Pateman coined the phrase "Wollstonecraft's dilemma" to describe women's fraught attempts to achieve citizenship within a model of citizenship designed for men. "From at least the 1790s [women] have . . . struggled with the task of trying to become citizens within an ideal and practice that have gained universal meaning through their exclusion. . . . On the one hand they have demanded that the idea of citizenship be extended to them, and the liberal-feminist agenda for a 'gender-neutral' social world is the logical conclusion of one form of this demand. On the other hand, women have also insisted, often simultaneously, as did Mary Wollstonecraft, that *as women* they have specific capacities, talents, needs and concerns, so that the expression of their citizenship will be differentiated from that of men"; Pateman, *The Disorder of Women* (Stanford, CA: Stanford University Press, 1989), 197.

110. Robin West, "Concurring in the Judgment," in *What Roe Should Have Said*, ed. Jack Balkin (New York: New York University Press, 2005), 141–42.

111. Brief for the Petitioner, *Struck v. Sec'y of Def.*, 409 U. S. 1071 (1972) (No. 72-178), at 34, quoted in Neil S. Siegel and Reva B. Siegel, "Struck by Stereotype: Ruth Bader Ginsburg on Pregnancy Discrimination as Sex Discrimination," in *The Legacy of Ruth Bader Ginsburg*, ed. Scott Dobson (Cambridge: Cambridge University Press, 2015), 50.

112. More explicit still is Sen. Elizabeth Warren's (D-MA) suggestion during a 2019 Democratic debate that abortion rights are "economic rights"; "Warren, Sanders, Klobuchar and Booker Talk Abortion Rights at Debate," *New York Times*, November 21, 2019.

113. See Erika Bachiochi, "Embodied Equality: Debunking Equal Protection Arguments for Abortion Rights," *Harvard Journal of Law & Public Policy* 34, no. 3 (2011): 889–950.

114. See Erika Bachiochi, "A Putative Right in Search of a Constitutional Justification: Understanding *Planned Parenthood v. Casey*'s Equality Rationale and How It Undermines Women's Equality," *Quinnipiac Law Review* 35, no. 4 (2017): 593–643.

115. *Planned Parenthood v. Casey*, 505 U.S. 833, 871 (1992). "We do not need to say whether each of us, had we been Members of the Court when the

valuation of the State interest came before it as an original matter, would have concluded, as the *Roe* Court did, that its weight is insufficient to justify a ban on abortions prior to viability even when it is subject to certain exceptions. The matter is not before us in the first instance, and, coming as it does after nearly 20 years of litigation in *Roe's* wake, we are satisfied that the immediate question is not the soundness of *Roe's* resolution of the issue, but the precedential force that must be accorded to its holding. And we have concluded that the essential holding of *Roe* should be reaffirmed" (871).

116. *Planned Parenthood v. Casey*, 856 (emphasis mine). The reference the *Casey* plurality cites for this claim, Petchesky, *Abortion and Woman's Choice*, discussed in this chapter, does not tend to support the Court's generalization here. See Bachiochi, "A Putative Right," 627–31.

117. Michael Stokes Paulsen, "Abrogating Stare Decisis," *Yale Law Journal* 109, no. 7 (2000): 1555.

118. The current literature is far more bullish on the effect of the pill on women's educational and professional advancement than on abortion. See, for instance, Lawrence Katz and Claudia Goldin, "The Power of the Pill: Oral Contraceptives and Women's Career and Marriage Decisions," *Journal of Political Economy* 110, no. 4 (2002): 730–70, detailing how the pill has had a much greater effect on women's career advancement than abortion. Martha Bailey and Thomas DiPrete, "Five Decades of Remarkable but Slowing Change in U.S. Women's Economic and Social Status and Political Participation," *RSF: The Russell Sage Foundation Journal of the Social Sciences* 2, no. 4 (2016): 14–15, surveying the literature and reporting that although abortion access has been shown to reduce the birthrate slightly, "evidence is more limited . . . that changes in abortion access translated into changes in women's labor-force outcomes." But see Richard Reeves and Joanna Venator, "Sex, Contraception, or Abortion? Explaining Class Gaps in Unintended Childbearing," Brookings, February 26, 2015, https://www.brookings.edu/research/sex-contraception-or-abortion-explaining-class-gaps-in-unintended-childbearing/. Reeves and Venator show that more well-off single women who are sexually active are far more likely to both use contraception and procure abortions than poor single women. They estimate that if poor women were to use contraception and abortion at the rates wealthier women do, the poor would decrease their rates of nonmarital birth substantially and so increase their chances for upward mobility. This data would seem to lend credence to the popular view that easy abortion access correlates with women's educational and economic opportunity. But like the *Casey* plurality, Reeves and Venator do not account for the much broader cultural effect of abortion access on increases in sexual risk-taking, discussed in the text presently (never mind the eugenic concerns discussed earlier in the chapter).

119. Economists suggest that as analogized to insurance, abortion offers "complete protection" against the risk of childbearing. But complete protection against risk, they argue, tends to lead to riskier behavior. Relatively easy access to abortion working therefore as a kind of secondary insurance to the primary insurance of contraception tends to "change [sexual actors'] behavior" in favor of greater sexual risk-taking, thus increasing "the likelihood of [abortion] being needed"; see Phillip Levine, *Sex and Consequences: Abortion, Public Policy, and the Economics of Fertility* (Princeton, NJ: Princeton University Press, 2007), 3–4. According to Levine: "The problem with the view [that abortion affects only the individual or couple] is that abortion decisions may also lead to something that economists call an 'externality,' in which the behavior of one individual has implications for the well-being of others . . . and that eternality may be positive or negative for society" (ibid., 5). See also Akerlof, Yellen, and Katz, "An Analysis of Out-of-Wedlock Childbearing in the United States"; Helen Alvaré, "Abortion, Sexual Markets and the Law," in *Persons, Moral Worth and Embryos*, ed. Steven Napier (New York: Springer, 2011), 261–71.

120. Alan Guttmacher, "Speech at the Law, Morality, and Abortion Symposium, Rutgers University Law School on March 27, 1968," *Rutgers Law Review* 22 (1968): 415, 437.

121. Levine, *Sex and Consequences*, 4: "Since using contraception or abstaining from sexual activity may be viewed as costly, women/couples may choose to do so less frequently, in essence substituting abortion for contraception, as abortion becomes even more accessible."

122. Richard Posner, *Sex and Reason* (Cambridge, MA: Harvard University Press, 1992), 143. Posner here refers to the dramatic increase in nonmarital childbearing beginning in the 1970s, from approximately 5 percent of all births in 1960 to 40 percent by the 1990s; see U.S. Department of Health and Human Services, "Report to Congress on Out-of-Wedlock Childbearing" (Hyattsville, MD: National Center for Health Statistics, 1995), https://www.cdc.gov/nchs /data/misc/wedlock.pdf.

123. Thomas J. Kane and Douglas Staiger, "Teen Motherhood and Abortion Access," *The Quarterly Journal of Economics* 111, no. 2 (1996): 467–506, https://doi.org/10.2307/2946685, finding that minor restrictions in abortion access, including the closing of abortion clinics and restrictions on Medicaid funding, were related to declines in teen pregnancy. Jonathon Klick and Thomas Stratmann, "Abortion Access and Risky Sex among Teens: Parental Involvement Laws and Sexually Transmitted Diseases," *The Journal of Law, Economics, & Organization* 24, no. 1 (2008): 2–21, doi:10.1093/jleo/ewm041, finding that parental involvement laws significantly reduce risky sexual activity among teenage girls. Josephine Jacobs and Maria Stanfors, "State Abortion Context

and U.S. Women's Contraceptive Choices, 1995–2010," *Perspectives on Sexual and Reproductive Health* 47, no. 2 (2015): 71–82, finding that women who lived in states with restricted abortion access were more likely to use highly effective contraception when compared with women living in states with greater abortion access. Jonathan Klick, "Econometric Analyses of U.S. Abortion Policy: A Critical Review," *Fordham Urban Law Journal* 31 (2004): 751, 764: "The most clear-cut finding of these econometric studies of the relationship between abortion policy and sexual behavior is that individuals, even young individuals whose sexual behavior is often considered to be driven more by emotion than by calculation, are sensitive to the costs of their sexual activity. When those costs increase, as predicted by the law of demand, individuals engage in less risky sex" (764). Andrew Beauchamp, "Abortion Costs, Separation, and Non-Marital Childbearing," *Journal of Family and Economic Issues* 37, no. 2 (June 2016): 182–96, finding that women who gave birth in states with greater abortion restrictions experienced sizable decreases in single motherhood and increased cohabitation rates.

These economic theories, detailed over the course of the last couple of decades, seem perhaps to be playing out in our day. Recent data have shown a significant decrease in the abortion rate over the last several years. Pro-lifers have credited recent legislative restrictions of abortion at the state level; pro-choicers have credited increased contraceptive use. Perhaps both are true: modest restrictions on abortion have made abortion a bit "more costly" and therefore have created incentives toward more responsible sexual activity, including more contraceptive use and greater avoidance of sexual intercourse, both of which have been reported recently.

124. Peter Arcidiacono et al., "Terms of Endearment: An Equilibrium Model of Sex and Matching," *Quantitative Economics* 7, no. 1 (2016): 117–56, finding that, when compared to girls, high school boys have a much stronger preference for relationships with sex. Mark Regnerus and Jeremy Uecker, *Premarital Sex in America* (New York: Oxford University Press, 2011), finding that, although there are exceptions, and not "deny[ing] in the least that women like sex, . . . the vast majority of them seem to like it less than men do and prefer to have it in a committed relationship" (ibid., 53); Lisa Wade, *American Hook Up* (New York: W. W. Norton, 2017): "In the hookup culture . . . [s]ince the ideal that is held up is a stereotypically masculine way of engaging sexually, both men and women aim to have 'meaningless sex,' expressing emotions is seen as weak. Hookup culture, strongly masculinized, demands carelessness, rewards callousness, and punishes kindness. In this scenario, both men and women have the opportunity to have sex but neither is entirely free to love. . . . The culture is designed . . . to the advantage of well-off, good-looking, white heterosexual men who feel comfortable treating sex as a game" (ibid., 244).

Women complain that "the guy kind of expects to get off . . . while the girl doesn't expect anything" or that hookups are "about allowing the male to use your body" (ibid., 158, 168). Elizabeth A. Armstrong, Paula England, and Alison C. K. Fogarty, "Accounting for Women's Orgasm and Sexual Enjoyment in College Hookups and Relationships," *American Sociological Review* 7, no. 3 (2012): 435–62, finding that women have orgasms more often in relationships than in hookups.

125. Many men seek to fulfill their responsibilities to their nascent children, and some grieve the loss of their children through abortion. See Catherine T. Coyle and Vincent M. Rue, "A Thematic Analysis of Men's Experience with a Partner's Elective Abortion," *Counseling and Values* 60, no. 2 (2015): 138–50.

126. Guttmacher, "Speech at the Law, Morality, and Abortion Symposium," 437. I've taken the liberty of replacing "husband" in the original with "man" since the consequences have extended far beyond relations within marriage.

127. See chapter 4, note 38.

128. Toni Weschler, *Taking Charge of Your Fertility*, 2nd ed. (New York: William Morrow, 2015). The efficacy of different methods varies substantially. Studies show, for instance, the Marquette Monitor Method is highly effective; see Richard J. Fehring, "Effectiveness of a Natural Family Planning Service Program," *The American Journal of Maternal/Child Nursing* 42, no. 1 (2017): 43–49 (98 percent efficacy for perfect use and 94 percent for typical use in 24 cycles). The symptothermal method (STM) is also highly effective; see Petra Frank-Herrmann et al., "The Effectiveness of a Fertility Awareness Based Method to Avoid Pregnancy in Relation to a Couple's Sexual Behavior during the Fertile Time," *Human Reproduction*, 22, no. 5 (2007): 1310–19, concluding that "the method effectiveness of the STM investigated in this study is comparable to the method effectiveness of modern contraceptive methods like oral contraceptives." But other methods are far less effective; for a comparison, see Rachel Peragallo Urrutia et al., "Effectiveness of Fertility Awareness–Based Methods for Pregnancy Prevention: A Systematic Review," *Obstetrics & Gynecology* 132, no. 3 (2018): 591–604. The website Facts about Fertility (https://www.factsaboutfertility.org/) collects medical information and current research on fertility awareness–based methods.

129. Gordon, *The Moral Property*, 362 (emphasis mine).

130. *Planned Parenthood v. Casey*, 505 U.S. 860.

131. Natalie Kitroeff and Jessica Silver-Greenberg, "Pregnancy Discrimination Is Rampant Inside America's Biggest Companies," *New York Times*, February 8, 2019, reporting that many of the nation's largest companies sideline pregnant woman as a matter of course, and sometimes even recommend abortion.

132. Deborah Dinner, "Strange Bedfellows at Work: Neomaternalism in the Making of Sex Discrimination," *Washington University Law Review* 91, no. 3 (2014): 526.

133. We ought not then be surprised when 180 CEOs take out a full-page ad in the *New York Times* and create a website proclaiming abortion as (workplace) equality, https://dontbanequality.com/. See also Doreen Denny, "For Liberal CEOs, Abortion Is Good for Business," *The Daily Signal*, June 27, 2019, https://www.dailysignal.com.

CHAPTER 9. SEXUAL ASYMMETRY, AMERICAN LAW, AND THE CALL FOR A RENEWED FAMILY ECOLOGY

1. Martin Luther King Jr., "Letter from Birmingham Jail," *The Atlantic Monthly*, August 1963, 78–88. Interview with Martin King Jr., in "The March in Mississippi," a CBS News Special Report, June 26, 1966.

2. Pope John XXIII, *Pacem in terris* (1963), nos. 98, 58.

3. Mary Ann Glendon, draft of unpublished essay, on file with author.

4. Marta Cartabia, "The Quiet Persuader between the Forum and the Tower," in *The Past, Present and Future of Comparative Law—Le passé, le présent et le futur du droit comparé*, ed. Katharina Boele-Woelki and Diego P. Fernández Arroyo (Paris: International Academy of Comparative Law, 2018), 11–19 (emphasis omitted).

5. Lorna Siggins, *Mary Robinson: The Woman Who Took Power in the Park* (Edinburgh: Mainstream Publishing, 1997), 203.

6. Mary Ann Glendon, *The Transformation of Family Law: State, Law, and Family in the United States and Western Europe* (Chicago: University of Chicago Press, 1989), 307.

7. Mary Ann Glendon, "A Glimpse of the New Feminism: From July 6, 1996," *America: The Jesuit Review Magazine*, July 6, 1996, https://www.americamagazine.org/issue/100/glimpse-new-feminism.

8. "The State of the Gender Pay Gap 2020," PayScale.com, reporting that, controlling for title, years on the job, industry, and location, women earn $0.98 to every dollar a man earns. One Harvard study discusses the persistent gender wage gap as a result of women's choices and preferences in the workplace. For example, the authors suggest that women tend to value "time away from work and flexibility more than men" and take "more unpaid time off using the Family Medical Leave Act (FMLA) and working fewer overtime hours than men." Women also prefer different kinds of work schedules, trying

to avoid weekend, holiday, and split shifts more than men. See Valentin Bolotnyy and Natalia Emanuel, "Why Do Women Earn Less Than Men? Evidence from Bus and Train Operators," working paper from Harvard University Department of Economics, November 28, 2018, https://scholar.harvard.edu/files /bolotnyy/files/be_gendergap.pdf.

Beyond these preferences, however, research suggests that motherhood explains most of the gender pay gap. "Economic studies now document the 'motherhood penalty'—that is, a severe and persistent economic penalty associated with motherhood. The wage gap between mothers and others is now larger than that between men and women, and motherhood accounts for much of the pay gap between men and women"; see Stephanie Bornstein, Joan Williams, and Genevieve Painter, "Discrimination against Mothers Is the Strongest Form of Workplace Gender Discrimination: Lessons from U.S. Caregiver Discrimination Law," *International Journal of Comparative Labour Law and Industrial Relations* 28, no. 1 (2012): 45–62.

9. Mill, *Subjection*, chap. 1. For instance, Ginsburg's 2016 autobiography begins its section on gender equality, women, and the law with an epigraph from this passage in Mill (Ginsburg, *My Own Words*, 119).

10. Mary Ann Glendon, *Rights Talk: The Impoverishment of Political Discourse* (New York: Maxwell Macmillan Press, 1991), 47–48. In a later article, Glendon writes: "The laws of the states, at the time of the founding and until the mid-twentieth century, were informed by more capacious notions of personhood, influenced in countless ways by biblical and classical understandings of human nature. Those local arrangements (which in some states even included established churches) were promoted and protected by the Constitution's federal structure. So, even though 'fraternity' (or, as we would say today, 'solidarity') was absent from the political vocabulary of the founders, habits of cooperative living were fostered in numerous ways by local laws and customs"; see Mary Ann Glendon, "Looking for 'Persons' in the Law," *First Things*, December 2006.

11. Consortium included a husband's common law prerogative to engage in sexual relations with his wife, a right that was not reciprocal. See Evans Holbrook, "The Change in the Meaning of Consortium," *Michigan Law Review* 22, no. 1 (1923): 1–9.

12. See West, *Political Theory of the American Founding*.

13. Glendon, *Transformation of Family Law*, 95.

14. Glendon points to the transition from *Griswold v. Connecticut* (1965) to *Eisenstadt v. Baird* (1972) as particularly consequential. *Griswold v. Connecticut* had struck down the Connecticut contraception law as an impermissible

governmental intrusion into the privacy of the family home, but *Eisenstadt* specified that the new "right to privacy" was a right held by the individual (i.e., "the right of the individual, married or single, to be free from unwarranted governmental intrusion into matters so fundamentally affecting a person as the decision whether to bear or beget a child"). The Court, Glendon writes, "abruptly severed the privacy right from its attachment to marriage and the family and launched it as a full-fledged individual right" (*Rights Talk*, 57). See Bachiochi, "A Putative Right," for further discussion of the legal significance of these decisions.

15. Mary Ann Glendon, *Abortion and Divorce in Western Law* (Cambridge, MA: Harvard University Press, 1987), 57.

16. Glendon, *Rights Talk*, 48.

17. Glendon, *The Transformation of Family Law*, 145–47.

18. Darlena Cunha, "The Divorce Gap," *The Atlantic*, April 28, 2016.

19. Marcia Pappas, "Divorce New York Style," *The New York Times*, February 19, 2006. Many reformers at the time saw the need to bring the strict divorce law on the books in line with the growing collusion of judges with spouses to invent grounds for what was actually an uncontested divorce, but Glendon's teacher, Max Rheinstein, whose own scholarship had inspired the trend, saw instead the opportunity for a "democratic compromise." In his view, the widely shared ideal of marriage as a lifelong commitment might stand in the law as an aspiration with a more lenient accommodation for those who either do not share or cannot live up to the ideal; see Mary Ann Glendon, *Traditions in Turmoil* (Washington, DC: Sapientia Press, 2006), 25.

20. Glendon, *Transformation of Family Law*, 297.

21. Mary Ann Glendon, "Irish Family Law in Comparative Perspective: Can There Be Comparative Family Law?" *Dublin University Law Journal* 9 (1987): 19.

22. Glendon, *Abortion and Divorce*, 134, citing the West German Federal Constitutional Court decision of July 7, 1970, as translated in Donald P. Kommers, "Liberty and Community in Constitutional Law: The Abortion Cases in Comparative Perspective," *Brigham Young University Law Review* (1985): 371, 403.

23. Tocqueville, *Democracy in America*, 270.

24. Glendon, *Abortion and Divorce*, 8.

25. Glendon, *Rights Talk*, 14.

26. One study, the Bright Horizons Modern Family Index (2017), describes these feelings collectively as the "mental load" felt by mothers. The study found that "69 percent of working moms say their responsibilities create a mental load," and that "52 percent are burning out from the weight of their

household responsibilities"; see "Modern Family Index 2017," Bright Horizons, https://solutionsatwork.brighthorizons.com.

27. See Wendy Wang and W. Bradford Wilcox, "Less Stable, Less Important: Cohabiting Families' Comparative Disadvantage across the Globe," *Institute for Family Studies*, March 12, 2019, https://ifstudies.org/blog/less-stable-less-important-cohabiting-families-comparative-disadvantage-across-the-globe. "In general, [our findings] correspond to research indicating that cohabiting families tend to be less stable for children than married families. Data from our 2017 World Family Map report indicate that children born to cohabiting parents in Europe and the United States are about 90% more likely to see their parents break up, compared to children born to married parents"; "The Cohabitation Go-Round: Cohabitation and Family Instability across the Globe," World Family Map 2017, http://worldfamilymap.ifstudies.org/2017/; Reeves, "Where's the Glue?," in Cahn et al., *Unequal Family Lives*, 217, reporting on the significant "stability gap" between cohabiting and married couples experienced in all countries, at every level of education.

28. The phrase "liquid modernity" comes from the Polish-British sociologist Zygmunt Bauman. In his 1999 book by the same name, he uses the phrase to describe the postmodern age characterized by what he sees as incessant mobility and change in society and in the lives of individuals; see Bauman, *Liquid Modernity* (Cambridge: Polity Press, 1999).

29. Email correspondence, February 15, 2019, on record with the author.

30. Mary Ann Glendon, "What Happened at Beijing," *First Things*, January 1996, 30–36.

31. The U.S. Census Bureau reports: "In 2018, there are 35.7 million single-person households, composing 28 percent of all households. In 1960, single-person households represented only 13 percent of all households"; see United States Census Bureau, "U.S. Census Bureau Releases 2018 Families and Living Arrangements Tables," United States Census Bureau, November 14, 2018, https://www.census.gov/newsroom/press-releases/2018/families.html. See also D'Vera Cohn, Jeffrey S. Passel, Wendy Wang, and Gretchen Livingston, "Barely Half of U.S. Adults Are Married—A Record Low," *Pew Research Center*, December 14, 2011, http://www.pewsocialtrends.org. See also Stefanie Marsh, "'The Desire to Have a Child Never Goes Away': How the Involuntarily Childless Are Forming a New Movement," *The Guardian*, October 2, 2017. In Europe, "around one third of households in the EU comprised single adults without children [in 2017]. . . . Since 2010, when the proportion of households with just one person was 31%, there has been a gradual rise of 2.4 percentage points to 34% in 2017 in the EU"; Eurostat, "Rising Proportion of Single Person Households in the EU," Eurostat, June 7, 2018, https://ec

.europa.eu/eurostat/web/products-eurostat-news/-/DDN-20180706-1?inherit
Redirect=true.

32. Richard V. Reeves, Isabel V. Sawhill, and Eleanor Krause, "The Most Educated Women Are the Most Likely to Be Married," Brookings, August 19, 2016, https://www.brookings.edu/blog/social-mobility-memos/2016/08/19/the-most-educated-women-are-the-most-likely-to-be-married/.

33. Sara McLanahan and Isabel Sawhill, "Marriage and Child Well-being Revisited," *The Future of Children* 25, no. 2 (2015): 3–9. Robert I. Lerman, Joseph Price, and W. Bradford Wilcox, "Family Structure and Economic Success across the Life Course," *Marriage & Family Review* 53, no. 8 (2017): 744–58; Kathryn Harker Tillman, "Family Structure Pathways and Academic Disadvantage among Adolescents in Stepfamilies," *Sociological Inquiry* 77, no. 3 (2007): 383–424; David Autor et al., "School Quality and the Gender Gap in Educational Achievement," *American Economic Review* 106, no. 5 (2016): 289–95; Melissa S. Kearney and Phillip B. Levine, "The Economics of Non-Marital Childbearing and the 'Marriage Premium for Children,'" working paper, National Bureau of Economic Research, Cambridge, Massachusetts, 2017; Donna J. Ginther and Robert A. Pollack, "Does Family Structure Affect Children's Educational Outcomes?," working paper, FRB, Atlanta, Georgia, 2001; Roger A. Wotjkiewz and Melissa Holtzmann, "Family Structure and College Graduation: Is the Stepparent Effect More Negative Than the Single Parent Effect?" *Sociological Spectrum* 31, no. 4 (2011): 498–521; Richard Reeves and Joanna Venator, "Saving Horatio Alger: The Data behind the Words (and the Lego Bricks)," *Brookings Social Mobility Memos*, 2014; Richard Reeves, "How to Save Marriage in America," *The Atlantic*, February, 13, 2014.

34. Reeves, Sawhill, and Krause, "The Most Educated Women Are the Most Likely to Be Married."

35. Mary Ann Glendon, "Rescuing Feminism from the Feminists," *First Things*, March 1996.

36. Cahn et al., *Unequal Family Lives*, a collection of scholarly papers from experts across disciplines and political perspectives, all of whom agree that "class inequality affects patterns of partnership and childbearing and, in turn, family change feeds economic inequality" (3); see also McLanahan, "Diverging Destinies"; W. Bradford Wilcox, Joseph Price, and Jacob Van Leeuwen, "The Family Geography of the American Dream: New Neighborhood Data on Single Parenthood, Prisons, and Poverty," American Enterprise Institute, October 17, 2018, http://www.aei.org; Robert I. Lerman and W. Bradford Wilcox, "For Richer, for Poorer: How Family Structures Economic Success in America," American Enterprise Institute and Institute for Family Studies, 2014, https://www.aei.org

/research-products/report/for-richer-for-poorer/; Sawhill, *Generation Unbound*, 76: "family formation is a new fault line in the American class structure."

37. Glendon, "What Happened at Beijing."

38. Glendon, *Rights Talk*, 51.

39. Ibid., 52. But, as Glendon points out, Mill's "harm principle"—when applied in the family arena—neglects to even follow Mill. In *On Liberty*, Mill writes: "Misplaced notions of liberty prevent moral obligations on the part of parents from being recognized, and legal obligations from being imposed, where there are the strongest grounds for the former always, and in many cases for the latter also"; see Glendon, *Traditions in Turmoil*, 246, quoting John Stuart Mill, *On Liberty*, in *Utilitarianism, Liberty and Representative Government* (New York: Dutton, 1951), 219–20.

40. Glendon, *Rights Talk*, xi.

41. See Glendon, *Abortion and Divorce*, 19. The first article of the 1975 French law thus announces: "The law guarantees the respect of every human being from the commencement of life. There shall be no derogation from this principle except in cases of necessity and under the conditions laid down by this law" (quoted at ibid., 16). The 1975 legislation permitted abortion in the first ten weeks of pregnancy without restriction (allowing the pregnant women to judge her "distress" herself), but heavily regulated abortion after this period, with allowances for "necessity" or otherwise serious cause similar to those permitted in the abortion reform laws struck down by *Roe* in 1973.

42. Claire de la Hougue, "Simone Veil . . . ," European Centre for Law and Justice, July 5, 2017, https://eclj.org/abortion/french-institutions/simone-veil-prcis-de-rcupration.

43. Glendon, *Abortion and Divorce*, 16.

44. Ibid., 26.

45. Ibid., 58.

46. *Planned Parenthood v. Casey*, 505 U.S. 833 (1992), which allowed state regulations to safeguard women's health so long as such regulations did not impose an undue burden on her right to an abortion.

47. U.S. abortion jurisprudence continues to be governed by the broadly worded health-as-well-being exception first announced in *Doe v. Bolton* in 1973. Thus, the prohibition of abortion to protect the lives of unborn children, even late in pregnancy, is still impermissible. But see *Gonzales v. Carhart*, 550 U.S. 124 (2007).

48. See, for instance, New York State's Reproductive Health Act (2019).

49. Glendon, *Rights Talk*, 65–66.

50. West, "From Choice to Reproductive Justice," 1411, 1409. West writes in the same section, "Someone tied to the needs of others is that much less free

to live the wealth-maximizing, self-regarding, autonomous life presupposed by, and valorized by, a free-market economy in the first place" (ibid., 1409).

51. Glendon, *Traditions in Turmoil*, 111.

52. Quoted in Dinner, "Strange Bedfellows," 486, citing Reply Brief for Appellant, *Geduldig v. Aiello*, 417 U.S. 484 (1974) (No. 73-640), 2, 13.

53. Dinner, *Strange Bedfellows*, 493.

54. Quoted in ibid., 499.

55. Ibid., 500.

56. 123 Cong. Rec. 29, 635 (September 16, 1977) (statement of Senator Biden).

57. Dinner, "Strange Bedfellows," 505, quoting Barbara Shack from the Women's Equity Action League, *What Constitutes Sex Discrimination in Insurance* (on file with the Women's Equity Action League Records, Schlesinger Library, Radcliffe Institute, Harvard University, Box 10, Folder 19).

58. *Troupe v. May Dept. Stores Co.* 20 F.3d 734, 738 (7th Cir. 1994).

59. As of September 2020, more than half the states and several localities have passed pregnancy worker fairness statutes that require reasonable accommodations for pregnant workers without a prior showing of comparative disability. A bipartisan bill awaits passage in Congress.

60. Oral argument in *California Federal Sav. & Loan Ass'n v. Guerra*, 479 U.S. 272 (1987), quoted in Gillian Thomas, *Because of Sex* (New York: St. Martin's Press, 2016), 123.

61. Christine A. Littleton, "Reconstructing Sexual Equality," *California Law Review* 75 (1986): 1279, 1306.

62. Ibid., 1306–7.

63. *California Federal Savings & Loan Assn. v. Guerra*, Director, Department of Fair Employment and Housing, 479 U.S. 272, 280 (1987).

64. Ibid., 290.

65. In 2003, Chief Justice Rehnquist, writing for the majority, upheld the family care provisions of the FMLA as a proper use of congressional power under section 5 of the Fourteenth Amendment; see *Nevada Department of Human Resources v. Hibbs*, 538 U.S. 721, 731 (2003).

66. See, for instance, Amber Lapp and David Lapp, "Work-Family Policy in Trump's America," *Institute for Family Studies*, December 12–13, 2016, https://ifstudies.org.

67. Mary Ann Glendon and William Galston, "The Second National Communitarian Teach-In, New York City, May 19, 1992: Opening Statements by Mary Ann Glendon and William Galston," *The Responsive Community* 2 (Summer 1992): 58.

68. The Communitarian Network, "A Communitarian Position Paper on the Family," Washington, DC: The Communitarian Network, 1992.

69. These included establishing paternity at birth and strengthening child support payments; supporting robust marriage preparation and revising divorce laws to be guided by the principle of "children-first"; finding ways to reduce sexual objectification, early sexualization, and teen pregnancy; and, finally, reforming welfare to reinforce family stability.

70. The first recommendation includes: "*The best place for infants is at home, where they can bond with their parents.* Most children who bonded with their parents in the first year of their lives are reported to be doing better by practically all social, intellectual, and other behavioral measurements than those who were largely brought up in the first year of their lives outside the home. Strong and growing evidence indicates that most infants (younger than age one) develop stronger attachments to their parents than to child care personnel. There may be a need for more study but we suggest that the accumulated evidence supports this conclusion. It follows that several measures should be enacted that would move us as quickly as possible toward enabling parents to be with their infants during the critical first years of life" (emphasis in original). A more recent appeal to infant-parent bonding (until age three) can be found in Erica Kosimar, *Being There: Why Prioritizing Motherhood in the First Three Years Matters* (New York: TarcherPerigee, 2017).

71. Smaller businesses were to be given tax incentives to encourage them to provide the same.

72. The reference to "working at home" here denotes parents caring for their children in the home. The scholars explained that an allowance was better than increased tax exemptions (though the latter was better than nothing) because the tax cut "discriminates against families that dedicate more time to their children and hence have less taxable income."

73. See, for instance, Marilyn Waring, *Counting for Nothing: What Men Value and What Women Are Worth* (Toronto: University of Toronto Press, 1999); Kathleen Cloud and Nancy Garrett, "A Modest Proposal for Inclusion of Women's Household Human Capital Production in Analysis of Structural Transformation," *Feminist Economics*, 3, no. 1 (2011): 151–77; "Promoting Women's Economic Empowerment: Recognizing and Investing in the Care Economy," issue paper, UN Women, May 2018, http://www.unwomen.org /-/media/headquarters/attachments/sections/library/publications/2018/issue -paper-recognizing-and-investing-in-the-care-economy-en.pdf?la=en&vs=2004. The work of Martha Nussbaum is an important exception.

Responding directly to this UN document, economist Catherine Pakaluk said: "Contemporary social science has very few measures of the value of children and value of carework outside of capitalistic measures (i.e., the kinds of things that can be measured in monetary, property, and labor market terms). We're stuck using this capitalistic language when we think about valuing things, but we can do better. Social science in general does measure many things that are difficult to measure, but that kind of creative work in the measurement and metric of things has not been applied to these areas of human life yet. I am optimistic that it can be done qualitatively—if we listen to women"; Catherine Pakaluk, "Valuing Unpaid Work and Caregiving," presentation at the Commission on the Status of Women by the Mission of the Holy See to the United Nations (March 15, 2019) (transcribed by the author).

74. Mary Ann Glendon, "Women's Identity, Women's Rights and the Civilization of Life," in *"Evangelium Vitae" e Diritto, "Evangelium Vitae" and Law: Acta Symposii Internationalis in Civitate Vaticana celebrati 23–25 maii 1996*, ed. Alphonsus Lopez Trujillo, Julianus Herranz, and Aelius Sgreccia (Roma: Liberia Editrice Vaticana, 1997), 74.

75. Glendon, *Rights Talk*, 126–27. Glendon well notes: "Putting children at the center of our family policy does not belittle or degrade childless individuals, or stigmatize other types of living arrangements. It merely recognizes the high public interest in the nurture and education of citizens" (ibid., 126).

76. Mary Ann Glendon, "Is the Economic Emancipation of Women Today Contrary to a Healthy, Functioning Family?," in *The Family, Civil Society, and the State*, ed. Christopher Wolfe (Lanham: Rowman & Littlefield, 1998), 93.

77. The Communitarian Network, "A Communitarian Position Paper on the Family."

78. Glendon, "Second National Teach-In," 56.

79. The Communitarian Network, "The Responsive Communitarian Platform," https://communitariannetwork.org/platform.

80. Glendon, *Rights Talk*, 137–38. Glendon continues: "The paradox of liberalism seems to be that the strong state, the free market, and a vital civil society are all potential threats to the individual citizens and to each other, yet a serious weakness in any one of them puts the entire democratic enterprise in jeopardy" (ibid., 138).

81. Mary Ann Glendon, "Pro-Life Strategies for the 90s," National Conference of Catholic Bishop Pro-Life Directors, March 26, 1993, on file with the author.

82. Benjamin R. Barber et al., "Forum: Who Owes What to Whom? Drafting a Constitutional Bill of Duties," *Harper's*, February 1991, 47.

83. Mary Ann Glendon, ed., "Intergenerational Solidarity, Welfare and Human Ecology," *Tenth Plenary Session of the Pontifical Academy of Social Sciences, Acta* 10 (2004): 339, http://www.pass.va/content/dam/scienzesociali/pdf/acta10/acta10-conclusions.pdf.

84. Glendon, *The Transformation of Family Law*, 308.

85. Mary Ann Glendon, "Looking for 'Persons' in the Law," *First Things*, December 2006.

86. Glendon, ed., "Intergenerational Solidarity," 367.

87. Glendon, *Rights Talk*, 120.

88. Robert D. Putnam, *Bowling Alone: The Collapse and Revival of American Community* (New York: Simon & Schuster, 2000). See generally the works of Michael Sandel.

89. See, for instance, Robert D. Putnam, *Our Kids: The American Dream in Crisis* (New York: Simon & Schuster, 2016); Charles Murray, *Coming Apart: The State of White America* (New York: Crown Forum, 2012); J. D. Vance, *Hillbilly Elegy: A Memoir of a Family and Culture in Crisis* (New York: Harper, 2016); Nicholas Eberstadt, *Men without Work*; Timothy Carney, *Alienated America: Why Some Places Thrive While Others Collapse* (New York: Harper, 2019).

90. Glendon, "Intergenerational Solidarity," 339.

91. Glendon, "The Right to Work and the Limits of the Law," in *Work & Human Fulfillment*, ed. E. Malinvaud and M. Archer (Ypsilanti, MI: Sapientia Press, 2003), 151. "An example of this type of law from labor history would be the U.S. labor legislation of 1935 which, in response to the circumstances of the time, promoted a particular type of mediating structure—unions—and tried to foster private ordering through collective bargaining, rather than minutely regulating the terms and conditions of employment as many other nations do" (ibid.).

92. See Mary Ann Glendon and Raul F. Yanes, "Structural Free Exercise," *Michigan Law Review* 90, no. 3 (1991): 477–550. "A structural reading of the Bill of Rights reminds us that the Founders attached particular importance to the kinds of rights that help create conditions for the exercise of others rights. . . . [T]hose features of the Bill of Rights that accord constitutional status to certain intermediate associations—religious groups foremost among them—were designed in part to promote self-government by fostering participation in public life, protecting the seedbeds of civic virtue, and educating citizens about their rights and obligations" (ibid., 543–44).

93. Glendon in 2001: "The men and women who hold key positions in governments, political parties, corporations, mass media, foundations and so on are often quite remote from the concerns of the average citizen. Strong ties to persons and places, religious beliefs, attachment to tradition and even family life are apt to be less important to those at the top than to the men and women whose lives they affect. Decision-makers have tended to be rather free in adopting measures that undermine the delicate communities on which others depend for practical and emotional support—as witness the organization of

work and schooling, the planning of cities, programs for public assistance, all too frequently designed without considering the impact on families and neighborhoods"; see Mary Ann Glendon, "The Ever-Changing Interplay between Democracy and Civil Society," in *Acta* 6 (Vatican City: Pontifical Academy of Social Sciences, 2001), 112.

94. Mary Ann Glendon, "The Cultural Underpinnings of America's Democratic Experiment," in *Building a Healthy Culture: Strategies for American Renaissance*, ed. Don Eberly (Grand Rapids, MI: Eerdmans, 2001). Reprinted in Glendon, *Traditions in Turmoil*, 73.

95. Glendon, *Rights Talk*, 134. Later, she writes: "One thing we have learned through trial-and-error is that intervention, even with the most benign motives, can have unintended and harmful consequences. . . . Evidence is accumulating that the idea of 'regulating' complex social systems (in the sense of controlling their development or ensuring desired outcomes) is an illusion. Interventions can shift probabilities, but often in unanticipated ways. Prudence thus suggests proceeding modestly, preferring local experiments and small-scale pilots to broad, standardized, top-down programs. Often, the principle of 'do no harm' will be the best guide. At a minimum, that would require attention to the ways in which governmental or business policies may be undermining fragile social structures, or discouraging persons who devote time and effort to the nurture of future citizens" (Glendon, "The Ever-Changing Interplay," 116–17).

96. Mary Ann Glendon, "From Culture Wars to Building a Culture of Life," in *The Cost of Choice*, ed. Erika Bachiochi (San Francisco: Encounter, 2004), 12.

97. In *A Nation under Lawyers*, Glendon writes that the "desegregation decisions [most famously, *Brown v. Board of Education*] took initiative in an area where ordinary democracy was not working. . . . Whereas *Brown* and the voting cases had been a response to insufficiently representative political processes, many later decisions [referring here to *Roe v. Wade*] seemed antagonistic to democratic decision making as such"; see Mary Ann Glendon, *Nation under Lawyers* (Cambridge, MA: Harvard University Press, 1994), 138, 141. In the same chapter, Glendon favorably notes Ruth Bader Ginsburg's assessment of the sex discrimination cases as akin to the desegregation cases in Ginsburg's own critique of the Court's decision in *Roe*, paraphrasing: "The Court would have done better, [Ginsburg] went on, to proceed as it had done in the sex discrimination cases, confining itself to instructing Congress and state legislatures to reexamine old classifications, and throwing the ball [now quoting Ginsburg] 'back into the legislators' court, where the political forces of the day could operate'" (ibid., 138–39).

98. Glendon, *Traditions in Turmoil*, 56.

99. Mary Ann Glendon, "A Challenge to the Human Sciences," in *A New Worldly Order*, ed. George Weigel (Washington DC: Ethics and Public Policy Center, 1992), 80.

CHAPTER 10. REIMAGINING FEMINISM TODAY
IN SEARCH OF HUMAN EXCELLENCE

1. Learned Hand, "The Spirit of Liberty" (1944), http://www.digital history.uh.edu/disp_textbook.cfm?smtID=3&psid=1199, paraphrased in Ruth Bader Ginsburg, "Confirmation Hearing Day 1 Part 1," C-SPAN video, at 1:36, July 20, 1993, https://www.c-span.org/video/?c4664217/justice-ginsburg -standard.

2. Learned Hand, "The Spirit of Liberty."

3. Wollstonecraft, *Rights of Woman*, 175.

4. John Adams wrote in a letter to his cousin Zabdiel Adams in 1776: "The only foundation of a free Constitution, is pure Virtue, and if this cannot be inspired into our People, in a greater Measure, than they have it now, They may change their Rulers, and the forms of Government, but they will not obtain a lasting Liberty"; see "John Adams to Zabdiel Adams, 21 June 1776," Founders Online, National Archives, https://founders.archives.gov /documents/Adams/04-02-02-0011. And in a speech at the Virginia Ratifying Convention on June 20, 1788, James Madison said: "Is there no virtue among us? If there be not, we are in a wretched situation. No theoretical checks, no form of government, can render us secure. To suppose that any form of govern-ment will secure liberty or happiness without any virtue in the people, is a chimerical idea"; James Madison, Virginia Ratifying Convention, June 20, 1788, in *The Founders' Constitution*, vol. 1, chap. 13, doc. 36, University of Chicago Press, http://press-pubs.uchicago.edu/founders/documents/v1ch13s36.html.

5. Harry Farley, "Sex Robots 'Will Make Women Interchangeable with Technology', Campaigners Warn," *The Telegraph*, July 28, 2018, https://www .telegraph.co.uk.

6. Today, a powerfully consumerist national identity guides putatively individual choice as much as any earlier national identity: corporations now equipped with big data can construct in consumers' minds a new, modern kind of "good society" or "good life," one unsurprisingly replete with the latest con-sumables, vacation destinations, pastimes, or even foods. In *The World beyond Your Head*, Matthew Crawford gives an especially troubling account of what he calls "affective capitalism." He demonstrates in particular detail the power

wielded by the "choice architects" in the gambling industry who manufacture experiences for the gambler to ensure their addictive quality; see Matthew Crawford, *The World beyond Your Head* (Boston: Macmillan, 2015), 89–112.

7. Of course, we still make societal judgments about ends all the time. To protect the inherent dignity of human beings, especially the weakest among us, we must. Though our capacity to make such judgments diminishes as the consumerist mindset grows in influence, we still acknowledge that some goods (e.g., human beings) and some services (e.g., child pornography) cannot licitly be bought or sold. Indeed, many progressives today articulate praiseworthy ends—and the personal and social self-restraint needed to attain them—when it comes to remedying the damage done to the environment or even promoting nutrition, health, and fitness. As Harvard philosopher Michael Sandel put it, "Without quite realizing it, without ever deciding to do so, we drifted from *having* a market economy to *being* a market society" (emphasis in original). He continues: "A market economy is a tool—a valuable and effective tool—for organizing productive activity. A market society is a way of life in which market values seep into every aspect of human endeavor. It's a place where social relations are made over in the image of the market"; Michael Sandel, *What Money Can't Buy* (New York: Farrar, Straus and Giroux, 2012), 10–11. More recently, social thinker Oren Cass wrote, "[My argument] recognizes the free market as a powerful *mechanism* for fostering choice, promoting competition, and allocating resources. But it does not regard creation of the freest possible market as an end unto itself or the most efficient outcome at any moment as necessarily the best one for the long run. . . . The first-order question must be what we want for our society and how we can best channel the free market toward accomplishing those ends"; Oren Cass, *The Once and Future Worker* (New York: Encounter Press, 2018), 8.

8. Linda Gordon, "Why Nineteenth-Century Feminists Did Not Support 'Birth Control' and Twentieth-Century Feminists Do: Feminism, Reproduction, and the Family," in *Rethinking the Family: Some Feminists Questions*, ed. Barrie Thorne and Marilyn Yalom (New York: Longman, 1982), 50.

9. Emily Shugerman, "A War over Sex Work Is Raging inside the Nation's Biggest Feminist Group," *The Daily Beast*, February 9, 2020, https://www.thedailybeast.com/the-national-organization-for-women-is-tearing-itself-apart-over-sex-work.

10. Lisa Wade, *American Hookup*; Mark Regnerus, *Cheap Sex*; Leah Fessler, "Can She Really 'Play That Game, Too'?" (college thesis, Middlebury College, 2015), retrieved from https://www.scribd.com/document/314719397/Can-She-Really-Play-That-Game-Too. See also note 124 in chapter 8 of this book.

11. Robin West writes: "There is no further reason to help a poor mother pay for [parenting] than there is to help a would-be recreational sailor buy a boat that will allow him to sail around the world, or to help the aspiring scholar with the expense of yet another graduate degree. [Parenting] is one lifestyle choice among several that happens to come with a hefty price tag" (West, "From Choice to Reproductive Justice," 1411).

12. Raj Chetty et al., "Where Is the Land of Opportunity? The Geography of Intergenerational Mobility in the United States," *Quarterly Journal of Economics* 129, no. 4 (2014): 1553–1623; Raj Chetty et al., "Race and Economic Opportunity in the United States: An Intergenerational Perspective," working paper, National Bureau for Economic Research, Cambridge, MA, 2018. See also Murray, *Coming Apart*; Putnam, *Our Kids*; Kay Hymowitz, *Marriage and Caste in America: Separate and Unequal Families in a Post-Marital Age* (Chicago: Ivan R. Dee, 2007); Sarah Halpern-Meekin, *Social Poverty: Low-Income Parents and the Struggle for Family and Community Ties* (New York: New York University Press, 2019).

13. Remember this beautiful insight of Wollstonecraft's: "I have vices, hid, perhaps, from human eye, that bend me to the dust before God, and loudly tell me, when all is mute, that we are formed of the same earth, and breathe the same element. Humanity thus rises naturally out of humility, and twists the cords of love that in various convolutions entangle the heart" (Wollstonecraft, *Rights of Woman*, 139–40).

14. Writing admirably about the human excellence manifest in the work of a short-order cook, philosopher Matthew Crawford similarly argues, "[One] wants to be seen as an individual, and recognized as worthy [of honor] on the same grounds on which he has *striven* to be worthy, indeed superior, by cultivating some particular excellence or skill. We all strive for distinction, [and] to honor another person is to honor this aspiring core of him" (Crawford, *The World beyond Your Head*, 255; emphasis in original).

15. Wollstonecraft, *Rights of Men*, 24, in reference to the "inhuman custom" and "atrocious insult to humanity" of the slave trade. Glendon first used the term "dignitarian feminism" in 1996; see Glendon, "Women's Identity, Women's Rights and the Civilization of Life," 63–75. If the term "human dignity" has fallen into disrepute because of its manifold (and often conflicting definitions), it enjoyed a rich heritage in the post–World War II period. As Glendon details in her definitive and critically acclaimed history of the Universal Declaration of Human Rights, *A World Made New*, "human dignity" reached its pinnacle as that principle upon which all could agree so long as agreement was not required with regard to its proper philosophical foundations; see Mary Ann Glendon, *A World Made New: Eleanor Roosevelt and the Universal Declaration*

of Human Rights (New York: Penguin Random House, 2002). Glendon received the National Humanities Medal for this book in 2005.

16. "[It may be that] human rights are grounded in the obligation of everyone to perfect one's own dignity, which in turn obliges one to respect the 'given' spark of dignity of others whatever they may have done with it. In other words, it may be our own quest for human dignity (individually and as a society) that requires us to refrain from inflicting cruel punishments on criminals, or from terminating the lives of the unborn and others whose faculties are underdeveloped or dormant" (Glendon, *Traditions in Turmoil*, 346).

17. Prudence Allen, *The Concept of Woman* (Grand Rapids, MI: William B. Eerdmans, 2017), 3:488 (emphasis in original): "It has taken over twenty centuries to shake off the devaluation of woman that took its systematic shape within an Aristotelian philosophy of nature. While Aristotle was correct to state that things in the world have a form/matter composite identity, and that living human beings have a *soul/body composite identity*, he made an error of judgment in claiming that while men contributed fertile seed in generation, women contributed no fertile seed in generation. This error led him to conclude that the female was a defective male and that man was naturally superior to woman. . . . The perpetuation of this complex Aristotelian error in judgment has been carefully traced through the[se] three volumes." Wollstonecraft herself, as we saw in earlier chapters, did much to correct this erroneous view in her implicit recognition of the profound integration of each man's and woman's equally rational (and unsexed) soul with his or her sexed body. Both men and women—different though they are from each other and different as each individual is from every other individual—are rational creatures whose common end is the development of wisdom and virtue.

18. The sort of habituation needed for development is widely recognized in athletics, music, and language: those with earned expertise (or at least proficiency) guide, nurture, and correct neophytes in the skills and practices standard to their particular discipline. Just so with the skills and practices of a good life: these too must be acquired through imitation and habituation.

19. Aristotle, *Nicomachean Ethics*, in *The Basic Works of Aristotle*, trans. W. D. Ross, ed. Richard McKeon (New York: Random House, 1941), 1162a16–29: "Between man and wife friendship seems to exist by nature; for man is naturally inclined to form couples—even more than to form cities, inasmuch as the household is earlier and more necessary than the city, and reproduction is more common to man with the animals. With the other animals the union extends only to this point, but human beings live together not only for the sake of reproduction but also for the various purposes of life; for from the start the functions are divided, and those of man and woman are different;

so they help each other by throwing their peculiar gifts into the common stock. It is for these reasons that both utility and pleasure seem to be found in this kind of relationship. But this friendship may be based also on virtue, if the parties are good; for each has its own virtue and they will delight in the fact. And children seem to be a bond of union (which is the reason why childless people part more easily); for children are a good common to both and what is common holds them together."

20. Wollstonecraft, *Vindication of the Rights of Woman*, 109.

21. Ibid., 159.

22. For a large minority of households in the United States, caregiving still manifests itself in a traditional or neotraditional scenario with married mothers with young children dedicating themselves full-time or part-time to taking care of the goods of the home; for many others, couples share in the breadwinning (with women still taking the lead on housework); and in an increasing number of other couples, we see a reversal of traditional roles, with the mother providing the lion's share of the income. "Employment Characteristics of Families Summary," April 21, 2020, U.S. Bureau of Labor Statistics, https://www.bls.gov/news.release/famee.nr0.htm: 62 percent of married mothers with children under three are in the labor force while 70 percent of married mothers with older children in the home work outside of the home; among employed mothers with young children, a quarter work part-time. Gretchen Livingston, "Stay-at-Home Moms and Dads Account for About One-in-Five U.S. Parents," Pew Research Center, September 24, 2018, https://www.pewresearch.org/fact-tank/2018/09/24/stay-at-home-moms-and-dads-account-for-about-one-in-five-u-s-parents/, reporting that 27 percent of mothers and 7 percent of fathers are "stay-at-home" parents. According to a *New York Times* analysis of data from the Census Bureau, 29 percent of married women in the United States earn more than their husbands, up from 18 percent in the 1980s; see Claire Cain Miller and Quoctrung Bui, "Equality in Marriages Grows, and So Does the Class Divide," *New York Times*, February 27, 2016. See also Karen Z. Kramer and Sunjin Pak, "Relative Earnings and Depressive Symptoms among Working Parents," *Sex Roles* 78 (2018): 744–59, finding that "an increase in one's share of family income is related to an increased level of depressive symptoms among mothers and a decreased level of depressive symptoms among fathers."

23. See, for instance, Ying Chen, Laura D. Kubzansky, and Tyler J. VanderWeele, "Parental Warmth and Flourishing in Mid-life," *Social Science & Medicine* 220 (January 2019): 65–72. McLanahan and Sawhill, "Marriage and Child Wellbeing Revisited," 4: "Most scholars now agree that children raised by two biological parents in a stable marriage do better than children in other family forms across a wide range of outcomes."

372   Notes to Pages 288–289

24. Philosopher Eva Feder Kittay explains how duties of care arise in these special relationships of dependency: "The needs of another call forth a moral obligation on our part when we are in a special position vis-à-vis that other to meet those needs. . . . [T]he moral claim arises not by virtue of the properties of an individual—construed as rights, needs, or interests—but out of a *relationship* between one in need and one who is situated to meet the need"; Kittay, *Love's Labor* (Philadelphia: Routledge, 1998), 55 (emphasis in original). "It is neither capricious nor misogynist nor disrespectful of individual rights when we insist that individuals who mother infants or young children defer their own desires, and even needs, to meet those of their dependent child" (ibid., 52). Family law and parents' special duties of care in tort law are grounded on philosophical underpinnings such as these.

25. In situations of adoption, biological parents fulfill their parental duties by transferring their parental rights to adoptive parents with the intention that the existential duties owed to their children can be better carried out by the same.

26. In 2014, statistics from the Census Bureau showed that 58 percent of children lived with their married biological parents, and an additional 4 percent lived with unmarried biological parents (U.S. Census Bureau, Current Population Survey, 2014 Annual Social and Economic Supplement).

27. Jeffrey Rosenberg and W. Bradford Wilcox, "The Importance of Fathers in the Healthy Development of Children," U.S. Department of Health and Human Services, Office on Child Abuse and Neglect, 2006. Rosenberg and Wilcox catalogue studies that show: Children whose fathers are attentive and present in their lives have better educational outcomes overall; fathers who nurture and play with their infants have children with higher IQs; toddlers have higher levels of academic preparedness; and adolescents have better verbal skills, intellectual functioning, and achievement in school. Fathers seem to be a determining factor in the emotional and social well-being of their children; children with caring fathers in intact marriages enjoy more security, more confidence in exploring the world, ability to deal with school stresses, and better social connections with peers. Fathers tend to engage their infants and preschoolers in stimulating, rough-and-tumble play, and researchers think this is a reason why their children more effectively regulate their feelings and behavior. See also Reeves, "Where's the Glue?," in Cahn et al., eds., *Unequal Family Lives*, 22. Calling upon a number of similar findings, Reeves concludes, "Boys seem to be influenced most strongly by the absence of a father."

In recognition of these benefits, Harvard Medical School and Massachusetts General Hospital initiated the Fatherhood Project to "improve the health and well-being of children by empowering fathers to be active, informed and emotionally engaged with their children and families." Their work involves training "professionals in healthcare, mental health, education, and social services about the critical role fathers play in child development and family life, and how to best support father engagement in their particular context"; developing programs for fathers and children; and undertaking research on topics surrounding fatherhood (The Fatherhood Project, http://www.thefatherhood project.org/).

28. National Fatherhood Initiative, Statistics on the Father Absence Crisis in America, http://www.fatherhood.org/father-absence-statistics.

29. Raj Chetty et al., "Where Is the Land of Opportunity? The Geography of Intergenerational Mobility in the United States," NBER Working Paper No. 19843 (January 2014): 41, finding that "the strongest and most robust predictor" of economic mobility in a community is the percentage of children living with single parents.

30. W. Bradford Wilcox and Steven L. Nock, "What's Love Got to Do with It? Equality, Equity, Commitment and Women's Marital Quality," *Social Forces* 84, no. 3 (2006): 1321–45; Daniel L. Carlson et al., "The Division of Child Care, Sexual Intimacy, and Relationship Quality in Couples," *Gender & Society* 30, no. 3 (2016): 442–66, finding that fathers' engagement with their children is "generally associated with more satisfaction with the division of child care, more satisfying sexual relationships, and higher quality relationships."

31. Petra Persson and Maya Rossin-Slater, "When Dad Can Stay Home: Fathers' Workplace Flexibility and Maternal Health," National Bureau of Economic Research Working Paper No. 25902 (May 2019), abstract: "We find that increasing the father's temporal flexibility reduces the risk of the mother experiencing physical postpartum health complications and improves her mental health. Our results suggest that mothers bear the burden from a lack of workplace flexibility—not only directly through greater career costs of family formation, as previously documented—but also indirectly, as fathers' inability to respond to domestic shocks exacerbates the maternal health costs of childbearing."

32. Wollstonecraft, *Rights of Woman*, 27.

33. David F. Bjorklund and Ashley C. Jordan, "Human Parenting from an Evolutionary Perspective," in *Gender and Parenthood: Biological and Social Scientific Perspectives*, ed. W. Bradford Wilcox and Kathleen Kovner Kline (New York: Columbia University Press, 2013): "While divorce rarely weakens a mother's affection for her children, it does frequently result in a deterioration of the father-child relationship" (73). See also W. Bradford Wilcox, "Marriage Facilitates Responsible Fatherhood," Institute for Family Studies, June 12, 2019, https://ifstudies.org/blog/marriage-facilitates-responsible-fatherhood.

34. Harry Benson and Stephen McKay, "Happy Wife, Happy Life," Marriage Foundation, September 15, 2019, https://marriagefoundation.org.uk/wp-content/uploads/2019/09/MF-Happy-Wife-Happy-Life-FINAL.pdf.

35. For a report of Family Responsibilities Discrimination (FRD) litigation, see Cynthia Thomas Calvert, "Caregivers in the Workplace," Work Life Law, UC Hastings College of Law, 2016, https://worklifelaw.org/publications/Caregivers-in-the-Workplace-FRD-update-2016.pdf.

36. For a critique of "consent" as a philosophical basis of parental duties, see Bachiochi, *Embodied Equality*, 930–34.

37. Carlson, *From Cottage to Work Station*, 163. "Family life survives only as the members of this small community defy, through tradition or intention, the incentives or pressures that would transform all human actions into market exchanges or subsume them to globalist economic goals. When the family structure surrenders to market organization, it disappears as a meaningful entity with the power to hold or shield its members from the depredations of rival centers of authority" (ibid.).

38. Claudia Goldin, "A Grand Gender Convergence: Its Last Chapter," *American Economic Review* 104, no. 4 (2014): 1091, noting among other findings that "hours of work for women increased in the market and decreased in the home relative to those of men" (ibid., 1092). But even before the 2020 recession, a large share of working-class men were without work at all (or were working far less than they would like); see Eberstadt, *Men without Work*.

39. See, for instance, *Chadwick v. Wellpoint*, 561 F.3d 38, at 45: "The essence of Title VII in this context is that women have the right to prove their mettle in the work arena without the burden of stereotypes regarding whether they can fulfill their responsibilities." Joan Williams writes that the United States is the best place to work for "tomboy women" (those who need only equal opportunity to succeed at work), but probably the worst for women living more "traditional feminine lives" (i.e., getting pregnant and caring for children); see Joan C. Williams, "Reconstructive Feminism: Changing the Way We Talk about Gender and Work Thirty Years after the PDA," *Yale Journal of Law & Feminism* 21, no. 1 (2009): 79–117. Williams's Center for WorkLife Law is the leading advocate for cases brought on the basis of Family Responsibilities Discrimination.

40. Susan J. Lambert, Peter J. Fugiel, and Julia R. Henly, "Schedule Unpredictability among Early Career Workers in the US Labor Market: A National Snapshot," Employment Instability, Family Well-being, and Social Policy Network, University of Chicago, 2014, https://ssa.uchicago.edu/sites/default/files/uploads/lambert.fugiel.henly_.executive_summary.b_0.pdf, finding that 41 percent of hourly workers age twenty-six to thirty-two years old are given

their schedules less than a week in advance. Joan C. Williams, Jennifer L. Berdahl, and Joseph A. Vandello, "Beyond Work-Life 'Integration,'" *Annual Review of Psychology* 67 (2016): 524. For solutions to just-in-time scheduling, see Williams et al., "Stable Scheduling Increases Productivity and Sales," Work Life Law, March 2018, https://worklifelaw.org/wp-content/uploads/2018/03/Stable-Scheduling-Study-Report.pdf; see also Eberstadt, *Men without Work*, showing that the work rate for American males age twenty-five to fifty-four was slightly lower in 2015 than at the tail end of the Great Depression.

41. Cass, *Once and Future Worker*, 33. See also Elizabeth Warren and Amelia Warren Tyagi, *Two-Income Trap* (New York: Basic, 2003), 8, arguing that families once counted on at-home mothers as a kind of "financial safety net" in case the family's father lost his job.

42. Williams et al., "Beyond Work-Life 'Integration,'" 522: "Blue-collar men's identities are intertwined with being a good provider, and often they see their jobs as means to an end—to support their families—rather than a totalizing identity." But see Kathryn Edin and Timothy J. Nelson, *Doing the Best I Can: Fatherhood in the Inner City* (Berkeley: University of California Press, 2013), 223, suggesting that low-income unwed fathers, often unable to provide adequately (or at all) for their children, seek to contribute to their children's upbringing in more traditionally maternal ways (e.g., nurture, spending time).

43. Slaughter, *Unfinished Business*, 60; Derek Thompson, "Workism Is Making Americans Miserable," *The Atlantic*, February 24, 2019. See also Mary Blair-Loy, *Competing Devotions: Career and Family among Women Executives* (Cambridge, MA: Harvard University Press, 2003).

44. Blair-Loy, *Competing Devotions*, 120; Williams et al., "Beyond Work-Life 'Integration,'" 530.

45. Thompson, "Workism Is Making Americans Miserable."

46. Ibid., reporting that the highest-earning men in America now work the longest, as compared to 1980 when they worked fewer hours than their middle-class and lower-income peers. Williams et al., "Beyond Work-Life 'Integration,'" 530. See also Erin Reid, "Why Some Men Pretend to Work 80-Hour Weeks," *Harvard Business Review*, April 28, 2015, https://hbr.org.

47. Youngjoo Cha and Kim A. Weeden, "Overwork and the Slow Convergence in the Gender Gap in Wages," *American Sociological Journal* 79, no. 3 (2014): 457–84.

48. Slaughter, *Unfinished Business*, 19: "What was once a manageable and enjoyable work-family balance can no longer be sustained—regardless of ambition, confidence, or even an equal partner." See also Claire Cain Miller, "Women Did Everything Right: Then Work Got Greedy," *New York Times*, April 26, 2019.

49. Abundant research shows that women (especially those with small children) more greatly value flexibility and shorter hours at work relative to men and/or sort into family-friendly firms or public sector jobs that provide these (but also lower pay). See Bolotnyy and Emanuel, "Why Do Women Earn Less Than Men?," finding that "women value time away from work and flexibility more than men, taking more unpaid time off using the Family Medical Leave Act (FMLA) and working fewer overtime hours than men" (1). Juliana Menasce Horowitz, "Despite Challenges at Home and Work, Most Working Moms and Dads Say Being Employed Is What's Best for Them," Pew Research Center, September 12, 2019, finding that more than half of mothers have had to reduce their hours at work; in terms of ideal hours, among mothers who work full-time, a majority would prefer to either work part-time or not work for pay at all, while a majority of mothers who work part-time believe part-time work is ideal; among stay-at-home mothers, a plurality believe working part-time would be ideal. "Women in America: Work and Life Well-Lived," Gallup, Inc., 2016, https://news-gallup-com.ezp-prod1.hul.harvard .edu/businessjournal/196058/kids-company-greatest-competition.aspx: "More than half of women (54%) who do not work and who have a child younger than 18 say their desire to stay home with their children is a 'major reason' why they are not working. Other factors are considerably less relevant, including the need to earn money, the cost of childcare and the ability to find a good job. . . . Among women who are employed and do not have a child under the age of 18, 70% would prefer to work outside the home. That number falls to 40% among women who are employed and do have a child under the age of 18." Arlie Hochschild and Anne Machung, "Afterword" (2012), in *The Second Shift* (London: Penguin, 2012), note that mothers with full-time jobs laughed less with their children than mothers who work part-time or only in the home and are less satisfied with how their children are faring (266).

50. Stephanie Bornstein, Joan Williams, and Genevieve Painter, "Discrimination against Mothers Is the Strongest Form of Workplace Gender Discrimination: Lessons from US Caregiver Discrimination Law," *International Journal of Comparative Labour Law and Industrial Relations* 28, no. 1 (2012): 45–62; Goldin, "Grand Gender Convergence," 1092: "The gender gap in pay would be considerably reduced and might vanish altogether, if firms did not have an incentive to disproportionately reward individuals who labored long hours and worked particular hours." Pregnancy discrimination is also still quite prevalent. See, for instance, Kitroeff and Silver-Greenberg, "Pregnancy Discrimination Is Rampant."

51. Bornstein et al., "Discrimination against Mothers," 48.

52. See Joan C. Williams, "Correct Diagnosis; Wrong Cure: A Response to Professor Suk," *Columbia Law Review Sidebar* 110 (2010): 24–34. "Women

who work part time get the worst of both worlds: They are assumed to be less warm than full time mothers, and less competent than full time workers" (ibid., 27). See also the collection of such research cited in Stephen Benard and Shelley J. Correll, "Normative Discrimination and the Motherhood Penalty," *Gender & Society* 24 (2010): 616, 616–17, 618. And yet, most women with children under eighteen believe part-time work would be the best option for their families, and a quarter of mothers remain out of the workforce altogether when they have young children in the home. See notes 22 and 49.

53. Katherine Weisshaar, "From Opt Out to Blocked Out: The Challenges for Labor Market Re-entry after Family-Related Employment Lapses," *American Sociological Review* 83, no. 1 (2018): 34–60.

54. Emily Oster, "End the Plague of Secret Parenting," *The Atlantic*, May 21, 2019, citing and quoting Emma Cahusac and Shireen Kanji, "Giving Up: How Gendered Organizational Cultures Push Mothers Out," *Gender, Work & Organization* 21, no. 1 (2014): 57–70. "Hiding being a mother and engaging in strategies for secrecy were ubiquitous themes in our interviews. . . . Many women who had gone back to work tried to conceal that they had small children or pretended that their children's interests were of little importance to them."

55. Bornstein et al., "Discrimination against Mothers," 53–54, noting that studies show that fathers who seek time off for family experience serious career penalties, perhaps even stronger than that faced by mothers. See also Jennifer L. Berdahl et al., "Work as a Masculinity Contest," *Journal of Social Issues* 74, no. 3 (2018): 422–48.

56. Jane Waldfogel and Susan E. Mayer, "Male-Female Differences in the Low-Wage Labor Market," Working Papers 9904, Harris School of Public Policy Studies, University of Chicago, 1999; Bornstein et al., "Discrimination against Mothers," 48.

57. Weisshaar, "From Opt Out to Blocked Out"; Pamela Stone, *Opting Out? Why Women Really Quit Careers and Head Home* (Berkeley: University of California Press, 2007).

58. Organisation for Economic Co-operation and Development (OECD), 2014, referenced in Williams et al., "Beyond Work-Life 'Integration,'" 518.

59. Sarah Jane Glynn, "Breadwinning Mothers Continue to be the U.S. Norm," Center for American Progress, May 10, 2019, http://www.american progress.org.

60. Philosopher Feder Kittay: "Radical visions in which dependency work is taken out of the family have left many women cold—largely, I suggest, because they have failed to respect the importance of the dependency relationship. . . . [W]omen [have tasted] the fruits of an equality fashioned by men— and [have found] it wanting. This equality has not left room for love's labors and love's laborers" (Kittay, *Love's Labor*, 188). Richard Reeves correctly notes,

"Very often policy is focused on extending the school day, or providing child care at unusual hours, essentially attempting to create job-friendly families, rather than family-friendly jobs" (Reeves, "Where's the Glue?," 22). Notably, 24 percent of children under five years old are cared for by a grandparent while parents work or are at school; see U.S. Census Bureau, "Who's Minding the Kids? Child Care Arrangements: Spring 2011," 2013, https://www.census.gov.

61. Many others have used this phraseology before. See, for instance, Deborah Dinner, "Vulnerability as a Category of Historical Analysis: Initial Thoughts in Tribute to Martha Albertson Fineman," *Emory Law Journal* 67, no. 6 (2018): 1149–63. "Law and society expected women as well as men to conform to the model of the industrial breadwinner" (ibid., 1160).

62. Eric Bettinger, Torbjørn Hægeland, and Mari Rege, "Home with Mom: The Effects of Stay-at-Home Parents on Children's Long-Run Educational Outcomes," *Journal of Labor Economics* 32, no. 3 (2014): 443–67, suggesting that "parental care is not easily substituted"; Michael Baker et al., "Universal Child Care, Maternal Labor Supply and Family Well-Being," *Journal of Political Economy* 116, no. 4 (2008): 709–45, finding that children were worse off on a variety of outcomes after the introduction of universal child care in Quebec. Baker et al., "The Long-Run Impacts of a Universal Child Care Program," *American Economic Journal: Economic Policy* 11, no. 3 (2019): 1–26, reporting worse health and life satisfaction and higher crime rate for children in early childcare care; see generally Kosimar, *Being There.*

63. See, for instance, Anne-Marie Slaughter, "A Toxic Work World," *New York Times*, September 18, 2015.

64. OECD, "Walking the Tightrope: Background Brief on Parents' Work–Life Balance across the Stages of Childhood," December 2016, 12 (fig. 7), http://www.oecd.org/social/family/Background-brief-parents-work-life-balance-stages-childhood.pdf.

65. Ibid. Marie Preisler, "Danish Parents Want Swedish Part Time Conditions," *Nordic Labour Journal*, March 3, 2016, http://www.nordiclabour journal.org/nyheter/news-2016/article.2016-03-02.3814454652, reporting that nearly three-quarters of Danes would like to grant parents the legal right to work part-time, urging the government to follow Sweden where parents of children younger than eight can work part-time, by right, since 1995. It may not be a coincidence that in the Netherlands, where children enjoy the highest subjective measure of life satisfaction among OECD countries, Dutch mothers are also the most likely to work part-time. "Subjective Well-Being and Satisfaction with Work-Life Balance," OECD Family Database (January 2015), chart LMF2.7. B; "Maternal Employment Rates" OECD Family Database (September 2016), chart LMF1.2. A.

66. OECD Family Database, "Maternal Employment Rates," September 2016, chart LMF1.2. A. See also U.S. Bureau of Labor Statistics, "Economic News Release," table 6, April 21, 2020, https://www.bls.gov/news.release/famee .t06.htm; and see notes 22 and 49.

67. Williams et al., "Beyond Work-Life 'Integration,'" 525, citing various studies.

68. Ibid., 531.

69. Ibid., 516, reporting that men's household contributions have doubled between 1965 and 2000, due to increases in time spent caring for their children. Frances K. Goldscheider and Sharon Sassler, "Family Policy, Socioeconomic Inequality, and the Gender Revolution," in Cahn et al., *Unequal Family Lives*, 207, reporting that U.S. fathers' share in housework and childcare are at levels similar to Nordic fathers. A particularly beautiful account of fatherhood was offered by Ryan Park, former clerk of Justice Ginsburg: "It goes without saying that work can be greatly fulfilling. It has been for me. But, as a general matter, mothers and fathers both report that time spent with their children is a far greater source of meaning and happiness than time spent at work. . . . The gender-equality debate too often ignores this half of the equation. When home is mentioned at all, the emphasis is usually on equalizing burdens—not equalizing the opportunity for men, as well as women, to be there" (Ryan Park, "What Ruth Bader Ginsburg Taught Me about Being a Stay-at-Home Dad," *The Atlantic*, January 8, 2015).

70. Williams et al., "Beyond Work Life 'Integration,'" 525.

71. Golden, "Grand Gender Convergence," 1117–18. See also Joan C. Williams and Marina Multhaup, "How Managers Can Be Fair about Flexibility for Parents and Non-Parents Alike," *Harvard Business Review*, April 27, 2018, https://hbr.org.

72. Williams et al., "Beyond Work-Life 'Integration,'" 525.

73. Ibid.

74. Goldin, "Grand Gender Convergence," 1117–18, reporting that, though not all positions can become more flexible, those in which employees can substitute easily for each other enjoy the greatest flexibility, the smallest gaps in pay, and the best proportionality of pay to hours worked.

75. Heather Schwedel, "Why Doesn't Apple's State-of-the-Art New Campus Include a Day Care?," *Slate*, May 16, 2017, https://slate.com.

76. Calvert, "Caregivers in the Workplace," 18–19, explaining that caregiving cases are brought currently using a "patchwork" of claims under state and federal antidiscrimination and leave laws. See also Ann C. Scales, "Towards a Feminist Jurisprudence," *Indiana Law Journal* 56, no. 3 (1981): 441.

77. Some of Betty Friedan's recommendations from *The Feminine Mystique* deserve a rehearing too. She suggested that universities recruit female

380 Notes to Pages 299–300

professors who have worked part-time at various stages of their lives, so that there might be a greater "presence of women on [college] campus[es] . . . who have babies and husbands and are still deeply committed to their work." At that time, she sought to enable college-age women to take their own education more seriously; today, serious-minded women (and men) need to see the possibility of "combin[ing] marriage and motherhood with the life of the mind," even if that means, as she said, "concessions for pregnancies" (Friedan, *The Feminine Mystique*, Kindle location 5994, 5998 of 8353).

78. See April Daniels Hussar, "New Study on Motherhood & Leadership Reveals What We Knew All Along," *Romper*, May 13, 2019, https://www .romper.com/p/new-study-on-motherhood-leadership-reveals-what-we -knew-all-along-17867642; Ann Crittenden, *If You've Raised Kids, You Can Manage Anything: Leadership Begins at Home* (New York: Avery Publishing, 2004); Stacey Epstein, "Five Reasons Your Company Needs More Moms," *Inc.*, June 7, 2012, http://www.inc.com/stacey-epstein/why-you-should-hire -more-moms.html; Lisa Evans, "How Motherhood Prepares You for Entrepreneurship," *Entrepreneur*, May 8, 2016, http://www.entrepreneur.com/article /245782.

79. NOW Original Statement; Appellant's Brief, *Reed v. Reed*, 404 U.S. 71 (1971), 430, on file with the Library of Congress, Ginsburg Collection, Accession 1, ACLU File, Box 6, at 20, no. 13 (quoting Pauli Murray); Ross Douthat and Reihan Salam, *Grand New Party: How Republicans Can Win the Working Class and Save the American Dream* (New York: Anchor, 2009).

80. Claire Cain Miller, "Americans Are Having Fewer Babies: They Told Us Why," *New York Times*, July 5, 2018.

81. Twenty percent of new mothers must return to work within days or weeks of a child's birth; see Alyssa Pozniak et al., "Family and Medical Leave in 2012: Detailed Results Appendix," Abt Associates Inc., prepared for U.S. Department of Labor, September 6, 2012, revised April 18, 2014. According to an article from FairyGodBoss.com, which lists 180 companies that offer the most paid leave, "Law firms, technology companies (particularly consumer technology companies), financial services firms as well as consulting firms tend to dominate this list of employers with generous parental leave policies" ("Paid Maternity Leave: 180 Companies Who Offer the Most Paid Leave," https://fairygodboss.com; Rebecca Greenfield, "More Companies Than Ever Offer Paid Parental Leave," Bloomberg, June 28, 2018, https://www .bloomberg.com).

As for paid leave for fathers, the Swedish experience with the use-it-or -lose-it "daddy quota" shows a significant increase in men's involvement with their young children. See Maria Stanfors and Frances Goldscheider, "The Forest and the Trees: Industrialization, Demographic Change, and the Ongoing

Gender Revolution in Sweden and the United States, 1870–2010," *Demographic Research* 36 (2017): 209; Richard J. Petts and Chris Knoester, "Paternity Leave-Taking and Father Engagement," *Journal of Marriage and Family* 80, no. 5 (2018): 1144–62.

82. U.S. Congress, Senate, Family and Medical Insurance Leave Act (FAMILY Act), S. 463, 116th Cong., 1st Sess., introduced in the Senate February 2, 2019; U.S. Congress, Senate, Economic Security for New Parents Act, S. 3345, 115th Cong., introduced in the Senate August 1, 2018; U.S. Congress, House, Cradle Act, H. R. 3865, 114th Cong., introduced in the House October 29, 2015. Liberal-leaning Brookings Institution and the more conservative American Enterprise Institute collaborated together to publish "Paid Family and Medical Leave: An Issue Whose Time Has Come," May 2017, https://www.brookings.edu.

83. The following detail some of these proposals over the past twelve years: U.S. Congress, Senate, American Family Act of 2019, S. 690, 116th Cong., introduced in March 6, 2019; Matt Bruenig, "Family Fun Pack," The People's Policy Project, 2019, https://www.peoplespolicyproject.org/projects/family-fun-pack/; Patrick T. Brown, "Leaning Out," *National Review*, March 11, 2019, https://www.nationalreview.com; Gladdin Pappin and Maria Molla, "Affirming the American Family," *American Affairs* 3, no. 3 (2019), https://americanaffairsjournal.org; Allan Carlson, "Expanding Child-Care Choices for All Families," *The Family in America* 1 (2009): 18–20; Douthat and Salam, *Grand New Party*; Allan Carlson, "Rise and Fall of the American Family Wage," *University of St. Thomas Law Journal* 4, no. 3 (2007): 571; U.S. Congress, Senate, Parents Tax Relief Act of 2007, S. 816, 110th Cong., introduced in the Senate March 8, 2007.

84. Although the work in which mothers and fathers are engaged is serious work, it is not remunerative work; indeed, as the early women's rights advocates well understood, such nonmarket labor could never rightly be valued by a wage. Rather, policies discussed here ought to be understood as seeking to manifest the deeply important work of the family, and thus lessen the economic burden on caregivers through sharing some of the burdens with the community at large. Mothers and fathers will know joys and privileges in caring for their children that will remain ever unknown to those beyond the family; just so, the community at large could not be expected to share in all of the costs associated with caregiving.

85. Gergely Szakacs, "Orban Offers Financial Incentives to Boost Hungary's Birth Rate," Reuters, February 10, 2019.

86. Douthat and Salem, *Grand New Party*, 171; Eva Feder Kittay, "A Feminist Public Ethic of Care Meets the New Communitarian Family Policy," *Ethics* 111, no. 3 (2001): 546.

87. See, for example, Brigid Shulte, "What Moms Always Knew about Working from Home," *The New York Times*, April 6, 2020; Angela Rachidi and Abby McCloskey, "A Future of Work That Complements Family Life," *Institute for Family Studies*, April 2, 2020; Eileen Reuter, "Learning the Right Lessons from COVID-19 Can Benefit Mothers after the Pandemic," *Public Discourse*, April 1, 2020; Helen Lewis, "The Coronavirus Is a Disaster for Feminism," *The Atlantic*, March 19, 2020; Marilyn Simon, "No, COVID-19 Is Not a 'Disaster for Feminism,'" *Quillette*, March 25, 2020.

88. "According to a 2017 report from Global Workplace Analytics, the number of U.S. workers who telecommute . . . has increased 115 percent in the past decade, to about 3.9 million workers, or about three percent of the U.S. workforce. . . . Forty percent of American employers indicate that they allow some workers the ability to work some regular paid hours from home" (Rachel Anderson and Katelyn Beaty, "Time to Flourish: Protecting Families' Time for Work and Care," Center for Public Justice, July 2018, 22–23). The Bureau of Labor Statistics indicates that those who work from home tend to be better educated and more well off. "Among workers ages 25 and older, 47% of workers with a bachelor's degree or higher worked from home sometimes . . . compared to just 3% of workers with only a high school diploma"; see Tara Law, "Americans are Being Encouraged to Work from Home during the Coronavirus Outbreak. For Millions, That's Impossible," *Time*, March 9, 2020.

89. Archie Hochschild writes in her 2012 afterword to *The Second Shift*: "Working from home, we also unclog freeways, save gas, and green our nation while saving precious time for giggling children at home." Other findings confirm the benefits of family time at home. For example, the Family Dinner Project (Massachusetts General Hospital, Psychiatry Academy) writes on their website: "Recent studies link regular family dinners with many behaviors that parents pray for: lower rates of substance abuse, teen pregnancy and depression, as well as higher grade-point averages and self-esteem. Studies also indicate that for young children, dinner conversation is a more potent vocabulary-booster than reading, and the stories told around the kitchen table help our children build resilience. The icing on the cake is that regular family meals also lower the rates of obesity and eating disorders in children and adolescents"; see https://thefamilydinnerproject.org/resources/faq/.

90. See, for instance, Chris Arnade, *Dignity: Seeking Respect in Back Row America* (New York: Sentinel, 2019); and W. Bradford Wilcox and Nicholas H. Wolfinger, *Soul Mates: Religion, Sex, Love, and Marriage among African Americans and Latinos* (Oxford: Oxford University Press, 2015).

91. Glendon, "Intergenerational Solidarity," 340.

SELECTED BIBLIOGRAPHY

"Adams Family Correspondence." In *Political Thought in the United States: A Documentary History*, edited by Lyman Tower Sargent. New York: New York University Press, 1997.

Adams Family Papers: An Electronic Archive. Boston: Massachusetts Historical Society, 2002. http://www.masshist.org/digitaladams/.

Akerlof, George A., Janet L. Yellen, and Michael L. Katz. "An Analysis of Out-of-Wedlock Childbearing in the United States." *The Quarterly Journal of Economics* 111, no. 2 (1996): 277–317.

———. "Men without Children." *The Economic Journal* 108 (1998): 287–309.

Allen, Prudence. *The Concept of Woman*. Vol. 1. Grand Rapids, MI: William B. Eerdmans, 1997.

———. *The Concept of Woman*. Vol. 3. Grand Rapids, MI: William B. Eerdmans, 2017.

———. "Metaphysics of Form, Matter, and Gender." *Lonergan Workshop Journal* 12 (1996): 1–26.

Alvaré, Helen. "Abortion, Sexual Market and the Law." In *Persons, Moral Worth, and Embryos*, edited by Stephen Napier, 225–80. New York: Springer, 2011.

Aristotle. *Nicomachean Ethics*. In *Basic Works of Aristotle*, translated by W. D. Ross; edited by Richard McKeon. New York: Random House, 1941.

Bailey, Martha J., and Thomas A. DiPrete. "Five Decades of Remarkable but Slowing Change in U.S. Women's Economic and Social Status and Political Participation." *RSF: The Russell Sage Foundation Journal of the Social Sciences* 2, no. 4 (2016): 1–32.

Beauchamp, Andrew, and Catherine R. Pakaluk. "The Paradox of the Pill: Heterogeneous Effects of Oral Contraceptive Access." *Economic Inquiry* 57, no. 2 (2019): 813–31.

Berges, Sandrine, and Alan Coffee, eds. *The Social and Political Philosophy of Mary Wollstonecraft*. Oxford: Oxford University Press, 2016.

Berges, Sandrine, Alan Coffee, and Eileen Hunt Botting, eds. *The Wollstonecraftian Mind*. New York: Routledge, 2019.

Blackstone, William. *Commentaries on the Laws of England in Four Books. Notes selected from the editions of Archibold, Christian, Coleridge, Chitty, Stewart, Kerr, and others, Barron Field's Analysis, and Additional Notes, and a Life of the Author by George Sharswood. In Two Volumes.* Philadelphia: J. B. Lippincott Co., 1893.

Bornstein, Stephanie, Joan Williams, and Genevieve Painter. "Discrimination against Mothers Is the Strongest Form of Workplace Gender Discrimination: Lessons from U.S. Caregiver Discrimination Law." *International Journal of Comparative Labour Law and Industrial Relations* 28, no. 1 (2012): 45–62.

Botting, Eileen Hunt. *Family Feuds: Wollstonecraft, Burke, and Rousseau on the Transformation of the Family*. New York: State University of New York Press, 2007.

———. "A Family Resemblance: Tocqueville and Wollstonecraftian Protofeminism." In *Feminist Interpretations of Alexis de Tocqueville*, edited by Jill Locke and Eileen Hunt Botting, 99–124. University Park: Pennsylvania State University Press, 2010.

———. "Mary Wollstonecraft's Contributions to Modern Political Philosophy: Intersectionality and the Quest for Egalitarian Social Justice." In *Feminist History of Philosophy: The Recovery and Evaluation of Women's Philosophical Thought*, edited by Marcy Lascano and Eileen O'Neill, 355–77. New York: Springer, 2010.

———. "Three Stages of Wollstonecraft's Philosophy of the Family." *The Review of Politics* 64, no. 1 (2002): 81–119.

———. *Wollstonecraft, Mill, and Women's Human Rights*. New Haven, CT: Yale University Press, 2016.

Botting, Eileen Hunt, and Christine Carey. "Wollstonecraft's Philosophical Impact on Nineteenth-Century American Women's Rights Advocates." *American Journal of Political Science* 48, no. 4 (2004): 707–22.

Brennan, Teresa, and Carole Pateman. "'Mere Auxiliaries to the Commonwealth': Women and the Origins of Liberalism." *Political Studies* 27, no. 2 (1979): 183–222.

Brodie, Jane Farrell. *Contraception and Abortion in Nineteenth-Century America*. Ithaca, NY: Cornell University Press, 1994.

Cahn, Naomi R., June Carbone, Laurie Fields DeRose, and W. Bradford Wilcox, eds. *Unequal Family Lives*. Cambridge: Cambridge University Press, 2018.

Callahan, Sidney. "Abortion and the Sexual Agenda: A Case for Pro-Life Feminism." *Commonweal*, April 25, 1986, 232–38.

Campbell, Amy Leigh. *Raising the Bar*. Printed by the author, Xlibris, 2003.

Carlson, Allan C. *From Cottage to Work Station*. San Francisco: Ignatius, 1993.

———. "The Productive Home vs. the Consuming Home." In *Localism in the Mass Age*, edited by Mark T. Mitchell and Jason Peters, 115–23. Eugene, OR: Cascade, 2018.

———. "What Happened to the 'Family Wage'?" *The Public Interest*, Spring 1986, 3–17.

Cass, Oren. *The Once and Future Worker*. New York: Encounter Press, 2018.

Cicero, Marcus Tullius. *De Legibus (On the Laws)*. Translated by David Fott. Ithaca, NY: Cornell University Press, 2014.

———. *De Officiis (On Duties)*. Translated by Walter Miller. Loeb Edition. Cambridge, MA: Harvard University Press, 1913.

Clark, Alice. *Working Life of Women in the Seventeenth Century*. London: Frank Cass, 1968.

Clark, Elizabeth B. "Matrimonial Bonds: Slavery and Divorce in Nineteenth-Century America." *Law and History Review* 8, no. 1 (1990): 25–54.

Cone, Carl B. "Richard Price and the Constitution of the United States." *The American Historical Review* 53, no. 4 (1948): 726–47.

Connelly, Matthew. *Fatal Misconception*. Cambridge, MA: Harvard University Press, 2008.

Cott, Nancy F. "Historical Perspectives: The Equal Rights Amendment Conflict in the 1920s." In *Conflicts in Feminism*, edited by Marianne Hirsch and Evelyn Fox Keller, 44–59. New York: Routledge, 1990.

Crawford, Matthew. *The World beyond Your Head*. Boston: Macmillan, 2015.

Croly, Jane Cunningham. *For Better or Worse: A Book for Some Men and All Women*. Boston, 1875.

Derr, Mary Krane, Rachel MacNair, and Linda Naranjo-Huebl. *Prolife Feminism: Yesterday and Today*. Bloomington, IN: Xlibris Corporation, 2005.

Dinner, Deborah. "Strange Bedfellows at Work: Neomaternalism in the Making of Sex Discrimination." *Washington University Law Review* 91, no. 3 (2014): 453–530.

Dodson, Scott, ed. *The Legacy of Ruth Bader Ginsburg*. New York: Cambridge University Press, 2015.

Douthat, Ross, and Reihan Salam. *Grand New Party: How Republicans Can Win the Working Class and Save the American Dream*. New York: Anchor Press, 2009.

Eberstadt, Nicholas. *Men without Work: America's Invisible Crisis*. West Conshohocken, PA: Templeton, 2016.

Edelman-Young, Diana. "Chubby Cheeks and the Bloated Monster: The Politics of Reproduction in Mary Wollstonecraft's *Vindication*." *European Romantic Review* 25, no. 6 (2014): 683–704.

Edin, Kathryn, and Maria Kefalas. *Promises I Can Keep: Why Poor Women Put Motherhood before Marriage*. Berkeley: University of California Press, 2005.

Edin, Kathryn, and Timothy J. Nelson. *Doing the Best I Can: Fatherhood in the Inner City*. Berkeley: University of California Press, 2013.

Eig, Jonathan. *Birth of the Pill: How Four Crusaders Reinvented Sex and Launched a Revolution*. New York: W. W. Norton, 2015.

Elshtain, Jean Bethke. *Jane Addams and the Dream of American Democracy*. New York: Basic Books, 2002.

———. *Public Man, Private Woman*. Princeton, NJ: Princeton University Press, 1981.

———. *Sovereignty: God, State, and Self*. New York: Basic Books, 2008.

———. "Women, Equality, and the Family." *Journal of Democracy* 11, no. 1 (2000): 157–63.

Ely, John Hart. "The Wages of Crying Wolf." *The Yale Law Journal* 82, no. 5 (1973): 920–49.

Farnsworth, Ward. "Women under Reconstruction: The Congressional Understanding." *Northwestern University Law Review* 94, no. 4 (2000): 1229–95.

Folbre, Nancy. "The Unproductive Housewife: Her Evolution in Nineteenth-Century Economic Thought." *Signs: Journal of Women in Culture and Society* 16, no. 3 (1991): 463–83.

Forsythe, Clarke. *Abuse of Discretion: The Inside Story of* Roe v. Wade. New York: Encounter Books, 2013.

Fortin, Ernest L. *Human Rights, Virtue, and the Common Good*. Edited by J. Brian Benestad. Lanham: Rowman & Littlefield, 1996.

Fox-Genovese, Elizabeth. *Feminism Is Not the Story of My Life*. New York: Nan A. Talese, 1996.

———. *Feminism without Illusions*. Chapel Hill: University of North Carolina Press, 1991.

Franks, Angela. "Consent Is Not Enough: Harvey Weinstein, Sex, and Human Flourishing." *Public Discourse*, November 26, 2017. http://www. thepublicdiscourse.com.

———. *Margaret Sanger's Eugenic Legacy*. Jefferson, NC: McFarland & Company, 2005.

Friedan, Betty. *The Feminine Mystique*. New York: W. W. Norton, 2013. Kindle.

———. *Life So Far: A Memoir*. New York: Simon & Schuster, 2006.

———. *Second Stage*. Cambridge, MA: Harvard University Press, 1988.

Gillman, Howard. *The Constitution Besieged: The Rise and Demise of* Lochner *Era Police Powers Jurisprudence*. Durham, NC: Duke University Press, 1995.

Gilman, Charlotte Perkins. *The Man-Made World: Or, Our Androcentric Culture*. New York: Charlton Company, 1914.

———. *Women and Economics: A Study of the Economic Relation between Men and Women as a Factor in Social Evolution*. Boston: Small, Maynard and Company, 1898.

Ginsburg, Ruth Bader. "Foreword." *Yale Journal of Law and Feminism* 14 (2002): 213–16.

———. "A Grand Ideal for the Future." *Oregon State Bar Bulletin* (August/ September 1993): 19–22.

———. "Remarks on Women Becoming Part of the Constitution." *Law & Inequality* 6 (1988): 17–25.

———. "Sex Equality and the Constitution." *Tulane Law Review* 52, no. 3 (1978): 451–75.

———. "Sexual Equality under the Fourteenth and Equal Rights Amendments." *Washington University Law Review* (January 1979): 161–78.

———. "Some Thoughts on Benign Classification in the Context of Sex." *Connecticut Law Review* 10 (1978): 813–27.

———. "Speaking in a Judicial Voice." *New York University Law Review* 67, no. 6 (1992): 1185–1209.

Ginsburg, Ruth Bader, and Barbara Flagg. "Some Reflections on the Feminist Legal Thought of the 1970's." *University of Chicago Legal Forum* (1989): 9–21.

Ginsburg, Ruth Bader, with Mary Hartnett and Wendy W. Williams. *My Own Words*. New York: Simon & Schuster, 2016.

Glendon, Mary Ann. *Abortion and Divorce in Western Law*. Cambridge, MA: Harvard University Press, 1987.

———. "The Ever-Changing Interplay between Democracy and Civil Society." Vatican City: Pontifical Academy of Social Sciences, *Acta* 6 (2001): 97–120.

———. *Forum and the Tower*. New York: Oxford University Press, 2011.

———. "A Glimpse of the New Feminism: From July 6, 1996." *America*, July 6, 1996.

———, ed. "Intergenerational Solidarity, Welfare and Human Ecology." Vatican City: Pontifical Academy of Social Sciences, *Acta* 10 (2004): 354–69.

———. "Irish Family Law in Comparative Perspective: Can There Be Comparative Family Law?" *Dublin University Law Journal* 9 (1987): 1–20.

———. "Is the Economic Emancipation of Women Today Contrary to a Healthy, Functioning Family?" In *Family, Civil Society, and the State*, edited by Christopher Wolfe, 87–98. Lanham, MD: Roman & Littlefield, 1998.

———. "Looking for 'Persons' in the Law." *First Things*, December 2006.

———. "Rescuing Feminism from the Feminists." *First Things*, March 1996.

———. *Rights Talk*. New York: Macmillan, 1991.

———. "The Right to Work and the Limits of the Law." In *Work & Human Fulfillment*. Pontifical Academy of Social Sciences. Ave Maria, FL: Sapientia Press, 2003.

———. *Traditions in Turmoil*. Ann Arbor, MI: Sapientia Press, 2006.

———. *Transformation of Family Law*. Chicago: University of Chicago Press, 1989.

———. "What Happened at Beijing." *First Things*, January 1996.

———. "Women's Identity, Women's Rights and the Civilization of Life." In *"Evangelium Vitae" e Diritto, "Evangelium Vitae" and Law*, edited by Alphonsus Lopez Trujillo, Julianus Herranz, and Aelius Sgreccia, 63–75. Roma: Liberia Editrice Vaticana, 1997.

———. *A World Made New: Eleanor Roosevelt and the Universal Declaration of Human Rights*. New York: Penguin Random House, 2002.

Glendon, Mary Ann, and David Blankenhorn, eds. *Seedbeds of Virtue*. Lanham, MD: Madison Books, 1995.

Glendon, Mary Ann, and Raul F. Yanes. "Structural Free Exercise." *Michigan Law Review* 90, no. 3 (1991): 477–550.

Goldin, Claudia. "A Grand Gender Convergence: Its Last Chapter." *American Economic Review* 104, no. 4 (2014): 1091–1119.

———. *Understanding the Gender Gap: An Economic History of American Women*. New York: Oxford University Press, 1990.

Gordon, Linda. *The Moral Property of Women*. Chicago: University of Illinois Press, 2007.

———. "Why Nineteenth-Century Feminists Did Not Support 'Birth Control' and Twentieth-Century Feminists Do." In *Rethinking the Family*, edited by Barrie Thorne and Marilyn Yalom, 140–53. New York: Longman, 1982.

Gordon, Lyndall. *Vindication: A Life of Mary Wollstonecraft*. New York: HarperCollins, 2005.

Greenhouse, Linda, and Reva B. Siegel. *Before* Roe v. Wade: *Voices That Shaped the Abortion Debate before the Supreme Court's Ruling*. New York: Kaplan, 2010.

Grimké, Sarah. "Letter II: Woman Subject Only to God, Newburyport, 7th mo. 17, 1837." In *Letters on the Equality of the Sexes*, http://www.worldculture.org/articles/12-Grimke%20Letters,%201-3.pdf.

———. "Marriage." In *The Grimké Sisters from South Carolina: Pioneers for Women's Rights and Abolition*, edited by Gerda Lerner, 303–9. Chapel Hill: University of North Carolina Press, 2004.

Hibbs, Stacey. "Liberty without License, Authority without Oppression: Women in *Democracy in America*." PhD diss., Boston College, 1999.

Hochschild, Archie. *The Second Shift*. New York: Penguin, 2012.

Hymowitz, Kay. *Marriage and Caste in America: Separate and Unequal Families in a Post-Marital Age*. Chicago: Ivan R. Dee, 2006.

Johnson, Claudia L., ed. *The Cambridge Companion to Mary Wollstonecraft*. Cambridge: Cambridge University Press, 2002.

Karst, Kenneth L. "Foreword: Equal Citizenship under the Fourteenth Amendment." *Harvard Law Review* 91, no. 1 (1977): 1–68.

Katz, Lawrence, and Claudia Goldin, "The Power of the Pill: Oral Contraceptives and Women's Career and Marriage Decisions." *Journal of Political Economy* 110, no. 4 (2002): 730–70.

Kelley, Florence. *Some Ethical Gains through Legislation*. New York: Macmillan, 1905.

Kerber, Linda K. *Women of the Republic: Intellect & Ideology in Revolutionary America*. Chapel Hill: University of North Carolina, 1980.

Kerry, Paul E. "Mary Wollstonecraft on Reason, Marriage, Family Life, and the Development of Virtue in *A Vindication of the Rights of Woman*." *Brigham Young University Journal of Public Law* 30, no. 1 (2015): 1–38.

Kittay, Eva Feder. "A Feminist Public Ethic of Care Meets the New Communitarian Family Policy." *Ethics* 111, no. 3 (2001): 523–47.

———. *Love's Labor*. New York: Routledge, 1999.

Lasch, Christopher. *Women and the Common Life*. Edited by Elisabeth Lasch-Quinn. New York: W. W. Norton, 1997.

Law, Sylvia. "Rethinking Sex and the Constitution." *University of Pennsylvania Law Review* 132 (1984): 955–1040.

Levin, Yuval. *The Fractured Republic*. New York: Basic Books, 2017.

———. *The Great Debate*. New York: Basic Books, 2013.

———. *Time to Build*. New York: Basic Books, 2020.

Levine, Phillip. *Sex and Consequences: Abortion, Public Policy, and the Economics of Fertility*. Princeton, NJ: Princeton University Press, 2007.

Littleton, Christine A. "Reconstructing Sexual Equality." *California Law Review* 75 (July 1986): 1279–1337.

MacIntyre, Alasdair. *Dependent Rational Animals*. Chicago: Open Court, 1999.

MacKinnon, Catharine. *Feminism Unmodified: Discourses on Life and Law*. Cambridge, MA: Harvard University Press, 1987.

Mansbridge, Jane J. *Why We Lost the ERA*. Chicago: University of Chicago Press, 1986.

McLanahan, Sara. "Diverging Destinies: How Children Are Faring under the Second Demographic Transition." *Demography* 41, no. 4 (2004): 607–27.

Motro, Shari. "The Price of Pleasure." *Northwestern University Law Review* 104, no. 3 (2010): 969–70.

———. "Scholarship against Desire." *Yale Journal of Law & the Humanities* 27, no. 1 (2015).

Mott, James, and Lucretia Mott. *James and Lucretia Mott: Life and Letters.* Edited by Anna Davis Hallowell. Boston: Houghton, Mifflin and Company, 1884.

Murray, Pauli, and Mary O. Eastwood. "Jane Crow and the Law: Sex Discrimination and Title VII." *George Washington Law Review* 34, no. 2 (1965): 232–56.

Pateman, Carole, *The Sexual Contract.* Redwood City, CA: Stanford University Press, 1988.

Paulsen, Michael Stokes. "Abrogating Stare Decisis by Statute." *Yale Law Journal* 109, no. 7 (2000): 1535–1601.

———. *The Constitution: An Introduction.* New York: Basic Books, 2015.

Petchesky, Rosalind Pollack. *Abortion and Woman's Choice.* Boston: Northeastern University Press, 1990.

Price, Richard. *A Review of the Principal Questions and Difficulties in Morals.* London: A. Millar, 1758.

Putnam, Robert D. *Bowling Alone: The Collapse and Revival of American Community.* New York: Simon & Schuster, 2000.

———. *Our Kids: The American Dream in Crisis.* New York: Simon & Schuster, 2016.

Regnerus, Mark, and Jeremy Uecker. *Premarital Sex in America.* New York: Oxford University Press, 2011.

Sandel, Michael. *What Money Can't Buy.* New York: Farrar, Straus and Giroux, 2012.

Sanger, Margaret. "Suppression." *The Woman Rebel* 1, no. 4 (1914).

———. *Woman and the New Race.* New York: Blue Ribbon Books, 1920.

Sapiro, Virginia. *A Vindication of Political Virtue.* Chicago: University of Chicago Press, 1992.

Sawhill, Isabel. *Generation Unbound: Drifting into Sex and Parenthood without Marriage.* Washington, DC: Brookings Institution Press, 2014.

Sayers, Dorothy L. *Are Women Human? Astute and Witty Essays on the Role of Women in Society.* Grand Rapids, MI: Eerdmans, 2005.

Scales, Ann C. "Towards a Feminist Jurisprudence." *Indiana Law Journal* 56, no. 3 (1981): 375–444.

Siegel, Neil S. "'Equal Citizenship Stature': Justice Ginsburg's Constitutional Vision." *New England Law Review* 43 (2010): 799–855.

Siegel, Reva B. "Home as Work: The First Woman's Rights Claims Concerning Wives' Household Labor, 1850–1880." *Yale Law Journal* 103 (1994): 1073–1217.

———. "She the People: The Nineteenth Amendment, Sex Equality, Federalism, and the Family." *Harvard Law Review* 115, no. 4 (2002): 945–1044.

Sharkey, Sarah Borden. *An Aristotelian Feminism*. New York: Springer, 2016.

Sharkey, Sarah Borden, and Christopher Manzer. "Feminism and Metaphysics." *eJournal of Personalist Feminism* 2 (2015): 1–30.

Slaughter, Anne-Marie. *Unfinished Business*. New York: Random House, 2016.

———. "Why Women Still Can't Have It All." *The Atlantic*, July/August 2012.

Sommers, Christina Hoff. *Freedom Feminism*. Washington, DC: American Enterprise Institute Press, 2013.

Stanton, Elizabeth Cady, Susan B. Anthony, and Matilda Joslyn Gage, eds. *History of Woman Suffrage*. Vol. 1, *1848–1861*. http://www.gutenberg.org/ebooks/28020.

Stoner, James R., Jr. *Common-Law Liberty*. Lawrence: University Press of Kansas, 2003.

Suk, Julie C. "Are Gender Stereotypes Bad for Women? Rethinking Antidiscrimination Law and Work-Family Conflict." *Columbia Law Review* 110, no. 1 (2010): 1–69.

Thomas, Gillian. *Because of Sex*. New York: St. Martin's Press, 2016.

Thomas, Tracy A. *Elizabeth Cady Stanton and the Feminist Foundations of Family Law*. New York: New York University Press, 2016.

Tocqueville, Alexis de. *Democracy in America*. Translated by George Lawrence. Edited by J. P. Mayer. New York: Harper & Row, 1969.

Wade, Lisa. *American Hookup: The New Culture of Sex on Campus*. New York: W. W. Norton, 2017.

Warren, Elizabeth, and Amelia Warren Tyagi. *The Two-Income Trap*. New York: Basic Books, 2003.

West, Robin. "Concurring in the Judgment." In *What* Roe *Should Have Said*, edited by Jack Balkin, 121–47. New York: New York University Press, 2005.

———. "From Choice to Reproductive Justice: De-Constitutionalizing Abortion Rights." *Yale Law Journal* 118 (2009): 1394–1432.

———. "Reconstructing Liberty." *Tennessee Law Review* 59 (1992): 441–68.

West, Thomas G. *The Political Theory of the American Founding*. Cambridge: Cambridge University Press, 2017.

Wilcox, W. Bradford, and Kathleen Kovner Kline, eds. *Gender and Parenthood: Biological and Social Scientific Perspectives*. New York: Columbia University Press, 2013.

Wilcox, W. Bradford, and Nicholas H. Wolfinger. *Soul Mates: Religion, Sex, Love, and Marriage among African Americans and Latinos*. Oxford: Oxford University Press, 2015.

Williams, Daniel K. *Defenders of the Unborn: The Pro-Life Movement before Roe v. Wade*. Oxford: Oxford University Press, 2016.

Williams, Joan. "Reconstructive Feminism: Changing the Way We Talk about Gender and Work Thirty Years after the PDA." *Yale Journal of Law & Feminism* 21, no. 1 (2009): 79–117.

———. *Unbending Gender: Why Family and Work Conflict and What to Do about It*. New York: Oxford University Press, 2001.

Williams, Joan, Jennifer L. Berdahl, and Joseph A. Vandello. "Beyond Work-Life 'Integration.'" *Annual Review of Psychology* 67 (2016): 515–39.

Williams, Wendy Webster. "The Equality Crisis: Some Reflections on Culture, Courts, and Feminism." *Women's Rights Law Reporter* 7, no. 3 (1982): 175–200.

———. "Equality's Riddle: Pregnancy and the Equal Treatment/Special Treatment Debate." *Review of Law & Social Change* 13 (1984–85): 325–80.

———. "Ruth Bader Ginsburg's Equal Protection Clause: 1970–80." *Columbia Journal of Gender and Law* 25 (2013): 41–49.

Wollstonecraft, Mary. *Complete Works of Mary Wollstonecraft (CWMW)*. Hastings: Delphi Classics, 2016. Kindle.

———. *A Vindication of the Rights of Woman*. Mineola, MN: Dover, 1996.

Woloch, Nancy. *A Class by Herself: Protective Law for Women Workers, 1890s–1990s*. Princeton, NJ: Princeton University Press, 2015.

Woodhull, Victoria. *Tried as by Fire*. New York: Woodhull & Claflin, 1874. Pamphlets from the Irvin Dept. of Rare Books and Special Collections.

Ziegler, Mary. "The Framing of a Right to Choose: *Roe v. Wade* and the Changing Debate on Abortion Law." *Law and History Review* 27 (2009): 281–330.

———. "Women's Rights on the Right: The History and Stakes of Modern Pro-Life Feminism." *Berkeley Journal of Gender, Law & Justice* 28, no. 2 (2013): 232–303.

Zimmerman, Joan G. "The Jurisprudence of Equality: The Women's Minimum Wage, the First Equal Rights Amendment, and *Adkins v. Children's Hospital*, 1905–1923." *The Journal of American History* 78, no. 1 (1991): 188–224.

INDEX

abolitionist movement. *See under* slavery

abortion, 172–73, 200–236, 303–4
  in *Abramowicz v. Lefkowitz*, 224–26
  as act of self-defense, 218
  as act of violence, 16
  the American Law Institute (ALI) Model Penal Code (1962) and, 210
  in *Doe v. Bolton*, 220, 348n75
  equal citizenship and, 223–33, 235–36
  the ERA and, 349nn86–87
  eugenics and, 15, 202, 204–5, 219–20
  the Fourteenth Amendment and, 18, 221
  in the 1960s and '70s, 207, 210–11
  before the nineteenth century, 201, 215–16
  in nineteenth-century America, 111–12, 115–16, 321n43, 323nn51–52
  NOW and, 344n48
  Planned Parenthood and, 204–5
  in *Planned Parenthood v. Casey*, 231–32, 236
  population control and, 205, 207–9, 220, 342n36
  reliance interests and, 231–32
  the right to privacy and, 348nn79–80, 349n81
  sexual behavior and, 233, 353n119, 353n123
  Wollstonecraft's view of, 50, 112, 202
  See also birth control; pro-life movement; *Roe v. Wade*

American Citizens Concerned for Life (ACCL), 263. *See also* pro-life movement

American Medical Association (AMA), 201–2, 211, 321n43

Adams, Abigail, 21–22, 24, 66, 68–69, 70–71

Adams, John, 21, 65–66, 69–70

Addams, Jane, 133–36, 297
  Hull House and, 133

Adkins v. Children's Hospital, 144–45
  Justice George Sutherland and, 144
  reversal of, 146

American founding, 4, 21–22, 26, 66–71, 82, 125–27, 250, 280, 367n4

Anthony, Susan B., 8, 93–95, 99

antisuffrage among women, 313n35. *See also* women's suffrage movement

Aristotle, 25, 29, 197, 229, 285–87, 317n13, 321n42, 370n17, 370n19

ERIKA BACHIOCHI

is a fellow at the Ethics and Public Policy Center and
a senior fellow at the Abigail Adams Institute,
where she founded and directs the Wollstonecraft Project.
She is the editor of *Women, Sex, and the Church:
A Case for Catholic Teaching* and *The Cost of "Choice":
Women Evaluate the Impact of Abortion.*

CPSIA information can be obtained
at www.ICGtesting.com
Printed in the USA
LVHW020858131122
733010LV00005B/54